Making social democrats

MANCHESTER
1824

Manchester University Press

Making social democrats

Citizens, mindsets, realities: Essays for David Marquand

Edited by

Hans Schattle and Jeremy Nuttall

Manchester University Press

Published by Manchester University Press
Altrincham Street, Manchester M1 7JA
www.manchesteruniversitypress.co.uk

British Library Cataloguing-in-Publication Data is available

ISBN 978 1 5261 2030 4 hardback
ISBN 978 1 5261 4588 8 paperback

First published by Manchester University Press in hardback 2018

This edition first published 2020

The publisher has no responsibility for the persistence or accuracy of URLs for any external or third-party internet websites referred to in this book, and does not guarantee that any content on such websites is, or will remain, accurate or appropriate.

Typeset by Toppan Best-set Premedia Limited

Contents

Contributors

Gideon Calder is Director of the social policy programme at Swansea University, and works on the application of political and ethical theory to issues of current social concern. He is author or editor of ten books – most recently *The Routledge Handbook of Philosophy of Childhood and Children* (2018) – and co-edits the journal *Ethics and Social Welfare*.

Michael Freeden is Emeritus Professor of Politics, University of Oxford and Professorial Research Associate, SOAS, University of London and, most recently, author of *The Political Theory of Political Thinking* and *Liberalism: A Very Short Introduction* (2013). He is the founder-editor of the *Journal of Political Ideologies* and is currently working on European conceptual history and on silence in political theory.

Andrew Gamble is Professor of Politics, University of Sheffield, and Emeritus Professor of Politics, University of Cambridge. His most recent book is *Can The Welfare State Survive?* (2016).

Clare Griffiths is Professor of Modern History at Cardiff University. Her publications include *Labour and the Countryside: The Politics of Rural Britain 1918–1939* (2007) and the co-edited collection of essays *Classes, Cultures, and Politics* (2011).

Will Hutton is Principal of Hertford College, University of Oxford, and Chair of the Big Innovation Centre. A columnist for the *Observer* and the *Guardian*, he was the author of *The State We're In* (1995).

Ben Jackson is Associate Professor of Modern History at Oxford University and co-editor of *Political Quarterly*. He is the author of *Equality and the British Left* (2007) and the co-editor of *Making Thatcher's Britain* (2012).

Neal Lawson is Chair of the good society pressure group Compass. He was author of *All Consuming* (2009).

David Marquand is Honorary Distinguished Professor in the School of Law and Politics at Cardiff University and former principal of Mansfield College, Oxford. He is a former parliamentarian at Westminster, a Fellow of the British Academy and author of nine books on British history, politics and political economy.

Kenneth O. Morgan has been Fellow of The Queen's College, Oxford,1966–89, Vice-Chancellor in the University of Wales 1989–95, a Labour peer since 2000 and visiting Professor at King's College London since 2013. His thirty-five books include *The Oxford Illustrated History of Britain* (1984) and biographies of Lloyd George, Keir Hardie, James Callaghan and Michael Foot.

Jeremy Nuttall is Senior Lecturer in Modern British History at Kingston University, London. He is author of the book *Psychological Socialism: The Labour Party and Qualities of Mind and Character* (2006), and of articles on British social democracy in leading journals like *Historical Journal* and *English Historical Review*.

David Owen is an Independent Social Democrat peer. He was Foreign Secretary (1977–79), Leader of the SDP (1983–90), and EU peace negotiator in the former Yugoslavia (1992–95), and is the author of *British Foreign Policy After Brexit* (2017).

Hans Schattle is Professor of Political Science at Yonsei University in Seoul, South Korea. He is the author of *The Practices of Global Citizenship* (2008) and *Globalization and Citizenship* (2012), both published by Rowman & Littlefield, as well as numerous academic journal articles on citizenship, civil society and democracy.

Stuart White is a tutor in Politics at Jesus College, Oxford. He is the author of *The Civic Minimum* (2003), *Equality* (2006), co-editor with Nik Seth-Smith of the e-book *Democratic Wealth* (2014), and is currently working on a book provisionally entitled *Democracy Over Wealth? Liberal Republican Political Economy*.

Tony Wright is a former Labour MP who is Professor of Government and Public Policy at University College London. His many books on politics and political ideas include, most recently, *British Politics: A Very Short Introduction* (2013).

1

Making social democrats

Jeremy Nuttall and Hans Schattle

Social democracy in the age (or moment) of 'Brexit' and Trump: decline or renewal?

It is intellectually fashionable to be gloomy about the current state of the political world and about British progressive and social democratic politics more specifically. There are some good grounds for this. The British Labour Party's electoral defeats since 2010, its profound internal divisions since the election of Jeremy Corbyn as leader in 2015, the collapse of the Liberal Democrats, the fragmentation of progressivism in Scotland and, above all, the 2016 referendum vote in favour of 'Brexit', are all situated in a broader international context in which social democratic and liberal parties have struggled to maintain traction amidst the rise of (mostly) right-wing populism, manifested most dramatically in the election of Donald Trump to the American presidency. These problems are also rooted in longer historical questions, since the arrival of democracy in Britain in 1918, regarding the persistence of inequalities, the limits of democratisation, and of the cultivation of a sense of active citizenship within the confines of the British state, and the Labour Party's patchy electoral success in the so-called 'Conservative century'. This book's honorand, the political thinker, historian, politician and public intellectual David Marquand, ranks among the most perceptive in drawing attention to many of these challenges, most notably in his acclaimed 1991 book *The Progressive Dilemma* (Marquand, 1992: 24–5).

These challenges are very real, yet the above picture is a partial one. It runs the risks both of conforming to the traditional tendency of many on the left, to focus primarily on the bleaker sides of social and political trends, and of magnifying relatively recent and short-lasting right-wing populist advances into something solidified, uniform and even irreversible. It is the contention of this volume that both political history and political present are more complex, multi-sided and essentially *mixed* than that, and social democrats need not resign themselves either to the inevitability or the endurance of the current state of affairs. As in times past, the constraints upon, and threats to, progress stand alongside achievements and new opportunities. While Labour won fewer elections than the Conservatives in the twentieth century, the extensions of welfare protection, civil liberties, democracy and educational opportunity to which its governments gave effect, most notably in office from 1945, 1964 and 1997, made a lasting impact, and often survived, at least in important measure, through long ensuing periods of Conservative rule. Social democracy's often diffuse societal, intellectual and cultural influences have exceeded and outlasted Labour's direct electoral success.

Moreover, even by the narrower electoral measure, it must be remembered that Labour's fall from power in 2010 came after, by far, its longest sustained period of electoral success. Albeit tentatively, the securing of the French presidency in 2017 by Emmanuel Macron, has suggested scope for a reinvigoration of centrist or centre-left electoral accomplishment, or at least, as also in recent elections in the Netherlands, and in the collapse of UKIP's vote in the 2017 British general election, the beginnings of a plateau and perhaps a diminution in the populist appeal. Even in the context of Trump's victory, it is too rarely remembered that the Democratic Party have still had the better of US presidential election results since 1992, and even more so in terms of share of the popular vote – as even in its defeats of 2000, and again in 2016 itself.

Most fundamentally, progressive and social democratic ideas rest on a broadly optimistic, albeit also nuanced and realistic, view of the potential and ultimate capacity for virtue, good sense and flowering of 'the people'. At the core of a new politics of 'mutual education', wrote Marquand in 1988, in his seminal *The Unprincipled Society*, 'lies the belief that men and women may learn if they are stretched; that they can discover how to govern themselves if they win self-government' (Marquand, 1988: 246). In many ways, this description goes to the heart of the meaning and the challenge of social democracy, and of progressive politics more broadly. It highlights that real progress, both social and individual advances, must in some profound sense be achieved *by* the people of a country, not just *for* them, that the people's role must be active, not passive. It also indicates that this advancement must ultimately be about more than a material or structural one, an increase in economic well-being or in the efficacy of particular policies or institutions. It must also encompass an uplift in the culture, values and indeed the very character of the citizenry.

Without this crucial double aspect of popular participation and ethical development, progressivism would both lack the depth of roots and power of momentum to sustain it and fail to provide to individuals that meaningful sense of inner, psychological fulfilment, involvement, and perhaps even happiness without which more economic-orientated or policy-orientated means of furthering progress seem pointless. The inescapable fate of the progressive, as Marquand articulated, is 'to gamble' on the ordinary people's ability to rise to this ambitious, participatory, learning process, and also to insist on this deeper agenda of progress through ethics, citizenship and values, not simply via the easier, more obvious or more tangible routes of 'manipulative short cuts to change, imposed "reforms", technocratic fixes' (Marquand, 1988: 246).

This approach suggests the basis of progressivism is to be found in values, culture and character as much as economics, institutions and structures – though also in the interconnections across all of these. That being so, developments like the rapid expansion of higher education, heightened civil liberties, home ownership and ambitions, not least for women and ethnic minorities, the more rapid, democratic and accessible dissemination of news and information, a seeming growing recent upsurge in grassroots political involvement and even more attentive approach to parenting *matter*. They may be just as conducive to social and political 'progress' as some of the more traditional, and more oft-cited measures of social democratic strength, such as the size of the organised industrial male working class, or the extent of state economic ownership. Moreover, many of these advances have been especially marked *since* the supposed high-water mark of social democracy (variously dated as 1951, 1970 or 1979). There are thus serious grounds for broadening and complicating narratives of social democratic decline and advance, which presently excessively privilege, and at times romanticise, the pre-1979 past.

With such considerations firmly in mind, this volume focuses less on the economic, institutional or policy issues that have produced much fruitful investigation elsewhere, and more on these questions relating to the popular values, mindsets and sense of citizenship needed to further social democracy, on that deeper enterprise of *Making Social Democrats*. The book also aims to provide an opportunity for its authors and readers to reflect broadly and deeply on the 'big picture' of social democracy and progressivism, both historical and contemporary. Encouraging the lifting of sights from the restrictions of either academic specialism or journalistic and political immediacy, contributors were asked to reflect, as Marquand has done over his long career, on what it is that lies at the 'heart' of progressive dilemmas, to consider social democracy over a broad historical and contemporary sweep.

These two aspects give the book both a distinctive unifying focus and an especially kaleidoscopic coverage of social democracy. Relatively few such broad explorations of British social democracy have been undertaken since turn-of-the-century edited collections like that of Tanner, Thane and Tiratsoo (2000). Worley's compilation (2009) is more recent, but more exclusively focused on the inter-war period, just as Hickson's (2016) is more specifically concentrated on contemporary social democratic policy and ideas. The most comparable collaborative work on the theme of social democracy is the book *In Search of Social Democracy* (Callaghan *et al.*, 2009), following a series of academic conferences in the mid-2000s on rethinking social democracy. This important volume is now ripe for reassessment; moreover, a large number of its contributions were in the sphere of economic policy. The book also offers a social democratic follow-up to the influential edited collection on Thatcherism by Jackson and Saunders (2012).

If the book seeks to attend to the large canvas of social democracy, it also pursues breadth in terms of its ideological inclusivity and its contributors. The term 'social democracy' serves as the unifying concept for the book, reflecting that in most major European countries, and certainly in Britain, the main social democratic political party has long been the primary focus of academic analysis, and broader public debate about the achievements and shortcomings of 'progressive' ideas – and indeed social progress as a whole. However, 'social democracy' is intended as a relatively expansive umbrella term, and it is one of the guiding assumptions that progressive ideas do not reside exclusively in any one ideology or party. Contributors (and themes) in the book range from socialists through social democrats to liberals, and, indeed, there is an acknowledgement in some of the discussion that conservatism has incorporated progressive dynamics. There is much divergence of viewpoint, reflecting the intellectual diversity of progressivism, past and present, as a whole. Although many of the chapters are written by academics and public intellectuals, several contributors hail from think tanks, journalism and government. In these respects, the book seeks to mirror its honorand, who has always bridged life's disciplinary, occupational and ideological divides. This is not to dispense, though, with an over-arching narrative, and a concern with the fluctuating mix of advances and retreats in progressive politics, and its essential ideas related to democratic empowerment and social equality permeates all the chapters. David Marquand's political approach and ideas provide the starting-point for many of the contributions. Equally, all the chapters open up fresh lines of enquiry of their own.

Progressive dilemmas: the historical long view

Part I takes the historical bird's eye view, exploring social democratic and liberal dilemmas that both pervaded the twentieth century and remain very much alive today. Jeremy Nuttall's chapter examines the many-sided relationship between social democracy and 'the people' in Britain. The issue of the people, the citizenry, the voters has long been a perplexing one for social democrats. Standing up for ordinary people is the very purpose of social democracy, and yet the people have frequently seemed to social democrats something of a disappointment, alternately insufficiently engaged with politics, or too conservative or individualistic when they do engage. Whilst highlighting this as a challenge and a problem, Chapter 2 also suggests that scholars and political analysts tend to under-play the extent to which progressivism and the voters have managed to operate in constructive harmony in the past, and the potential in the present moment for them to do so again.

For all the contemporary allure of populism, the British people have been, and are, on the whole, *better* than some of the worst sentiments aroused by the 'Brexit' project indicate, and their better instincts are open to more forward-looking political agendas. The chapter also contends, however, that channelling this more progressive side of the people will require social democrats to raise their game, too. If the people have sometimes disappointed social democrats, social democracy has also often failed properly to serve the people, tending, in its class outlooks, conservatism and internal obsessions, to itself lag behind some of the growing yearning for modernity, opportunity and affluence of the society it is claiming to wish to change. Both the people as a whole, then, and social democracy as an ideology, need to re-acquaint with, and refresh, the more forward-looking, constructive, optimistic sides of their respective natures.

A crucial part of this process will be intellectual and ideological re-thinking and reinvigoration, and more specifically an attention to the enduring intellectual and political divisions within progressivism. In Chapter 3, Michael Freeden probes this divide within liberalism whilst also addressing its implications for social democracy. Tracing liberalism's, and especially New and social liberalism's, distinctive offer of a fusion between social interdependence and individualism, Freeden assesses the failure of this liberalism to become the over-arching driver of twentieth-century politics. Too often, liberalism remained divided between its two wings, and insufficiently intellectually bold and imaginative in building on the ideological syntheses that Leonard Hobhouse, in particular, had articulated in the early part of the century. Such visions had been unable fully to break through amid alternative, more technocratic conceptions of the state, or adulations of the market, as well as the sheer magnitude of the challenges of the historical day to day. Nonetheless, Freeden sees two grounds for optimism. One is that liberalism has enjoyed a greater, albeit somewhat covert, influence than the rather limited later twentieth-century electoral success of the Liberal Party implies. In particular, liberalism long infused social democracy, notably in its Croslandite and New Labour variants. Second, the resilience and durability of liberalism, for all its apparent minority status, has been under-estimated, and it may well prove its fortitude at this contemporary populist moment, just as it appears under such strain and attack.

A third set of historical progressive dilemmas is explored, in Chapter 4, by Andrew Gamble through a re-visiting of Marquand's 1977 biography of Ramsay MacDonald. An extensive historical work, which sought to rescue MacDonald from the simplistic cries from his own party of betrayal for his heading of the coalition National Government in 1931, the book was also intended to offer clear lessons for what Marquand viewed as a Labour Party in the 1970s undermining itself though its class warfare, trade union sectionalism and doctrinal narrowness. Gamble argues that the dilemmas observed and lived out by both MacDonald and by Marquand, as his biographer, endured throughout the twentieth century and, indeed, remain unresolved today. How could the Labour Party protect the labour interest, yet also resonate beyond it, to a middle class and national audience? To what extent could it retain high ideals whilst also not shirking the practical responsibilities of actual government and the pursuit of electoral success? The answers to these questions, Gamble notes, divided left and right in the party. Yet, in other ways, they also united intellectuals of left and right in their frustration with the perceived conservatism, and intellectual inertia of the party's 'pragmatic' tradition. In today's context, then, there is the challenge of how to reconcile Corbynism with Blairism, yet also of how to reconcile the metropolitan liberalism which these present and past leaders have in common with some of the discontents of the party's northern working-class heartlands. Nearly one hundred years on, MacDonald offers, if not outright answers, some insights into the way in which, in times arguably even more challenging than our own – as the infant Labour Party sought to solidify its very existence – he grappled for an extended period with these delicate political balancing acts.

Forever a rolling stone: the life and endeavours of David Marquand

Before introducing some of the more contemporary dilemmas examined in the book's later chapters, we pause here to reflect on the contribution of the book's honorand. It is no contradiction to say that two of the most striking aspects of David Marquand's intellectual contribution are its breadth and its depth. In terms of the former, it is that ability to cross life's spheres, to combine and synthesise intellectual and political schools, that most impresses. He has been a politician *and* a thinker, a historian *and* a political theorist, a contributor to both left and centrist ideological traditions and, latterly, and increasingly, engaged with issues of democratic republicanism, civic engagement, identity and social history as much as the state and high policy. If it is achievement enough to excel at one thing, Marquand has been unusually successful in contributing in highly original ways to several, and perhaps most distinctively in creating something interesting from the points of intersection between them.

This breadth and variety did not, however, come at the expense of intellectual and moral depth, of unity and coherence, a sense of the big picture, the main event. He was not, as he put it of the Labour intellectual Richard Crossman, merely 'the progressive as gadfly', pricking intriguingly at disparate points, attacking, 'but when the demolition was over, the site was left vacant' (Marquand, 1992: 137–8). Marquand has always sought to address the large canvas, to search for the crux of things. What was most at the crux of things was the importance of values. His progressivism was determinedly, in Peter Clarke's distinction, 'moral', not 'mechanical'.

Although Marquand has attained considerable laudation and standing, the extent of his contribution remains somewhat under-estimated. This reflects that, lacking the perspective of hindsight, we tend to under-value the achievement of that which is closest to us in time, and Marquand's major works, most of which were published well into his 40s and beyond, remain relatively recent. It, perhaps, also stems from his refusal to dwell in a single, easily definable political or professional home. It also indicates his own, in many ways very British sense of reserve (although he testifies in his own chapter for this volume to presently feeling less comfortable with this particular identity). In any case, Marquand should certainly be considered one of the most important of British political thinkers and public intellectuals in the twentieth and early twenty-first centuries.

David Marquand's ever-evolving political and intellectual life reads as a history of many of the pivotal dilemmas of British progressivism as a whole, with which this book seeks to engage. He was born in Cardiff in 1934, son of Hilary Marquand, a professor of industrial relations and subsequently a minister in Clement Attlee's post-war Labour government. Marquand describes his as a sort of 'intermediate generation', too late to fight in the Second World War, yet matured too early to be a child of the culturally dynamic 1960s (Marquand, 1997: 7). What was formative and, to the young Marquand, normalised was the statism, collectivism and welfarism of the 1940s, the character of which has been the focus of much of both his most forceful critiques and his most passionate defences. Following National Service, he arrived at Oxford in 1954, where he studied history under A. J. P. Taylor. Already a bookish sceptic, who knew that 'revolutions devour their children', he was nonetheless determined not to swing to the other extreme of the dry empiricism he witnessed within the dreaming spires. Here, already, was the Marquandian search for the synthesis of apparent opposites, how, he had written in a pre-university paper, 'to find a way of applying scepticism to politics without destroying devotion' (Marquand, 1997: 8–9).

The answer seemed to lie initially with fellow Welshman Aneurin Bevan, or the New Left, but soon he became converted to the social democratic revisionism of Tony Crosland's *The Future of Socialism* (1956), which remained broadly his bible into the 1980s. Crosland was a fellow reconciler of values, believing a firm egalitarianism could be fused with a commitment to freedom and democracy, within a mixed democracy, given a capitalism that had been firmly tamed. This also suited the political optimism of the times, with a welfare state established, the economy booming, and globalisation and relative economic decline still some way around the corner. Marquand became a Gaitskellite *Guardian* leader-writer, and also worked briefly in academic posts at Berkeley, Oxford and Sussex.

In 1966 he became Labour MP for Ashfield, which he remained for eleven years. He would later write of his ill-suitedness to the 'feverish inconsequence' of parliamentary life, but it was characteristic that he was drawn to the two sides of the coin, to complement, and enhance his intellectualising about politics with practical experience of its realities (Marquand, 1997: 12). This period also witnessed the early stirrings of some of the themes that were to preoccupy him from the 1980s – how to reinvigorate British democracy, the limitations of the various British economic models of the 1960s, and the growing importance of both a political and a psychological Europeanism. He argued for devaluation with David Owen and John Mackintosh, before Harold Wilson was forced into it in 1967.

Crucially, Marquand was also one of the sixty-nine Labour MPs to rebel against a three-line whip to support new Conservative Prime Minister Edward Heath's policy of membership of the Common Market in 1971, a figure crucial to the outweighing of the anti-European Conservative MPs who voted against. By this time, Marquand was most admiring of the leader of this rebellion, another Welshman, Roy Jenkins, who had increasingly shown himself a more skilful and serious politician than his friend and fellow leading revisionist Crosland, as well as bolder in challenging the growing dogma and conservatism of his own party in the 1970s. As Jenkins fairly recalls, 'it was remarkable to hold sixty-nine Labour members against the pressures from constituencies, trade unions, whips, and the leadership, which all exploited the simple atavistic appeal to party loyalty and solidarity'. It reflected, ultimately, 'the politics of principle as opposed to those of place' (Jenkins, 1991: 311).

The problem, as Marquand now saw it, was not just that his revisionist social democratic middle way was losing ground to both a revitalised Labour left and a resurgent New Right, but that this revisionism had itself run out of intellectual steam, and now shared that outmoded over-reliance on ever-rising public expenditure and statism that also characterised Wilsonian labourist pragmatism and the Bennite left. Even the old hero Crosland had been reduced by this time, as Marquand saw it, to 'the progressive as [party] loyalist' (Marquand, 1992: 166). Here, was the first dramatic revelation for Marquand that the revisionism in which he had believed was not the final answer. The very mindset of questioning and fresh thinking that had given birth to revisionism now needed to be applied to its reinvention. Social democracy 'would go on losing until revisionism had been revised' (Marquand, 1997: 18).

Marquand resigned his seat in 1977 to work as adviser to Jenkins, now President of the European Commission, the same year as his biography of MacDonald was published. But the wide-ranging work of political thinking needed to grapple with the enduring historical dilemmas he had showcased through MacDonald had to be put on hold as he played a leading role as a founder member of the Social Democratic Party (SDP) in 1981. There are some valid criticisms of the SDP, and the Alliance it formed with the Liberal Party. Despite a striking public flirtation with its brand of less class-polarised, more centrist politics, culminating in a momentarily remarkable Gallup opinion poll rating of 51 per cent in December 1981, it fell well behind Labour's seat share in the 1983 election, and slid steadily in support thereafter, as Labour returned gradually to moderation under Neil Kinnock (Crewe and King, 1995: 144). The somewhat socially rootless Liberal Alliance, and its leaders, over-estimated the pace of the decline of class-based party loyalties (real as it was). There is also something in the charge that the SDP, in its early years, was too much an updated version of 1950s' Croslandism, insufficiently attuned to the more socially mobile, less deferential society of the

1980s, with its yearning for home and share ownership, and self-employment, although it was certainly more attentive to these than the Labour Party. As Crewe and King (1995: 116) shrewdly observed, those in the SDP 'were founding a new party, but in many cases they were not quite sure how new they really wanted it to be'.

But, when all this is allowed for, one is more impressed by the political and intellectual insight and boldness of the SDP than its failings. In the highly polarised political and social environment of the late 1970s and early 1980s, it sought to provide a thoughtful middle way, which fused the best of both social justice and economic dynamism. Its founders were also brave – intellectually, politically and, not least, personally. Especially for those, like Marquand, who were, as he put it, 'cradle Labour' (Marquand, 1997: 8), it meant being willing to tear away from long-held institutional and personal loyalties and emotions. The split from Labour at this point remains perhaps the most dramatic and important instance in which Marquand exhibited, in a very direct and personal way, his commitment to the politics of independent thinking, to confronting uncomfortable new truths head on, and being willing to break with the past. In hindsight, it seems improbable that there was ever a serious chance of the Alliance 'breaking the mould' of two-party politics at this point, but this is because its ideas were essentially ahead of their time. They later found fruition in both the governing New Labour Party, and the resurgent new Liberal Democrat Party, in the 1990s and 2000s, the creation of which, in 1988, out of the old Alliance, Marquand was surely, in any serious view of practical party politics, correct to support.

When that next book, *The Unprincipled Society* (1988), his finest, did eventually appear, it was, therefore, the culmination of much pent-up thought, 'two – perhaps three – books in one', as he saw it (Marquand, 1997: 26). It critiqued the then electorally dominant neoliberalism, rejected the fading neo-socialist alternative, but crucially also pointed to the limitations of the post-war Keynesian consensus, too statist and mechanical, and lacking the moral self-definition, and self-confident philosophical defence of the virtues of the public realm to defend itself in hard times. A new, more communitarian, participatory and conversational politics of 'mutual education', as described earlier in this introduction, was his view of the way forward (Marquand, 1988: 246).

With the intellectual weight of *The Unprincipled Society* allied with the more politically focused *The Progressive Dilemma* (1991), both works proving that moral and ideological profundity could go hand in hand with readability and indeed, for the reader, excitement, Marquand was now at the height of direct influence on the intellectual climate of politics. Suffering its fourth consecutive general election defeat in 1992, Labour, under the neo-Croslandite John Smith, and then the ultra-moderniser, Tony Blair was readier to engage with new and challenging thinking.

The revised, 1992 edition of *The Progressive Dilemma*, updated in the light of Labour's election defeat, sought in Marquand's typical fashion to deter the party from any lazy, cosy reassurance they might derive from their modest advance from the 1987 election. Instead, he poured directly over its face the harsh cold-water realities of a diminishing core manual working-class base, and accompanying growing aspirational class to whom Labour's collectivism did not automatically appeal (Marquand, 1992: viii). More than this, he insisted that the party's problems were not confined to the specifics of the 1980s. More fundamentally, Labour had failed to fully construct the sort of broad-based, national progressive alliance which had been achieved by the nineteenth- and early twentieth-century Liberal Party. The reasons why included the conservatism and group loyalty of the labourist sectional tradition, the party's reservations about embracing the progressive intelligentsia and new ideas, and the implausibility of Labour's claim to be ready for government. A new progressive coalition was now needed, both intellectual and political, 'social democratic in its ethic but liberal in its practice', inspired by values of citizenship and community, and transcending both the old ideological categories of left, centre and right, and the rigid existing party lines (Marquand, 1992: x).

Partly through the intellectual intermediary of David Miliband, the broad thrust of *The Progressive Dilemma* chimed with, and influenced the early thinking of Tony Blair and New Labour (Marquand, 2010: 42). Disagreeing with the Liberal Democrats' policy of equidistance from Labour and the Conservatives, because he believed it under-valued the achievement of Neil Kinnock in reforming his party, Marquand left the party after the 1992 election, and re-joined Labour after Blair became leader, firmly approving the re-writing of Clause Four of the party's constitution, succeeding where Hugh Gaitskell had failed. For all Marquand's later criticisms of New Labour, he was one of its most important intellectual influences, especially in its early, dynamically reforming years.

In high policy terms, the *zeitgeist* was in favour of combining an acceptance of aspects of the market economy with a new emphasis on rebuilding the public realm and public services, the sort of balance that had essentially characterised the SDP. Marquand's long advocacy of democratisation and constitutional reform also found fruit in the 1997 government's long list of modifications to the Westminster Model, from devolution to reform of the House of Lords. Perhaps most fundamentally, the early Blair demonstrated that Marquandian essential of sheer governing competence, finally demonstrating conclusively that one could be progressive and bold, without shedding the ability actually to manage things, and keep grasp of the detail, especially on the economy.

But there was also a new recognition in both social democratic and liberal circles that high policy was not enough. For progress to be real and sustainable, progressive values needed to have roots in, and participation from the people: the citizenry as much as the approval of the political elites. This meant social democracy must broaden its scope to incorporate an interest in culture, citizenship, community values and character, as well as to democratise political and other institutions to allow the people's attributes to flower.

Even in his fleeting New Left days at Oxford, Marquand had been drawn by 'their view that socialism was about culture as well as about economics' (Marquand, 1997: 9). Later, as his enthusiasm for parliamentary and constitutional reform grew, it was qualified by the knowledge that 'institutional changes would make little difference' without 'a culture of negotiation and power-sharing' (Marquand, 1997: 13). Policies, institutions, material changes could only advance things so far. Even ideological or doctrinal refinements did not quite get to it; something still more fundamental, to do with the very attitude, approach and mentality was needed. 'Republicanism', Marquand was reflecting by 2010, 'is not so much a doctrine as a cast of mind' (Marquand, 2010: 42). All this was testimony to the relentlessly challenging and insightful quality of Marquand's work. The eminent social historian, Arthur Marwick, in his hugely popular Penguin history of post-war Britain, labelled *The Unprincipled Society* 'perhaps the most interesting political critique' of its era (Marwick, 1990: 379).

Yet, as with any body of thought, there are criticisms and omissions in Marquandism. Lauding Marquand's vision of a 'principled society' in place of the unprincipled one, Marwick observed that 'just how this was to be achieved was less clear' (Marwick, 1990: 379). It is a fair criticism that Marquand, for all his hard realism and historical sensitivity in some respects, at times under-estimates the real-life obstacles to the achievement of political ideals, and the constraints that practising politicians face. That leads him to under-value the 'mixed result' that is the outcome of so many, probably most governmental projects, certainly in modern British history. In more recent years, in particular, his appraisals of some of the more centrist post-war social democratic figures, like Crosland and Blair, appear to insufficiently allow for the circumstances of the time, or of the achievement and building blocks contained within steady, if undramatic social and political progress.

Second, while Marquand, along with Roy Jenkins, was to the fore in the 1970s in articulating a case for Labour to shed its labourist conservatism, and adapt to meet a changing society, this also, by the 1980s, had its limits. Again like Jenkins, and representative of the SDP as a whole prior to David Owen's more forward-looking leadership, Marquand gave a nod to the way in which heightened social mobility, rising wages, home ownership and educational opportunity were empowering many formerly Labour-supporting, and now Thatcher-supporting working-class families, but it was a somewhat half-hearted one. As Black's penetrating research has shown, socialists have long struggled to come to terms with the modernities of affluence and social change. Crucially, this did not have to mean abandoning a critique of brash materialism. But by, at times, seeming uneasy with affluence altogether, the left missed the chance to define, appropriate and shape a politics of affluence on its own terms, to the detriment of both the quality of its policy and its electoral performance (Black, 2003).

Third, if Marquand's intellectual focus has moved increasingly beyond high politics – and his writings certainly point powerfully to the need for a very broad definition of what is political – there remains a trace in his work of the 'mechanistic' preoccupation with political groupings and institutions, and state machinations of which in other ways he disapproves. The interest in broader social and psychological themes, in education, mindset, character and outlook that characterises some of this book's chapters is, thus, partly building on foundations Marquand has established, but also moving in directions he only tentatively signposted.

In 1996, Marquand became Principal of Mansfield College, Oxford. This post was a fitting appointment: Mansfield is known for its democratic, egalitarian and informal culture – the scouts had the same access to the wine cellar as the dons; high table is situated no higher than the rest of the hall; the chapel points north instead of east, as in all the Anglican colleges, and as David's wife Judith once noted with a sense of glee at a festive Mansfield event (at which Roy Jenkins spoke) commemorating Oliver Cromwell, Mansfield, had it existed in the seventeenth century, would have backed Cromwell in the Civil War, in contrast with many of the other Oxford colleges at the time.

Mansfield was also where the two editors of this volume were to enjoy the benefits of Marquand's doctoral supervision. This was a richly rewarding, if at times somewhat daunting, experience. The high intellectual stimulation provided and the sense of being in the presence of a rapier-like mind, may be unsurprising to readers. More noteworthy, although one certainly felt one had to be at the top of one's game, and emphatically not inadequately prepared, that feeling coexisted with a striking degree of genuine warmth and absence of pretension, given what one might have expected in the presence of either the head of an Oxford college or a leading public intellectual, let alone both. During his years in Oxford, Marquand led path-breaking efforts, both at Mansfield and across the university, to admit higher proportions of applicants from state schools, in no small measure delivering upon the principles of equity, inclusion and pluralism he has long championed in his writings.

Upon his retirement from Mansfield in 2002, Marquand did not rest on his laurels or ride off into the sunset but immediately catapulted himself into the most prolific decade of his career, publishing four books from 2004 to 2014 and keeping a high public profile with frequent commentaries in *Prospect*, *New Statesman* and *The Guardian*. The first book in this more recent assemblage, *Decline of the Public*, compiles a series of essays that looked searchingly at the erosion of engaged citizenship and the attrition of the public domain in the face of neoliberalism, or 'market fundamentalism', as well as the more populist strands within the then-Blair government, which Marquand criticised with increasing ferocity as Blair lapsed into excessive deference to American President George W. Bush. Although *The Unprincipled Society*, *The Progressive Dilemma* and *Ramsay MacDonald* are often considered as Marquand's most significant books, *Decline of the Public* has received the most academic citations, according to Google Scholar, among his many publications.

Next came *Britain Since 1918* (2008), the *magnum opus* in Marquand's more recent writings: a comprehensive and multifaceted history of the political development and political economy of Britain that contains within it the intriguing proposition that successive British governments throughout the twentieth century shifted repeatedly across four particular conceptions of the British state: Whig imperialism, Tory nationalism, democratic collectivism and, his preferred model, 'democratic republicanism'. Like all of Marquand's books, the story combines lively narrative with rich interpretation that in this case was a long time in the making: Marquand shared his early prospectus of what eventually became *Britain Since 1918* with one of this volume's editors in the spring of 1998 as he first made contact with Marquand while preparing to embark upon his studies.

Alongside his incessant writings on British history and politics, Marquand has written two noted books on European integration. First he popularised the now-common phrase 'democratic deficit' in *A Parliament for Europe*, published in 1979, the same year in which reforms led the way for the Parliament's representatives to be elected directly by the citizens rather than being dispatched by the respective national assemblies of the member states. Then, in 2012, amid the Eurozone crisis and the malaise that accompanied the palpable decline of solidarity across the member states in an overstretched European Union, Marquand published *The End of the West*, which excoriated the architects of the single European currency for forging ahead with monetary union without a corresponding fiscal union (an incongruity that the European Union has since partially corrected) and argued that the larger project of European economic and political integration can only go forward productively by pursuing a federal model. He also made the point that as the centre of gravity in the global economy shifts in the direction of Asia, Europe and the transatlantic 'West' must abandon its old and false sense of superiority over the 'East'. Whilst in *Britain Since 1918*, Marquand calls for a democratic constitution for the United Kingdom, in *The End of the West* he calls for a corresponding move for the European Union. His argument encountered some criticism from those who prefer to cast the European Union as largely intergovernmental both in empirical and normative terms (Moravcsik, 2011), but the present difficulties facing the European Union leave one suspecting that Marquand's diagnosis about the status quo was all too prescient.

Most recently, Marquand published the polemical *Mammon's Kingdom: An Essay on Britain, Now* (2014), a blistering and blunt yet colourful and historically informed attack on the ways in which he believes today's governing and business elites have abdicated any sense of pursuing a common good in favour of the greedy pursuit of immediate self-interest as well as crass self-gratification; indeed, Marquand uses the word 'hedonism'. Echoing the themes of *Decline of the Public*, in terms of his worry, even despair with regard to the continued hollowing out of the public domain, *Mammon's Kingdom* is a clarion call for market individualism and outright consumerism to be swept away once and for all into a renewed politics of the public interest and public trust. Portions of this book, in the eyes of some of the reviewers, seemed too rosy-eyed about the past, while indifferent to recent progress, both in moral and social terms, as well as new wellsprings of activism and altruism. As Rowan Williams, the former Archbishop of Canterbury and now the head of Magdalene College, Cambridge, noted in a review (Williams, 2014): 'the irritable dismissal of late-Sixties radicalism, especially R. D. Laing and Edmund Leach, is not entirely fair: there were oppressive family structures, violent domestic arrangements and corrupt habits to be challenged, even if some of the challenges ended up generating new and equally corrupting follies'. Still, when it comes to the imperatives of renewing a social market economy, a vibrant democracy, and a morally vigorous public realm, in many respects, our 'Making Social Democrats' theme in this volume picks up exactly where

Marquand left off at the close of *Mammon's Kingdom* (2014: 220), when he articulated several core values of social democracy as urgently vital at this moment in time:

> We face formidable challenges, but given determination and courage we can meet them. We can break with the arid fancies of Chicagoan economics. We can begin to master markets instead of allowing them to master us. We can start to rebuild the battered public realm and halt the drift toward a market society. We can put the ethic of stewardship ahead of profit, empathetic understanding ahead of command and control, and sustainability ahead of growth ...
> Sceptics may wonder if such a philosophy can fly in the harsh world of the twenty-first century. The answer is straightforward. We can't go on as we are.

David Marquand, for his part, has never found contentment in going on as he is. The eminent historian Kenneth Morgan, a contemporary of Marquand's and one of the contributors to this volume, has noted (2014) with a mixture of irony and affection that 'at various times, Marquand has pursued all sorts of lost or struggling causes – the SDP, the Lib Dems, proportional representation, English regionalism, Milton's republicanism, "stakeholder society", European federalism'. And, most recently, Welsh nationalism and independence, in the event that his dream of a federal Britain in a federal Europe should die at the hands of Brexit. This latest cause traces back to September 2013, when David and Judith visited Cardiff, where David was born, and found themselves energised by the open, bottom-up, locally oriented democratic political culture still very much in its emerging stages. As Marquand later recounted:

> Some time ago a civil servant in the devolved Welsh administration tried, in my hearing, to distil in a few words the crucial difference between the political culture of Wales and that of the United Kingdom as a whole. The overarching theme of United Kingdom governance, he said, can be summed up as 'choice, customer, competition'. The Welsh equivalent, he thought, is 'voice, citizen, collaboration'. Instead of endlessly looking over her shoulder at her English neighbour, the task for Wales is to make a reality of that magnificent trio. (Marquand, 2015)

Excited by this political outlook, David and Judith proceeded to buy a flat close to the oceanfront Esplanade in Penarth; so began their foray into Wales and, ultimately, their decision together in 2016 to ditch Labour and join Plaid Cymru in its efforts to bring about a renewal of democratic socialism and further devolution within the United Kingdom. Never one to rest on his laurels, David Marquand is now writing a book on the disparate histories and indeterminate prospects facing each of the four nations of the United Kingdom.

Citizenship, republicanism and democracy

Any construction of a new public philosophy and resurgence for progressive politics in the years ahead will depend on the capacities of citizens to take responsibility for the public good in multiple, overlapping communities, from local to global. Prospects for open and just societies ultimately rest in the hands of citizens, and in this sense, citizens are the glue in this collection of essays binding together mindsets and realities with regard to social democracy. Part II of this book, which concentrates on citizenship, republicanism and democracy, looks at citizenship as a set of practices carried forth by everyday people in politics and civil society – what Alexis de Tocqueville (1966: 286–7) famously termed the 'habits of the heart' – as well as the institutional and public policy changes that have thrown into jeopardy the entitlements and protections that necessarily accompany any meaningful social democratic citizenship.

Hans Schattle's opening chapter for this section, Chapter 5, takes stock of these issues in a global context, particularly with regard to the breaking of the post-war-era social contract across the 'Western' democracies alongside the dominance, since the Reagan–Thatcher era, of neoliberalism and its tenets of deregulation, privatisation and unfettered trade. The legions of dislocated industrial workers who comprised an essential base of support for social democratic parties throughout the twentieth century have been relatively neglected by left and centre-left parties at the dawn of the twenty-first century as party leaders have shifted the balance of their strategies and public outreach toward the more affluent professional classes. As Robert Ford and Matthew Goodwin have documented in their path-breaking book, *Revolt on the Right*, the UK Independence Party (UKIP) gained large numbers of voters from Labour's historically white, working-class base who concluded they had been left behind by the Blair government and by New Labour. As Ford and Goodwin put it:

> Symbolic and substantive commitments to helping the poor and economically insecure workers were downplayed in favour of commitments to tough spending discipline and free market reform of 'inefficient' state services. The needs of traditional Labour voters – for affordable housing, secure work, higher incomes and access to training – were marginalised in rhetoric and often in policy too … New Labour were seen as a party which neglected the poor and the working class, and courted minorities and the right. (2014: 129, 134)

Likewise, across the Atlantic, when Bill Clinton first campaigned for the US presidency in 1992, he pledged to restore economic opportunity for the 'forgotten' working classes, yet his economic policies had the effect of further widening social and economic inequalities and eroding opportunities for the working class. Schattle also reckons with the sobering reality that exclusionary variants of right-wing populism have tapped the public resentment against the excesses and inequities of economic globalisation far more effectively than a renewed model of social democracy. Indeed, the likes of Marine Le Pen and Nigel Farage share with many (but certainly not all) social democrats an aversion to the same international economic institutions and arrangements. Le Pen and her National Front party have taken on board social welfare policies more commonly associated with politicians on the French left, and across the Atlantic. Although Donald Trump and Bernie Sanders articulated dramatically different visions for the United States in the 2016 presidential campaign, they drew supporters from the same wellspring of economic frustration – the still-forgotten voters shunted into the margins by every American president since the waning days of the Cold War.

How, then, can social democratic citizenship be transformed for the new technologically driven, digitally interconnected world of the twenty-first century? Schattle argues that empowerment, equity and engagement are three lodestars for the re-making of social democratic citizenship and illustrates how new voices and venues are emerging in pursuit of more auspiciously deployed governing institutions and public policies. It isn't enough for today's social democrats merely to follow the directives of party leaders or trade union bosses. In fact, this isn't even on the cards, since many of today's voters who lean toward a social democratic ideology belong neither to a trade union nor to a political party. Yet new local, transnational and virtual venues – from online petitions to social movement campaigns that confront local problems using global platforms – have great potential in filling the vacuum and creating new public spaces for deliberation and contestation. Indeed, this is the most promising way to tap into righteous anger over economic injustice while preventing it from simmering into the toxic, xenophobic brew fuelling much (but again, not all) of today's 'new' populism. Schattle emphasises that although today's social democrats inevitably operate in capitalist frameworks, there are indeed real divides in interests between labour and capital: the business sector, by its nature, has never sought to take on benevolence, and social democrats must take up the challenge of modulating, managing and regulating capitalist economies in ways that protect the interests and uphold the well-being of the general public; this imperative of social democracy is timeless.

Stuart White shifts the critical scrutiny, in Chapter 6, to the extensive body of thought from David Marquand on citizenship, and especially Marquand's civic republican vision for a far more energised and engaged public in Britain. Taking stock of how Marquand's thinking about citizenship in relation to governing institutions has evolved throughout the past three decades, he shows how Marquand's preferred democratic republicanism, as set forth especially in *Britain Since 1918*, elevates civic virtue as not only instrumental toward the pursuit of social and economic justice but also as an end in itself in political life. At the nexus of citizenship and democracy, in Marquand's thinking, is public deliberation in the search for a common good as well as the public embrace of duties alongside rights. All this ties into Marquand's close affinities, especially in his writings published in the years preceding New Labour's 1997 election, with 'communitarian' critics, such as Alasdair MacIntyre (1980) and Michael Sandel (1996), of an excessively individualistic and atomistic model of liberalism. Marquand decisively positions himself against both market individualism and moral individualism as impediments to establishing a shared public philosophy with a common public purpose.

Echoing the language of J. G. A. Pocock, the path-breaking historian of the civic republican tradition who wrote of the 'Machiavellian moment' (1975), White argues that the beleaguered United Kingdom is ripe for a 'Marquandian moment' that would help usher in a new configuration of governing institutions, along the lines of federalism and pluralism, thereby living up to civic republican principles far more readily than the existing, highly centralised, 'winner-take-all' British state. White cautions, however, that civic republican processes of public deliberation and responsive decision-making do not necessarily yield social democratic outcomes. Civic republicans can just as easily lean toward conservativism or a radically individualistic brand of liberalism. In light of this, White maintains that today's social democrats need to focus on rendering state institutions more accessible and accountable to the myriad interests of the public, and that the English, in particular, need to cultivate a civic nationalism that will enable England's increasingly diverse population to shape a newly unifying, socially inclusive political narrative.

For all the emphasis in this volume upon the practices and accompanying mindsets of citizenship, state institutions and their respective configurations also matter decisively in determining whether or not social democratic agendas go forward in government decisions and policies. Many chapters, therefore, place great weight upon possible ways to reshape governing institutions in Britain in ways that would point toward Marquand's conception of democratic republicanism and better serve the public: towards more federal, plural, decentralised arrangements that spur public participation and account more fully for the interests and problems facing a diverse and stratified, even fractured population. Other questions that take a high profile in this section include the extent to which it is feasible for capitalism and democracy to operate in mutual harmony, and what it will take for the political left in Britain to regroup, regain power and, eventually, govern more effectively than before, in whatever institutional arrangements it might inherit.

Ben Jackson is preoccupied, in Chapter 7, with possible changes in the configuration of the United Kingdom: he confronts head-on the looming possibility of Scottish secession from the United Kingdom in the aftermath of the Brexit referendum. Jackson sees this development as a long time in coming and critiques the thinkers behind Charter 88 for giving the Scottish question 'short shrift' in their landmark document on constitutional reform Although the spectre of secession might sound ominous, Jackson points out that Scottish nationalism has evolved in a way highly compatible with the imperatives of republican social democracy, and that somewhat ironically, Scottish independence from the United Kingdom could have the effect of finally shifting England into more pluralist and republican forms of governance; it could also prompt England, he argues, to forge a stronger link between democratic reform and economic reform that Marquand has long advocated in his writings. Jackson takes seriously the Scottish nationalist critique that the United Kingdom, as it currently exists, is 'unreformable', and he sees the Scottish nationalists as the furthest along, of all the political parties in Britain, on the path to a democratic-pluralist vision of governance.

The principled society: mindsets and values

Part III seeks to apply Marquand's search for the 'principled society', and his favouring of a moral over a mechanical politics to some crucial contemporary, as well as broad historical contexts. It also takes Marquand as a starting-point for some new departures, in particular his previously mentioned reflection that the route to political advancement, or democratic republicanism lay not so much in 'a doctrine as a cast of mind' (Marquand, 2010: 42). The importance of mindset in politics, and of psychological attributes of outlook or good character, whether their presence or absence, to the success, or failure, of political projects has begun to receive attention in recent years, especially from modern British historians. In his seminal work on nineteenth-century 'public moralists', Stefan Collini pointed to the prominence of the ideal of character in Victorian thought (Collini, 1991: 94). Collini adjudged this less central to twentieth-century thinking, but in fact political thought, on the left, right and centre has remained very interested in the question of the virtue and character of the citizenry, and of politics as values and outlook, not simply ideas and policies. The Labour Party's historical approach to the theme of character was explored in Nuttall's work on *Psychological Socialism* (Nuttall, 2006), and the relevance of character and outlook to contemporary politics is touched on in several chapters beyond this section, including Nuttall's own.

In Chapter 8, Clare Griffiths probes the historical and political implications of the social and psychological concept of 'neighbourliness', especially as it played out in that pivotal moment of apparent social democratic ascendancy, the 1940s, and the 'People's War'. In line with the revisionist historiography on this period, Griffiths warns us against romanticising the decade, and exaggerating the degree of good will and community spirit that really existed. 'Neighbourliness' was often constructed, whether to boost the case for the war effort or, later, for socialism or town planning. It could also at times be invasive and snooping. Yet, she insists, we should not ignore the importance of the aspiration to neighbourliness, albeit imperfect and half-formed, as it was a persistent theme at government and intellectual levels, but also in ordinary, everyday conversations. Part-hidden in the seemingly more statist 1960s and 1970s, it has nevertheless re-emerged in the contemporary political era. Above all, it shows the important relationship between values and emotions on the one hand and political objectives on the other, as well as subjects like housing policy and community life somewhere in between. 'The *idea* of neighbourliness', notes Griffiths, 'opened up a different political territory, between the private sphere of the home and the public sector of government'.

Gideon Calder's intersecting themes of political contestation, care and the temper of the country examine the public good less as a fixed entity but rather as an evolving conversation taking place across a wide range of social settings, not least in the flux and informality of everyday life. Drawing on Marquand's belief that progressivism was as much about process as outcomes, Calder suggests that it is also not just about doctrine, but also, as R. H. Tawney articulated, dependent on a certain 'temper' in the country at large. Progress required not just structural or economic change, but good relationships, not just the espousal of social democracy, but the making of social democrats. Consequently, Calder concludes his chapter with ten suggestions for progress not via policy, but through conversation. One is to converse as if listening were as valued an attribute as speaking; another is not to speak as if the status quo tightly defines all available horizons.

Sharing Calder's view that social democracy must be lived and practised as a never-ending quest for improvement, Neal Lawson, in Chapter 10, probes the historical reasons why the ethically driven, pluralist politics espoused by Marquand has yet to be fully adopted and assesses its relevance to the present. For much of the twentieth century, he argues, a mechanistic politics (and economics) were variously reflected in the power of, and importance attached to the state, the big company, the political 'centre', hierarchy and the machine. Fordism and Fabianism went hand in hand, but in the early twenty-first century they have given way to an uncertain situation in which capitalism is discredited, yet social democracy has not worked out a persuasive alternative. The need, in Lawson's eyes, is to bend modernity to social democratic values, neither ignoring modernity, like Jeremy Corbyn, nor bending the values to modernity, as with Tony Blair. The less hierarchical, more communicationally and informationally connected modern society offers grounds for optimism about the prospects for more democratic and egalitarian approaches. However, this must entail making moral choices, in favour of Marquand's vision of active citizenship over turbo-consumerism. In terms of political means, it also entailed a more pluralist and decentralised politics, and the creation of a progressive, cross-party alliance.

In the final chapter of Part III, Kenneth Morgan explores the significance of Christopher Addison, a still relatively neglected figure, whose long career illuminates many of the central dilemmas of the broad progressive tradition in the first half of the twentieth century, as well as offering some lessons for Labour's faction-ridden army today. Unusual in being a Lloyd George coalition Liberal who crossed over to Labour and not the Conservatives, Addison symbolises that there was, in his case and others, a fusion of the socialist and liberal progressive traditions, even if it did not lead to a merger of the parties. Addison was very much a practical social democrat, 'mechanical' in some ways, Morgan suggests, from work with local authorities, through the cooperative movement, to collaboration with the professions over national insurance. Yet he was driven by a clear moral purpose. This was an illustration that mechanical and moral routes to progress could be complementary, and that, as Morgan notes, an excessively abstract or pious moralism (as with some Victorian moralists) was of little benefit without a substantial practical agenda to give it concrete thrust. A further lesson for social democrats today is that Addison was far removed from a grandstander, drawn to conflict for its own sake. He pursued ideals, but was also grounded in the possibilities of the moment. As Morgan concludes, 'a quiet medical man of the Edwardian centre-left could be re-emerging as a prophet of practical socialism in our time, dreaming his dreams but always basing them on existing realities'.

Whither social democracy in Britain?
Prospects, reflections and realities

Academic history and political theory at times show too little understanding of practical political constraints and realities, just as practitioners can lose sight of vision and the broader horizons. Any project on reinvigorating social democracy must therefore reckon with the practical hurdles, pitfalls and obstacles that inevitably accompany and, at times, inhibit or foreclose public policy innovations and reforms in the configurations and objectives of political institutions. It is equally essential to come to terms with the very rough and tumble of political bargaining and partisan jockeying in the corridors of government and beyond. Hence the chapters in Part IV combine scholarly insights with more practical sources of wisdom culled from the analysis of everyday politics – akin to Harold Lasswell's immortal take on politics as 'who gets what, when, how' (1936) – as well as decades of hands-on, lived experiences across the arenas of politics and government, business, civil society and academia.

The hands-on challenges involved in building up genuinely democratic mechanisms of self-government in Britain take a high profile in Tony Wright's essay (Chapter 12) focused on the *democracy* aspects within social democracy. In Wright's view, today's social democrats must probe the depths of this fundamental question: what kind of state is important and for what purpose? Mediating public interests and private interests is cast in this chapter as a central task of social democracy, along with checking corporate power for the good of the public. Like it or not, Wright notes, the Brexit referendum was a remarkably successful democratic uprising, regardless of whether leaving the European Union is truly in the long-term interest of Britain and its citizenry. The defeat for the 'Remain' campaign underscored the weaknesses of the Labour Party in the 'politics of place and identity', and renewed the imperative for social democrats to defend the *liberal* tradition in the face of nationalist and populist attacks.

Social democracy is no longer (if it ever was) the route to a resolutely socialist future but rather to democratic outcomes that fulfil the needs of the general public in liberal democratic political systems. Achieving this goal in Britain is a challenge, Wright says, not only because of the government's 'centralised and concentrated' power but also because any real sense of active citizenship across the United Kingdom continues to languish in a state of underdevelopment. Yet despite all the setbacks that have undermined social democracy throughout the past generation, its 'permanent revisionism' is needed more than ever, Wright says, as the continuous restructuring of the economy in the hypercompetitive global marketplaces breeds tremendous insecurity for all segments of workers

– professionals as well as the working class. Wright also notes that for all the problems, social democrats can take pride in the hard-fought public goods won through the years – better jobs, cleaner air, affordable health care – and forge ahead for a wholesale democratic revolution in Britain that renders a government more 'decentralised, pluralised and participatory'. As Wright aptly puts it, 'If democracy is about enabling people to exercise some power and control over the forces that impact on their lives, then social democrats should be those who are constantly looking for ways to make this a reality.'

David Owen, in Chapter 13, reflects upon the underlying concerns that he and David Marquand share in principle: creating conditions to foster a more equitable distribution of wealth and resources in Britain, as well as a bottom-up, republican social democracy championing the virtues of justice and equality. Despite their incompatible positions on Europe, with Marquand supporting a federal Britain embedded in a federal Europe and Owen having campaigned for Brexit, the two erstwhile parliamentary colleagues converge in placing priority, in tandem, on democratic empowerment and economic reform and see these two goals as thoroughly interconnected. Can Britain manage to hang together in a post-Brexit Europe and also shift to a republican civic culture? Owen sees this prospect as still within reach, despite the obstacles.

David Marquand, in Chapter 14, revisits the trajectory of his thinking and writing across his varied life experiences – as a history student tutored by A. J. P. Taylor, journalist at the *Guardian*, parliamentarian, European Union official, Oxford don, public intellectual and, most recently, Welsh nationalist, as a convert to Plaid Cymru as of 2016. Among the revelations here is that Marquand places such a high priority on transforming Britain into a more robustly democratic and civic culture that he turned down the 'half-offer' of a peerage some years ago, noting that 'I couldn't have lived with myself if I had accepted.' He also traces his pro-European leanings back to his period of national service in the RAF, contrasting the fates of his Russian language teachers who had been displaced from their homes and their career paths with his own fortunate circumstances:

> I couldn't help realising that, but for the lucky chance of a few miles of salt water, their fates might have been mine. As a result, I came to feel that the smug, condescending and self-righteous notion that Britain was different from and better than the rest of the European continent was both false and disgraceful. The seeds of my lifelong commitment to the vision of a united Europe were sown in the unlikely setting of a camp of leaky wooden huts perched on the edge of Bodmin moor.

Above all, Marquand places value on the 'mutual learning' that goes with pluralist democracy as well as the potential, through public deliberation, for citizens to transform their outlook, perspectives and maybe even their very natures as human beings by taking on board the perspectives of others that they encounter in political conversation, even in the most informal of settings. This is what worries Marquand most about populism: that populism of any kind has the effect of extinguishing the potential for dynamic political education, mutual respect, public empowerment and moral advancement. It is also why Marquand, in his chapter, issues a ringing endorsement of pluralist democracy and a sharp denunciation of populism in which its leaders, or, in many cases, demagogues, falsely claim to speak 'for the people', when they are merely speaking *to* the people, while also fraudulently framing the people as a 'homogenous and monolithic whole'.

Mindful of Britain's uncertain prospects – both as a member state of the European Union and as an intact United Kingdom – Marquand concludes by observing that the outlying nations of the United Kingdom are now far more poised for this kind of pluralist democracy than the prevailing sentiment across most of England. Should Brexit actually go forward, Marquand writes, then 'I would want Wales to become an independent nation state within a proto-federal European Union instead of being chained for ever to a hard-right, chauvinistic and xenophobic England'. Can a reinvigorated, pluralist, republican social democracy emerge in a still-United Kingdom no longer part of the European Union? Marquand has all but given up on this possibility, and in doing so he is sounding the alarm bell for progressives in general and the Labour Party in particular.

Will Hutton, in Chapter 15, levels indictments against the existing British state and its elected dictatorship as a 'Gothic, feudal horror' as well as the political left for lapsing into a state of 'bankruptcy' under current Labour leader Jeremy Corbyn. (His attack on Corbyn is reminiscent of Thomas Jefferson's charges against King George III as written in the US Declaration of Independence.) In contrast, despite all the malfeasance documented within the business sector in the years surrounding the 2008–9 financial crisis – a global cataclysm that discredited 'market fundamentalism' even as this ideology remains largely dominant in the present day – Hutton adopts a far softer tone on the business sector and maintains that harmony between vigorous capitalism and reinvigorated self-government is entirely within reach.

Government leaders, in Hutton's view, ought to engage business, broadly speaking, in positive terms as a public institution with the purpose of placing 'human betterment' over profit, and accordingly, he suggests that the role of government is to orchestrate a harmonious relationship between democracy and capitalism: he is seeking a capitalist rendition of social democracy, not a socialist version. On the other hand, Hutton acknowledges that the post-war social contract has been 'unpicked' in the course of the past generation and worries that the existing political and economic system in Britain – and especially the way the system tilts toward Tory governments that perpetuate injustices not even supported by the majority of the public – inhibits (at best) and perhaps even forecloses the possibility of reform. Hence, Hutton concludes by claiming that successful democracy and successful capitalism both require a massive shift in political power in the United Kingdom away from top-down centralisation and domination – which Hutton specifically cautions Labour to avoid, not embrace, whenever it regains power – and toward bottom-up participation and wealth generation. All told, Britain's social democrats face the immediate challenge of crafting a new set of guiding principles and compelling programmes that will help the left (including the centre-left) regain power and inspire the entire country across its many lines of asymmetry and diversity.

Taking stock of citizens, mindsets, realities

The overarching theme of this book, *Making Social Democrats*, brings together the intersecting notions of citizens, mindsets and realities. How do these three keywords relate with the ongoing challenge of reviving and reshaping progressive politics?

Citizenship, of course, is one of *the* central political concepts, an idea that partisans across the ideological spectrum in any democracy claim to champion even as they disagree on its essence. As many thinkers, including David Marquand, have long noted, citizenship encompasses multiple duos: rights and responsibilities, status and practices, membership and participation. Liberals and social democrats often place priority on rights, entitlements and protections, with a strong role for governing institutions in securing public goods and implementing social welfare provisions, whilst conservatives tend to give more weight to the marketplace and civil society as well as the good character of individual human persons. It is our premise in this book, though, that the state–society divide offers nothing more than a false and unhappy choice: meaningful democratic citizenship of any kind necessarily transcends the realms of state and society. It is not enough for social democrats merely to implement public policies defending the interests of the middle classes and working classes without cultivating the qualities of actively engaged and responsibly empowered citizens. Likewise, it is folly to offload the responsibility for maintaining social welfare primarily to the citizenry while rolling back the involvement of the state in safeguarding social and economic rights. Ultimately, in free societies, we citizens get the government we seek, regardless of whether the resulting collective of leaders and their decisions yield us the government we deserve. This is why citizenship and democracy worth having depend so heavily on the actions, judgements and indeed the prevailing spirit of the citizenry.

The notion of mindsets spins off, in many respects, from the concept of citizenship, since mindsets – as in dispositions, perspectives and outlooks – constitute a vital element of citizenship. Citizenship encompasses ways of thinking as well as ways of living, and this has been widely recognised by political and social theorists. As T. H. Marshall (1963: 8) famously noted, citizenship, at least in the national sense, depends on 'a direct sense of community membership based on loyalty to a civilisation which is a common possession'. What kind of mindset might take precedence among the citizenry at any given moment therefore becomes a crucial question: mindsets can be either narrow or broad; inclusive or exclusive; short-sighted or far-reaching; ignorant or enlightened. Mindsets can either privilege or downgrade various constellations of liberty, equality and democracy; mindsets can also have the effect of justifying either engagement and activism or apathy and indifference. Because mindsets amount to far more than the composite pulse of the citizenry at any given time, translating into imperatives for governing institutions and their resulting policy choices, mindsets hold fundamental importance in shaping the destinies of political communities at all levels.

In some ways, 'realities' might come across as banal and disheartening as a subtitle – as nothing more than a series of hard knocks to undercut whatever lofty mindsets might fortuitously spring forth from the public – but it requires only passing reflection to realise the extent that political realities are anything but preordained. To be sure, as shown in the chapters that follow, some of today's realities are challenging for social democrats: several authors relay incidence upon incidence of dislocation and disempowerment of unjustifiably marginalised segments of the public. Many of today's biggest problems lie well beyond the capacities of individual states to solve on their own, yet also elude the necessary global coordination: the endurance of neoliberalism in spite of its failures, the intensification of global warming, the spread of suicide terrorism and the accompanying chill this places upon civil liberties, resurgent militarism and nuclear proliferation in an emerging and potentially unstable multipolar world, the persistence of sexism, racism and discrimination against cultural minorities, to name a few. Such realities impose new challenges on all political leaders, not only social democrats, while also rendering the principles of social democracy all the more necessary.

And yet although today's problems are daunting, the present stockpile of realities is far from uniformly bleak; as also noted by several authors in this volume, all of us can take solace in the many ways in which social progress has taken hold over the past generation on many fronts: advances in the rights of women, children, ethnic and sexual minorities, as well as persons with disabilities; greatly improved access to higher education; higher quality and more accessible health care; longer life expectancies thanks to improved nutrition and heightened scientific knowledge and medical capacity; and greater comfort, convenience and choice in many facets of everyday life. As economist Branko Milanović (2012) is fond of pointing out in his expositions on inequality, societies were far more equal when almost everyone lived barely above subsistence level. Lastly, we can also think about realities in an aspirational sense: what unacceptable realities must today's social democrats confront most forcefully and, correspondingly, what kinds of new realities should progressives strive to bring into existence? We hope the essays in this volume cast light upon such questions and help point the way toward a renaissance for social democratic politics.

References

Black, L. (2003) *The Political Culture of the Left in Affluent Britain, 1951–64* (Basingstoke: Macmillan).

Callaghan, J., Fishman, N., Jackson, B. and McIvor, M. (eds) (2009) *In Search of Social Democracy: Responses To Crisis and Modernization in The Western European Left* (Manchester: Manchester University Press).

Collini, S. (1991) *Public Moralists: Political Thought and Intellectual Life in Britain 1850–1930* (Oxford: Oxford University Press).

Crewe, I. and King, A. (1995) *SDP* (Oxford: Oxford University Press).

de Tocqueville, A. (1966) *Democracy in America*, J. P. Mayer (ed.) and G. Lawrence (translator) (New York: Harper & Row).

Ford, R. and Goodwin, M. J. (2014) *Revolt on the Right: Explaining Support for the Radical Right in Britain* (London: Routledge).

Hickson, K. (ed.) (2016) *Rebuilding Social Democracy* (Bristol: Policy Press).

Jackson, B. and Saunders, R. (eds) (2012) *Making Thatcher's Britain* (Cambridge: Cambridge University Press).

Jenkins, R. (1991) *A Life At The Center* (New York: Random House).

Lasswell, H. D. (1936) *Politics: Who Gets What, When, How* (London: Whittlesey).

MacIntyre, A. (1980) *After Virtue* (South Bend: University of Notre Dame Press).

Marquand, D. (1988) *The Unprincipled Society* (London: Fontana).

Marquand, D. (1992) *The Progressive Dilemma* (London: Heinemann).

Marquand, D. (1997) *The New Reckoning: Capitalism, States and Citizens* (Cambridge: Polity).

Marquand, D. (2008) *Britain Since 1918: The Strange Career of British Democracy* (London: Weidenfeld & Nicholson).

Marquand, D. (2010) 'Progressive dilemmas after the election: David Marquand interviewed by Ben Jackson', *Renewal*, 18, 3–4, 36–46.

Marquand, D. (2014) *Mammon's Kingdom: An Essay on Britain Now* (London: Penguin).

Marquand, D. (2015) 'Returning native', *openDemocracy* (15 December). www.opendemocracy.net/uk/david-marquand/returning-native (accessed 15 May 2017).

Marshall, T. H. (1963) *Citizenship and Social Class* (Cambridge: Cambridge University Press).

Marwick, A. (1990) *British Society Since 1945*, 2nd edn (London: Penguin).

Moravcsik, A. (2011) 'Capsule review: the end of the West: the once and future Europe', *Foreign Affairs*, 90(5), 183.

Milanović, B. (2012) *The Haves and the Have-Nots: A Brief and Idiosyncratic History of Global Inequality* (New York: Basic Books).

Morgan, K. O. (2014) '*Mammon's Kingdom*: An essay on Britain, now by David Marquand', *Independent*, 15 May. www.independent.co.uk/arts-entertainment/books/reviews/mammons-kingdom-an-essay-on-britain-now-by-david-marquand-book-review-9378002.html (accessed 12 May 2017).

Nuttall, J. (2006) *Psychological Socialism. The Labour Party and Qualities of Mind and Character, 1931–The Present* (Manchester: Manchester University Press).

Pocock, J. G. A. (1975) *The Machiavellian Moment: Florentine Republican Thought and the Atlantic Republican Tradition* (Princeton: Princeton University Press).

Sandel, M. (1996) *Democracy's Discontent: America in Search of a Public Philosophy* (Cambridge: The Belknap Press of Harvard University).

Tanner, D., Thane, P. and Tiratsoo, N. (eds) (2000) *Labour's First Century* (Cambridge: Cambridge University Press).

Williams, R. (2014) 'Business as usual: how we are dominated by the language of markets', *New Statesman*, 20 May. www.newstatesman.com/culture/2014/05/business-usual-how-we-are-dominated-language-markets (accessed 12 May 2017).

Worley, M. (ed.) (2009) *The Foundations of The British Labour Party: Identities, Cultures and Perspectives, 1900–1939* (Farnham: Ashgate).

Part I

Progressive dilemmas: the historical long view

2

Social democracy and the people

Jeremy Nuttall

The dilemmas of democracy

At the start of the twenty-first century, the British ... had plenty of public spirit. Large numbers of them were involved in a wide range of voluntary organizations and informal social networks. They had outgrown political paternalism, ... but they were not isolated from their society or from each other. This did not mean that they were itching to transform the political order. The servility and snobbery that Tawney had seen as the most contemptible vices of his fellow countrymen were much less obvious than they had been in his day, but the culture of Channel 4's Big Brother and Murdoch's Sun were not exactly Tawneian. ... But ... Tawney's stolid, pragmatic, unimaginative and somewhat anti-intellectual Henry Dubb was stirring in his sleep ... [T]he beat was changing. (Marquand, 2008: 407).

This concluding passage from David Marquand's *Britain Since 1918*, published in 2008, a historical work focused on the evolution of British politics since the arrival of democracy, is characteristically Marquandian in two ways. First, it identifies a dilemma right at the heart of historical and contemporary progressivism, in this case the role of 'the people' in the furtherance of progress or social democracy – the central focus of this chapter. Second, it offers a complex and many-layered appraisal of the character and condition of the contemporary British citizen, one somewhere between hero and villain, which resists the straightforward or comfortable answer as to what will happen next. Marquand's own concluding assessment, which is implicitly recommended to the reader, is that we need to keep thinking, still embarked, as he had put it over a decade earlier, on that intellectual and personal 'journey to an unknown destination' (1997: 7).

Historians in the past quarter-century have displayed growing interest in how British social democrats, as well as liberals and Conservatives, responded to the challenges of the arrival (broadly) of democracy in 1918. For the historian, this meeting between social democracy and the people fascinates as an ongoing, evolving encounter between political ideas and idealism on the one hand, and the realities of the human condition on the other. For the political scientist and contemporary observer, the interest lies in the fact that it is a relationship that continues to be of central importance to the state of British politics today. Existing work exploring social democracy and the people has focused on relatively short, contained historical periods. This chapter seeks to examine the issue over a longer time span, from the late nineteenth century to the present. It offers five main observations, a mix of historical patterns and dilemmas, and reflections on the present and possible future.

The first is a dilemma: to achieve their ends, social democrats needed the people, yet they were often disappointed by them. Contemporary progressives' dismay about the twin democratic events of 2016, the British people's vote for 'Brexit', and the American people's election of Donald Trump has a long ancestry. Since social democracy saw itself as an ideology *for* the mass of the people, designed to better their lot, it had a recurring interest in the people. That meant an interest in their conditions and living standards. Just as important, though, was an interest in how virtuous, engaged, egalitarian-spirited and reflective the people were, because, in the end, without a virtuous, engaged citizenry there could *be* no social democracy. Yet, as with Marquand's reference to the culture of *Big Brother* and the *Sun*, social democrats have frequently viewed the people as falling short, and been unsure about how, or even whether to come to terms with the electorate.

Historians of the 'constraints school', most persistently Steven Fielding, have shown how social democrats were forced to come to terms with the fact that 'the people', the voters, including even the working-class ones, were far from uniformly social democratic or politically engaged, and incorporated considerable conservative as well as apathetic strains. This was perhaps most dramatically illustrated at that supposed crowning moment of social democratic achievement in 1945. Here, Labour effected considerable policy and social structural change, most notably through the creation of a welfare state, but it was not able, in Fielding's words 'to make socialists', that is to create a nation of egalitarian-minded citizens, thus sustaining the apparently collectivist, classless spirit of wartime (Fielding *et al.*, 1995: 213). Drawing on the work of earlier revisionists questioning the extent to which 1939–45 really witnessed a 'People's War', he reminded us that developments such as the evacuation of working-class children to middle-class homes aroused antagonism as much as cross-class reconciliation. Moreover, Labour's majority in 1945 exaggerated the extent of its lead over the Conservatives, and concealed the fragility of its support among the more prosperous classes, who turned once again to the Conservatives just six years later. The party's stated desire to forge a new citizenry, engaged in more 'wholesome' political and leisure pursuits, foundered on people's appetite instead for privacy, individualism and 'escapist' entertainments (Fielding *et al.*, 1995).

Second, the case of the 1940s shows especially strikingly what was to be a recurring theme. Social democracy is about economic and institutional change, but it is as much, more even, about the pursuit of change in hearts and minds. It has articulated a vision for better *conditions* for people, but ultimately it wants better *people*, better, fuller, happier lives. The arrival of democracy in 1918 seemed to create the theoretical political support base for constructing a more egalitarian economy and society. But because economic and social structural changes were unlikely to be achieved, and certainly not meaningfully sustained, without an accompanying elevation in popular values and engagement, the pursuit of social progress has proved a much more elongated process than many of its adherents had hoped, raising interesting questions about the time-frames and periodisation of social democratic history (Nuttall, 2013). This sense that, as Marquand puts it, 'institutional change would get nowhere without a change of mentality and feeling' was evident throughout social democracy's history (Marquand, 2008: 74). But the sense of it, the appreciation of the absence of 'quick fixes' has also grown. It helps explain the broader progressive movement's (certainly including liberals', and exhibited especially strongly by Marquand himself) rising interest in themes of political reform, decentralisation and citizenship, the heightened belief that change needed to be political, not just economic. But, in truth, it is deeper still. Social democracy has been, and remains, a project in the liberating, raising and nurturing of values, and, in fact, of character. More crucial than even the most nuanced of economic policies is an increase in the stockpile of kindness (Nuttall, 2006).

Third, however, if social democrats were sometimes disappointed with the people, the disappointment was not only one way. There is an equal case for pointing to how social democracy has at times let down the voters. Here, the people's most recurring reservation about social democracy has been whether, in its focus on poverty and disadvantage, it has been attentive enough to the also legitimate desires for social mobility, affluence and 'getting on' (Black, 2003). This did not just create a problem of electability for social democrats, although it did do that: the rise across the twentieth century of a home-owning middle class, and the later shrinkage of Labour's traditional male, unionised working-class support base posed an increasing sociological challenge to social democracy. But, no less importantly, it was also that, as Clapson has argued, suburbanisation and its accompanying changes have been profoundly empowering for many people, not least those from working-class and ethnic minority backgrounds (Clapson, 2000). For social democracy to find a way to accommodate, and indeed speak for, these individual ambitions and aspirations was thus not just good electoral calculation, but good policy and, indeed, morally desirable. When Labour has neglected these aspirations, by turning its gaze away from 'the people', or, worse, in its more class warrior-like moments, actively opposed them, it has not just lost elections, but also arguably exhibited a deficiency in moral and intellectual vision.

That said, this chapter argues that this is also, crucially, a matter of balance. Embracing social mobility and affluence did not then need to entail complacency about poverty, or about the working-class 'core vote'. It is arguable that early New Labour showed considerable adeptness in achieving this balance between agendas of equality and social mobility, and between engaging working- and middle-class support. Labour's estrangement from the people had finally become, through Tony Blair's popularity with the voters in the later 1990s, 'like a love affair', as he described it (Blair, 2010: 29). Yet, by the later New Labour years, pursuing the love affair seemed to have become too much the end in itself, and the accompanying vision had retreated alongside, especially in the sphere of economic and workplace rights, that sense of the importance of maintaining touch with working-class voters. After defeat in 2010, what seemed initially like a need just for the normal, cyclical rebuilding of the party took on a more all-embracingly problematic, urgent dimension with the extent of the party's defeat in Scotland in 2015, the 'Brexit' vote in 2016 and the rising threat from UKIP, and then, under Theresa May, the Conservatives in working-class seats. All this illustrated that the pursuit of social democracy was an enduring dilemma of synthesis: how best to combine compassion and aspiration, electability and ideals, an attentiveness to people's ambitions, without fostering a populist subservience to 'the people', or losing sight of one section of the people in the pursuit of another. As so often in history, having neglected one side of the equation, the danger was then over-compensating by neglecting the other.

Fourth, the relationship between social democracy and the people was thus a two-way flow. That relationship has been, and is, a central dilemma and problem for social democrats. But, crucially, the chapter does not just see it as a problem. Historians, political scientists, political commentators and social democrats themselves are correct to highlight social democratic dilemmas. But they are also apt somewhat to underplay both the achievements and, importantly, the adaptability of social democracy, and of progressivism more broadly. Liberal and Labour governments since 1905 have left a considerable legacy of social welfare, educational expansion, civil liberties, democratisation and greater access to culture and the arts. The undoubted limits to the *electoral* success of parties other than Conservative between 1918 and 1992 can obscure the extent to which many of these accomplishments have endured, in whole or at least in part well beyond the progressive government which implemented them. In his work on the evolution of the 'Conservative Century', Anthony Seldon perceptively argues that while this description is apt in terms of the Conservatives' governmental dominance, it is less uniformly true of its setting of the overall intellectual agenda of politics (Seldon, 1994: 17). Progressive parties, seeking as they do to *change* society, often have a more inherently difficult task in winning elections than more conservative parties, more apt to mirror society as it is. Yet progressives' activity rate in government is often higher. Albeit that the government's longevity may be shorter, we may under-estimate the extent to which the cultural and attitudinal shifts it has cultivated are preserved. It will be argued that the social democratic tendency to under-estimate itself is especially true of the past twenty years in social democratic history, and of the analysis of the historical legacy of New Labour. As Tomlinson (2009: 227, 249) points out, a belief that the current or most recent era is the one of most alarming decline is a historically recurring one, and one which may reveal as much about the observer as the period under observation.

If this under-estimation and excessive declinism points to the desirability of a more nuanced and proportionate perspective on social democracy, it also implies the need for such a perspective on the political history of 'the people' themselves. Social democrats tend to look back on supposed golden ages of a more left-leaning and participatory citizenry, whether to the 'Blitz spirit' of the 1940s, or the more highly unionised, pre-Thatcher workforce of the 1960s and 1970s. The research discussed here, qualifying this romanticised picture of 'the people' in these earlier decades, has been increasingly accompanied by important new findings cautioning against excessively bleak or one-dimensional portrayals of the populace in more recent decades. The fact that the voters granted Labour by far its most sustained period in office between 1997 and 2010 is the most manifest demonstration of this. But, more broadly, recent studies of political or civic participation (Lawrence, 2009; Hilton, 2011: 232, 268) have emphasised the complexity of people's levels of engagement in different spheres. The decline of mass membership political parties or in a, largely male, working-class trade union culture is not the same as a broader decline in public political interest or social responsibility.

This points also to the need for a greater focus on the progressive contribution of moderate, middling sentiments among the public – those quieter, unspectacular building blocks of social improvement which, cumulatively, could amount to significant advances. As Lawrence has observed, the British people's frequently deliberative '"peaceable-ness" was not the same as passivity' (Lawrence, 2009: 128). The history of the people is also not static. Marquand's sense of the changing of the 'beat' of popular politics in his aforementioned book's last line is a reminder that social democrats, for all their frustrations, have enduringly had hope and – more than that – a certain underlying confidence in the people's ability, albeit somewhat incrementally, to learn and to grow.

Finally, if much of the above has highlighted the ideological and intellectual dilemmas for social democracy, there were also dilemmas of outlook, mood and style. Put simply, social democracy has often been at its best (1945, 1964, 1997) when it has seemed most optimistic and upbeat about the society it is simultaneously seeking to represent and to change. This was partly a matter of communicational attributes. Laura Beers, for example, demonstrates that while the Labour Party, and wider labour movement, have certainly oscillated across the century between revulsion towards, and embrace of modern methods of media and communication, we tend to under-recognise those times when social democracy *has* engaged constructively and successfully with modernity in these respects, and sought to turn it to progressivism's advantage. This was evident in Ramsay MacDonald's use of colourful visual images in party posters in the pre-First World War years. Effective use of the media was also part of Labour's success in capturing the public mood at the 1945 election (Beers, 2010). But the point is also broader. Apt to focus on the deficiencies of the society and economy, social democrats have too often conveyed a rather negative, even joyless air. This negativity has at times become self-fulfilling, both by impeding constructive and thoughtful approaches to finding solutions to problems, and by evincing a sense of low confidence, which the voters, often drawn to the perceived 'strength' of politicians, have then punished. If, as argued here, social democrats have more reasons for optimism than they presently think, it is important to display that optimism, indeed to live it.

Social democracy meets the people: 1889–1939

The outcomes for the different political parties from democracy have frequently surprised, and are replete with paradoxes. The Liberal Party turned out to have the most to fear from what approximated to universal suffrace in 1918. They had been electorally ascendant in the middle decades of the nineteenth century, were buoyed by their landslide victory in 1906, and were home to many of the most creative and constructive political minds in the first half of the twentieth century, both governmental (Herbert Asquith, David Lloyd George) and intellectual (Leonard Hobhouse, John Maynard Keynes, William Beveridge). But the twentieth century's more overtly class politics saw them lose middle-class supporters to the Conservatives, and working-class ones to Labour. The New Liberal Hobhouse, who straddled the liberal and social democratic traditions, had already expressed concerns about the character of the increasingly democratic electorate in his *Democracy and Reaction* (1904), reflecting that whereas

> both the friends and enemies of democracy inclined to the belief that when the people came into power there would be a time of rapid and radical domestic change ... [a]s it turned out, almost the first act of the new British democracy [following the suffrage extensions under the 1884 Reform Act] was to install the Conservatives in power, and to maintain them with but partial exceptions for nearly twenty years. (Hobhouse, 1973: 49–50)

This was, Hobhouse believed, partly because rising living standards had blunted the people's appetite for reform, and partly because democracy heightened the influence of 'the Press and the platform', the typical Briton, what Hobhouse termed 'the man-in-the-street is the man in a hurry; the man who has not time to think and will not take the trouble to do so' (Hobhouse, 1973: 2, 67, 71).

For Conservatives, the pattern was in reverse, pessimism about democracy's implications giving way to the discovery of frequent synchronicity with the people's appetites and ambitions. The late nineteenth-century Prime Minister, Lord Salisbury had been profoundly gloomy about how the propertied classes would fare in the twentieth century. Even as late as March 1924, in a speech to the Cambridge Union, the dominant Conservative leader of the inter-war era, Stanley Baldwin could still express concern about 'the emotions of the ignorant mob' (Baldwin, 1926: 96). Yet, increasingly the party was benefiting, as McKibbin notes, from that late Victorian and early twentieth-century shift of middle-class allegiance away from nonconformist liberalism towards Conservatism, with its associated wariness of rising taxation (McKibbin, 2010: 9–10). It would be a mistake simply to attribute inter-war, and subsequent twentieth-century Conservative electoral success purely to good fortune, or reaping the rewards of an increasingly prosperous and propertied society, however. The party showed an ability to engage with 'modernity', sometimes, through its more socially liberal and one nation strains, enthusiastically, at other times with skilful tactical acumen, adopting, at various points measures of state intervention, support for meritocracy and opportunity, and even, at times (as most recently with gay marriage), promotion for elements of social liberalism. By their recurring ability over the course of the century to relate to a relatively wide range of British society, and by developing Benjamin Disraeli's mantra of 'trust the people', the Conservative Party, as Ball and Holliday (2002: 2, 12) have shown, 'made the advent of democracy an opportunity rather than a peril'.

Social democrats, and in particular the Labour Party, experienced neither the near-destruction meted out by the people to the Liberal Party, nor the surprising embrace offered up to the Conservatives. Their relationship with the people was more mixed, hesitant, sporadic, conditional and slow burning, and for these reasons especially socially and politically interesting and revealing. In the late nineteenth century, before either full democracy or the Labour Party itself had even come into existence, it was understandable that some social democrats exhibited a certain uncomplicated optimism about how straightforwardly the full enfranchisement of the people would result in their opting for social democracy or socialism. For Fabian Sidney Webb (1962: 93), in the seminal *Fabian Essays* (1889), 'so long ... as democracy in political administration continues to be the dominant principle, Socialism may be quite safely predicted as its economic obverse'. This confidence rested on the (as it turned, out too simple) double assumption that social democracy represented the workers' interests, and that the workers were conscious of what their interests were.

Nonetheless, even at this relatively early stage, there were signs of recognition that there might be a disparity between what social democrats envisioned for the people and the people's own actual wishes, appetites or 'stage' of development. This was often heavily caveated, as in the following from William Morris in 1894, by the point that the people were not themselves the authors of their limitations, but the victims of the social and economic circumstances that dictated their lives: 'civilization has reduced the workman to such a skinny and pitiful existence, that he scarcely knows how to frame a desire for any life much better than that which he now endures perforce' (Morris, 1894: 245). Similarly, to take the endlessly illuminating Hobhouse, illustrative as much of the social democratic as of the liberal outlook, 'what are we to expect from the mechanical training in the elements of learning which is all that we are able to give to the public at large?' (Hobhouse, 1973: 72–3). It was possible, and a recurring social democratic perception, then, to observe the people as possessing a powerful latent potential, yet one that was either not immediately realisable, or needed a level of nurture that was presently denied to them. But whether the cause lay in environment, history or character, the sense that the people could be a barrier to progress was already beginning to formulate: whether the people had *potential* for the future was of little immediate practical political use.

Moreover, this feeling that the people mattered was intensified by the continuously strong moral dimension to British social democratic thought. Throughout, this vied with – as well as complemented and overlapped with – more 'mechanical' definitions of social democracy in terms of economics, class or institutional change. But the ethical dimension was almost always potent enough to push social democrats to the conclusion that without virtue, engagement and, indeed, plain good character being shown by the people, no material, structural or policy change could really be adequate on its own. This was why it was so important to 'make socialists', as Morris urged, for 'preaching and teaching' was 'the only rational means of attaining to the New Order of Things' (Morris, 1890: 226).

By the end of the First World War, with democracy, from 1918, now a living reality, and with Labour moving from its foundational stages to its first, fleeting, experience of actual government in 1924, it was less possible to be so sanguine about the inherent desire of the people for social democracy as Webb had been. This is what makes the pivotal Labour figure of this period, Marquand's biographical subject, Ramsay MacDonald, so fascinating. As both a serious social democratic thinker and the party's leader and first prime minister, MacDonald was the first front rank social democrat to have to grapple seriously with that central dilemma: how to preserve and redefine the meaning of social democracy whilst engaging with the political reality of what the new democratic electorate actually wanted. Given this, and MacDonald's penchant for intellectual honesty, his appraisal was unsurprisingly more hard-headed than Webb's had been about the citizenry, not least in the context of the nationalist fervour on display in the immediately post-war 1918 'coupon election', which considerably bolstered the strength of the Conservative Party. 'Even if we regard the election of December, 1918, as being a special manifestation of passionate blindness,' he wrote in 1919, 'elections have not shown on the part of the masses that vigilant watchfulness and that consistency in thought and interest which James Mill assumed [in his article on *Government* (1820)]' (MacDonald, 1919: 2). Indeed, Webb himself, writing in 1923, had also begun to accommodate himself to the voters' more complicated nature, referring to 'the inevitable gradualness of our scheme of change ... why because we are idealists, should we be supposed to be idiots? ... How anyone can fear that the British electorate ... can ever go too fast or too far is incomprehensible to me' (Webb, 1923: 11).

The implication of this was that it would take much longer for the Labour Party to achieve the really broad electoral appeal than many social democrats had hoped for, or that Conservatives, like Salisbury had feared. More fundamentally still, there was a growing realisation that the prevalence of the sort of cooperative and egalitarian values on which social democrats had pinned their hopes was less manifest than had been thought, and not just among the increasingly well-organised middle classes, but within the working classes themselves. As leading ethical social democrat R. H. Tawney reflected in his *Equality* (1931), 'an indifference to inequality ... is less the mark of particular classes than a national characteristic' (Tawney, 1952: 27).

Tawney encapsulated in heightened form that essential social democratic duality in its view of the people. He was an idealist, yet, having known and fought alongside the workers during the First World War, also a realist. He admired that archetypal English citizen, Henry Dubb, but did not romanticise him. Tawney, for Marquand the democratic republican par excellence, was, as Marquand puts it, 'an unillusioned Dubbite ... He knew that there could be no democratic culture without Dubb, and he hoped against hope that Dubb would one day help to build it. But he did not allow his hopes to become dupes' (Marquand, 2008: 73). Both the strength and the weakness of British democracy has been what Marquand terms its 'crablike progress' (Marquand, 2008: 5). This gave it a powerful, organically evolved solidity, yet also meant it was partial and incomplete. The further problem, to return to Henry Dubb, was that the formal and institutional establishment of democracy in 1918 did not mean people had become overnight imbued with fully formed democratic or egalitarian values. Here, Marquand suggests, 'Dubb was caught in a vicious circle. Democracy without a democratic culture was a contradiction in terms. But Dubb and his fellow citizens had been shaped by a profoundly undemocratic one' (Marquand, 2008: 73). Ultimately, the central dilemma of democracy, first enunciating itself in these inter-war years, was 'how to bring the heart into line with the garments; and this was a cultural and moral question far more than an economic or even a political one' (Marquand, 2008: 73–4).

Interestingly, Tawney extended his critique of the dearth of egalitarian spirit to 'even those groups which are committed by their creed to measures to mitigating its more repulsive consequences' (Tawney, 1952: 27). This, of course, meant social democrats themselves. One of the recurring objections of the people to being told of their failings by social democrats has been that social democrats themselves have too often allowed a mix of personal animosity, ideological dogma and class rhetoric to come in the way of their exhibiting the fraternity they preached. With a certain cyclical symmetry, the tendency of the Labour Party to fratricide was to be especially evident in the early 1930s, early 1950s, early 1980s and the most recent 2015–17 period. This may seem a trivial or incidental point, but in fact goes to the heart of the matter. For if indeed, as many, most social democrats have believed, social democracy depended not only on the articulation of abstract theories but on the actualities of a cooperative spirit and kindness of character, then the limitations in the actual existence of these qualities mattered fundamentally. Tawney, in a powerful passage in the context of the party's early 1930s' flirtations with neo-Marixism, internal conflicts and cries of betrayal over the 1931 split, sought to remind colleagues that virtue did not rest solely on the apparent radicalism of one's pronouncements:

> What matters most is not what men say, and the language in which they say it; it is what they mean to do, and the intensity with which they mean it. The important point is not that they should express – or even hold – opinions as to policy which attract attention as extreme. It is that they should show extreme sense in reaching them, extreme self-restraint in keeping their mouths shut till the opinions are worth stating, and extreme resolution in acting on them when stated. (Tawney, 1952: 226)

A further problem was that if social democrats were beginning to engage more with the practical question of what the people, their potential voters were really like, and what they wanted, this had still, even by the 1930s, only reached relatively primitive stages, if the party was serious about regularly challenging the Conservatives for power. Most crucially, there remained an (albeit modified) instinct to assume that some dramatic event or economic downturn would suddenly jolt the masses into appreciating the need for a more radical politics, an inclination to wait, as Morris had put it, for 'when the crisis shall come' (Morton, 1984: 25). This contributed to an under-estimation of how much the people, and their circumstances, had changed since 1900. This was true of the middle classes, through rising educational opportunities and the spread of home ownership and suburbia. But it was also true of the workers, most of whom, for all the horror and trauma of both the war and then the depression were, in most cases, enjoying steadily, if unspectacularly rising wages, as well as the benefits of the Edwardian Liberal welfare reforms, and inter-war Conservative-dominated governments' consolidation of these. Thus, when George Bernard Shaw claimed in 1930 that socialism 'reverses the policy of Capitalism … The change involves a complete moral *volte-face*', or Labour's leader in 1937, Clement Attlee, insisted that the party's aim was to 'replace' an existing society that was 'wrong', whilst they undoubtedly articulated a widely felt sense of particular social grievances, they almost certainly underplayed a coexisting consciousness of improvement and progress (Shaw, 1930: 3; Attlee, 1949: 120).

This reluctance to acknowledge, and indeed embrace, such social advances for fear that this would undermine a mono-narrative of grievance and injustice, allied to that sense of the people as a frequent disappointment, their being, variously, too conservative, selfish, apathetic or unthinking, gave social democracy, at times, a character at once negative, melancholy and somewhat prescriptive. It was a problem shared with late Victorian liberalism. Investigating the local politics of Wolverhampton in the later nineteenth century, Lawrence shows the appeal of a popular Conservatism built around promising to protect men's leisure pursuits from the moral strictures of Liberal nonconformists (Lawrence, 1998: 7). Hobhouse's later warning, in 1904, that 'no social revolution will come from a people so absorbed in cricket and football' may have contained a germ of truth, but it was rather sweeping, and arguably not the best way to advertise progressivism's willingness to fuse moral seriousness with an openness to pleasure (Hobhouse, 1973: 76).

Through the negative, somewhat tired and staid vibe this gave to voters, and the associated unwillingness of the left to engage with modern presentational and communication techniques, this pessimism could be electorally self-fulfilling (Beers, 2010: 5–6). It also meant defining progress too narrowly, seeing its further-ance only in terms of governmental or collectivist measures, and dismissing the consequence of, or even sneering at, more individually driven or socially autonomous changes, especially suburbanisation. Again, while Hobhouse drew valid attention to how the march of the middle classes could have some conserva-tive political implications, it was quite a stretch, and a revealing one to claim that 'while the private life of the suburb is no doubt comfortable and blameless, politically it is a greater burden on the nation than the slum' (Hobhouse, 1973: 68). In part, to be fair, this reflected an inherently difficult balancing act for any party of reform, that had both to represent ordinary people as they *were*, and simultaneously to outline a better future. As Lawrence (1998: 263) has put it, social democrats 'wish[ed] both to speak for the people, and to change them'. But by appearing at times only to condemn the contemporary society, liberals and social democrats risked the voters granting them the opportunity to do neither.

By the eve of the Second World War, then, social democracy had been confronted both by some harsh electoral realities and some of its own limitations. One *could* adjudge the record of British social democracy by 1939 a disappointment, given that Labour had managed to govern for just three years, never with a majority, and with relatively limited legislative or policy achievements to show for it. But the truth is more complex. For all these very real dilemmas and problems, there are also three grounds for pointing to the resilience and adaptability of social democracy in these years, as well as its rootedness in the people themselves.

The first is the importance of a sense of historical perspective and proportion. As Fielding has argued, articulating the 'constraints school', political history is too often divorced from social history, from context, the difficult and entrenched societal realities which constrain political agendas for progress (Fielding, 2003: 26–7). Between the wars, only five out of every thousand pupils in English elementary schools went on to university, almost two-thirds of householders still rented from a private landlord, and even by 1938 only three million people were entitled to a paid holiday (Stevenson, 1990: 193, 228, 257). This no doubt reflected some of the failings and injustices of inter-war governance. But it cannot only be a commentary on maldistribution. It must also tell us something about the overall limits of the country's resources, and of the people's own expectations and horizons, whether for property ownership, leisure time or, indeed, social justice and equality. This is not to downplay the inter-war increase in working-class political organisation and consciousness, both industrial and political. It is to suggest that democratic and egalitarian ideals remained in a relatively infant state at this time, and that when we write abstractly about the 'failure' of social democracy, or even politicians more generally, to create a land of equality, prosperity or opportunity, greater credit should be given to a more plausible sense of the possible, and of prevailing societal norms.

Awareness of such constraints places social democracy, with its transformative aspirations, in a better sense of perspective, and lends weight to those who, like George Bernard Shaw, offered social democracy 'not in one lump sum, but by instalments' (Shaw, 1962: 218). The leading Labour expert on colonial affairs, Leonard Woolf elaborated on this lengthening of social democratic time-frames in his little cited *After The Deluge* (1931), suggesting that both defenders and opponents of the newly emerging British democracy should pause for thought about how much they expected it to deliver, and how quickly. Ultimately, the 'man in the street [could] … become … as cultured and intelligent and politically sagacious as any member of the present cabinet', but it would take time (Woolf, 1937: 209, 213–15, 217).

Second, a historically under-estimated social democratic strength and relevance was in fact evident in Labour's strikingly rapid adaptation to 'mainstream' politics. For all its flirtations with Marxism, extra-parliamentarianism and syndicalism, it is in many ways remarkable how readily this ideology of social discontent, representing the most downtrodden and disadvantaged, was able to rise to the political challenges and maturity of embracing political constructiveness, liberal democratic methods and a focus on detailed, practical policy formulation. For all the very real factional disputatiousness, and at times opposition-mindedness of the party's subsequent history, this coexisting practicality and desire to *do* things always re-surfaced. 'The Labour Party recognises the defects of the Parliamentary machine', acknowledged MacDonald in 1920, 'but in no ways abandons Parliament as the embodiment of the civic life of the community, the citizen as the unit to be represented, or public opinion as the only creator of social change which is to last' (MacDonald, 1920: 75). Socialism is 'not "class war" but the ancient doctrine of human brotherhood', echoed Webb (Webb, 1923: 15). The quiet economic policy development of figures like Hugh Dalton, G. D. H. Cole and Evan Durbin was, in the end, a more representative portrait of inter-war British social democracy than the 1926 general strike or the Marxist dabbling of John Strachey and Harold Laski. The fact, as Marquand narrated (1992: 18–19), that none of the 'Big Five' in MacDonald's Cabinets had attended university, and all had experienced poverty was testimony both to working-class political advance, and to that class's leaders' adaptability to democracy and governmentalism. Alongside this, though, as Marquand also observed (1992: 18–19), Labour's other considerable achievement in this period was increasingly to win over sections of the liberal middle classes and intelligentsia. What was most striking was how balanced, in important ways, social democrats managed to be. If an instinctive, and sometimes indiscriminate anti-capitalism remained, it coexisted with a constructive sense that the social and economic history of the preceding half-century had not been without its gains. To turn again to MacDonald (1920: 183): 'the Labour movement takes Society as it is, with its good and bad, its triumphs and failures, its gains to be conserved and its errors to be removed, and ... it seeks to transform it into a greater perfection'.

Of course, what one commentator may judge to be laudable practicality, another may suggest is succumbing to the allure of the establishment. Marquand, sharing the Tawneian dislike of flummery, observes the striking extent to which Labour and trade union working-class leaders in the 1920s, like J. H. Thomas and J. R. Clynes, became comfortable within the established political class, and admiring of the conventional institutions of British parliamentary democracy. For railway workers' leader, Thomas, in 1924, 'a constitution which enables an engine-driver of yesterday to be a Secretary of State today is a great constitution' (Marquand, 2008: 39). 'The House of Commons', Marquand reflects, 'was as good at instilling old norms into new members as any public school, officers' mess or miners' lodge' (Marquand, 2008: 39). 'In old days they hanged the leaders of popular movements. Now they ask them to dinner – a method of painless extinction which has proved far more effective' (Hobhouse, 1973: 76). Yet on balance, and in the main, this social democratic preference for engaging with, not withdrawing from, parliamentary democracy and governmental practicality, for voice, not exit, was an aid to the furtherance of social democracy's ethical objectives, not a betrayal of them.

Last, while social democrats were 'getting to know' the people whose lives they theoretically sought to transform, and in part this was a sobering experience, it was by no means a wholly negative process of discovery. This is where the concept of the mix becomes important. Much social democratic history, especially that of the period after 1979, considers the problem of the individualistic, capitalistic, even selfish attitudes that are assumed to have pervaded dominant governing ideologies, and also, in some accounts, the wider populace themselves. Undoubtedly, this was a problem for social democrats. But this is also too one-dimensional a view of the people. An understanding of the people as exhibiting a complex mix of motives and outlooks, part collectivist, part individualist, part vices, part virtues, seems more consistent with the spread of support across different parties, the varying outcomes of elections and, ultimately, with social democrats' own accounts of the people they scrutinise. The location of the people somewhere between romantic, utopian conceptions and ultra-conservative, individualist portraits, built around individual sin, makes for a citizenry both more historically interesting, and more hopeful for social democrats: not straightforwardly amenable to the social democrat case; but not out of its reach, either.

It was not, therefore, romantic or delusional of social democrats to seek to build on the cooperative and enlightened side of 'the people', so long as this did not entail the assumption that this was *all* people were about. Cooperation was an actually existing, real, historically grounded part of life. This was a point well made in 1889 by Sydney Olivier in *Fabian Essays* (Olivier, 1962: 144): 'The social instinct, the disposition to find comfort in comradeship independently of its material advantages, is of such evident antiquity in Man that we are justified in speaking of it as one of his fundamental and elementary characteristics.' This instinct was not, therefore, necessarily shallow, or reliant on wanting 'to be thought a good fellow', it was often bound up with people's very being, an intuitive generosity 'simply because it gives him immediate pleasure so to act' (Olivier, 1962: 145).

This did not preclude an awareness of people's coexisting individual appetites. Nor did it suppose a super-human level of altruism. The mixed view of the people has long held a prominent place within social democracy, an appraisal in which their virtues were modest, but still firm, real and of potential political benefit to progressivism. The working-class trade unionist Ernest Bevin (1942: 136) captured this well in a radio broadcast on 30 January 1934, noting the under-estimated 'understanding, ability and courage' of ordinary people. Herbert Morrison, who was able to execute social democratic power as leader of the London County Council in the 1930s, captured its dual aspect, pragmatically forward-looking, whilst not exactly socialist:

> It was essential that we should provide London with clean, efficient, progressive and public-spirited local government. The people were more interested in good administration and socially beneficial results than in theories and dogmas, and in effect they had put us into power to try us out. Next time they would be judging us on results. (Morrison, 1960: 144)

Here, then, was social democracy already in power, working with the people as they actually were, yet seeking to harness their better, more progressive instincts. The evolving relationship between social democracy and the people was not easy, straightforward or always harmonious. But this period had certainly begun to show that there was potential for the two to live together.

The people and the state: 1939–79

It is customary to begin discussions of the forty-year era of mixed economy, welfare statist 'consensus' politics by mentioning the achievements of the Attlee government, and then to follow this with an analysis of how statism collapsed and failed. This section reverses that order. It assesses how the state did become an insufficient vehicle for people's needs and ambitions by the 1970s. Yet it accompanies this with the distinction that *insufficiency* is not the same as failure, and that neither the role nor the relevance of the state ended in 1979. If the state was over-stepping its role in some respects by the late 1970s, this was as nothing compared to how much its value had been underplayed before the 1940s. The key point is that both the criticism and the laudation of the state should be approached with a greater sense of proportion. A second important point is that whilst the state and the people are often seen in this period (as today) as juxtaposed against each other, in conflict even, as the state takes power and taxes away from the people, it has in fact been just as much a vehicle *for* the people – embedding their better ideals, protecting them at their most vulnerable – as well as simply being a practical way of organising their needs. The state and the people were not alternatives, or polar opposites.

The relationship between the people and the state captures much of the essence of social democracy's history in what might be termed the middle phase of its evolution to date – both social democratic achievements and failures. This was the heyday of straightforward confidence in what the state could do, much less developed, before 1940, and much more ambiguous in its confidence after 1979. The failures and dilemmas have tended to receive rather more attention, and they were certainly real. One was the insufficiency of social democratic engagement with rising 'affluence', and with it of an expanding middle class. This is becoming a more familiar argument following the work of Black, yet it is still one which many social democrats, and indeed historians of social democracy, remain reluctant to take fully seriously (Black, 2003). Yet, less commonly noted, these were developments to which social democracy had itself substantially contributed, raising expectations and opportunities through educational expansion and the welfare state.

Denis Healey was one of the earliest to spot this, reflecting by 1970 on how 'the Labour Party had still failed to adapt its thinking to the profound social changes it had itself initiated through the Attlee Government after the war'. He noted that 'class feeling was receding. Living standards had risen substantially and most of the British people now felt they had something to conserve … The trade unions were now emerging as an obstacle both to the election of a Labour Government and to its success once it was in power' (Healey, 1990: 346). There were a significant number of voters who, whilst drawn to social democracy in its generous funding of education and health care, were increasingly worried about the more dogmatic side of egalitarianism, whether in the form of rapidly rising taxes, the more doctrinaire of 'experimental' teaching methods, or an apparent social democratic apathy about supporting the desire to own a home or business. The six aims listed in Labour's February 1974 manifesto, *Let Us Work Together*, which reflected the rising influence of Tony Benn and the grassroots left, and famously included the promise of a 'fundamental and irreversible shift in the balance of power and wealth in favour of working people and their families', and to 'eliminate poverty', said literally nothing about the more affluent, the middle class, or indeed the increasingly aspirational skilled working class (Labour Party, 1974).

This critique needs to be carefully made, because it can be overdone, and indeed, under New Labour, it *was*, by the end, somewhat overdone. There are important caveats. Twice in this period, in 1945 and 1964 Labour was in tune with the people, their wishes and aspirations, and significant advances in both social equality *and* aspirational social mobility resulted. The two were far from incompatible. Moreover, one has to be precise in defining 'aspiration'. To many on the right, aspiration has often had rather exclusively competitive, private sector and ruggedly masculine connotations. If one incorporates into one's definition of aspiration the ambition to high quality professionalism or public service, care for one's family and others, and ambitions for a better society, one produces a more rounded understanding of the concept, and one in which social democracy scores higher.

But it is still the case that social democracy was too often falling short in its engagement with the concept as a whole, a failing first properly evident in the 1950s, and more blatantly so in the 1970s and 1980s. The human side of this was movingly, humorously, alarmingly, and somewhat mockingly captured by the left-wing director Mike Leigh, in his play, *Abigail's Party*, first televised in 1977, two years before the onset of Thatcherism. Portraying the insecurities, snobbery and pretentiousness of the newly emerging middle-class world of home-owners, computer-operators and estate agents, what was almost entirely missing from the drama was the more laudable side of these people who had striven to rise. The play simultaneously captured socialism's insight and its blind spot: its sense of the superficiality of status competition, yet also its reluctance fully to engage with the liberating aspects of social mobility. What social democrats also needed to draw from the drama was that these were voters whose parents may well have been Labour, and who were now being lost. As the soft left-winger Bryan Gould recalled, he had concluded by the 1983 election that the Conservatives were now seen as 'the liberator of working-class ambitions', and that 'Labour could not hope to be re-elected if we allowed ourselves to be seen as a party which stopped people from doing things, which prevented them from realising their aspirations' (Gould, 1995: 152).

A further problem for social democracy was linked to the first, yet also distinct. By the 1970s it had become too one-dimensional in its reliance on the state and public spending as a solution to social ills. An ideology that had often prided itself on its pluralism now, ironically, seemed reductionist, too inclined to reduce all problems to material disadvantage, and all solutions to central government action. It was the younger generation of Labour revisionists, like David Marquand, John Mackintosh and David Owen who saw this most clearly. Marquand's 'Inquest on a Movement', published shortly after Labour's pivotal 1979 defeat, argued that post-war statist Fabian social democracy had borrowed insufficiently from the New Liberal commitment to moral persuasion and individual autonomy. Social democrats 'seemed more anxious to do good to others than to help others to do good to themselves' (Marquand, 1979: 9–11).

What was increasingly clear, at least to the more perceptive new generation of social democratic thinkers, was that while structural changes, whether in the economy or social institutions could take social democracy so far, mindsets, values and, indeed, the very character of the people also needed to change. To take one of the most central and emblematic policy changes of the 1960s, the move to comprehensive secondary education: formally equalising educational structures in this way, by theoretically enabling people of different social-class backgrounds and academic levels to attend the same school, was undoubtedly liberating for many who had failed their 11 plus, and languished in the old secondary modern schools. But it could not really compensate for disadvantages of a still deeper nature, like a lack of books in the home to provide stimulus, or of the parental nurturing, encouragement and expectation of achievement that varied greatly both between social classes and within them. Equality and opportunity were in the mind, not just the pay packet (Nuttall, 2006).

What had been lost by the 1970s was, again, that sense of ideological balance. Conservatives have often tended to under-value state and social support, and over-play the role of 'character', or more specifically its ability to flourish without social nurturing, as well as to over-rate the extent to which Conservatives possessed all those virtues of good character. The left has been correspondingly apt to under-play the importance of individual character, effort and ambitions in shaping life-chances and achievements. Social democracy at its best sought a middle way between the two, in which good character *and* improved social environment, individual endeavour *and* state support were harmonised. The politically active philosopher Bertrand Russell, who straddled the divide between liberalism and socialism, put it well in 1952. He noted the polarisation of views between those who believed that changing institutions would 'bring the millennium', and those who felt everything depended upon a 'change of heart' (Russell, 1969: 221–2). The truth, Russell objected, was that 'institutions mould character, and character transforms institutions. Reforms in both must march hand in hand' (Russell, 1969: 222).

Russell's analysis is a reminder that an active state and engaged, character-possessing citizens were not mutually exclusive. This has implications for how we view the record of the state and social democracy itself, in this period. Critics since the 1970s have at times somewhat denigrated 'the state' – always a rather opaque concept – especially as it extended its reach in those decades, the 1960s and 1970s, when confidence in its benign role was at its most uncomplicatedly high. As suggested, this critique of the state was *both* necessary *and* overblown. It helped social democracy after 1979 to renew its interest in those other branches of its creed, fraternity, community and political de-centralisation. These had long roots, not least in Morris, who had been clear in 1890 that 'I neither believe in State Socialism as desirable in itself, nor, indeed, as a complete scheme do I think it possible' (Morris, 1890: 225).

Yet, there is also a powerful argument that the critique of the state by the end of this period, and gaining ground thereafter, even among some post-1979 social democrats themselves, has been too sweeping and undifferentiating, and has undermined social democrats', and the people's confidence in government and collective action more than is proportionate. This is partly because the 1939–79 period, and its Labour governments in particular are too often judged from the viewing station of the 1978–79 'Winter of Discontent', so that the failures and contradictions of this near-four-decade era tend to receive more exposure than their very real achievements. Given the constraints imposed by the physical and economic devastation of the Second World War, the achievements of the 1945–51 Labour government in constructing a welfare state and National Health Service, and setting a framework for full employment were very real indeed. Even the leading left-winger Aneurin Bevan, never given to easy praise, could, in 1952, label the Attlee government in which he had served a 'success' (Bevan, 1978: 125).

The 1964–70 Wilson government has been less universally applauded, partly, unfairly, because the problems it faced were less dramatic than in 1945, and therefore required more subtle remedies. Relative poverty has been, in an odd way, a more intellectually taxing problem to combat than absolute. But here the achievements were greater in the social and cultural spheres, in educational reorganisation and expansion, and liberalising measures in the areas of race relations, sexuality, capital punishment and divorce. At the same time, perfectly respectable levels of economic growth were maintained, helping the country transition through imperial decline, and structural economic adjustment, with, in many ways, remarkable social unity and stability.

These social, cultural and educational accomplishments were also a reminder that the 'state' was not the one-dimensional, malign creature sometimes portrayed, solely concerned with its own power and enlargement. The state was, in fact, many things. It was certainly a means of centralising power and resources to further social protection and create more equalised standards. But it was also, through educational provision, empowering, a liberator of individual ambition and potential. Further, it was, in those socially liberalising reforms in areas like race and sexuality, a vital means of fostering more enlightened outlooks, albeit that changes of attitude often lagged some way behind changes in law. The state was also, more mundanely, but no less crucially, a vehicle for the practical dissemination of information, and for regulation on subjects like smoking or the wearing of seat-belts, without which many people might simply not even consider the topic of importance at all. Indeed, much of the extension in public provision and regulation came as an exercise in practical necessity as ideology, and support for it was shared across parties. As Sidney Webb noted as early as 1923, 'the candid Liberal' and 'the honest Unionist' still spoke the language of individualism, but often in practice adopted 'a Collectivist solution': 'the whole nation has been imbibing Socialism without realizing it!' (Webb, 1923: 10, 12).

Given these social democratic achievements, and given how recently the new, post-1945 welfare state-market mix had come to replace the still relatively *laissez-faire* inter-war approach, it is striking how ready Conservatives and Liberals were to present the expansion of the state as so vast and all-embracing that it was becoming a terrible menace, stifling initiative and freedom at every point. This is what stands out in the most sustained critique, Friedrich von Hayek's *The Road To Serfdom* (1944). It is not that all Hayek's criticisms of some of the excesses of state control at that time were unjustified, it is that he presents every intervention by the state in such extreme and disproportionate light. When it came to specifics, we see that Hayek was prepared to acknowledge that 'the preservation of competition is [not] incompatible with an extensive system of social services' (Hayek, 1944: 28). Yet, in the book's wider analysis, almost everything becomes general and absolute. German collectivist and statist ideas had everywhere crowded out English ones, 'such that it is Germany whose fate [that is to say, the rise of the Nazis] we are in some danger of repeating' (Hayek, 1944: 1, 16). Indeed, National Socialism was essentially just one of the 'rival socialist factions', and 'planning leads to dictatorship' (Hayek, 1944: 6, 52).

Even those on the moderate, modernising wing of the Conservative Party, such as leading thinker Quintin Hogg, were apt to portray social democracy and the state in a dramatically menacing way. To Hogg, by 1947, 'the great heresy of our age is no longer self-interest, it is State Worship' (Hogg, 1947: 62). Moreover, local, community and voluntary endeavours, 'each and all, one by one, are to be swallowed in the capacious maw of the omnivorous Socialist State' (Hogg, 1947: 67). Even more firmly centrist figures were prone to lose the sense of balance that was otherwise so central to their political outlook when it came to appraising the role of central government. Liberal leader Jo Grimond, in his *The Liberal Future* (1959), writing after nearly a decade of *Conservative*, not social democratic government, that had hardly presided over state spending run rampant, nonetheless painted a picture of 'endless welfare benefits to be handed out by the grandmother state' (Grimond, 1959: 22, 72).

None of this is to deny that the state could be guilty of excesses of control, spending and regimentation. Rather, the point is that state excesses have almost always been more readily and rapidly publicised, and more dramatically exaggerated than market ones, social democratic failings more ruthlessly highlighted than Conservative ones. The British welfare state by the early 1960s remained relatively modest in scale, and certainly very youthful in its age. Relatively unbridled capitalism had existed a great deal longer, yet it was often the former that was presented as vast and interminable. Emblematic of this, during the 1976 IMF crisis, when the IMF had made a loan to Britain conditional on public expenditure cuts, the Treasury had in fact significantly over-estimated the size of the Public Sector Borrowing Requirement, and thus, in fact, the very need for the loan that seemed so to symbolise the 'crisis' in post-1945 welfarist social democracy (Thorpe, 1997: 194).

Social democrats, as so often, have themselves contributed to the under-valuing of their record. Harold Wilson famously likened the Labour Party to a stage-coach, at its best when travelling with great speed and purpose, at its worst when it stopped to self-indulge in internal dispute and self-flagellation. This was characteristically funny, but it also contained a profundity. Social democrats' tendency to oppositionism and self-criticism has been both virtue and vice. As Marquand's career exemplifies, intellectual nonconformity and questioning were essential virtues of the progressive, being forever, as he put it, 'a rolling stone', a permanent revisionist, in the knowledge that 'no one party or faction ever has a monopoly of the truth' (Marquand, website). This outlook also stemmed from the legitimate desire to analyse what was wrong with society. There, surely, always needed to be something of the temperamental dissenter and critic in a true social democrat, and even an inherent uneasiness about the holding of power, and its associated ethical concessions. Even Roy Jenkins, the archetypal establishment liberal, was simultaneously a Celtic rebel, who reflected on 'the question of how much I was truly at ease with power' (Jenkins, 1991: 562). On the left, Richard Crossman, in his Fabian tract, *Labour in the Affluent Society* (1960), argued that the party needed to remind itself that its primary purpose was to provide a political voice for nonconformist critics and the socially disadvantaged. There were dangers in elevating electability and pragmatism into the supreme virtues (Crossman, 1960: 5–6).

But it is also the case that this too often lapsed into negativity. Even the Attlee government was not free, for instance, from the perennially critical Crossman's frustration, formulated by 1959, about 'how great were its failures' and 'how much further it might have taken us towards a true Socialist welfare state' (Crossman, 1959). John Strachey, writing in 1952, drew attention to the unattractive habit of both left and right to 'see the crisis of the contemporary world as "total"', and to luxuriate in the repetition of words such as 'desperate', 'catastrophic' and 'absolute'. Instead, he advocated 'a cooler temper and a lower claim' (Strachey, 1952). Yet, the self-denigration was to continue. One set of memoirs, in 1971, described the 1964–70 government of Harold Wilson as a period of 'disappointment after disappointment': the memoirs were Wilson's own (Wilson, 1974: 18).

Social democrats have been too bashful about the successes of this era, and too ready to see their own ideology as having failed *en totale*. Tony Crosland, here, is an interesting antidote. He had moved, between the 1950s and 1970s, from being an arch-revisionist to a rather worldly party loyalist, scolding those apt to denigrate the 1964–70 government's achievements, or prone to factional in-fighting or intellectual despair, and pointed, in his *Social Democracy in Europe* (1975) to the dangers of an 'intellectual fashion in the Western World today [which] is deeply pessimistic'. He acknowledged that 'people make more and more incompatible (and often unreasonable) demands on government; and they grow sullen when their expectations, which they now see as entitlements, are not met' (Crosland, 1975: 13–14). Yet his main contention was that 'there is another side to the picture. There is little evidence either from casual observation or opinion surveys that people are less generally contented than they were … little evidence of a general flight of faith from democratic parties and institutions'. Ultimately, he concluded, 'I find the current pessimism to be much exaggerated' (Crosland, 1975: 13–14). In troubling times, then as now, this was a valuable reminder to progressives to retain their nerve, and their sense of proportion.

The people take the lead: 1979 – the present

Margaret Thatcher's election victory in 1979 symbolised the fading of both old-style Fabian, state-directed social democracy and old-style hierarchical, paternalist Conservatism. The people's ambitions and expectations, both for themselves, and of government had risen to the point where they were less content to be told what to do, what was best for them, or where lay the limits to their 'place'. The evidence of this had already begun to mount in the 1970s, and carried on firmly through the 1980s. It was apparent in the increasingly assertive trade union and Labour grassroots left, and the women's liberation movement. The emerging leader of the Labour left, Tony Benn, reflected as early as 1970, that 'more people want to do more for themselves, and believe they are capable of doing so' (Benn, 1970: 1, 9–10, 16, 28).

But it was just as manifest in the growing working- and middle-class aspiration for social mobility and home-ownership, which helped fuel the advance of Thatcherism. As Middlemas notes, rising public expectations and assertiveness made it ever harder for the old political elites to pursue the top-down fine-tuning and balancing of interest groups that had characterised the 1950s and 1960s. This was a concern to some centrist politicians and civil servants of the consensus years, who began to fear 'they had helped create, not a balanced polity but one dominated by a Frankenstein monster of public ingratitude, wantonness and greed' (1986: 353–4).

In fact, this less deferential, more assertive popular will did not necessarily favour the political 'extremes'. On the whole, it would make it increasingly difficult for governments – even, in many ways, Thatcher – to ignore that archetypal centrist, 'floating voter'. A politics more responsive to the people has, therefore, for most of this time, not been the same as *populism*. Nonetheless, the 'Brexit' vote does mean that this nearly forty-year era of a less top-down politics has culminated in the most dramatic reminder that it is not the politicians who are the ultimate masters and mistresses, but the people themselves.

We should not romanticise this more restless populace, nor ignore the difficulties it posed to progressive politics. It has fostered elements of both sharp, ultra-competitive individualism and, as the Brexit vote partly shows, illiberal populism. It also meant that Labour could no longer rely on the voting strength of that now numerically declining, relatively homogenous male, unionised working class to be enough – if ever it could. There were also important limits to the enhanced popular assertiveness and decline of deference, and, interestingly, Benn himself acknowledged that 'the new citizen' still exhibited 'fears and doubts and lack of self-confidence' (Benn, 1970: 1, 9–10, 16, 28).

But the opportunities should not be overlooked either. The steady erosion of deference and hierarchy, the growing appetite for education, not least among women, and the reduction in automatic class voting was creating a more fluid, contestable politics. This politics was not *innately* favourable to social democracy, but rather a complex mix. Britain was decreasingly politically or socially monolithic, but rather, as Brooke observes of the 1980s 'a society based upon ... contradiction ... partly neoliberal, partly social democratic, partly individualist, partly collectivist' (Brooke, 2014). But this contestable mix opened up possibilities for a social democracy that was in tune with the new social patterns, attentive to support in the middle ground, and persuasively led. This was most clearly evidenced by Labour's three consecutive election victories from 1997, an achievement that would have been unthinkable to many in the party across the twentieth century. Just as significant, of course, have been the electoral defeats the party has endured in this period, both from 1979, and since 2010.

The fundamental question is: was this because the people fell short of Labour's progressive ideals, or because Labour fell behind a socially modernising public? Both, perhaps. But, certainly, there have been, and remain, some crucial ways in which Labour has been insufficiently intellectually imaginative and constructive in seeking to forge an alliance with the electorate, to make the most of the progressive dimensions contained within the 'mainstream', and to turn that many-sided 'modernity' to its advantage. This did not mean pandering to every popular sentiment, but switching off from the voters was always likely to be electorally fatal.

An important indicator of when social democrats have struggled in their relationship with the people is their tendency to reduce politics to supposedly malign or betraying leaders. The names of Margaret Thatcher and Tony Blair bestride both the academic and the broader public discussion of social democracy since 1979. This is curious, because social democrats tend to pride themselves on not viewing history solely as the actions of leaders. By creating culpable demons at the top, social democrats have sometimes avoided an engagement with the deeper societal changes and popular sentiments that allowed Thatcherism and New Labour to develop. Again, these were not uniformly attractive sentiments, but by overlooking them in favour of a focus on the leader, social democrats have too often disengaged from the social changes around them, and the opportunities for moulding them in progressive directions. For while leaders undoubtedly shape society, they are, in democracies at least, also reflections and products of it, symbols of attitudes and approaches that are usually much more widely shared.

In this vein, Ewen Green has suggested that 'Thatcher was a creature of her time and not the creator of it' (Green, 2006: 196). In many ways, the more aspirational, socially mobile, individualistic culture which helped sustain Thatcherism, and the broader popular Conservatism for four successive elections, had its roots in the 1960s and 1970s. The increasing affluence and consumerism of those decades, accompanied by rising educational expectations, reduced deference, and even the protection and confidence afforded by expanding state welfare, were all motors for the expansion of people's horizons and ambitions. As Labour had witnessed to its benefit in 1964 and 1966, and again, though to a receding extent, in 1974, these rising ambitions could help fuel support for the election of Labour governments, and for collectivist political projects. But they could also provide the dynamic for more individualistic and Conservative ones. Whether the effect was to push politics left or right depended in part, no doubt, on a certain cyclical swing of the ideological pendulum and the popular mood. But the implications of these ambitions were also contingent. They reflected that mix of individual ambition and social conscience that characterises, perhaps, most people, and they were thus open to being channelled by whichever party, and leader seemed best to articulate that sense of forward-looking dynamism and modernity at the time. In the 1960s, that was manifestly Harold Wilson. In the 1980s, it was Thatcher. As that most perceptive of social democratic journalists, Peter Jenkins, wrote at the time, Thatcher had 'excited expectations of a certain kind. She had taught more people to want to own their homes, to want to own a stake in things, to want a better chance for their children' (Jenkins, 1989: 379). But if she helped reinforce such aspirations, they had also long preceded her.

This is not to say that the popular spirit of the 1980s was by any means unambiguously laudable. In some respects, indeed, it validated the long-standing reservations of progressives about the people as carriers of saloon-bar prejudices. The portrayal of the decade in terms of an amoral City and rampant materialism was a caricature, but not without *some* basis in reality. Further, the fact that the government was able to enact Section 28 of the Local Government Act (1988) stating that local authorities should not 'promote' homosexuality, including in their schools was indicative that although Thatcher did not reverse the broad thrust of the liberalising social legislation of the 1960s, popular attitudes in these areas often lagged significantly behind the initial legal change. Thatcher, the first female prime minister, was also notoriously unsympathetic to government support for working women, leaving female–male pay differentials in Britain higher than elsewhere in Europe, and access to child care more limited (Beers, 2012: 118). Again, this is a critique of popular attitudes as much as of government. Women themselves were not clamouring to change this. Beers notes the striking duality at this time that whilst 'women were increasingly working outside the home ... the vast majority still held conservative views about the gender order' (Beers, 2012: 124).

Yet, there were also more pragmatic, middle-of-the-road popular outlooks which at this time Thatcher proved more adept at moulding to her advantage than social democrats. For female voters, still at this stage more prone than men to vote Conservative, especially middle-aged and older ones, this was true on issues of economic management and education. On the former, Labour has historically had difficulties, yet its inability to garner votes on the latter at this time was striking testimony to how far social democracy's association with the socially mobile, educationally expansive 1960s had eroded. Here, polling suggests that Thatcher scored especially well among women on education, not so much through ideology but by 'her presentation of her ... education policies as a logical outgrowth of her common sense approach', favouring standards and choice over what was not entirely unfairly perceived as elements of left-wing dogma in schools, and ongoing teachers' strikes (Beers, 2012: 131).

Of course, what was 'common sense' and what was 'dogma' was highly contestable, and it was often harder for parties of change to present their ideas as a 'norm' than conservative ones. But voters' perceptions mattered. Moreover, Labour figures in the 1980s did at times do little to help themselves in making what was progressive seem sensible, practical and mainstream. The tendency to portray Thatcher and Thatcherism en bloc as an almost evil, menacing force too often degenerated into an implicit (or indeed explicit) *en totale* condemnation of the society over which she presided, and its values. 'This awful monetarist philosophy, which is nonsense', reflected Tony Benn in his diary entry of 26 March 1980; Thatcher's speeches were (15 May) 'rumbustious, rampaging, right-wing' (Benn, 1991: 505, 587). Benn was opposed to 'the current philosophy, that is to say the philosophy of profit' (Benn, 1991: 196). Few social democrats would disagree that Thatcher over-lauded the one-dimensional pursuit of profit. But social attitudes as a whole in the 1980s were not one-dimensional, so that such portrayals of social attitudes risked under-estimating the significance of other ambitions at this time, more modest, less ruthlessly competitive and sometimes rather altruistic, but the holders of which nonetheless saw Thatcher, not social democracy, as in some way speaking for them.

This outlook also entailed a missed opportunity for Labour to engage more positively with affluence and aspiration, and, indeed, to redefine these crucial concepts in more social democratic, more collectivist terms. Bryan Gould pointed to housing policy as an illustrator of the point. Labour had opposed council house sales on the grounds that they had led to a shortage of available cheaper housing. But there was no reason why the party could not have supported both the sales and the building of more houses as a replacement. Instead, its policy had been to deny to working-class people the benefits of home ownership, 'which were seen as a birthright by everyone else' (Gould, 1995: 152).

But it was an opportunity that Tony Blair did finally and boldly seize by the mid-1990s. Here, it seemed, was the epitome of social democracy as balance, those third way syntheses between the individual *and* the community; rights *and* responsibilities. The electoral potency of this fusing of Labour's traditional support base with a substantial section of those aspirational supporters of Thatcher in the 1980s has been frequently noted. Here was a conscious assertion that Labour was not only for the deprived, the cities, the left and the North, but also for the more comfortable, the suburbs, the centre and the South. 'When I hear people urging us to fight for "our people"', Blair told the party's 1995 conference, in the words that best captured the essence of this popular re-connect, 'I tell you, these are our people' (Blair, 1995). Yet, there was a moral rationale to this attempt to broaden the party's appeal too. Labour's drift in the 1970s and 1980s towards a more class-based, socially, industrially and politically conflictual approach undoubtedly contained elements of ideological dogma, class warfare, and exclusion of a disliked 'middle England', as well as an undoubted strain of rugged masculinity that was not simply antithetical to the broad coalition needed to win elections, but also, in a profound sense, *morally* deficient. In its early heyday, New Labour was repeatedly emphatic about its claim to be raising the ethics, not just the electability of the party. 'It wasn't at all about changing the basic values or purpose of progressive politics;' insisted Blair, 'on the contrary, it was about retrieving them from the deadweight of political and cultural dogma that didn't merely obscure those values and that purpose, but also defeated them' (Blair, 2010: 91).

At its best, earlier and middle phases, New Labour was also genuinely intellectually and ideologically innovative. This was perhaps most strongly evident in education policy, which was New Labour's substitute for nationalisation as the crucial springboard to greater opportunity and equality. Here, again, the balanced coupling of values and methods was the key: widening access and encouraging excellence; better funding of schools, but also more rigorous inspection. In essence, as Blair put it, 'more support, and, in return, more demand for achievement' (Blair, 1995).

The 1997–2010 Labour government established a significant and wide-ranging legacy of public service investment, economic growth, constitutional democratisation, more socially liberal attitudes and extended access to museums and the arts. It also demonstrated, finally and conclusively, that progressivism and the people could sustain each other over a prolonged period. Blair could legitimately claim in his final conference speech in 2006 that 'our core vote is the country' and that he had gone some way to resolving the party's enduring and 'ridiculous self-imposed dilemma between principle and power' (Blair, 2006). The dilemmas of social democracy's long-standing encounter with the people seemed, for a time, finally to have been resolved.

What New Labour did not manage, however, was to articulate a narrative about the importance of public services and the public realm that was embedded sufficiently into the political culture to make it resistant to Conservative spending cuts from 2010. Nor, indeed, did it even manage to secure the endurance of its values, or pride in its legacy within the Labour Party itself. Indeed, all of Labour's leaders since 2010, in fact since 2007, have been obsessed with seeking to prove that they are emphatically *not Blair*. This partly reflects Blair's own failings: the excessive closeness to George Bush, the over-confidence in the Westernisation of Iraq and, by the end, his tendency excessively to laud the market. New Labour became guilty of the error of over-compensation. So eager was it to demonstrate that it now valued the virtues of enterprise and the market alongside those of public services, that in its later years it began to give the impression that it valued them more. Blair, in particular, was repeatedly, and increasingly inclined to draw a distinction between a dynamic market sector that almost inherently 'shifted fast under … social pressures' and a 'public sector [which] got stuck' (Blair, 2010: 90). Not only was this a crude generalisation, it contradicted not simply traditional social democracy, but New Labour's own third way, which was supposed to combine and fuse the best virtues of public and private, not subordinate one to the other. New Labour had, by the end, lost the balance that had been its very rationale.

But if Blair is culpable for errors during his time in office up to 2007, he cannot be held accountable for the party's failure to articulate a compelling new intellectual vision over the decade since. The party's fixation with him since his departure is both a back-handed compliment as to the size of the ideological hole he left, and an indication that Labour has since spent too much time enunciating what it is not, and too little crafting innovative policies for the future. The lack of distance from this time, as so often with contemporary history, leads academic accounts and contemporary Labour figures to over-state the New Labour government's failings and under-estimate the constraints under which it operated. The generalised claim, in one of the most influential studies of the government, that it presided over 'losing Labour's soul' is indicative of the long-standing tendency to romanticise the unremitting moral rectitude of a socialist past that never was, and to reduce all policy errors to moral decline and betrayal (Shaw, 2007). Similarly, with Jeremy Corbyn's Shadow Chancellor John McDonnell's description in 2015 of 'this drivel' of 'all the old Blairite mantras that Labour has failed to be a party of aspiration, to occupy the middle ground and appeal to middle England' (McDonnell, 2015). Tom Watson's 2016 conference speech as deputy leader, seen as a rallying of Labour moderates, perceptively warned that 'trashing our own record is not the way to enhance our brand' (Watson, 2016).

New Labour's broad idea of a third way, synthesising aspiration with social conscience, ambition with equity, seems of considerable continuing applicability. But New Labour's admirers must also now move on from the past, and start articulating the values and policies of the present and future. As Ed Miliband had promised in his 2010 party leadership campaign, though he found it a difficult balance to sustain, the task was a twofold one of 'retaining what New Labour got right but moving on from what it got wrong' (E. Miliband, 2010). What dilemmas and conclusions remain in the present and future for Labour's relationship with 'the people'? We end here by pinpointing two, the first relating to social democracy, the second to the people themselves.

First, for social democrats, the post-New Labour challenge was to retain, and indeed enhance, that positive outlook towards aspiration and enterprise, whilst exhibiting greater self-confidence in advocacy of the values and virtues of the public sphere. There were hints of this in David Miliband's final draft of what would have been his victory speech in the Labour leadership contest of 2010. His insistence that he would have 'no truck with the prejudice of public bad, private good' was a response to a bias which had characterised late New Labour, not just the Conservatives (D. Miliband, 2010). There were even, in fact, some hints of it on the centre-right. In a tonal shift from the austerity under David Cameron, Theresa May's leadership campaign launch speech reassured the swing voter that 'we don't hate the state, we value the role that only the state can play'. She also spoke of new agendas of placing employees on company boards, and addressing slow wage growth, and excessively high ratios of CEO to average worker pay levels (May, 2016). This was also a reminder that New Labour had been more active on social, welfare and educational policy than on the economy and the workplace. Addressing the inequalities in the latter in a bolder way is both right in itself, and a means of countering the populism (on right and left) that has thrived in part on those economic injustices.

This entails social democracy recovering both its moral vision and its connection with the people. Throughout Labour's history, and certainly since 2010, it was not so much that moral purpose and electability came into conflict, as that social democracy, under both late Blairism and its successors lost hold of both of these desirables simultaneously. Social democracy's most successful phases have tended to come when it has been both popular and intellectually visionary. Labour should be in tune with the people's aspirations, but also have a vision to lead the people. For the historical evidence marshalled in this chapter suggests, on the whole, that the British people will support a vision, whether of centre-right or centre-left, which stretches and challenges them, not one that simply flatters them for their prejudices (like UKIP), or promises to remedy their every grievance (to which the left is sometimes prone). In the end, values and vision are always indispensable.

As ever, the challenge was also one of mood and outlook. There is surely no historical coincidence that Labour's greatest moments have tended to coincide with a broader optimism and dynamism in the national outlook and culture: the 'Blitz' spirit, the 'Swinging Sixties, 'cool Britannia'. Not only do voters like optimism in itself (it is no coincidence that Tony Blair, Bill Clinton and Barack Obama, with seven victories out of seven, all exuded this), it is also often a necessary mindset for constructive and intelligent policy formulation. Social democrats, then, should, on the whole, be optimists – not uncritical optimists (the nonconformist, questioning strain is rightly too powerful for that) – but positive and constructive in their outlook. They should engage with a long-overdue scrutiny of their tendency towards pessimism, looking backwards, and a lack of internal fraternity – the danger, as Robin Cook warned, that 'leftist analysis by tradition tends to the gloomy ... end of the spectrum' (Cook, 2004: 375). More than this, holding together vision and popular appeal meant maintaining a certain energy and boldness, a politics of fast tempo.

Forging ahead in 1964 with an agenda of expanded social welfare, the National Plan, and comprehensive education, despite an initial Commons majority of just four, Harold Wilson (1974: 42) told his first Cabinet that 'we should ... press on with all the policies in which we believed', and 'live dangerously'. 'The only way to do it is to maintain the momentum', advised Neil Kinnock (Kinnock: 2016). Michael Heseltine made a perceptive observational aside in the 1980s, which was that the Labour Party would start to win again when it really wanted to. The right appetite and outlook would precede and generate the policy programme for achieving it (Rawnsley, 2017).

Second, if social democrats can raise their game, can the people themselves correspondingly rise to the challenge? Over the years covered by this chapter, the British people have exhibited a complex mix of conservatism and progressivism, ambition and apathy, generosity and prejudice. Social democrats, liberals and even liberal Conservatives are often gloomy about how the Brexit vote, Labour's electoral defeats since 2010, and on a broader, international scale Donald Trump's victory in 2016 appear to indicate the ascendancy of that less progressive, darker side to the people. But, as is social democrats' wont, this meant tending to ignore the more encouraging countervailing evidence. Between 1997 and 2010, Labour had enjoyed by far its longest sustained period in office. After thirteen years in government, it was perhaps unsurprising that people had become weary of the party by 2010, but its influence and legacy have been by no means dismantled *en totale*. Most notably, voters have remained reluctant to grant the Conservatives a blank cheque to pare back the welfare state: it is surprisingly infrequently observed that the election-winning machine which presided over the 'Conservative century' underwent seven general elections between 1992 and 2017 without winning a majority above 21.

There are also significant divisions between liberal, mainstream and right-wing Conservatives, which seem likely to intensify as the negotiations over Brexit proceed. The farther right, in the form of UKIP, presently seems to have been electorally weakened, not strengthened by the very fulfilment of its purpose on Brexit, just as the alarming advances of the British National Party in the 2009 European election also relatively rapidly receded. This is not to advocate complacency. Rather, it is a reminder that the combination of the Brexit vote and Trump's victory in 2016 constitute a historical moment, not, as yet, an epoch, that popular political outlooks are, as the closeness of the Brexit vote illustrated, divided, complex, mixed and closer to the centre than sometimes portrayed, and that much remains in play.

More fundamental still, though, than the people's voting habits, is their deeper underlying condition, values and character. The people have always been crucial to political and social progress. Improving their lives was its rationale, the people's support and active participation was the means to achieving it, and the people's limitations were always the most important fundamental constraint on it. Populism, in attributing all problems to a malign elite or minority, whether of capitalists, immigrants, bankers, European technocrats or London liberals obscures this, distracting the broad mass of the people from their own, ultimately determining role in the state of the nation, for both good and ill.

If much of this section has portrayed that political role of the people as becoming more assertive, ambitious and demanding, that can also be exaggerated. As throughout the previous century, the full picture in the immediate present is more many-sided, with this heightening of the people's engagement coexisting with the lingering of substantial deference, insecurity and inertia. That sense of a certain middle-of-the-road mediocrity, of 'getting by', but not reaching the heights remains a frequent component in the national identity and in people's personal self-definitions. It is, perhaps, especially emblematic of the past quarter-century, which has seen a diminution in the starkness of the old class and ideological divides, but which retains a nagging sense of hopes frustrated and constrained. It was, maybe, no coincidence, that the 'satisfactory', middling C grade at GCSE was, since 1990, consistently that most commonly achieved (GCSE Results: Joint Council). Blair (2010: 272–3), for all his reverence for the people, reflected intriguingly that whilst the public 'could accept radical reform in the event of chronic failure, most would not accept that radicalism in the case of passive mediocrity'. This sense of contradictory strains in the people is echoed in Marquand's 2008 passage, with which the chapter began, in which the culture of *Big Brother* and *The Sun* coexisted with a declining deference and resilient public spirit (Marquand, 2008: 407). Marquand, possessing the dual assets of the idealism of the political theorist with the realism of the historian, has often charted this mix, alerting fellow social democrats to harsh realities, yet also charting possible routes out of them. For him, British democracy, and, importantly, the elite and popular outlooks which underlay them remained, as they had throughout the period of this chapter, fourfold and contradictory in their character, a blend of evolutionary Whiggism, democratic collectivism, Tory nationalism, and Marquand's favoured, more participatory and egalitarian democratic republicanism: 'democratic politics in Britain have been the politics of rival *democracies*, not of one, all-embracing democracy' (Marquand, 2008: 75).

Yet Marquand also sensed that the tempo of public political engagement and interest seemed to be rising, 'the beat was changing' (Marquand, 2008: 407). Nearly ten years on, the sense of that more politically engaged public is perhaps greater still, though the competing impulses also remain evident. On the nature of that beat, much rests. For social democracy at its best has *asked* something of the people, not just offered it. The 1945 government asked voters to sustain the 'Blitz spirit' of togetherness and cooperation into peacetime. The 1964 government sought a new, modern, classless spirit, to be observed by both sides in the workplace. New Labour spoke of community and citizenship. This is also why the level of priority accorded to education – so central in 1964 and 1997, yet fading in prominence in the party's agenda subsequently – is often a barometer of social democracy's intellectual vibrancy.

It is in these ways that Marquand's work is especially pertinent, located at that intersection where social democracy as ideas and values meets social democracy as popular participation. Social democracy was 'demanding', insisted

Marquand in his *The Unprincipled Society* (Marquand, 1988: 246). Here was his call 'to substitute the politics of mutual education for the politics of command and exchange' (Marquand, 1988: 246-7). In the end, the people had to do it for themselves, social democrats must 'gamble … on [people's] … sociability and capacity for growth' (Marquand, 1988: 246-7). Ultimately, there is no other way, for politics must in some profound sense be a reflection of the character of the people and the timbre of the times. If politicians and political thinkers will continue to seek to make social democrats, it is also now – as, in truth, it always has been – the challenge for the people to make social democracy.

References

Attlee, C. R. (1949) *The Labour Party in Perspective – And Twelve Years Later* (London: Victor Gollancz).

Baldwin, S. (1926) *On England: And Other Addresses* (London: Philip Allan).

Ball. S. and Holliday, I. (2002) 'Introduction', in Ball, S. and Holliday, I. (eds), *Mass Conservatism. The Conservatives and The Public Since The 1880s* (London: Psychology Press).

Beers, L. (2010) *Your Britain. Media and The Making of The Labour Party* (London: Harvard University Press).

Beers, L. (2012) 'Thatcher and the Women's vote', in B. Jackson and R. Saunders (eds), *Making Thatcher's Britain* (Cambridge: Cambridge University Press), 113–31.

Benn, A. (1970) *The New Politics: A Socialist Reconnaissance*, Fabian Tract 402, September.

Benn, T. (1991) *Conflicts of Interest. Diaries 1977–80* (London: Arrow).

Bevan, A. (1978) *In Place of Fear* (London: Quartet Books).

Bevin, E. (1942) *The Job To Be Done* (London: Heinemann).

Black, L. (2003) *The Political Culture of the Left in Affluent Britain, 1951–64* (Basingstoke: Macmillan).

Blair, T. (1995) Labour Party Conference speech, 3 October.

Blair, T. (2006) Labour Party Conference speech, 26 September.

Blair, T. (2010) *A Journey* (London: Hutchinson).

Brooke, S. (2014) 'Living in "New Times": Historicizing 1980s Britain', *History Compass*, 12 (January), 20–32.

Clapson, M. (2000) 'The suburban aspiration in England since 1919', *Contemporary British History*, 14, 151–74.

Cook, R. (2004) *The Point of Departure* (London: Simon & Schuster).

Crosland, C. A. R. (December 1975) *Social Democracy in Europe*, Fabian Tract 438.

Crossman, R. H. S. (28 Nov. 1959) *The New Statesman*.

Crossman, R. H. S. (June 1960) *Labour in The Affluent Society*, Fabian Tract 325.

Fielding, S. (2003) *The Labour Governments 1964–1970* (Manchester: Manchester University Press).

Fielding, S., Thompson, P. and Tiratsoo, N. (eds) (1995) *'England Arise!' The Labour Party and Popular Politics in 1940s Britain* (Manchester: Manchester University Press).

GCSE results, at Joint Council for Qualifications at: www.jcq.org.uk/ examination-results/gcses (accessed 2 February 2016).

Gould, B. (1995) *Goodbye To All That* (London: Macmillan).

Green, E. H. H. (2006) *Thatcher* (London: Bloomsbury Academic).

Grimond, J. (1959) *The Liberal Future* (London: Faber & Faber).

Hayek, F. A. (1944) *The Road to Serfdom* (London: Routledge).

Healey, D. (1990) *The Time of My Life* (London: Penguin).

Hilton, M. (2011) 'Politics is ordinary: Non-governmental organizations and political participation in contemporary Britain', *Twentieth Century British History*, 22, 230–68.

Hobhouse, L. T. (1973) *Democracy and Reaction* (New York: Harper & Row).

Hogg, Q. (1947) *The Case For Conservatism* (Harmondsworth: Penguin).

Jenkins, P. (1989) *Mrs Thatcher's Revolution* (London: Pan).

Jenkins, R. (1991) *A Life At The Center* (New York: Random House).

Kinnock, N. (2016) *Conversations: Interview*, BBC Parliament channel, 24 July.

Labour Party (1974) *Let Us Work Together*, General Election Manifesto (February).

Lawrence, J. (1998) *Speaking For The People: Party, Language and Popular Politics in England, 1867–1914* (Cambridge: Cambridge University Press).

Lawrence, J. (2009) *Electing Our Masters: The Hustings in British Politics From Hogarth To Blair* (Oxford: Oxford University Press).

MacDonald, J. R. (1919) *Parliament and Revolution* (Manchester: National Labour Press).

MacDonald, J. R. (1920) *A Policy For The Labour Party* (London: Leonard Parsons).

McDonnell, J. (2015) *The Guardian*, 12 May.

McKibbin, R. (2010) *Parties and People. England 1914–1951* (Oxford: Oxford University Press).

Marquand, D. (July 1979) 'Inquest on a movement: Labour's defeat and its consequences', *Encounter*, 53, 8–18.

Marquand, D. (1988) *The Unprincipled Society* (London: Fontana).

Marquand, D. (1992) *The Progressive Dilemma* (London: Heinemann).

Marquand, D. (1997) *The New Reckoning: Capitalism, States and Citizens* (Cambridge: Polity).

Marquand, D. (2008) *Britain Since 1918. The Strange Career of British Democracy* (London: Weidenfeld & Nicolson).

Marquand, D., website at http://davidmarquand.com/.

May, T. (11 July 2016) Conservative leadership candidate launch speech.

Middlemas, K. (1986) *Power, Competition and The State: Vol 1: Britain in Search of Balance, 1940–61* (London: Macmillan).

Miliband, D. (10 June 2010) Final draft of victory speech for Labour leadership contest, 2010, *The Guardian*.

Miliband, E. (2010) *The Observer*, 29 August.

Morris, W. (15 November 1890) 'Where are we now?', *Commonweal*, in A. L. Morton (ed.) (1984) *Political Writings of William Morris* (London).

Morris, W. (16 June 1894), 'How I became a Socialist', *Justice*, in A. L. Morton, (ed.) (1984) *Political Writings of William Morris* (London).

Morrison, H. (1960) *Herbert Morrison. An Autobiography* (London: Odhams).

Morton, A. L. (ed.) (1984) *Political Writings of William Morris* (London: Lawrence & Wishart).

Nuttall, J. (2006) *Psychological Socialism. The Labour Party and Qualities of Mind and Character* (Manchester: Manchester University Press).

Nuttall, J. (2013) 'Pluralism, the people and time in Labour Party history, 1931–1964', *Historical Journal*, 56, 729–56.

Olivier, S. (1962) 'Moral', in G. B. Shaw (ed.), *Fabian Essays in Socialism* (London: Dolphin Books).

Rawnsley, A. (2017) *The Observer: Interview with Tony Blair*, 30 Apr.

Russell, B. (1969) *The Autobiography of Bertrand Russell, 1944–1967*, vol. 3 (London).

Seldon, A. (1994) 'Conservative century', in Seldon, A. and Ball, S. (eds), *Conservative Century. The Conservative Party Since 1900* (Oxford: Oxford University Press).

Shaw, E. (2007) *Losing Labour's Soul?: New Labour and The Blair Government 1997–2007* (London: Routledge).

Shaw, G. B. (1930) *Socialism: Principles and Outlook*, Fabian Tract, 233 (London: Fabian Society).

Shaw, G. B. (1962) 'Transition', in G. B. Shaw (ed.), *Fabian Essays* (London).

Stevenson, J. (1990) *British Society 1914–45* (London: Penguin).

Strachey, J. (29 July 1952) *The Guardian*.

Tawney, R. H. (1952) *Equality* (London).

Thorpe, A. (1997) *A History of The British Labour Party* (London: Macmillan).

Tomlinson, J. (2009) 'Thrice denied: "Declinism" as a recurrent theme in British History in the long twentieth century', *Twentieth Century British History*, 20, 227–51.

Watson, T. (2016) *Speech To Labour Party Conference*, 27 September.

Webb, S. (1923) *The Labour Party On The Threshold*, Fabian Tract, 207 (London: Fabian Society).

Webb, S. (1962) 'Historic', in G. B. Shaw (ed.), *Fabian Essays* (London).

Wilson, H. (1974) *The Labour Government 1964–70* (Middlesex: Penguin).

Woolf, L. (1937) *After The Deluge: A Study In Communal Psychology* (Harmondsworth: Penguin).

3

British liberalism in search of ideological recalibration

Michael Freeden

The Liberal Party has been much less successful than the Liberal creed. (Marshall, 2004: 2).

The salience of ideas in British political culture has too often been obscured by discursive misreadings, an exaggerated focus on leaders and institutions, or a dogmatic adherence to a mythical notion of pragmatism (Blackburn, 2017). The mounting invisibility of liberal thinking in public consciousness – if not perhaps among scholars and academics – following the heyday of political liberalism a century ago is the outcome of those tendencies, combined with the additional need to look under and through political labels that mask liberalism's considerable intricacies (Grayson, 2009). Probing at the macro-level of ideological discourse, rather than in the small print of detailed policy proposals, reveals the tortuous ideological roads trodden by British liberalism at a time where it has been squeezed and overshadowed by more powerful and vocal ideological rivals, often due to its own ideological retreat from the pinnacles of its social vision. That retreat had already gathered pace in the 1930s, witnessed in the texts of the Liberal Party and the writings of its intellectuals and publicists, but became more pronounced in the post-1945 era. The inter-war years' bifurcation between the social liberalism of the Hobhouses and Hobsons of the liberal, welfarist left on the one hand, and the centrist liberalism of Ramsay Muir, Keynes and the 1928 Yellow Book on the other, now found the spokespeople of 'official' liberalism articulating a frequently weary and repetitive discursive stance, peppered nonetheless with small doses of the older liberal humanist tradition, and with a few flashes of fervour and invention (Freeden, 1986).

The ideationally powerful social liberalism, in many ways still the innovative progressive voice of twentieth-century Britain from today's vantage point, increasingly came to be lodged at the heart of a broader social democratic tradition, long before a group of dissatisfied Labour and Liberal Party members attached that sobriquet to the short-lived Social Democratic Party (the least liberally inclined of the putative contenders for a radical progressivism). If, in the United Kingdom, the liberal tradition had been a proud and confident one a century and more ago, its resettlement in social democratic terrain would have come as no surprise to those acquainted with Swedish welfare thinking. There, social democracy had always contained policies closely akin to Britain's new liberalism – Ernest Wigforss, Leonard Hobhouse and J. A. Hobson spoke in similar registers – but the different connotations and contexts of the descriptor 'liberal' made it a politically awkward word among northern European progressives. By contrast, in Britain both left and centrist liberalism before 1945 had a historic profile well-known to progressives, and the word 'liberal' retained a political cachet, yet the difficulty was that the two increasingly drifted apart, leaving the application of that label more confusing and controversial than desirable.

Left-liberalism had absorbed not only a social but a communitarian element in its vigorous reinterpretation of J. S. Mill's legacy. It rewrote the liberal agenda of fundamental human rights to include all reasonable claims to a wholesome and full individual existence, while encouraging mutual aid and state enablement of the less fortunate. Inter-war centrist liberalism reverted to a more cautious, property-promoting and free-trade oriented ideological position, while honouring elements of a social liberalism in a much-muted voice (Freeden, 1986). Post-1945 liberalism gradually reconfigured the balance of its elements to espouse a more conventionally 'political' creed, highlighting constitutional reform and local government-cum-devolution, while its social justice policy went down diverging routes. In the initial post-war years, the electoral dullness and ideational paucity conveyed by the term 'liberalism' was plainly evident to all except its most fervent supporters, while the spirit of welfare liberalism continued its post-1918 trajectory by means of 'Labourite' programmes and debates, through which it controlled an expanding discursive space at the expense of that commanded by what was now publicly perceived as a reduced liberalism.

For the researcher, this state of affairs is problematic. The term 'liberal' occupies three different dimensions. The first is its prevalent usage in ordinary political language, associated with a strong historically anchored emphasis on individual liberty, human rights, tolerance, and the rule of law. The second is the party-political connotation, which oscillates according to party fortunes and policies, and has been shared between the older Liberal Party and the late twentieth-century Liberal Democratic Party. The third, the most difficult to appreciate for those who subscribe to dominant public discourses, is the more inclusive and often silent ideological identification of the conceptual combinations that can be understood as liberal. In unpacking that complexity of liberalisms, the porousness obtaining among the three levels must also be taken into account.

To compound such difficulties, an inaccurate distinction has emerged between 'economic liberalism' and 'social liberalism'. It is not only that, if the division relates to a welfarist tendency versus a market tendency, there have always been elements in the one liberal variant that are present in the other (Grayson, 2009: 11). Rather, the common obfuscation among commentators between 'liberalism' and 'liberalisation' has permitting an elision between liberal and libertarian-conservative ideologies. Thus Vincent Cable regards economic liberalism as 'the continuation of the Thatcherite reforms of the 1980s' (Cable, 2009: 165). Yet liberalisation alone does not make for liberalism. Decontextualised from its ideational environment that shored up a typical conservative-capitalist agenda, liberalism appeared to drift apart from the moral injunctions with which nineteenth-century liberals had encircled free trade and private enterprise (Freeden, 2015).

A more useful distinction is that between a political-civic liberalism and a welfare liberalism. The former focuses on political reforms of greater inclusiveness and participatory citizenship, equal opportunities for self-development (not only for economic success), and the protection of people from harm and unreasonable intrusion, entailing a strong emphasis on the divide between private and public, all those within the framework of legal and constitutional safeguards. The latter incorporates much of the former, without being dogmatically wedded to an impermeable private–public fault-line. It entertains a more comprehensive understanding of participation, centring on a generous interpretation of Mill's 'free development of individuality' to include human flourishing in a social environment of mutual assistance and enablement (Mill, 1910: 115). Since the late twentieth century such flourishing has also absorbed the group uniqueness of ethnic, religious, cultural and gender identities. To that extent, liberals regard such groups as 'individuals' writ large. Not least among those enablers was the state, transformed in the minds of welfare liberals from a potential threat whose power may be abused to personal detriment, to an agency devoted in part to removing hindrances to a full share in social life for everyone. Individual activity would be enhanced by putting the beneficial goods a society creates at the disposal of all, for individuals to use (or not use) as they pleased. There is obviously an economic element in all that, but it does not have to receive top billing in the ranking of liberal values.

Back to basics or treading water?

The conscious and public ideological blending of liberalism and social democracy in the second half of the twentieth century proceeded unevenly. The split between welfarist liberalism and centrist liberalism continued after 1945. Official Liberalism, as demonstrated in Liberal Party manifestos, underwent a further reduction in its range and ambitions, initially appearing more as a rearguard holding pattern than sponsoring a dynamic and progressive agenda (Sloman, 2015). Liberalism felt short as an ideology that could employ the kind of visionary language it had radiated prior to the First World War. True, its ideals still emanated periodically through the editorials of the *Guardian*, in the spirit of its previous illustrious incarnation, the *Manchester Guardian*, but even there it was rarely identified as liberal. The force of late-twentieth-century ideological rhetoric had diminished in relation to the sweep and flair of its bygone elegance. The passion of progressive language that Hobhouse had admired in 1911 was still available; sadly, though, not among self-defined liberals. The resounding rhetorical notes were struck instead during the Crosland years and the early years of Blairite labourism.

In mid-century, the party mantra was that of a 'break on class bitterness' as Conservatives and Socialists locked horns in class-conscious slogans (Liberal Party Manifesto, 1951). Any active return to a policy of nationalisation was abandoned. Beveridge's full employment and a commitment to maintaining the social services were tempered by the call to practise thrift and achieve full production. Political reform: proportional representation, the House of Lords, separate parliamentary assemblies for Scotland and Wales, and a pledge to conform to the United Nations Declaration of Human Rights, as well as a curiously antiquated and gendered reference to the party's 'unanimous adoption of a programme for women drawn up by women Liberals' made up the rest. By contrast, the first 1974 manifesto included a section on equality of opportunity and equal treatment for women (Liberal Party Manifesto, February 1974). As the winds of decolonisation gathered in the 1950s, liberals sought to apply their principles of human development and equality to the prospect of 'real partnership between races in the colonies' in an attempt to secure the prosperity of 'the resident local multiracial population'. In parallel, the programme contained a vigorous reassertion 'of the rights of the individual, his liberty to live his own life subject to respect for the rights of others, to hold and express his own views, to associate with others of his own choice, to be granted all possible freedom of opportunity and to be subject to no penalty or discrimination by reason of his colour, race or creed' (Liberal Party Manifesto, 1955).

In view of the Brexit referendum, the pro-European persuasion of liberalism as its main international plank deserves emphasising. Whereas in the 1950s and 1960s, decolonisation of sorts preoccupied foreign-policy liberal thinking and had found a prominent place in Liberal Party manifestos, the role of the EU and its organisational predecessor, the EEC, became more pronounced. Significantly, in the light of current concerns, the 1966 manifesto contended that: 'To play our part in Europe would not only be of great economic benefit it would make us a pioneer in the first supranational community where States have agreed to share some of their sovereignty'; and the 1970 manifesto spelled it out: 'In Western Europe we want the closest possible political unity. We see Britain's joining the Common Market as a part of this unity' (Liberal Party Manifestos, 1966; 1970). In pooling resources and sovereignty, it endorsed a selective collectivism in defined areas that social liberals had previously welcomed in the domestic arena, but that British liberalism was increasingly disinclined to pursue at home. Of course, the EU was precisely the kind of partnership without a central state (its critics notwithstanding) with which many liberals had found favour, but it also displayed the kind of self-imposed compulsion that had riven British liberalism for over a century.

How did the mid-twentieth-century liberal mission compare with Hobson's famously eloquent and ambitious painting of the path of progress as combining individual liberty and a self-development 'adjusted to the sovereignty of social welfare', all leading to 'free land, free travel, free power, free credit, security, justice and education', without which 'no man is "free" for the full purposes of civilised life to-day' (Hobson, 1909: xx)? One clue can be gleaned from a collection of essays published in 1957, entitled *The Unservile State*, mirroring Hilaire Belloc's 1912 attack on the liberal social reform agenda, *The Servile State*, and billing itself somewhat grandiosely as 'the first full-scale book on the attitudes and policies of British Liberalism' since the Yellow Book. The writers reflected the opinions of a largely anti-statist stream of liberal thought, of which Elliott Dodds, then vice-president of the Liberal Party and editor of the *Huddersfield Examiner*, was a prominent member. In a cleverly crafted chapter on 'Liberty and Welfare', Dodds began by affirming the social reform record of the new liberals and objected to the contrast between economic and political-cum-civic liberalism. In his words, 'true liberalism ... regards Liberty and welfare as complementary'. Liberals were conscious that individuals are 'involved in a complex of social relationships ... stressing their interdependence as much as their independence' (Dodds, 1957: 15–16).

But then the reservations began to pile up. In particular, the Unservile State liberals stepped back from the early twentieth-century rosy-eyed endorsement of the state. The notable honeymoon between liberalism and the state was definitely over, replaced by an uneasy cohabitation. 'A vast amount of red tape', 'bureaucratic methods', 'inordinate tax burdens' and a fear of state provision leading to augmented state control, were recurring themes. As the mouthpiece of the group, Dodds borrowed – somewhat selectively – William Beveridge's phrase in summing up their position: 'our aim is a "Welfare Society" rather than a "Welfare State".' Private endeavour and voluntary mutual aid were called on 'to diminish the role of the State' (Dodds, 1957: 18–19). That diminution was required because 'a State monopoly in Welfare has certain illiberal consequences'. Employing Belloc's term, a 'distributism' based on localism, spontaneous organisation, and the spread of private property was proposed instead (Jackson, 2016). That was more broadly expounded in Liberal circles through various proposals for 'ownership for all', a theme already mooted before 1945 by Ramsay Muir and others (Freeden, 1986: 258–66). They comprised twinning the dispersal of ownership and of the power it entailed, and adopting forms of mutualism rather than collectivism, through co-ownership, co-partnership and profit-sharing.

In his convoluted essay, Alan Peacock juggled with formulating a liberal welfare policy while trying to hold the state at bay. In a grudging acknowledgement of the inevitability of some state activity in order to provide 'reasonable comfort' to its citizens, Peacock allowed for transfers of income through progressive taxation. He also conceded that some minimal public regulation was necessary in an imperfect world that ran short of the 'Liberal Utopia' that would have seen private individuals fulfilling their responsibilities to health and education. But he avoided delivering public provision in health by means of the centralised state, opting instead for local control and local services. Free education and health services, compulsorily financed through taxation, were for Peacock emergency wartime measures, 'fundamentally illiberal' on a regular basis (Peacock, 1957: 118–19).

Winding up the volume, Nathaniel Micklem, the former Principal of Mansfield College, Oxford and about to be President of the Liberal Party, grandiloquently proclaimed, in terms that were oddly out of step with progressive liberalism: 'We are Liberals because we believe the fundamental principle of Liberalism to be right and in accord with the ultimate nature of things.' Micklem saw liberalism (as he did all creeds of political reform) as an elite political philosophy, elevating liberty to 'the supreme political good', resisting equality except the 'right to equal consideration', emancipating workers 'by making property-owners of them all', and filling the vacuum caused by 'the recession of collectivist ideas'. All that was enveloped in 'the supreme issue of the time. Liberalism aims at the moralising of power through the enlargement of liberty' (Micklem, 1957: 308–15).

Tellingly, in the entire volume, subtitled 'Liberty and Welfare', there was no mention of either Hobhouse or Hobson. It is one of the bizarre peculiarities of the liberal tradition as the twentieth century unfolded that any solid historical appreciation of the transformative role of the new liberalism, as an intellectual and political movement, went missing in the 1920s and was only rediscovered in the 1970s. That may partly be accounted for by the rise of a monopolising Labour discourse that had no truck with ideological neighbours and affinities. But, as *The Unservile State* illustrates, it was also due to a process whereby liberals shut out *their* own intellectual history, to a shrinkage of vision and ideological aspiration, and not least to the sheer ignorance of those who articulated the typical liberal thinking of the mid-twentieth century, unaware that the alien 'collectivist' ends they now targeted had been embedded in much liberal discourse itself. It is one thing to express an individualist version of liberalism when it is an element in a vanguard radicalism. It is quite another to disregard later progressive aspects of an ideological family when that advanced progressivism is a salient component of its evolving profile. Caution, balance and criticism all have their essential place, but not at the cost of a proper consideration of the full range of arguments marshalled by some of the most prominent liberals themselves.

As for prominent liberals, one conspicuous absence in the British ideational landscape of the second half of the twentieth century is that of any major left-liberal thinker. Among the British intelligentsia, once the prolific supplier of radical liberal ideas, the most prominent liberal was Isaiah Berlin, who displayed a remarkable lack of interest in the twentieth-century history of British liberalism. Indicatively, Berlin recollected: 'I was not deeply impressed by him [T. H. Green], nor by Hobhouse, admirable as they are' (Cherniss, 2013: 157–8; Berlin, 2016). Hobson did not get a look-in. The new liberals were unfamiliar territory for Berlin. Nor did the momentous post-war welfare legislation of the Labour Party, with its left-liberal antecedents, leave much of a mark on Berlin's appreciation of the path liberalism had adopted. Rather, his view of the immediate post-war world was strikingly encapsulated in a survey he wrote on the year 1949:

> Everywhere the doctrine of social responsibility was gaining ground at the expense of self-assertive individualism and liberal humanism alike. In particular, disciplines were encouraged whose purpose it was to mould human beings in ways likely to make them fit more effectively, and eagerly, into preconceived patterns of social life; and this ideal was advanced at the expense of conceptions of existence

in which men were left – or at any rate expressed the wish to be left – relatively undirected to achieve their own triumphs and failures. Avoidance of misery was on the whole cultivated as a goal worthier than the development of independence of character with its record of conflict and frustration … This growing primacy of social over individual problems – the conception of the individual as an element in this or that social situation or pattern rather than vice versa – was part of the doctrine upon an extreme form of which the Soviet Union had been expressly built, and it had, in fact, advanced further in the west than the survival of cultural forms fully developed in a more individualist age might at first suggest … the culture of a liberal bourgeoisie would soon be only an interesting but hardly a haunting memory. (Berlin, 1950: xxii–xxxi).

Berlin's antagonism, or at least considerable ambivalence, towards a social liberalism was focused in the British instance solely on T. H. Green. Berlin's had misread Green's idea of liberty as entailing the true self-realisation of an individual through enforced perfectionist social standards, rather than – as Green had intended – in conjunction and cooperation with others, and not subject to a higher external authority, whether political or ideational. Green, and the new liberals a generation later, employed Mill's developmental conception of human nature, with the proviso that a properly constituted society was one in which collective mutual aid – not a top-down regulatory state, general will, or ideal-type – would help to remove various hindrances to the full exercise of evolving individual powers. Berlin's famous resurrection of the distinction between negative and positive liberty opted for the latter's totalitarian implications and anti-pluralism without appreciating that British social liberalism did not aspire to superimpose a correct model of human nature, but employed a rationed state coercion with the explicit aim of blocking impediments to the exercise – by generically energetic human beings – of free enlightened choices. Indeed, the new liberals were far more supportive than Green of the role of the state in such an enabling process, while enlisting a gentler positive liberty that the one Berlin feared. Social liberals objected to the minimalism involved in the negative libertarian's unshackling of 'static' individuals to exercise their will in a social vacuum, without taking into account the broad range of obstructions to the movement of that will. Those impediments were now more generously construed than Mill or Green had done, embracing material deprivations such as poverty or avoidable ill-health that disabled self-development.

In the absence of liberal philosophers, the focus shifts to the ideologists and commentators nearer the front line. Thus, Jo Grimond, leader of the Liberal Party from 1956 to 1967, was keen to employ the term 'Left' for the spectrum of ideas to which both liberals and socialists belonged (Sloman, 2015: 204–29). Together, he declared, they embrace three values: equality, freedom and participation. The first was emblematic of the socialist left; however, when the liberal left adopted it, equality was divested of its exaggerated materiality, and redirected to the kind of limited equality of opportunity that saw 'the abilities of the better equipped used for humane purposes'. Participation, however, was the idea 'which needs developing most as far as Britain is concerned'. It denoted 'the right and the obligation to take some positive part in running affairs' in all areas of social life, not just in politics, ultimately 'to create a society which is at once skilful and humane' (Grimond, 1963: 19, 23–6). As for freedom, it was 'slowly eroded by the State'; ambivalently, though, Grimond also insisted that 'the State cannot stop at removing obstacles to freedom, nor at the enforcement of law and order'. On the contrary, in many fields 'it is impossible to visualize all government withering away'. In reinforcing a qualified allegiance to liberal social reform ideals, what is telling was Grimond's need to re-dismiss the 'extreme doctrines of *laissez-faire*', as if liberals still needed to challenge that chimerical argument, which the new liberals thought they had rejected for once and for all in the 1890s. (Grimond, 1963: 30–1; Freeden, 1989: 17–19).

Political realignments amidst ideological division

The Liberal Party continued to maintain that 'the great issue facing all nations in this century is how to combine the collective activity of the state, necessary for the welfare of the people with democratic freedoms and an opportunity for individual initiative in economic enterprise'. And it increasingly advocated that 'minority and individual liberties should be guaranteed through a Bill of Rights' (Liberal Party Manifesto, February 1974). But by 1983, the Liberal-SDP Alliance attempted to disaggregate the ideological pedigree of the

> political ideas and momentum which are now carrying the Alliance forward. One was Liberalism, a long and honoured political tradition from which we draw not only the philosophy of individual freedom but also a record of achievement in the establishment of the modern welfare state and the championing of local communities. [Second], the SDP combines a commitment to social justice and ending poverty with a dynamic approach to wealth creation and its leaders have extensive experience of government. (Alliance Manifesto, 1983)

This oddly worded and empirically inaccurate amalgam, with its Venn diagram listing, identified liberty as the liberal component, social welfare as the shared policy and wealth-creation and political experience as the SDP contribution. In effect, the elements of choice, responsibility and scepticism about state provision were now highlighted as the Alliance credo, strengthening the movement of stand-alone post-war liberalism towards a more individualistic core.

A spate of books from the founding ideologues of the SDP goes some way to making sense of the ideological cocktail introduced into British liberalism from the 1980s. In *Politics is for People*, Shirley Williams hailed 'progressive liberalism' as American, sharing with social democrats the goals of 'economic growth, full employment, the abolition of poverty and equality of opportunity'. Tediously, British left-liberalism was yet again ignored by the political intelligentsia. Appealing to gradualism and to antipathy towards 'big government', Williams, too, associated cultural and political pluralism with transferring welfare state functions to local communities, with 'greater individual liberty and to fraternity' and with 'a pluralist economic system, a mixed economy', even praising Milton Friedman for extolling market economies as 'a highly-decentralized form of decision-making' (Williams, 1981: 17, 33, 46, 150, 207).

In *Face the Future*, David Owen's case for radicalism was focused, likewise, on 'over-centralized Government' and the simultaneous promotion of social equality and the free market – a slogan whose rhetorical facileness masks its ideological complexity (Owen, 1981: xiv, xviii). The idea of community, once a statement about the organic solidarity of a liberal nation, was shifted to local structures and communities, Owen referring to both 'liberties' and 'communities' in the plural, as conservatives were increasingly wont to do when repainting their traditionalist colours (Owen, 1981: 8; Freeden, 1999a: 42–51). He continued the move to consign the liberal faith in the state to the margins, identifying it as 'an impediment to further change towards the development of a participatory democracy'. For the social liberals the issue had never been what Owen implied was a choice between 'the state as an enabling rather than a controlling force', but one of a choice between methods and degrees of enablement (Owen, 1981: 10, 246).

Other Liberal-Democratic messages about the allegiance to state welfarism were even more muted. In 2004, *The Yellow Book* inspired a second iteration, *The Orange Book*, which, despite the mix of yellow and red of its title and cover, exhibited little more than a veneer of social democratic ideological stances and attempted to shift liberalism to the right-of-centre. Its authors attempted to bolster the business, market-oriented tendency within British liberalism; 'hard-headed in [its] economic liberalism', in the words of the then leader of the Liberal Democrats, Charles Kennedy (Kennedy, 2004: 13). It was detailed by David Laws, the chief advocate of elevating an anti-statist 'economic liberalism' to the position of liberalism's leading theme, as 'the belief in the value of free trade, open competition, market mechanisms, consumer power, and the effectiveness of the private sector' (Laws, 2004: 20). Extolling the 'creativity unleashed by competition' or 'consumer power' was a poor reward for generations of liberal thinkers who sought to tame the dehumanising nature of much competition and the inequality and occasional irrationality of such power, and whose inclusive participatory category was that of citizens, not consumers.

Laws latched on to Grimond's later views of the 1980s when the latter bemoaned 'this new brand of politics, sometimes represented as democratic socialism, to which many liberals are addicted', a democratic socialism run by those whom Grimond had earlier referred to as 'planners' – people irritated by the democratic process (Grimond, 1963: 28). Laws singled out Grimond's utterances that state-owned monopolies were 'millstones round the neck of the economy', and that 'Much of what Mrs Thatcher and Sir Keith Joseph say and do is in the mainstream of Liberal philosophy' (Laws, 2004: 29). Concurrently, Laws tarnished the social liberal heritage with the libertarian label 'nanny-state liberalism' (Laws, 2004: 40). Cable's more circumscribed approach also questioned whether, given the normality and inevitability of market failures, the cost of governmental regulation would not 'destroy the entrepreneurial and competitive impulses on which the private enterprise system depends'. Like most post-war centrist liberals, Cable approved of the principle of regulating collective goods relating to public services such as health, defence, welfare and education, but came to focus on the excessive bureaucracy, centralisation and unintended consequences of economic regulation (Cable, 2004: 143, 146, 155). The word order of his chapter heading, 'Liberal Economics and Social Justice', indicates the secondary ranking the latter was accorded, briefly concentrating on tax reforms to benefit those with low incomes, but lacking any generous vision of social justice.

Inching close to neoliberalism, the *Orange Book* allowed the market to replace swathes of democratic control and policy-making. The promise of decentralisation, for example, though presented as a means to secure greater local accountability, was promoted by Edward Davey in terms of 'the opportunity to embrace the choice agenda' (Davey, 2004: 50). The multiplication of options that competition engenders, as most liberals know, is not a necessary good, and the libertarian capacity to choose does not ensure that the choices will be liberal ones, stimulating human development and fairness: liberals, far more than conservatives, have always recognised that individuals have to be rescued from the consequences of some of their bad choices. As David Marquand, one of the UK's most prominent liberal voices of the past half century, has maintained: 'today's liberals seem strangely reluctant to distinguish between good and bad choices, to make clear how they envisage the individual, or to define the proper relationship between individual freedom and the public good' (Marquand, 2004).

Davey also extolled decentralisation, which had become central as a *political* devolutionary requirement among liberals and beyond. But in an unusual linguistic, he portrayed it as a *social justice* mechanism 'for checking state power' (Davey, 2004: 44). In support, Davey quoted the following excerpt from Hobson's *The Crisis of Liberalism*: 'Liberalism will probably retain its distinction from Socialism in taking for its chief test of policy the freedom of the individual rather than the strength of the State', but he mischievously omitted the second part of that sentence: 'though the antagonism of the two standpoints may tend to disappear in the light of progressive experience', as well as ignoring the end of that chapter in which Hobson stated: 'When society is confronted, as it sometimes will be, by a breakdown of competition and a choice between private monopoly and public enterprise, no theoretic objections to the State can be permitted to militate against public safety' (Hobson, 1909: 94–5).

Liberalism in camouflage

There is a larger picture. In the 1930s, British liberalism was floundering, owing to a substantial institutional failure of the left. As Marquand observed, 'Labour's inability to establish itself as the electoral heir of the Edwardian Liberal Party was, in large part, the product of its indifference to the intellectual legacy of Edwardian liberalism' (Marquand, 1999: 47). In the era of the cold war, the negative association of state ownership and regulation with communism and the 'Labourite left' had gained considerable public purchase. It had led Dodds to maintain, implausibly, that: 'By any strict use of language Liberals are the true Left, the real progressives', a claim hardly substantiated by *The Unservile State* (Dodds, 1957: 25). Ironically, when Dodds, just a year after Tony Crosland had published *The Future of Socialism* (1956), asserted that the upsurge in Liberal ideas has been noteworthy far beyond the Party he may have been right, but not for the reasons he had assumed (Dodds, 1957). Social-democratic thinking, replicating many of the features of social liberalism, always contained liberty and equality of opportunity within a broader agenda, but then all the major parties did, attaching diverging means to the terms. If the success of an ideology lies in its proliferating impact rather than its purity, the story of British liberalism shifts to the torchbearers of the moderate left. Yet again, liberal ideas were the product of an intelligentsia, but many members of that loose grouping were located within the cultural orbit of the Labour Party. Core liberal concepts figured prominently in Labour discourse, often as liberalism *sans le nom*. Ideologically speaking, social democracy was outdoing post-war liberalism at its own game, in areas where liberalism had in the past established major beachheads.

It may seem odd to claim that Crosland's *The Future of Socialism* was a remarkable book in the history of British liberalism, but its so-called 'revisionism' constituted a resurrection of many of the new liberal themes from which post-war liberalism had disengaged itself, as well as echoing some of the more recent liberal ideological retreats. It was a sign of ideological continuity as well as a tract for party-political reform; 'hallowed', as Crosland described it, 'by an appeal to the past' (Crosland, 1963: 62). The overlap between Crosland's five socialist principles and the social liberalism of the early twentieth century is striking. The first, 'a protest against the material poverty and physical squalor which capitalism produced', was the central theme of liberal social reformists from Hobson to Beveridge. The second, 'a wider concern for "social welfare" – for the interest of those in need', drove the ideology of welfarism at the heart of the liberal welfare state. The third, 'a belief in equality and the "classless society"' combined with workers' rights and responsibilities was compatible with those features of the new liberalism that emphasised non-sectionalism and workers' participation (Freeden, 1978: 150–8; 1986: 45–77). The fourth, 'a rejection of competitive antagonism and an ideal of fraternity and co-operation', was conditionally acceptable to social liberals, as long as it pertained to the sharper end of competition and did not rule out private initiatives. The fifth, a protest against capitalist inefficiencies (notably not against capitalism in toto), and in particular mass unemployment, was also a social liberal theme. Most significantly came Crosland's emphatic qualifier: 'underlying the social and economic aspirations was a passionate belief in liberty and democracy. It would never have occurred to most early socialists that socialism had any meaning except within a political framework of freedom for the individual' (Crosland, 1963: 67–8).

Crosland offered a glimpse of his conception of freedom in the conclusion to his book, in which he advocated a more expressive view of liberty, supported by a culturally qualitative increase in the choice of lifestyles, in effect a pluralist version of the Millite avowal of self-development. Taking to task a Fabian-inspired asceticism and collectivist centralism, he wrote: 'the time has come … for a greater emphasis on private life, on freedom and dissent, on culture, beauty, leisure, and even frivolity. Total abstinence and a good filing system are not now the right sign-posts to the socialist Utopia.' Crosland observed that much legislation in matters sexual and in the area of censorship 'should be highly offensive to socialists, in whose blood there should always run a trace of the anarchist and the libertarian, and not too much of the pig and the prude'. Socialism was not about the sacrifice of private pleasure to public duty. Nor was it, importantly, about the suppression of dissent (Crosland, 1963: 354–7).

Much of Crosland's economic theory reflected the approach of centre-of-the-road liberalism (Freeden, 1999b: 151–65). He resurrected the importance of incentives as a psychological constituent of human activity. The 'psychologisation' of profit redeemed it as an aspect of human nature, which respect for individual needs would have to legitimate. He bracketed the welfare state together with the paternalist tradition, targeting social welfare at a specific deprived sector of the population, rather than interpreting it as a general feature of human flourishing. The fundamental needs which welfare had to satisfy were reduced to address-ing need in the sense of primary and secondary deprivation, thus significantly decoupling welfare from a broader idea of equality underpinned by the free and universal provision of social goods (Crosland, 1963: 54–7, 80–91). Nonetheless, Crosland defined a socialist as one who accorded welfare exceptional priority over other claims, and his expansive understanding of equality of opportunity was in line with new liberal and moderate socialist ones (Jackson, 2007: 169–76). As with the new liberals, the state was still the prime mover: government had to allow space for private corporations, but it needed to manage them as a reflection of democratic responsibility and popular control (Crosland, 1974: 33–5). Still, it was an etiolated redistributive version of the fuller concept available to social democrats, as indeed it would have fallen short of the implicit trust in the state harboured by the new liberals.

Given that *The Future of Socialism* is still considered to be the most important work on British social-democracy in the past sixty years, the fact that its prominent liberal components are largely misidentified to this day is an indicative lack that underscores prevailing misconceptions about the ideological cartography of Britain. We should not, of course, conclude that any direct and concrete link existed from Crosland back to the new liberal thinkers and their writings; it did not. But, in Marquand's perceptive words about *The Future of Socialism*, 'In effect (though, of course, without acknowledgement) socialism was redefined to mean updated Hobhousian New Liberalism' (Marquand, 1997: 75). As is often the case with ideological filtration, the new liberalism was subtly diffused into public discourse throughout the twentieth century through a plethora of channels, all the while fluctuating in its intensity and spread. Crosland's antennae picked up that mode of political reasoning to considerable effect.

The Hobhouse moment

The recognition by the British political class of the liberal commonalities embedded in British social democracy, normally dormant, flared up briefly in 1996. A conscious acknowledgement of the link between New Labour and the early twentieth-century new liberalism – contrary to Crosland's conspicuous silence – was voiced in Tony Blair's astonishing 1995 lecture to the Fabian Society, where he claimed that the new liberalism provided a 'bridgehead' between an older liberalism and New Labour. '[L. T.] Hobhouse and others', argued Blair, 'saw the nineteenth century conception of liberty as too thin for the purposes of social and economic reform ... So they argued for collective action, including state action, to achieve positive freedom ... They did not call themselves socialists, though Hobhouse coined the term "liberal socialism", but they shared the short-term goals of those in the Labour Party' (Blair, 1995: 11). Crucially, Blair continued, the New Liberals were people who were both liberals with a small 'l' and social democrats, also in lower case (Blair, 1995). That echoed Hobhouse's shrewd observation in 1926 that

> if we divided parties by true principles, the division would be like this:
>
> | Communist | Ordinary Labour | Bad Liberal | Diehard |
> |---|---|---|---|
> | Theoretical Socialist | Good Liberal | Ordinary Tory | |
>
> But traditions and class distinctions kept many 'good Liberals' outside Labour. Now Labour has grown so much that it tends to absorb them and to leave the 'bad' Liberals who incline to the Tories, and a mass of traditional Liberals who can't desert a party of that name. (Hobson and Ginsberg, 1931: 66)

Barring the relative magnitudes, that remained the story of most of the twentieth century.

A year later, the *Guardian* ran a whole page feature under the heading 'Question for all British voters: Is Tony Blair a Liberal?', following a number of interviews the future Prime Minister had given, in which he indicated that he planned a political appeal to Liberals, Liberal Democrats and Social Democrats. The *Guardian*'s political correspondent, Michael White, claimed that 'what is striking about Mr Blair's quest is that he carries little ideological baggage from the past', referring to the Labour Left, the trade unions, Gaitskell and Crosland (White, 1996). Martin Kettle added shrewdly of the Labour leadership that the 'ism that really gave them trouble' wasn't socialism but liberalism. However, although – in Kettle's words – Blair was driven 'towards the historic reunification of the Liberal and Labour traditions', that window of ideological awareness closed as quickly as it had opened (Kettle, 1996).

Elsewhere, Blair had envisaged 'a strong, united society which gives each citizen the chance to develop their potential to the full' (Blair, 1994: 7). In those halcyon days, it appeared that under New Labour, in Marquand's words, 'the doctrinal quarrel between liberalism and socialism ha[d] been settled in liberalism's favour' (Marquand, 1997: 79). For a while, the New Labour ideological mixture represented much late twentieth-century left-centre thinking. It was also more self-confident and far bolder than the hesitant political thoughts of those who spoke in the name of liberalism alone. As usual, the issue was not the presence or absence of an ideological theme within either the liberal or social-democratic families – they shared many ideas – but the relative weight accorded to the diverse components and clusters that make up an ideological credo.

It was often contemporary liberals who reduced individualism to economic initiative and to the pursuit of vaguely defined opportunities, a considerable step away from the developmental paths of personal growth and intellectual vigour that humanist liberals had envisaged. And it was often contemporary liberals who reduced the alluring power of a flourishing society promoting human well-being, and enabled through a vibrant welfare state, to the more insipid terminology of fairness, in which government would 'provide the essential requirements that everyone needs to make real choices in their lives' (Liberal Democrat Party Manifesto, 2005). True, Liberal manifestos formulated various micro-policies intended to enhance both liberty and well-being. And, in 2015, Tim Farron, the then Liberal Democrat leader, sounded a more Beveridgian welfarist note in writing: 'Liberalism is about championing the individual against the powerful ... But it's also about protecting individuals from those giant evils that rob people of their freedom: poverty, poor housing, inequality' (Farron, 2015). But, as a whole, official Liberalism lacked the crucial element of rhetorical power and emotional conviction that Labour social democrats were sporadically able to summon up.

Conclusion

A proper assessment of an ideology needs to take its most complex and mature manifestations as the benchmark from which to evaluate its course. The liberal idea of open-ended progress does not necessarily apply to its own ideological development. Political and economic circumstances may have conspired to limit its capacity to build on its ideational successes, and some forms of liberal thought and practice became stagnant or even retrogressive. It may be correct that 'since the Grimond era, most Liberal and Liberal Democrat leaders have identified the party closely with social liberal political thought' (Sloman, 2014: 41–50). But it is also the case that the vagaries of post-war liberalism are located in the varying intensity, even ambivalence, of that commitment, watered down. Certainly, some of the liberal thinking after 1945 went over old ground in a less than imaginative or original manner. There were, of course, important innovations on devolution, the environment and post-colonialism. Yet looking back across seventy years, much of the liberal sparkle had disappeared. The last vestiges of liberal organicism, accentuating social interdependence as the flipside of individualism, had gone. The expectations directed at the state had been knocked back, as mounting political and economic complexities, and indeed the aspirations of social reform itself, had foregrounded administrative encumbrances and the perceived loss of negative liberty at the expense of collective solidarity and mutual care. The state as stultified bureaucracy was threatening to overshadow the state as the repository of a common purpose; the fear of big government was displacing the vigour of an enabling polity. The belief in the unifying power of a rational liberal society functioning as a centripetal group had dissolved under the centrifugal and fragmenting impetus of a minorities-sensitive ethos that extolled difference more than it fostered commonality.

Whether any of those could be found in social-democratic thought is another matter, as much political thinking become bogged down in the technical economic challenges that increasingly overshadowed policy and dominated discourse. Perhaps it was also a lack of vision, as if vision had gone out of fashion amidst the daily grind of economies lurching from crisis to crisis, technocracies stumbling from fix to fix, and an electorate unable to separate liberalism from the fluctuating fortunes of the Liberal-Democratic Party. And while social liberalism still existed, it now needed to be sought in its percolations and permutations; no longer as a unified and cohesive body of thought.

If there is hope for British liberalism, it is this. Ideologies are made of layers of their own histories and mutations. Sometimes one layer floats to the top; sometimes another. Sometimes one combination of ideas takes charge of an ideology; sometimes another. Ideologies are vulnerable to enormous fluctuations in their appeal and creativity, and in troubled times such as those the UK is experiencing at the moment of writing, it might seem that the odds are stacked against liberal voices, that the passions inspired by tolerance, generosity and humanism are making way for bigotry, provincialism and populist demagoguery of a ferocity rarely seen in recent decades. Yet the liberal tradition, here and abroad, has proved remarkably resilient. Far from being the expression of universal ethics that some philosophers hold it to be, liberalism has derived strength from being attacked and marginalised, and from having to fight its corner against potent rivals. In the battle of ideas, even in its own European homeland, liberalism has been bruised and often silenced, but its stamina has nonetheless been maintained across two centuries. More often than not a minority creed, despite the empty invocations one hears of a liberal world order, a British liberalism with its back against the wall may be more likely to gather its diffuse forces and be spurred on to a revival. One way of achieving that will be to hammer home the message that a liberal social democracy is not about majoritarian winning but about the respect, consideration and protection afforded to the losers as well as the winners, whoever they may be. Another will be to ensure the vigilant monitoring of public political discourse, so that it is not overrun and monopolised by intemperate and irresponsible language. The ideational wherewithal is there; the will, spirit and moral confidence need to be mustered.

References

Berlin, I. (1950) 'The year 1949 in historical perspective: the trends of culture', *1950 Britannica Book of the Year* (London: Encyclopaedia Britannica, Inc.).

Berlin, I. 'In Conversation with Steven Lukes', www.jstor.org/stable/40549054 (accessed 14 December 2016).

Blackburn, D. (2017) 'Still the Stranger at the Feast? Ideology and the Study of Twentieth Century British Politics', *Journal of Political Ideologies*, 22, 116–30.

Blair, T. (1994) *Socialism*, Fabian Pamphlet 565 (London: Fabian Society).

Blair, T. (1995) *Let us Face the Future: The 1945 Anniversary Lecture*, Fabian Pamphlet 571 (London: Fabian Society).

Cable, V. (2004) 'Liberal economics and social justice', in P. Marshall and D. Laws (eds), *The Orange Book: Reclaiming Liberalism* (London: Profile Books).

Cable, V. (2009) 'Classical liberalism in a modern setting', in K. Hickson (ed.), *The Political Thought of The Liberals and Liberal Democrats Since 1945* (Manchester: Manchester University Press).

Cherniss, J. L. (2013) *A Mind and its Time: The Development of Isaiah Berlin's Political Thought* (Oxford: Oxford University Press).

Crosland, C. A. R. (1963) *The Future of Socialism*, rev. edn (New York).

Crosland, A. (1974) *Socialism Now* (London: Cape).

Davey, E. (2004) 'Liberalism and localism', in P. Marshall and D. Laws (eds), *The Orange Book: Reclaiming Liberalism* (London: Profile Books).

Dodds, E. (1957) 'Liberty and welfare', in G. Watson (ed.), *The Unservile State: Essays In Liberty and Welfare* (London: George Allen & Unwin).

Farron, T. (2015) 'My Values – My Liberalism', www.markpack.org.uk/files/2015/05/ Tim-Farron-Credo-document-Lib-Dem-leadership-contest-2015.pdf.

Freeden, M. (1978) *The New Liberalism: An Ideology of Social Reform* (Oxford: Clarendon Press).

Freeden, M. (1986) *Liberalism Divided: A Study in British Political Thought 1914–1939* (Oxford: Clarendon Press).

Freeden, M. (1989) (ed.), *The Minutes of the Rainbow Circle, 1894–1924* (London: Royal Historical Society).

Freeden, M. (1999a) 'The ideology of New Labour', *Political Quarterly*, 70, 42–51.

Freeden, M. (1999b) 'True blood or false genealogy: New Labour and British social democratic thought', in A. Gamble and T. Wright (eds), *The New Social Democracy* (Oxford: Blackwell).

Freeden, M. (2015) *Liberalism: A Very Short Introduction* (Oxford; Oxford University Press, 2015)

Grayson, R. S. (2009) 'Social liberalism', in K. Hickson (ed.), *The Political Thought of The Liberals and Liberal Democrats Since 1945* (Manchester: Manchester University Press).

Grimond, J. (1963) *The Liberal Challenge* (London: Hollis and Carter Ltd).

Hobson, J. A. (1909) *The Crisis of Liberalism: New Issues of Democracy* (London: P. S. King & Son).*Liberal Party Manifestos*, www.politicsresources.net/area/uk/man/ lib51.htm.

Hobson, J. A. and Ginsberg, M. (1931) *L. T. Hobhouse, His Life and Work* (London: George Allen & Unwin).

Jackson, B. (2007) *Equality and the British Left: A Study in Progressive Political Thought, 1900–1964* (Oxford; Oxford University Press).

Jackson, B. (2016) 'Currents of neo-liberalism: British political ideologies and the New Right, c.1955–1979', *English Historical Review*, 131, 823–50.

Kennedy, C. (2004) 'Foreword', in P. Marshall and D. Laws (eds), *The Orange Book: Reclaiming Liberalism* (London: Profile Books).

Kettle, M. (1996) 'He regards the party he leads as a failure', *Guardian*, 18 September.

Laws, D. (2004) 'Reclaiming liberalism: A liberal agenda for the Liberal Democrats', in P. Marshall and D. Laws (eds), *The Orange Book: Reclaiming Liberalism* (London: Profile Books).

Marquand, D. (1997) *The New Reckoning: Capitalism, States and Citizens* (Cambridge: Polity Press).

Marquand, D. (1999) *The Progressive Dilemma*, 2nd edn (London: Phoenix).

Marquand, D. (2004) *Decline of the Public: The Hollowing Out of Citizenship* (Cambridge: Polity).

Marshall, P. (2004) 'Introduction', in P. Marshall and D. Laws (eds), *The Orange Book: Reclaiming Liberalism* (London: Profile Books).

Micklem, N. (1957) 'The challenge of liberalism', in G. Watson (ed.), *The Unservile State: Essays in Liberty and Welfare* (London: George Allen & Unwin).

Mill, J. S. (1910) *On Liberty* (London; Dent).

Owen, D. (1981) *Face The Future* (Oxford: Oxford University Press).

Peacock, A. (1957) 'Welfare in the liberal state', in G. Watson (ed.), *The Unservile State: Essays in Liberty and Welfare* (London: George Allen & Unwin).

Sloman, P. (2014) 'Partners in progress? British Liberals and the Labour Party since 1918', *Political Studies Review*, 12.

Sloman, P. (2015) *The Liberal Party and the Economy, 1929–1964* (Oxford: Oxford University Press).

Watson, G. (1957) (ed.), *The Unservile State: Essays in Liberty and Welfare* (London: George Allen & Unwin).

White, M. (1996) 'Question for all British voters: Is Tony Blair a Liberal', *Guardian*, 18 Sept.

Williams, S. (1981) *Politics is For People* (Harmondsworth: Penguin Books).

4

A labour of Sisyphus:
the quest for a great Labour Party

Andrew Gamble

Labour's dilemmas: intellectualism, governmentalism and leadership

One of the central preoccupations of David Marquand's writing has been the Labour Party, its tortured trajectory, its achievements and its failures, its capacity to inspire and disappoint. He has written eloquently about the progressive dilemma (Marquand, 1991), whether progressives in British politics should support and work within the Labour Party as the best available vehicle for achieving political, economic and social reform. This was, and remains a dilemma because progressives, both social democrats and socialists, have tended to be drawn from the radical intelligentsia, enthused by ethical ideals and political theories as to how society might be made better, and committed to a politics founded on principles and clear ideological views of the world, whereas the Labour Party was created by the trade unions primarily to represent the labour interest in Parliament, and appealing for support on the basis of working-class solidarity, identity and culture.

When the Labour Representation Committee was established in 1900, its objective was to establish a distinct Labour group in Parliament, with its own whips, able to agree its own policy. Labourism, the ideology of the Labour movement, was conservative, pragmatic, realist and defensive, rather than radical and transformative. Progressive intellectuals often came into conflict with Labourism, and many despaired of the party and left it (Dowse, 1966; Seyd, 1987), but for more than a hundred years the Labour Party has been the main focus for progressive politics in Britain, the indispensable party for both the left and centre-left. The enthusiasm of different groups of progressive intellectuals for the party has ebbed and flowed, as some leave in despair and others join (or rejoin) in hope.

David Marquand's understanding of the progressive dilemma was shaped both by his parliamentary experience and also, crucially, by the research for his biography of Ramsay MacDonald (Marquand, 1997). The aim of this chapter is to analyse Marquand's interpretation of MacDonald, and his social democratic critique of Labourism, contrasting it with the very different interpretation by Ralph Miliband in his socialist critique of Labourism, *Parliamentary Socialism*, first published in 1961. Marquand and Miliband articulate different accounts of the progressive dilemma, which resonate in today's Labour Party, where for the first time in its history the left of the party has elected its candidate, Jeremy Corbyn, as leader, but they agree about the recurring problems which have beset Labour throughout its history (Miliband, 1964: 16). Miliband argued that Labour had a chronic inability to act as an effective opposition, an inherent ambiguity of purpose and a persistent inability to adjust to new circumstances. For him, Labourism was a barrier preventing the Labour Party developing as a socialist party. Those progressive intellectuals who wanted a socialist transformation of Britain were repeatedly frustrated and disappointed by the timidity and conservatism of the Labour Party. Those, like David Marquand, who wanted a social democratic transformation of Britain, constitutional and social reform and a new social democratic citizenry, were also often despairing of the Labour Party as a vehicle for social reform. Marquand left the Labour Party in 1981 and joined the Social Democratic Party created by Roy Jenkins, Shirley Williams, David Owen and Bill Rodgers. This was an attempt, ultimately unsuccessful, to replace Labour as the main vehicle for progressive reform in British politics (Crewe and King, 1995).

David Marquand's most extended reflection on the progressive dilemma and the nature of the Labour Party is the biography he wrote of Ramsay MacDonald, Labour's first prime minister. He started writing the book in the early 1960s, the 'high noon' as he puts it of the Keynesian era (Marquand, 1997: xvi). It was finished and published in 1977, when dusk was falling on Keynesianism and the post-war era of 'tamed' capitalism, when the fissures in the Labour coalition had become so great that the Labour government was 'incapable of governing effectively' (Marquand, 1997: xvi). This was a time of great political and economic turmoil. A Labour government was struggling to manage the fallout from the severe stagflation which was gripping western economies, a broad left insurgency had won control of the National Executive of the party and the party conference, opening a major rift between the parliamentary party and the party members

(Kogan and Kogan, 1982). Marquand resigned his safe seat in Ashfield in Nottinghamshire in 1976 to work for Roy Jenkins as his chief adviser at the EU Commission. The seat was lost to the Conservatives at the ensuing by-election. The government had already lost its parliamentary majority and become reliant on the Liberals for survival. The divisions over membership of the EEC, over nationalisation, over devolution and over foreign policy, particularly unilateral nuclear disarmament and membership of NATO, were deep and polarising. The ground was being laid for the split in the party which occurred after the election defeat in 1979.

Ramsay MacDonald had died in 1937, yet forty years later his memory was still toxic in the Labour Party. Marquand was even warned by a rising Labour politician that no one foolish enough to write a biography of Ramsay MacDonald could expect a future in Labour politics (Marquand, 1997: xv). That did not deter him. MacDonald had once been such a commanding figure in the Labour Party, and so important in shaping its development, its strategies and its purposes, that the party's amnesia about him seemed very odd then, and still does today. Labour has always had a problem with its leaders, especially some of its most successful ones. In its earliest days the party resisted having a Leader in the way that the Conservatives and Liberals did. It instead vested power in secretaries, who were responsible to the party's Committees. The post of Chairman of the Parliamentary Labour Party was subject to annual election, and was expected to rotate. The party wanted no cult of personality, and distrusted the powers that a permanent Leader might accrue (Pelling, 1961; McKenzie, 1955). It was one of MacDonald's achievements to persuade the party that it needed to give the parliamentary leader more powers and a longer tenure if Labour was to become an effective parliamentary force against the other parties. He served as Leader between 1911–14 and 1922–31, and was twice Labour Prime Minister, in 1924 and 1929–31, although never with a parliamentary majority. He established Labour as the main rival to the Conservatives, the alternative party of government, displacing the Liberals. These were extraordinary achievements, which in hindsight are treated as inevitable, because of the extension of the franchise in 1918. But as Marquand argues, in the politically fluid circumstances of the 1920s they were never guaranteed. Other outcomes, particularly a revival of the Liberal party were also possible. The new salience of class politics and class identity after 1918, the quadrupling of the electorate, and the deep split in the Liberal party allowed Labour to break through (Marquand, 1997: 488). But seizing that opportunity required the welding of Labour into a coherent electoral and parliamentary force. That owed much to MacDonald.

Yet no Labour Leader, not even Tony Blair, has been more vilified by his own party. In 1929 Egon Wertheimer wrote, after witnessing MacDonald's performance and reception at the Labour Party conference, that he was 'the focus of the mute hopes of a whole class' (Marquand, 1997: 488). But two years later he was a pariah, for choosing to stay on as prime minister and form a national government with the Conservatives and the Liberals, and go against majority opinion in the Labour Party. His fault was compounded when he then stood against Labour in the 1931 General Election and called on its voters to vote for National Government candidates rather than Labour ones. He, along with the few ministers and MPs who had supported him, were expelled from the party and formed the National Labour group. National Labour proved not to be a significant split. It soon withered and died. The Labour Party regrouped and although it was reduced to 52 seats after the 1931 election, leaving the National Government dominated by the Conservatives with a huge majority, it still had 30.6 per cent of the vote, a higher percentage than the party had achieved in 1918 or 1922, or indeed in 1983, 2010 or 2015. It steadily rebuilt during the 1930s, but although there was a radical break from MacDonald the individual, there was no radical break from his strategy and vision for the party. That continued. It was just that its author was no longer acknowledged. He was a class traitor who had joined not a national government but a Wall Street government. Undone by his vanity and snobbery, he allowed himself to be seduced by the aristocracy and, out of social cowardice, abandoned his class and his colleagues.

Marquand has no difficulty in showing how inaccurate that popular caricature was. The reason for MacDonald's decision was much more complex and goes to the heart of the debates on the political purpose of the Labour Party. The issue which brought down the Labour government was the threatened implosion of Britain's public finances following the runs on the banks and spiralling unemployment occurring across Europe during 1931. The need for some fiscal adjustment was plain, but the government played for time by appointing the May Commission. When the Commission finally reported, its recommendations were stark. In line with Treasury orthodoxy it recommended that the bulk of the adjustment should come from spending cuts, in particular cuts in the benefit paid to the unemployed and in the wages of public employees. Borrowing was ruled out because the budget had to balance if the confidence of the financial markets in the pound and the gold standard was to be preserved. Similarly, there was general agreement, even among radical economists like Keynes, that income taxes could not be raised because that would also affect confidence and risk making the slump worse.

The Cabinet was deeply divided on the May Commission proposals. In the wider Labour movement the trade unions signalled strong opposition, but without offering any alternative policies. The government lacked a majority in Parliament and therefore needed the support of the Opposition parties to get any package through Parliament (Skidelsky, 1967). MacDonald and Philip Snowden, the Chancellor, spent much time trying to craft such a package, but when it was clear that a significant minority of the Cabinet led by Arthur Henderson, the Foreign Secretary, were implacably opposed, the government was forced to resign. Henderson's view was that Labour's priority should be to keep the two wings of the Labour movement, the parliamentary party and the trade unions united, and since that could not be done if the government accepted a package to stabilise the public finances which loaded the cost disproportionately onto the unemployed and public employees, it was better for Labour to go into opposition and let the Conservatives and the Liberals take responsibility for implementing the cuts.

MacDonald saw the force of this argument, and his first inclination was to resign and go into opposition. But he also believed that would be a defeat of everything he had been trying to achieve. Only if Labour showed it could act in the national interest, if necessary overriding the sectional interests of its own supporters, could it plausibly become not just a minority but a majority party of government. If the party abdicated responsibility whenever tough decisions had to be made, it would never win the respect, trust and support of the great swathe of middle opinion in Britain which it needed to convince if it was to gain their votes and win parliamentary majorities in general elections. If the Labour Party preferred the comfort of opposition to the realities of power it would never reach its full potential. The same argument has raged about every subsequent Labour government.

Marquand brings out very clearly MacDonald's own frustration with the Labour Party and with his Cabinet colleagues. There were radical ideas for dealing with the unprecedented economic crisis which was engulfing the country, ideas that had been put forward both by Oswald Mosley, then a Labour minister, in the Memorandum he circulated to his colleagues (Skidelsky, 1967), and by Lloyd George in *We Can Conquer Unemployment* (1929). In addition, Keynes was strongly advocating the imposition of a revenue tariff, which would have avoided the need to target the unemployed for cuts. Keynes argued that the British economy was locked into a collapsing world economy and had to break free by leaving the gold standard. McDonald dithered over the Mosley Memorandum. He saw its merits, but Snowden and the Treasury as well as the Department of Transport were implacably opposed to the proactive interventionist role it proposed for government in resolving the crisis. MacDonald lacked the political strength or conviction to overrule them. Mosley resigned from the government and put his case to the parliamentary Labour Party, but received little support. Only 29 MPs supported him, 210 were against. On the revenue tariff MacDonald became convinced that this was what had to happen, but a majority of the Labour Cabinet were opposed. Most Labour ministers, particularly Snowden, were free traders. Free trade for them was an ethical policy, a demonstration of internationalism, rather as free movement is today. MacDonald was defeated. This meant there was no policy which could save the government.

MacDonald could very easily have saved himself, however. He could have followed the Henderson line, and resigned rather than implement the cuts which the May Commission was recommending. The later accusations about the aristocratic embrace, and his fondness for country house weekends, are unconvincing. The personal appeal from the King was more telling. MacDonald accepted that it was a betrayal of everything he had worked for if he was to refuse to act in the national interest. His critics argued that there was no national interest, only class interest. He was either on the side of one class or the other. Politics was binary. But MacDonald had never accepted that. His idea of a Great Labour Party was that Labour had to show that it was genuinely a national party which could govern in the best interests of the whole community. His critics argued that was impossible and that he was governing in the best interests of the bankers.

When he decided to accept the King's call to stay as prime minister and head an emergency National Government he thought it would be only for a short time until the immediate financial crisis had been dealt with. The Rubicon was crossed when he acceded to the demands of his new coalition partners, the Conservatives, for an early general election. His relationship with the Labour Party never recovered and there was no way back. He endured fierce criticism, often from former friends and allies, and he retaliated, as Marquand (1997: 609) shows, with his own withering assessment of what Labour had become. He complained that it had retreated to a Poor Law frame of mind:

> The Socialist Movement in this country is going to rack and ruin, because it is being controlled by people who are nothing more than critics of the Government, inspired by the idea that all you have to do is to hand out largesse to the community.

He wrote in his diary (Marquand, 1997: 645): 'The Labour party will run away from two things – the orders of the TUC and an awkward crisis.' By running away, he complained, they left everything unprotected. 'If this is the best Labour can do then it is not fit to govern except in the calmest of good weather' (Marquand, 1997: 653). Later, he concluded despairingly: 'It looks as though all our work has gone into the creation of a petty and passionate class movement whose ideal of socialism is not much more than public subsidies (Marquand, 1997: 674). The TUC's position on the other side was equally blunt. Resigning rather than cutting employment benefit was what *Labour* Ministers should do (Marquand, 1997: 646). MacDonald had surrendered to the City and defied the Labour ethic of loyalty to majority decisions. It did not help that the Conservative election battle cry in 1931 was that the National Government had saved the nation from the Labour Party. MacDonald was naive about that. He complained that 'the Tories imagine that they are the only people with national views – that the Tories are the Nation' (Marquand, 1997: 746) but by lending his authority and prestige to the National Government he had contributed to the sharp reduction in Labour support and to the defeat of four out of five of its MPs. Reflecting on these events later he ruefully noted: 'Anyone in my position at the time, knowing all that I did, would have acted as I acted. However I sometimes wish that someone else had been in my position at that time (Marquand, 1997: 685). This is the lonely position many Labour leaders have since found themselves in.

Labourism, liberalism and national appeal

The important point, which Marquand emphasises, is that MacDonald was never an exponent of Labourism, subordinating everything to the Labour interest as expressed by the trade unions. If he had been, he would have acted as Henderson did, and cheerfully accepted the view that it was better to be in opposition than in government, if being in government meant doing things that were against the labour interest. MacDonald was a progressive intellectual who had a vision for the Labour Party and what it might become – a party of reform and democratic citizenship – if it could transcend the narrow politics of the labour interest. At the same time, he was the politician who more than anyone else had spent his career seeking to find ways in which the trade unions and the progressive intellectuals of the socialist societies, particularly the Fabians and the Independent Labour Party (ILP) could work together. As the first secretary of the Labour Representation Committee he worked extremely closely with the trade unions. He saw the labour interest as integral to the Labour Party, the foundation on which everything else rested. But he believed that a politics of labourism, which some of the unions often seemed to want, focused exclusively on defending the interests of trade unions as corporate bodies, was insufficient, and might not even achieve what its advocates hoped. Being a permanent minority in Parliament did not interest MacDonald. It meant that Labour would always be excluded from making decisions and shaping the institutional framework of society and the state. It would be a pressure group rather than an alternative government.

MacDonald's political career was devoted to showing that Labour could become an alternative government, could aspire to be not just the second party of the state but the leading one. To do this, he had to persuade the unions to support and fund a much broader kind of party than many of them initially wanted to do. This has remained a tension down to the present. The party even under Jeremy Corbyn often wants to do things which the unions do not support. MacDonald made a close working relationship of the leader with the trade unions a cornerstone of the Labour Party, yet in the two great political crises of his career, 1914 and 1931, the relationship broke down. In 1914 it was the issue of war, which the unions supported, as did Henderson, who was elected leader in Ramsay MacDonald's place and went on to join the war cabinet. MacDonald stayed true to the principles of the ILP and the second international in opposing the war and calling for the international solidarity of the working class to prevent it. This stand not only cost him the leadership and isolated him from the labour movement, but also made him a target for the right-wing nationalist press. He lost his seat in Leicester at the 1918 election having been branded a pacifist and traitor. But his hounding increased his standing within the ILP, and their continuing support gave him a route back when he fought and won Aberavon in 1922. Once back in Parliament he was re-elected leader. The party was much larger now than it had been before 1918, and the weakness of the Liberals and the level of labour unrest and political upheaval gave Labour a huge opportunity. Among the Labour parliamentary leaders MacDonald was the most clear-sighted about what Labour needed to do in order to consolidate its new found strength and develop a strategy to advance.

At the heart of MacDonald's vision for the Labour Party was the example of the Liberal Party. Under the old limited franchise the Liberal Party had assembled a broad, cross-class coalition, which had rallied to it all the non-Conservative and anti-Conservative forces in the country. These included the Nonconformist churches, Wales and Scotland, the northern industrial working class, and many industrialists. The radical wing was republican, anti-imperialist, anti-landlord, anti-the established Anglican Church and anti-aristocracy. The more mainstream wing supported the Empire and property, but all Liberals were against protection and supported free trade, as well as political devolution within the UK, the most potent symbol of which was Irish Home Rule. The strength of this Liberal Party was that it did not depend on a single interest but drew a wide range of different social groups into the party and created a broad party of reform. Labour succeeded in doing this three times in the twentieth century – in 1945, in 1964 and in 1997, and won office as a result. Its present plight is that for the moment it is no longer able to do so.

Many parts of the Labour movement were originally part of the Liberal coalition. The reason why socialists like Keir Hardie and MacDonald were determined to break away and establish separate representation of the labour interest in Parliament was because they thought the Liberal Party was no longer capable of properly representing the Labour interest. As MacDonald put it before 1914: 'In this country, as on the continent, the fight … will be … between a Great Labour party and a strong reactionary party, with a small liberal party standing between, cut off from every source of inspiration and opportunity of growth' (Marquand, 1997: 162). It was a hard task to persuade many trade unionists that separate representation was indeed necessary, since few were socialists or favoured the various kinds of social transformation advocated by the Fabians, the Independent Labour Party, or the Social Democratic Federation. What created the Labour Party was the Taff Vale decision in 1901, which allowed unions to be sued for damages if they launched strike action. The determination to reverse Taff Vale led directly to the formation of the Labour Party and the winning of 29 seats in Parliament in 1906, rising to 40 seats in 1910.

The new Labour Party was very small and inexperienced and not considered a big threat to the Liberals, who in 1906 won one of their most emphatic election victories. In the system of multi-member constituencies, which existed in many parts of the country, the Labour Party's electoral successes was often dependent on persuading the Liberals to allow a Labour member to stand unopposed. MacDonald devoted considerable energy to cultivating good relations with the Liberal Party and its chief whip, in order to maximise Labour representation. He was criticised for this strategy at the time by those who wanted the Labour Party to make a clean break from liberalism, and present itself as a socialist, working-class party. MacDonald resisted this approach, because he argued, first, that Labour could not make headway without the tacit support of the Liberals, and, second, that it needed to attract Liberal votes. MacDonald saw Labour from the outset as the natural successor to the Liberal Party, taking on its mantle and completing its programme, rather than marking a complete ideological and political break from it. The future of progressive politics in Britain lay in Labour taking over from the Liberal Party as the party of orderly progress through the ballot box (Marquand, 1997: 329). The wheel has now turned full circle. The future of progressive politics in Britain may require the emergence of a new party to replace Labour, if it continues its decline.

This also influenced his view of the complex issues around class and representation. Labour was a class party in a much more obvious sense than the Liberal Party had been. Labour identity and purpose were rooted from the outset in the distinctive identity and culture of the British working class, particularly in the great industrial centres of London, the Midlands, the North, Wales and Scotland. This world of labour which G. D. H. Cole wrote about before 1914 (Cole, 1913), had been created by a hundred years of British industrial and commercial supremacy. Britain was a free trade nation and an imperial nation, and by 1900 had the largest urban and industrial population anywhere in the world. Numbers working on the land had shrunk to very low levels, and this gave Britain's industrial workers a potentially decisive political strength, if it could be mobilised. This strength was viewed apprehensively by many in the governing class, who feared that extending the suffrage to all citizens would mean the political supremacy of the working class in Britain, as Marx had predicted.

The first half of the twentieth century was dominated by this looming clash, and an increasing political polarisation along class lines. The Liberals hoped ths clash could be averted by persuading British workers that a party devoted to the reform of capitalism rather than its transformation into socialism would better serve their interests. There was no inevitability about the conjoining of the labour interest with socialism in capitalist industrial societies. It occurred almost universally across Europe, but notably failed to do so in the United States. Many socialists welcomed class polarisation because they saw it as leading to a decisive confrontation which would lead to the displacement of the existing ruling class and its replacement by the representatives of the workers.

MacDonald, Ralph Miliband and the left

MacDonald and many like him thought that liberalism had done its work. They wanted an independent *labour* party, committed to a socialist philosophy and a socialist programme, but they were also deeply opposed to class polarisation. Ralph Miliband argues that the kind of labour party which socialists like MacDonald and the trade unions created between them made Labour 'not just opposed to revolution, violence and exacerbation of class conflict but the best bulwark against them (Miliband, 1964: 119). MacDonald always argued, however, that revolution and class war were dead ends for the labour movement. He was critical of the Russian Revolution which transformed socialist politics and parties across Europe: 'the cruelty and fanaticism of the Bolsheviks is not accidental but the inevitable consequence of the Leninist creed (Marquand, 1997: 256). He accepted that the Conservatives were implacable class warriors and constantly fought for the interests of property. But he thought it would be folly for Labour to reciprocate. Instead, it should adopt the high ground of the national interest, and appeal to the goodwill and idealism of all citizens. Socialism was about moral belief not class interest, a position shared by many later social democrats, including Hugh Gaitskell, John Smith and Tony Blair. Resorting to the same tactics against property which the Conservatives were prepared to use against Labour would result either in the defeat of the labour movement, because its members were ultimately not prepared to support a violent overthrow of the state, or in a socialist dictatorship as in Russia. Neither outcome would bring about the socialism which MacDonald believed in. His socialism involved a cultural and moral change, in which aggression and acquisitiveness would be replaced by trust and solidarity, strengthening communities and ensuring that no one was left behind. Public ownership and redistribution were means to achieve this, although the policy details were often vague. Marquand (1997) notes that while MacDonald had a clear strategy for gaining power, he never developed a clear strategy for using it.

This was partly because there was a strong strand of determinism and fatalism running through much early twentieth-century socialist thought. The belief in the inevitability of gradualness was an important part of the socialist belief. One form it took was the idea that whatever defeats might be suffered, the progress and ultimate victory of the working class was assured. Fifty years later this belief was still strong, as Eric Hobsbawm (1981) argued. It was also why so many Bolsheviks thought that a proletarian seizure of power in Russia would be premature because Russia had not yet passed through all the necessary stages of economic development. While never a Marxist, MacDonald did believe that the world was moving in a socialist direction. Economies were becoming more interdependent and more socialised. The need for government intervention and regulation was increasingly recognised, and public opinion was, as a result, steadily moving towards socialist conclusions. Today the reverse is true. Gradualists like MacDonald argued that socialists should not accelerate the process. They should steadily build up their strength and persuade more and more of their fellow citizens that a socialist organisation of society was not only right, but also efficient, and in tune with the way that the economy and society were evolving. *Labour and the Nation* in 1928 saw socialism as the creed of practical men and women, and labour as a movement of all classes, a movement of democratic citizens, against the small minority of property owners. It argued a moral case for gradualist socialism, applying the resources of science to bring civilised and dignified existence within the reach of all. Those who advocated class war and revolution were misreading the political moment, and had to be resisted.

The platform of James Maxton, the radical Clydeside MP, and Fenner Brockway, which became increasingly the majority position in the ILP through the 1920s, called for a radical programme of public ownership to implement socialism immediately. But for MacDonald, whose original political base had been the ILP, this only made sense if Britain was ripe for revolution. The failure of the General Strike in 1926 was blamed by many socialists on the betrayal of the workers by the trade union leaders. Ralph Miliband's view was that betrayal was the inherent and inescapable consequence of Labour leaders' whole philosophy of politics (Miliband, 1964: 144). But MacDonald thought the trade union leaders, having blundered into a confrontation with the government, were forced to blink because they recognised that the majority of their members would not support an attempt to organise the overthrow of the government and seize power. He had always believed that if the unions tried to coerce the state, the state would win. The only alternative to parliamentary socialism was revolutionary socialism, and in a democracy revolutionary socialism was a disastrous cul-de-sac (Marquand, 1997: 423). Once the government chose to define the General Strike not as an industrial dispute over the miners' terms and conditions, but as a challenge to the constitution and the elected government, the trade unions either had to go through with that challenge or admit defeat. As Jimmy Thomas, the leader of the rail union, and one of the ministers who joined the National Government in 1931, put it: 'I have never disguised that in a challenge to the constitution, God help us unless the Government won' (Miliband, 1964: 134).

All these themes were present in the famous speech which MacDonald delivered to the Labour Conference in 1930, as the slump and the financial crisis were gathering force. It was to be his last address to a Labour Party conference (Marquand, 1997: 569):

> So, my friends, we are not on trial; it is the system under which we live. It has broken down, not only in this little island, it has broken down in Europe, in Asia, in America; it has broken down everywhere, as it was bound to break down. And the cure, the new path, the new idea is organisation – organisation

which will protect life, not property ... I appeal to you, my friends, today, with all that is going on outside – I appeal to you to go back on to your Socialist faith. Do not mix that up with pettifogging patching, either of a Poor Law kind or of Relief Work kind. Construction, ideas, architecture, building line upon line, stone upon stone, storey upon storey; it will not be your happiness, it will certainly not be mine to see that fabric finished. It will not be your happiness, and it will certainly not be mine, to see that every stone laid in sincerity has been well laid. But I think it will be your happiness, as it is mine, to go on convinced that the great foundations are being well laid ... and that by skilled craftsmen, confident in each other's good will and sincerity, the temple will rise and rise and rise until at last it is complete, and the genius of humanity will find within it an appropriate resting place.

The retort from the left was that a gradualist strategy was interminable, and delivered little of benefit to workers, who needed relief from their sufferings and a better society now. Right from the beginning in the Labour Party there had been those who argued that the industrial power of the worker class had to be mobilised to force through the implementation of a socialist programme. Since any Labour government would be subjected to huge pressures from business and finance and the media, Labour's only weapon was to deploy the power which it possessed. This critique was not only of Labour's parliamentary leaders but also of its industrial ones. The syndicalists, in particular, did not just reject the parliamentary road, and the need for parliamentary representation. They also disputed the need for traditional trade unionism, with its patient incremental bargaining. Instead, they favoured the general strike as a means to force the propertied class to capitulate.

Many on the Labour left did not go as far as the syndicalists. But they did have a very different view to MacDonald of the proper balance between parliamentary and extra-parliamentary activity. In the 1920s, the Clydesiders, the group of Scottish MPs led by James Maxton and John Wheatley believed that Labour MPs were elected to articulate the grievances and aspiration of the class they represented. Parliament was a soap box and debates in Parliament were skirmishes in the class war. It followed that this war had to be fought outside, as well as inside, Parliament (Middlemas, 1965; Dowse, 1966). The purpose of engaging in Parliament was not to gain power through office, but to use it as a platform to mobilise not the uncommitted voters but the militant, class-conscious workers who were already Labour voters (Marquand, 1997: 288).

This was also the view of the Communist Party which emerged as a rival to the left of Labour in the 1920s. The Communists rejected the 'reformist view that a Social Revolution can be achieved by the ordinary method of Parliamentary Democracy' (Miliband, 1964: 86). Instead, they saw parliamentary and electoral action as providing a means of propaganda and agitation towards the revolution. Communist representatives in Parliament, the party declared, held a mandate from the party not from the constituency. If they violated party decisions they would be called on to resign from Parliament (Miliband, 1964: 86). The gulf between the Labour leadership and the Communist leadership was very wide, with the Communists advocating the adoption of the Soviet system to replace parliamentary democracy. Repeated attempts made by the party to affiliate to Labour in the 1920s and 1930s were regularly rebuffed.

There have always been many in Labour's ranks, like the Clydesiders and like Jeremy Corbyn, who agree with the Communists about the priority that should be given to extra-parliamentary agitation and campaigns, rather than parliamentary activity to build a platform on which to win office. Many in the ILP, MacDonald's initial base and ideological home, were sceptical about Parliament, and argued that the ILP should be a purely propagandist force, spreading 'sound and thorough' socialist opinion through the country (Miliband, 1964: 30). Fred Jowett rejected the 'jiggery pokery of party government played like a game for ascendancy and power' (Miliband, 1964: 29). Socialists should always stand on principles, and vote on the merits of the issues before them.

MacDonald's legacy: social democracy today

These divisions go deep in Labour's culture and have resurfaced in every generation. The advocates of the extra-parliamentary road point to the slim achievements which the parliamentary road has delivered. Every Labour government, including that of 1945, was disparaged at the time for being too cautious and defensive, never enacting bold and transformative policies, and soon being overwhelmed by problems and collapsing to defeat. Even before 1914, socialists grumbled that the Labour MPs elected to Parliament were invisible, and were achieving very little. It has been a refrain heard many times since. The lifelessness of Parliament is contrasted with the energy and vitality of the movement.

The two conceptions of politics are far apart. Marquand's appreciation of the divide was no doubt sharpened by his experience of Labour's factional struggles in the 1970s. MacDonald grappled with it at a time when the parliamentary road was still in its infancy and had not proven itself. In MacDonald's time it never delivered a majority Labour government. His achievement nevertheless was considerable in laying the foundation of a parliamentary road which would yield majority Labour governments in 1945, 1950, 1964, 1966, 1974, 1997, 2001 and 2005, although only five of these were substantial parliamentary majorities (Gamble, 2017).

MacDonald's Great Labour Party did eventually come into existence, and for periods it dominated British politics, 1945–51, 1964–70, 1974–79 (much less securely) and 1997–2010, Labour's longest period of electoral success, during which it won three consecutive general elections, all with substantial majorities. But all these periods of government are disparaged unreasonably by many in the contemporary Labour Party, with the partial exception of 1945–51. The Attlee government has been rehabilitated largely because it created the National Health Service. Unlike the Conservatives, Labour has always found it difficult to look back with pride on the achievements of its previous leaders and governments. That started with its treatment of MacDonald.

MacDonald would have been pleased that a Great Labour Party came into existence, but he would have been dismayed that after a high-water mark in the decades after 1945, the trend turned decisively against the kind of solidaristic, non-materialist, non-acquisitive community he thought that history would deliver (Abrams, 1959; Hobsbawm, 1981). His basic intuition about British politics, however, was proved correct. Support for the kind of class-war politics that the Communists and parts of the Labour left advocated was always limited. Even Ralph Miliband admits it in a revealing passage in *Parliamentary Socialism* on the record of the ministers in the first Labour government in 1924. He wrote: 'There was much that could be held against them on socialist grounds. But then most Labour supporters were not socialists, only anti-Conservatives' (Miliband, 1964: 119).

MacDonald's strategy was to rally anti-Conservatives and non-Conservatives to Labour, and convince them that Labour could stand for them and would govern for them. MacDonald's supporters in the unions argued that if workers would not vote for a Labour Party pursuing constitutional methods to effect social reform, they would be unlikely to support industrial action to achieve political demands. MacDonald and the Labour leadership were always aware that a large percentage of the working class in Britain voted Conservative. Labour was far from monopolising the support of the class it claimed to represent. Philip Snowden expressed it in his usual trenchant manner on entering government in 1924: 'We should not adopt an extreme policy but should confine our legislative proposals to measures that we were likely to be able to carry … We must show the country that we were not under the domination of the wild men' (Miliband,

1964: 101). It was to be Snowden, never one for understatement, who in the 1931 General Election described the manifesto of his former colleagues in the Labour Party, as 'Bolshevism run mad'.

MacDonald's legacy to the Labour Party was not destroyed in 1931, even though his own reputation was, and he was no longer given the credit for the party he had created. In the 1920s, Labour was still a loose federation of local bodies and special interests, rather than a cohesive unitary organisation with a single purpose. The unions provided the party with an anchor and a connection with the working class, but the unions were themselves divided, on strategies and policies. MacDonald, when he returned to Parliament in 1922, quickly stated the essence of the problem: 'the failure of the party in the last Parliament was that it never was an Opposition, and was never led as an Opposition. It never impressed itself upon the country as an alternative Government with an alternative policy' (Marquand, 1997: 287). Similar complaints are voiced today. MacDonald was determined to rectify that. He wanted to complete the work he had started before 1914, changing Labour from a pressure group for working-class interests into a national party capable of winning and building power (Marquand, 1997: 231). Labour's opportunity in the 1920s was not to be distracted by the calls for class war and revolution but to focus on building an alliance between the organised labour movement and the radical wing of the Liberal Party (Marquand, 1997: 247).

In a new introduction, written in 1997, the year of Blair and New Labour's great triumph, Marquand reflected once more on Ramsay MacDonald's place in Labour's history and on his own assessment of him made twenty years before. Macdonald, he wrote, like Blair, had contrived to make the Labour Party appear both adventurous and safe. In the course of the 1920s under his leadership Labour had forged decisively ahead of the Liberals not just in one but in several elections. The party system had been reshaped and Labour had become the main alternative to the Conservatives. MacDonald's strategy of building Labour as a constitutional party grounded in the trade unions and the labour interest but appealing to progressive intellectuals and progressive opinion far beyond the labour movement, sufficient to make Labour a contender for power, had succeeded.

There still remained the issue of what that power was for. In his first edition Marquand accepted that he had interpreted MacDonald and the great crisis of 1931 through a Keynesian lens. Robert Skidelsky, in his *Politicians and the Slump*, published in 1967, had argued that a Keynesian solution to the slump existed, and was articulated by politicians like Oswald Mosley, before he turned to the advocacy of direct action with the establishment of the British Union of Fascists.

But the political leadership, including MacDonald, were too cautious, and failed to grasp the opportunity, with calamitous consequences (Skidelsky, 1967). In 1977 Marquand shared much of that analysis. By 1997 he had doubts. Much of the confidence in the post-war social democratic project had dissipated. The assumption that it was possible gradually to transform capitalism – the assumption both of MacDonald and post-war social democrats – no longer seemed to hold. The harsh dilemmas facing earlier generations of social democrats had been forgotten after 1945, trying to pursue projects of social justice in a global economy ruled once again by an unbridled, untamed capitalism. Now that great period of capitalist success and excess has ended in another crash equal in scale to the crash of 1929. Social Democrats have once more had to struggle to cope with hard times, and across Europe have been on the defensive. MacDonald would not have been surprised. He always thought that socialism depended on the success of capitalism, not its failure (Marquand, 1997: 454). If citizens were freed from want and insecurity they might become non-materialist and non-acquisitive, and create true fraternal and solidaristic communities (MacDonald, 1908; 1972).

Problems beset both the electoral, and the governing strategies of social democrats. Is the best vehicle for progressive politics still a party which is anchored in the labour interest? Many of today's labour parties are being hollowed out as working-class voters defect, and progressive intellectuals and professional elites increasingly dominate. Trade unions are much weaker than they were, and changes to work and households have undermined the assumptions on which the politics of labour movements were based. Right-wing populist parties across Europe have begun to invade their electoral territory. The progressive coalition which underpinned the idea of a Great Labour Party has begun to fragment. In the British Labour Party, the trade unions, so long the anchor which kept the party in touch with working-class opinion, have ceased, at least for the moment, to fulfil that role. The party has fallen to a new left insurgency, led by young urban cosmopolitans and older sympathisers of the party's broad left. Many of Labour's working-class voters voted for Brexit in the referendum in 2016, with immigration a key issue. The cultural and political gulf between the old labour working-class communities and the new cosmopolitan intellectuals (Blairites and Corbynites alike) has become stark. Although only 37 per cent of Labour voters voted for Brexit, their concentration in particular constituencies means that on some estimates over 70 per cent of Labour-held constituencies voted for Leave, almost all of them in the north of England, Wales and the Midlands.

The progressive dilemma only existed in the past because the labour interest was such a powerful electoral and industrial force, and aligned to a policy of gradual progressive political change. But the new identity politics which is dividing the centre-left makes establishing a secure connection between the different parts of the progressive coalition much harder. In that sense the Blairite and the Corbynite factions in the British Labour Party, although locked in a fight to the death, also share many assumptions about politics. They represent different wings of the progressive intelligentsia which has come increasingly to dominate the party and has lost touch with the labour interest and the cultural politics it represented. The Labour coalition has shrunk, and Labour is ceasing to be a credible party of government.

The same is true of governing strategy. Marquand in 1977 was implicitly critical of MacDonald for not realising that the future was Keynesianism and grabbing it with both hands. By 1997 he was more sceptical. It was always anachronistic, he writes (Marquand, 1997), to think that MacDonald could have implemented a Keynesian solution in 1931. But now he goes further. There is no reason to think, he argues, that a Keynesian solution attempted in 1931 would have worked, The external conditions were too unfavourable. The problem was that faced with a series of increasingly unpalatable options MacDonald opted in the end for the orthodox policy, because that at least might preserve Labour's reputation as a responsible (which means constitutional, non-revolutionary) governing party, prepared to play by the rules devised by others. The governing dilemma for social democrats is that if they behave responsibly, as MacDonald did in 1931, they risk losing their party. If they are perceived as acting irresponsibly, they risk losing their voters, which has happened to Labour in 2010, and again in 2015, and even more since. The response of many Labour Party members, dismayed at the party's electoral reverses has been to support a new version of the ILP platform from the 1920s, one that gives priority to the extra-parliamentary struggle rather than to Parliament. The policy platform of this new insurgency calls itself once again socialist, although it is a pale, if still recognisable, reflection of the socialism of the ILP in the 1920s. The 1928 ILP programme *Socialism in Our Time* proposed a national living wage, nationalisation of the banks, the railways, the mines, the land, electricity generation, and the import of food and raw materials. Taxation on the rich would be increased to pay for supplements to working-class incomes, and the unemployment allowance substantially increased. The problem with this programme, as with all its successors, is: could a Labour government be elected on it, and if that hurdle is cleared, could it be implemented and democracy preserved, given the intense resistance which it would arouse?

These tensions and these dilemmas, around governing, around socialist purpose, around representation and electability, have recurred many times in Labour's history, and in those of other centre-left parties and movements around the world. Sisyphus, in the Greek legend, was punished by being forced to roll a huge boulder up a steep hill, and then watch it roll back down again, repeating this cycle endlessly. David Marquand, through his many writings, but particularly in his great biography of Ramsay MacDonald, offers many deep insights into these social democratic dilemmas. The possibility of social democratic renewal through changes in the hearts and minds of citizens is always present because of the arrival of new generations and new circumstances. But that time is not yet. In his latest work (Marquand: 2014), Marquand presents an increasingly bleak and disenchanted view of Britain and British politics, rather like MacDonald himself, who wrote in his diary: 'In youth one believes in democracy; later on one has to accept it … I read for consolation Gibbon's Decline and Fall and the minor Prophets' (Marquand, 1997: 246).

References

Abrams, M. and Rose, R. (1959) *Must Labour Lose?* (London: Penguin).

Cole, G. D. H. (1913) *The World of Labour: A Discussion of The Present and Future of Trade Unionism* (London: G. Bell & Sons).

Crewe, I. and King, A. (1995) *SDP* (Oxford: Oxford University Press).

Dowse, R. (1966) *Left in the Centre: The Independent Labour Party 1893–1940* (London: Longmans).

Gamble, A. (2017) 'The progressive dilemma revisited', *Political Quarterly*, 8(1), 136–43.

Hobsbawm, E. (1981) *The Forward March of Labour Halted?* (London: NLB).

Kogan, D. and Kogan, M. (1982) *The Battle for The Labour Party* (London: Fontana).

MacDonald, J. R. (1908) *Socialism and Society* (London: ILP).

MacDonald, J. R. (1972) *Political Writings* (London: Allen Lane).

McKenzie, R. (1955) *British Political Parties: The Distribution of Power Within The Conservative and Labour Parties* (London: Heinemann).

Marquand, D. (1991) *The Progressive Dilemma* (London: Heinemann).

Marquand, D. (1997) *Ramsay MacDonald* (London: Richard Cohen Books).

Marquand, D. (2014) *Mammon's Kingdom* (London: Allen Lane).

Middlemas, K. (1965) *The Clydesiders: A Left Wing Struggle for Parliamentary Power* (London: Hutchinson).

Miliband, R. (1964) *Parliamentary Socialism* (London: Merlin).

Pelling, H. (1961) *A Short History of the Labour Party* (London: Macmillan).

Seyd, P. (1987) *The Rise and Fall of the Labour Left* (London: Palgrave).

Skidelsky, R. (1967) *Politicians and The Slump: The Labour Government of 1929–31* (London: Macmillan).

Part II

Citizenship, republicanism and democracy

5

Globalisation, the breaking and re-making of social democratic citizenship

Hans Schattle

Introduction: the erosion of social democratic citizenship

Social democratic citizenship can be regarded as the fulfilment of not only civil and political rights but also social and economic rights – rights to education, health care, living wages, unemployment insurance and pensions – and it is all too obvious that these rights have eroded severely in recent decades across the 'developed' world. The gutting of trade unions, the reduction of full-time jobs paying decent living wages in favour of temporary and part-time under-employment, the mounting unaffordability of essential public goods such as education and housing, the widening gaps in health care and social welfare provisions, and the continuing disparities in access to key decision makers in government – with the wealthiest campaign contributors and corporate lobbyists pulling far more leverage than ever in comparison with everyday people –have all eroded citizenship from the vantage point of social democracy. In fact, social democratic citizenship began to fade even before the start of the Reagan and Thatcher years and the ideological ascendancy of neoliberalism and its tenets of deregulation, privatisation and unfettered trade as the driving forces of the global economy.

For a time in the 1990s, it seemed the 'baby boomer' generation intended to take up the challenge of revitalising social democracy and creating the conditions for empowered, engaged and equitable citizenries ready to take the 'West' into a new global, post-industrial era. The 'third way' rhetoric of Tony Blair and Bill Clinton, however, quickly evaporated into a mirage that tacitly handed the game over to big business and the global 'super rich' – and short-changed the key constituents of their respective centre-left political parties: the middle class and the working class. This was a huge setback for citizens everywhere, as like it or not, conditions in the United States and Great Britain often set the tone for the world economy. For all the excitement in recent years behind the rise of 'global civil society' and the impact of online social networks in inspiring new generations of citizens to mobilise and campaign on a host of compelling issues, particularly related to protecting the environment, advancing human rights and alleviating world poverty, it is simply not enough for citizens to project their voices on a global scale using the tools of digital communication if this does not translate directly into appropriate laws and policies that safeguard public interests and hold wealthy and powerful economic actors more accountable to an encompassing public good. Governments at all levels must carve out new competencies in exerting genuine oversight over economic actors, especially multinational corporations well on their way to monopolistic power, if we have any real prospect of moving beyond the 'new gilded age' (Bartels, 2007) and ushering in a renewed model of social democratic citizenship in the years to come.

This chapter first takes stock of the decline in social democratic citizenship, tracing in particular how economic restructuring and public policy shifts accompanying globalisation in recent decades have harmed the middle-class and working-class populations essential in sustaining democratic self-government – and, more recently, have prompted many citizens on both sides of the Atlantic to gravitate toward right-wing variants of populism rather than social democracy. Next the chapter seeks to light candles, rather than curse the darkness, by bringing forward some of the new voices and emerging venues for political participation amid today's global transformations in politics, economics and culture that suggest the potential for a long overdue revitalisation of social democratic citizenship. The conclusion underscores how empowerment, engagement and equity serve as three lodestars in the larger endeavour, still ongoing and perhaps set to continue indefinitely, of remaking social democratic citizenries.

Impunity as well as inequality: the breaking of social democratic citizenries

Well, we're waiting here in Allentown For the Pennsylvania we never found
For the promises our teachers gave – If we worked hard, If we behaved
So the graduations hang on the wall, But they never really helped us at all
No they never taught us what was real: Iron and coke And chromium steel …
But they've taken all the coal from the ground, And the union people crawled away
Billy Joel, lyrics to 'Allentown' (1982)[1]

Written and performed by Billy Joel during the relatively early phase of the manufacturing exodus that has drained the economic lifeblood from so many communities, the classic hit song 'Allentown' blisteringly captures not only the breaking of the 'old' post-war era social contract but also the mechanical ways in which industrial workers were supposed to live up to their side of the bargain: behave, obey, follow directions and work hard (often at rather menial, repetitive tasks). These social democratic citizens 'made' in the post-war era generally were *not* taught to take risks, to innovate, to make new discoveries, to question the legitimacy of authority figures; they were not taught the sorts of 'critical thinking' skills extolled by political economist Robert Reich in his book *The Work of Nations* (1991), as essential for the knowledge workers – the creative and strategic individuals that he labelled as 'symbolic analysts' – who would prosper in the post-industrial age.

Published long after the rug had been pulled out from under the steelworkers depicted in 'Allentown', Reich's book offered a formula for the rising generation of young adults to gain a foothold in the global economy, but it was too late for many of their elders who could not retool themselves as readily. These skills became 'what was real' in terms of what it took to get ahead, plus network connections for those lucky enough to be accepted into prestigious academic institutions and the investment banks, consulting firms and start-up ventures of what David Marquand labelled the 'techno-managerial elite' (1997). Note also how Joel directs his contempt at the union people who 'crawled away' – not at the corporate masters who flew away as they outsourced jobs in countries with much cheaper workers and lower standards on the environment as well as workplace health and safety. This foreshadows how the public would desert trade unions but not politicians bankrolled by corporate interests; in fact, for the past 40 years, working-class voters have flocked repeatedly to candidates whose policies were totally out of sync with their economic interests.

Mainstream politics and the relentless dismantling of the middle class

The ways in which neoliberalism and its proponents overtook social democracy have been widely documented and need only a brief recap here. The 'New Deal' that helped the United States lift itself from the Great Depression of the 1930s, Labour's reshaping of the UK toward a 'New Jerusalem' following the Second World War, and the rise of the 'European social market' on the continent all can be seen in hindsight as deploying, in specific ways, a new social contract, unprecedented at the time, that finally provided necessary but long neglected measures of well-being and protection for middle-class and working-class citizens, as well as the means for advancement through greatly improved access to higher education.

For a period of nearly thirty years after the war, this new social contract held together with bipartisan consensus in America and Britain, at least with respect to general principles and specific programmes such as the GI Bill, Social Security and Medicare in the United States and the National Health Service (NHS) and free university education in the UK. Some of these provisions are still considered indispensable. Yet by the 1970s, amid the OPEC oil shocks and the double whammy of 'stagflation', with its high inflation and rising unemployment, the Anglo-American consensus on economic policy veered in pursuit of efficiency above all else. The conservative Reagan presidency and Thatcher government ushered the era of global neoliberalism, which still reigns supreme today with its imperatives of deregulation, privatisation and unfettered trade. The sting of ravaged economic opportunities could be seen as clear as day in the decimated industrial enclaves of both countries; look no further than the film *Billy Elliot*, for instance, to remember the grim and ultimately brutal outcome of the 1984 coal miners' strike in County Durham.

The negative consequences of global neoliberalism on the middle and working classes became a 'front burner' issue in both the United States and the UK by the early 1990s. A landmark publication in 1992, titled *America: What Went Wrong*, by *Philadelphia Inquirer* journalists Donald Bartlett and James Steele, provided the most extensive documentation at that time of how deregulation and tax cuts had provided a boon for corporations and the wealthiest individuals while 'dismantling the middle class'. One of their many statistical findings showed that from 1980 to 1989, the combined salaries of Americans earning $20,000–$50,000 per year increased by 44 per cent, while the combined salaries of people being paid $1 million or more per year soared by 2,184 per cent (Bartlett and Steele, 1992: 4). Published first in newspapers across the country and subsequently in book form, this investigative reporting helped set the agenda for the presidential race that year. Indeed, George H. W. Bush appeared to be coasting smoothly toward re-election, flush from his military triumph in swiftly driving Saddam Hussein's Iraqi army out of Kuwait, until the economic dislocation caused substantially by the exodus of manufacturing jobs became the number one issue in the 1992 presidential campaign.

Upstart Democrat Bill Clinton defied the early conventional wisdom and won the election with promises to 'cut taxes for the middle class and make the rich pay their fair share' and to 'make sure American workers can get training and retraining throughout their careers – so that America can achieve a high-skill, high wage economy'. (Clinton campaign brochure, 1992) Clinton's slogan, 'It's the Economy, Stupid!' as well as the related catchphrase 'Fighting for the Forgotten Middle Class' helped catapult him past Bush, who at times seemed oblivious to the problems even as he faced an insurgent Republican Party challenger, Pat Buchanan, a former White House speechwriter and communications adviser who won the high-profile New Hampshire state primary by railing against Bush's inattentiveness to the plight of the working classes. With its emphasis on economic dislocation and its promises to reduce immigration and avoid international trade agreements, Buchanan's campaign prefigured Donald Trump's presidential victory in 2016.

Bill Clinton handily won the presidency, also defeating independent candidate Ross Perot, but once in office, he failed to deliver on his promises to help the 'forgotten' constituencies that had been crucial to his election. Instead, Clinton devoted his energy to the passage and initiation of the North American Free Trade Agreement, which had the effect of shifting an estimated one million jobs from the United States to Mexico (Wallach, 2014), as well as the formation in 1995 of the World Trade Organization (WTO), and the granting of 'most favoured nation' status to China, which in 2001 joined the WTO. These latter two developments set the stage for even more American manufacturing jobs to move to China and Southeast Asia; according to the Economic Policy Institute, China's entry into the WTO alone led to the displacement of yet another 3.2 million American jobs from 2001 to 2013 (Kimball and Scott, 2014). When Robert Reich became Secretary of Labor in the Clinton administration – the two men had met in 1968 when they enrolled as fellow Rhodes scholars at Oxford – Reich sincerely placed the economic rebounding of the middle and working classes as his top priority. After he got 'locked in the cabinet', as Reich aptly titled his memoir from this period (1998), Reich found his agenda side-lined by Clinton's economic globalisation imperatives as well as his politically calculated shift toward reducing the federal budget deficit as a means to help secure re-election in 1996.

Clinton's economic policy of neoliberalism continued during the George W. Bush and Barack Obama administrations; even though Obama managed to pass legislation easing the way for Americans to obtain health insurance, the Patient Protection and Affordable Care Act remained a market-based system still centred on profit-making insurance corporations. In his stirring oratory before becoming president and in his policies while governing, Obama consistently placed the goal of unifying America's divergent ethnic, cultural and ideological segments of the population ahead of any endeavour to change America's economic policies to help those Americans long falling behind. Although Obama helped the United States rebuild its image in the world after the George W. Bush presidency and pulled the country out of the economic downturn and financial collapse that resulted from both G. W. Bush's and Clinton's policies, Obama simply did not attempt a decisive righting of the ship when it came to taming capitalism for the good of the general public. This, of course, helped lead to the election of Donald Trump, and a similar pattern of neoliberalism giving way to right-wing populism has emerged in the UK. Upon Labour's successful 1997 election, Tony Blair promised to usher in a 'third way' that would reconcile free-market economics with social democracy. In practice, however, the 'third way' defaulted to free-market economics and unfettered capitalism. As David Marquand observed in a *New Statesman* essay (2015), contrasting Blair and his ilk with earlier social democrats:

> Unlike the communist parties of the (postwar) era, social democrats did not attempt to abolish capitalism; they knew that any such attempt would end in tears as it had done in the Soviet Union. But they also knew that, although the capitalist market economy could be a good servant, it was a disastrous master. They were the chief architects of the reformed capitalism – the capitalism of welfare states, mixed economies and capacious public realms – that straddled the developed western world in the postwar period. Today's governmental social democrats, by contrast, have not just acquiesced in capitalism's return to the wild; they have connived in it. In doing so, they have spurned the left-behind.

New Labour presided over an era in British history that widened social and economic disparities and facilitated the dramatic expansion of a 'nouveau riche' elite class that has contributed to the virtual uncoupling of London from the remaining segments of the United Kingdom and its population. This is not entirely New Labour's fault – many 'global cities' worldwide have become entities unto themselves. London, however, stands as an especially egregious case: look no further than the forbidding apartment towers along the Thames owned by the global 'super rich' (often left largely uninhabited as mere investment properties) and the skyrocketing of housing prices that has reaped windfalls for some but driven out the next generation of its would-have-been middle-class residents. London has become more dynamic, diverse and inclusive than ever, but at the cost of displacing many of its long-time residents and also enlarging the gulf between Britain's southeastern region and the remainder of the country.

The same problem has emerged in the United States, with gentrified global magnets such as New York, Boston and San Francisco now thriving for those with the initiative and good fortune to prosper as 'symbolic analysts', and who coexist within these cosmopolitan enclaves alongside an underclass of workers, many of them immigrants, who prop up the local economies with their cheap and flexible labour. Just a short drive away from these prosperous hubs languish their less-competitive counterparts: the Allentowns of the world. Now, in the days (if not exactly the era) of Brexit and Trump, these long decaying communities have become much more than hotbeds of discontent; these no-longer 'forgotten' citizens have led the charge in an outright abandonment of the mainstream political parties – the centre-right as well as the centre-left. Left up in the air is whether these parties will regroup in ways that adapt to the needs and demands of the voters who have now forsaken them. Marquand saw all this coming; as he warned New Labour in his 1997 book, *The New Reckoning*, published shortly after Tony Blair's ascendancy to the prime minister's seat:

> The lion's share of the extraordinary productivity gains associated with the current capitalist renaissance has gone to the owners of capital, to a new techno-managerial elite and to a handful of stars in the increasingly global entertainment industries … Confronting them are the losers: the anxious middle classes, threatened by proletarianisation; the increasingly casualised working class; and the burgeoning underclass. That faultline runs through the new Labour coalition. No project for social inclusion will work unless it captures some of the winners' gains and redirects them to the losers. (Marquand, 1997: 25)

Neoliberalism's wreckage: exploitation, stratification, alienation and polarisation

The inequality spurred along by global neoliberalism has only become more vast since Marquand wrote that observation two decades ago; we now can see, in even starker terms than before, how thoroughly citizens have lost ground in economic well-being, and by extension, political efficacy. As economists Thomas Piketty, Emmanuel Saez and Gabriel Zucman (2016) reported in a recent study, the top one per cent of the working population in the United States in 1974 earned 10.5 per cent of the total national income, while the bottom half of the working population in this year earned 20 per cent of the national income. Forty years later, in 2014, these two per centages had reversed, with the top one per cent raking in the top 20 per cent of national income and the bottom half of the working population left with 12.5 per cent. Adjusted for inflation, meanwhile, the salaries of the lower middle class and working class have been falling steadily over the past 40 years: Piketty and his colleagues found that workers in the bottom 50 per cent of the US population have seen their average pre-tax earnings increase by only 2.6 per cent since 1974, meaning that they have been shut out of any growth in income during this period. In stunning contrast, the pre-tax earnings for US citizens in the top 10 per cent of the population increased by 231 per cent from 1974 to 2014.

Compounding this sharp increase in inequality, the tax system in the United States has become far more indulgent toward the wealthier segments of the population in recent decades (courtesy mainly of tax reductions, for the richer segments, initiated in the 1980s by the Reagan administration) and likewise more hostile, even confiscatory for the poorer segments. At the end of the Second World War, the average income tax rate for the top one per cent of the population was approximately 45 per cent, while the corresponding rate for the bottom 50 per cent was 15 per cent; by 2014, the average tax rate for the top one per cent had fallen to 36 per cent while the rate for the bottom 50 per cent had risen to 24 per cent (Piketty, Saez and Zucman, 2016). All this shows that the 'Occupy Wall Street' movement and its global counterparts did not emerge from nowhere: the very people who have been bearing the brunt of wage stagnation and declining economic opportunity for the past 40 years have also been bearing a higher burden in paying the nation's income taxes: a core duty of citizenship that their wealthier citizens have been tacitly shirking.

As another indicator in the United States, economist Timothy Smeeding (2016: 268–9) has found that the income gap between average households in the top 20 per cent of the population and the middle 40–60 per cent of the population nearly tripled (in inflation adjusted dollars) from $68,000 in 1979 (one year before Ronald Reagan's election as US president) to $169,000 in 2010. This illustrates clearly how inequality is not only about the proverbial one per cent – that the top 20 per cent have been decisively uncoupling from their fellow citizens for some time. Worldwide, even as rapid economic development in much of Asia and Latin America has lifted generations out of poverty and raised living standards, the overall spread of inequality is even more stark than in domestic contexts: a study by Oxfam International in 2016 found that the 62 richest people in the world now own the same wealth as the poorest 3.6 billion; the richest one per cent of the global population now hold more wealth than the remaining 99 per cent of humanity combined – including at least US$7.6 trillion in assets tucked away in tax havens (Hardoon, Ayele and Fuentes-Niva, 2016).

The socio-economic divide across the world's developed countries has become so thoroughly entrenched, in the eyes of Piketty and his colleagues, that public policies focused on redistributing wealth will not be sufficient to overcome the diminished life chances for these citizens caught in the lower half of the income curve. What would work, they argue, is a concerted effort to raise the incomes of the American working and middle classes. This would translate into rebuilding the bargaining power of trade unions, improving access to quality education and job training programmes for the entire population, and returning to more progressive taxation by sharply increasing income taxes for the wealthier segments and sharply reducing taxes for lower income brackets. Such solutions challenge the arguments from many political philosophers and social scientists in recent years placing priority on 'bottom-up' civil society initiatives rather than 'top-down' state policies, that it is more important to focus on the moral and civic character of good citizens (Sandel, 1996) and strengthen 'social capital' mainly through voluntary associations and community programmes (Putnam, 2000).

In the field of psychology, meanwhile, recent studies have led to the popularity of buzzwords – such as 'growth mindset' (Dweck, 2007) and 'grit' (Duckworth, 2016) – intended to capture the importance of passion, perseverance, tenacity and straightforward hard work, coupled with a positive 'can do' attitude receptive to lifelong learning and adaptation, especially in the face of adversity. While social capital and the character formation of good citizens are undoubtedly important, these elements are just part of the equation in explaining what it takes for individuals to flourish, they simply do not compensate for the absence of strong public policies that set out in earnest to boost the prospects for the segments of the population that really have been neglected for far too long. (Of course, redistributive policies are not even likely at the moment, given the direction the political winds are blowing.) One can have a 'growth mindset' and abound with passion and perseverance yet find oneself cast aside simply by not being in the right place at the right time and, related to this, lacking access to the right kinds of network connections. A 'gritty' person with a 'growth mindset' can all too easily fall into a lousy job because it's the best break one can find at a given moment.

Unfortunate examples of exploitation in the world's 'post-industrial' countries are no longer centred on stereotypical fifth-rate employers such as low-end retailers and fast-food chains; instead, high-end brand names are now routinely exposed as perpetrators of the same fundamental crimes that accompany the 'gig' economy of easily disposable freelance workers and per diem contract labour: Hermès, for instance, became the target of critical scrutiny in July 2016 in Britain for failing to pay the living wage of £7.20 per hour to its couriers who deliver the high-end fashion accessories that its customers purchase online. Couriers provided evidence that they were actually earning roughly £6.00 per hour and as little as £5.50 per hour; and, since they were classified as self-employed, none received paid holidays, sick pay, or pension contributions. In practice, however, the workers are self-employed in name only; as one courier based in Yorkshire told the *Guardian*: 'I don't feel like I am self-employed at all. Every aspect of this job is dictated to me. The customer says when they want the parcels delivering; Hermès says they want us to work to a set way of doing things. If they are going to treat us like employees, make us employees.' Despite the apparent exploitation of the 'self-employed' category as well as the people essentially trapped within this unenviable status, the *Guardian* reported that the exemption of 'self-employed' couriers from the mandatory living wage had been approved by Her Majesty's Revenue and Customs and is, in fact, common in the internet shopping industry. The public advocacy group Citizens Advice Bureau (2015) has estimated that as many as 460,000 persons across the UK are wrongly classified as self-employed, and that the employment benefits they have forgone would be worth a total of £600 million in holiday pay (£1200 per worker annually, on average) and £314 million in lost national insurance.

Even flagship companies in the (no longer entirely) 'new economy' pay some of their lower-level workers far too little money to escape conditions of squalor. Online retailer Amazon, already notorious for its exceptionally high-pressure workplace culture for its professional employees, received newly unwelcome attention in December 2016 for the tent settlements that some of its temporary seasonal workers had set up outside a warehouse in Dunfermline, Scotland, because they couldn't afford the cost of nearby housing on their wages of £7.35 per hour (Smith, 2016). In the epicentre of today's high-tech paradise – comparatively balmy but stratospherically pricey San Francisco – the long-standing problem of homelessness has recently become more visible as several tent camps that long existed in empty lots have been displaced in the current construction boom, moving the tents to sidewalks just below one-bedroom apartments that typically are rented for US$4,500 per month (Duane, 2016).

Local resentment in San Francisco has also been building over the private buses that transport Google, Apple, Facebook and e-Bay employees each day from their gentrified neighbourhoods (where, as in London, many locals can no longer afford to live) to their respective corporate 'campuses' in Silicon Valley. Contrast the sidewalk tents with the so-called 'velvet rope' economy now emerging for the super-rich: visitors to crowded theme parks can now pay extra fees in order to jump the otherwise inevitable queues, while Delta Airlines now shuttles its premium-class passengers from terminal to terminal at the Atlanta airport with the 'surprise and delight' service of a Porsche. Clearly there is a market for these kinds of perks, but this also illustrates the ways in which today's elites opt out of normal social interaction (Schwartz, 2016). Such new manifestations of class segregation are a far cry, for instance, from the daily routine of the late television news presenter Peter Jennings, who rode the city bus each morning in Manhattan on his way to work.

Adding insult to injury, the 'Panama Papers' disclosures in the spring of 2016 revealed how numerous corporations and wealthy individuals – including the father of former British prime minister David Cameron – have funnelled massive amounts of wealth into offshore accounts. As political economist Jeffrey Sachs noted with stark clarity, these revelations further underscored how today's 'new gilded age' stems in no small measure from sheer impunity, which in turn has exacerbated the widening inequality:

> Impunity is epidemic in America. The rich and powerful get away with their heists in broad daylight. When a politician like Bernie Sanders calls out the corruption, the *New York Times* and *Wall Street Journal* double down with their mockery over such a foolish 'dreamer'. The *Journal* recently opposed the corruption sentence of former Virginia governor Bob McDonnell for taking large gifts and bestowing official favours – because everybody does it. And one of its columnists praised Panama for facilitating the ability of wealthy individuals to hide their income from 'predatory governments' trying to collect taxes. No kidding. (Sachs, 2016)

To substantiate his allegation of 'impunity', Sachs singled out his alma mater, Harvard University, for accepting a gift of US$400 million from hedge-fund manager John Paulson after he was found to have concocted, along with Goldman Sachs, a portfolio of 'toxic assets' that were sold to unwitting investors so that Paulson could then 'bet against the portfolio' and, once the 2008 financial crisis hit, turn a profit of US$1 billion in doing so. As Sachs noted: 'Yet Harvard was delighted last year to take $400 million of Paulson's ill-gotten gains, leave Paulson with the rest, name its engineering school after Paulson, and declare Paulson to be 'the epitome of a visionary leader'. Sachs could have also mentioned that Harvard includes a series of 'moral reasoning' courses within its undergraduate core curriculum, yet the university readily accepted funds in this instance from an individual implicated in a major incidence of financial corruption.

The anxiety and exasperation of 'forgotten' citizens

In the year of Brexit and Trump, political analysts disagreed on whether racism functioned as a more prevalent driving force than economic outrage in driving disaffected, beleaguered white, working-class voters toward right-wing populist candidates as well as authoritarian sentiments. Combing through years of cross-national public opinion data, political scientists Ronald Inglehart and Pippa Norris (2016) argued that Brexit and Trump are mainly the result not of economic deprivation but of 'cultural backlash' against a range of progressive values – not only opposition to immigration and multiculturalism but also resistance to rising gender equality and progressive cultural norms such as same-sex marriage. However, economic outrage is a substantial and inescapable part of the equation. Immediately after Donald Trump's victory in the 2016 US presidential election, activist and author Naomi Klein described the political dynamics this way:

> Here is what we need to understand: a hell of a lot of people are in pain. Under neoliberal policies of deregulation, privatisation, austerity and corporate trade, their living standards have declined precipitously. They have lost jobs. They have lost pensions. They have lost much of the safety net that used to make these losses less frightening. They see a future for their kids even worse than their precarious present.
>
> At the same time, they have witnessed the rise of the Davos class, a hyper-connected network of banking and tech billionaires, elected leaders who are awfully cosy with those interests, and Hollywood celebrities who make the whole thing seem unbearably glamorous. Success is a party to which they were not invited, and they know in their hearts that this rising wealth and power is somehow directly connected to their growing debts and powerlessness.
>
> For the people who saw security and status as their birthright – and that means white men most of all – these losses are unbearable. (Klein, 2016)

All this is not lost on the millennial generation (Generation Y) as well as the rising post-millennial generation (Generation Z). They have seen many of their parents, aunts and uncles get 'expelled' from their placings in the middle class and have also observed the sheer impunity and hypocrisy of many wealthy and powerful individuals. This has prompted some in the younger generations to become involved politically, but many view both the political and business worlds with a mixed sense of resignation and cynicism. Economist and journalist Noreena Hertz argues that a more fitting label for the post-millennial generation is 'Generation K', after Katniss Everdeen, a character in *The Hunger Games*:

Like Katniss, they feel the world they inhabit is one of perpetual struggle – dystopian, unequal and harsh ... This generation is profoundly anxious. In the US, the Center for Disease Control and Prevention reported that 17 percent of high school students had seriously considered killing themselves. In England, there has been a threefold increase during the past 10 years in the number of teenagers who self-harm ... This generation does not believe that life is a meritocracy. In fact, not one teenager surveyed (by the World Health Organization) agrees with the statement that 'society is fair and everyone has an equal chance'. Instead, they believe that it's the colour of their skin, their sex, their parents' economic status and their social standing that will determine their future. Depressingly, the data bears this out. (Hertz, 2016; for WHO data, Inchley *et al.*, 2016)

By no means is the disillusionment among today's younger generations exclusive to the 'West'; it also simmers across the 'Asian tigers' states. Many people in the West presume that these economies are still on fire, but along the Pacific Rim, too, economic inequality is widening and the Asian middle classes that have risen in the past thirty years are already endangered. In South Korea, for example, the younger generations (the equivalents of Generations Y and Z in the West) have taken to calling their country 'Hell Joseon', with 'Joseon' the name of Korea's *ancien régime*, the dynasty that ran the (then-unified) peninsula for 500 years (from 1392 to 1897) and epitomised oriental feudalism. It was a world in which a tiny, powerful, rigidly hierarchical elite hoarded all the privileges for themselves and shamelessly dominated the masses who remained, quite literally, nameless slaves. Of course, today's Korea is not nearly this bad, and many (elder) stalwarts think the 'Hell Joseon' crowd are a bunch of spoiled brats who have no idea of how well they have it compared with the absolute poverty of the not-so-distant past. However, like the children in the United States and Europe who can feel the palpable decline in their prospects compared with their parents' generation, large numbers of twentysomethings – and even thirtysomethings – in today's Korea are under-employed in part-time jobs (which are, in fact, typically full-time jobs that pay part-time wages and are totally lacking in benefits), living with their parents and either postponing or abandoning the possibilities of long-term relationships and having children. Indeed, South Korea's birth rate, at 1.24 on average (as of 2015) for women of childbearing age, is the lowest in the OECD (Yon and Noh, 2016), while its suicide rate has been the highest in the OECD since 2003, and the country consistently ranks near the bottom of OECD countries in Gallup's yearly World Happiness Report (Fifield, 2016; Moon, 2016).

Once again, unhappiness to the point of exasperation can be easily traced: as of 2016, according to the International Monetary Fund, South Korea had the most severe income inequality among the twenty-two Asia-Pacific countries, approximately one-third of adults in their early thirties remain stuck in temporary or part-time jobs, and the country's youth unemployment rate (covering persons under the age of 30) rose to 12.5 per cent in February 2016 (Moon, 2016). A 'Hell Joseon' Facebook page has drawn more than 5,000 members who swap stories and fantasise about leaving South Korea for other countries where, they presume, the grass is greener or at least the air is cleaner. Air pollution in Northeast Asia has worsened in the past five years because of China's rapid increase in 'dirty' coal-fired plants. A novel about a young woman who leaves South Korea for Australia – titled *Because I Hate South Korea* – is a recent best-seller. Despite this collective yearning for 'Exit', the country's young adults have shifted in droves to 'Voice', recalling Albert Hirschmann's treatise (1970), in taking to the streets in truly massive weekly Saturday evening rallies, in the fall of 2016 and winter of 2017, drawing as many as 2 million people at a time to demand the removal of the country's conservative president, Park Geun-hye, after she became implicated in a massive influence-peddling scandal. As Park's approval rating plunged to 4 per cent, public opinion surveys indicated that as many as 9 million of the country's 50 million people have participated in at least one of the rallies, which have turned out to be remarkably peaceful with hardly any arrests, and have called attention to the country's economic disparities and abuses in corporate power as well as political corruption. It all suggests that at least in some of the world's constitutional democracies, the citizens are ready and willing as ever to push for social democratic change, constructively yet forcefully, when they decide that 'enough is enough'.

New voices, emerging voices and the gradual re-making of social democrats

Do I consider myself part of the casino capitalist process by which so few have so much and so many have so little, by which Wall Street's greed and recklessness wrecked this economy? No, I don't. I believe in a society where all people do well. Not just a handful of billionaires. (Bernie Sanders, advocate of 'democratic socialism', responding to a presidential debate question asking whether he was a capitalist. [13 October 2015])

Citizens around the world are more than ready, even hungry, for governments to offer a social democratic corrective to the excesses of neoliberalism; this is why Bernie Sanders won over so many supporters, especially among younger voters, in the 2016 presidential campaign and now stands among the leading progressive voices to challenge Donald Trump and the Republican US Congress. Many American pundits initially could not grasp his appeal and wrongly gave Sanders short shrift: at age 74 during his presidential campaign, Sanders would have been the oldest president in US history, and he totally lacked the media polish usually associated with candidates for national office ever since the advent of television. Yet this also speaks to his very strength: not only does he challenge the system and its faults head-on, but his voice carries authenticity and sincerity that make it clear that his intended policies (i.e. universal health care, free education at state universities, shifting to alternative energy alternative sources in an effort to stop global warming) are for real and that he genuinely seeks to advance the interests of everyday people rather than well-heeled campaign contributors.

Yet Sanders is one of a small number of exceptional voices among elected officials in the United States – Massachusetts senator Elizabeth Warren is another – and both their stars have risen accordingly. For the most part, the momentum in many constitutional democracies (with Canada as one exception) is with the right-wing populist camp whose candidates claim to offer the easiest answers. Social democrats and their political parties still have an uphill climb ahead, both in reaching consensus among themselves and convincing their respective publics that they have a coherent governing strategy on offer, ready to put in place, that will actually succeed in improving the lives of the working-class and middle-class citizens who were formerly their core constituents, and do so in ways that will strengthen the political effectiveness and economic vitality of their countries. At the moment, they don't.

Many political observers, including Neal Lawson and Tony Wright (Chapters 10 and 12 in this volume), even doubt that the next progressive revival, whenever it does emerge, will come in the form of social democracy or amount to some other model, perhaps more original, innovative and in tune with the times. Given the economic restructuring, technological change and cultural transformations of the past half-century, with far more ethnically diverse societies than yesterday's social democrats were positioned to serve, it is clear that the post-war model of social democracy with its 'mechanistic' world of mass production and overarching dominance of industrial trade unions is not coming back; the challenge now lies in re-imagining social democracy for the twenty-first century. Social democratic voices and venues abound; we need to identify them, see what we can learn from them and think about how best to leverage them for the good of all. Presently, the voices and venues that could feed into a revitalised version of social democracy are quite diffuse and dispersed; hence this section of the chapter presents a small selection of these voices and emerging venues and offers a few thoughts about how they might fit into the revitalising of social democracy.

For starters, the array of new media platforms over the past two decades has yielded a mixed bag for democratic citizenship: new media brings new minefields, such as rampant incivility ('cyber-bullying'), narcissism and misinformation and utter trash readily available online. It has virtually shunted far too many of us into 'echo chambers', with individuals gravitating to like-minded sources of information and conversation, weakening if not wiping out the capacities of citizens to comprehend (or even notice the existence of) perspectives divergent from their own. As legal scholar and political theorist Cass Sunstein (2009: 223) has written, today's new era of personally tailored news and information, delivered on an individual basis through social media 'newsfeeds', weakens the very essence of political freedom since higher social fragmentation undermines the collective task of self-government, at least in the American context: 'Perhaps above all, a republic, or at least a heterogeneous one, requires arenas in which citizens with varying experiences and prospects, and different views about what is good and right, are able to meet with one another, and to consult.'

Even seemingly dazzling opportunities offered by the new public spaces of the internet often fall flat: joining millions of people around the world to sign online petitions, for example, on websites such as change.org or avaaz.org to reform the Bretton Woods international economic institutions or to demand that governments make a more concerted effort to curb global warming or to free political prisoners in China or to stop the US Electoral College from selecting Donald Trump as president does not mean the intended recipients will listen, even if the points in the petition are well taken. Likewise, using the internet to mobilise street demonstrations does not mean the repressive national authorities in question will step down or mend their ways. As technology writer Evgeny Morozov (2011: 26) has cautioned, 'the more Western policymakers talk up the threat that bloggers pose to authoritarian regimes, the more likely those regimes are to maneuver space where those bloggers operate'. What is more, the internet has not brought about a more equal basis for participation; the flaws in E. E. Schattschneider's elusive 'pluralist heaven' (1960), which have long enabled the more affluent interests to dominate in national politics seem to be enduring in the new media age (Bartels, 2007; Schlozman, Verba and Brady, 2012).

Nevertheless, any quest to re-make social democratic citizenship simply must include a new media dimension, considering the strength of new media platforms in mobilising activists and also given the need for closer public scrutiny, holding new media empires more accountable to their professed good intentions that often fall short in practice. Online juggernauts such as Facebook, Twitter and Google are now de facto gatekeepers and passive disseminators of news content – since so many of their one billion plus users access information through articles that their friends and acquaintances forward through these online platforms – and this cultural shift has stripped news operations of their former revenue streams (imperilling the future of professional journalism) and has also eased the way for fraudsters and manipulators (the wrong kinds of voices from the vantage point of social democracy) to circulate bogus content to millions of readers – even contributing to the Brexit and Trump outcomes in 2016. Since challenging concentrated power is what social democrats are supposed to do well, insisting that Facebook *et al.* stop such abuses within their platforms has become an important task.

Although the limits of 'clicktivism' are now highly apparent – Morozov sardonically titled his latest book *To Save Everything, Click Here* (2013) – the internet at least provides today's budding social democrats with unprecedented venues to take collective action for good causes, rather than sit out as free riders. A recent study by management scholar Ethan Mollick (2016) that examined the impact of popular crowdfunding outlet Kickstarter estimated that it has generated, since its launch in 2009, more than US$5.3 billion in economic value for project creators, 29,000 full-time jobs and 283,000 part-time jobs. All in all, the numbers are not massive in a world of 7 billion people, but they are certainly not to be dismissed. Kickstarter's board has embraced its social role, voting unanimously in September 2015 to become a 'public benefit corporation' that obligates it to account for the social impacts of its practices and decisions; the board also pledged at that time to donate 5 per cent of its after-tax profits to arts and music programmes for children and young adults, with half the donations going to 'organizations addressing systemic inequality' (Kickstarter, 2015).

Meanwhile, the micro-lending (*via* crowd-funding) outlet Kiva (the Swahili word for 'unity'), launched in San Francisco in 2005 after its founders were inspired by the work of Bangladeshi banker and social entrepreneur Muhammad Yunus, has supported more than 2.3 million borrowers across 82 countries with US$965 million in loans – with a 97 per cent repayment rate as of January 2017 (Kiva, 2017). Clearly, contributions on an ad hoc, individual basis are not the same as designing and implementing large-scale social welfare programmes or redistributing wealth, and crowd-funding and micro-lending do not qualify as substitutes for bad macro-economic policy. However, these new opportunities for creating new wealth by sharing wealth can help foster the habits of mind that lead people to see the value in public policies that open up opportunities for individuals who otherwise would find themselves left on the margins. The time has come to view social democracy and entrepreneurship as compatible in many ways; both can promote bottom-up participation in economic, political and social life, and reward initiative and ingenuity, while also providing social 'safety nets'.

Since this chapter has drawn attention to some problems in South Korea, it is worthwhile also to present a positive example in which the country's regulators used their teeth to help level the economic playing field, which tends to favour the country's dominant conglomerates. In early 2013, a South Korean government regulatory agency, the Korea Commission for Corporate Partnership (KCCP), agreed to prevent bakeries either owned or franchised by large corporations from opening up new shops within 500 metres of an existing independent bakery and also restrict total increases in corporate-affiliated bakeries nationwide to 2 per cent each year. The new regulations had the effect of spurring many bakers either to open up new shops or step up investment in their existing bakeries, and many citizens across the countries noticed the upsurge in quality and the greater choice of bread. As noted by Won-jae Lee, the President of the Hope Institute, a 'social innovation' think tank based in Seoul, while the policies were business-friendly, at least on a small scale, they also included necessary regulation: 'There are times when you need to build fences – if only to preserve entrepreneurial spirit. You don't put a lion in the same cage with a cow and expect the cow to save the meadow with its "creativity" and "entrepreneurship". It isn't just about protecting the weak – it's also about product diversity' (Lee, 2016). Whether these locally owned bakeries would qualify as meaningful venues of a revitalised social democracy might be in the eye of the beholder, but the regulation definitely helped numerous independent business people get ahead, sparing them from losing out to the concentrated corporate power that extends from neoliberalism, making it almost impossible for smaller players to enter the marketplace. This example also illustrates why social democrats need to think about 'pro-business' policies that encourage small-scale enterprises, and this goal is indeed very much compatible with a reconfigured, 'post-mechanistic' vision of social democracy.

Online media also provide many important virtual venues for today's social democrats to inform the public on crucial issues – and here social democrats have an opportunity to link more closely with environmentalists who have already used the internet effectively in this way. Consider the website AQICN.org, a voluntary social enterprise project dating back to 2007 that tracks, in real time, microscopic air pollution levels in more than 600 major cities (in 70 countries). This has helped advance public understanding of the severity of the problem while also providing a vital public health function in countries and cities prone to pollution (especially in Eastern Europe and all across Asia) as to whether the conditions in their neighbourhoods at any given moment are hazardous. Another such online, bottom-up initiative, this one specific to the UK, is CleanSpace, which relies on volunteers to carry tags conveying information on the state of the air in their immediate surroundings; this information is then compiled in real time and circulated online. Such online venues for sharing information offer plenty to a revived social democratic citizenship reliant on voluntary participation from the bottom up to call attention to serious problems in ways that ought to push them to the top of government agendas.

Today's social democrats also have important work to do – and ready-made supporters in waiting – in strengthening fair employment standards in the new workplaces of the twenty-first century. Workplaces can either be important venues of social democracy – under the right kinds of collaborative and respectful conditions – or key adversaries for social democrats to fight through legal channels as well as the informal courts of media and public opinion. High-tech companies and start-up ventures, while major sources of jobs and innovation, often fall woefully short in terms of how they treat their people – even coming across as clueless. Consider the voice of American journalist and author Dan Lyons, who became so frustrated with his employment at software developer HubSpot that he published a book (Lyons, 2016a), which quickly rose to the best-seller list, calling out the ways in which his colleagues blatantly discriminated against him as an older worker. He was 52 years old at the time, while the average HubSpot employee was 26 years old. His comments remind us that workplace diversity extends into the integration of elder workers – all the more important since our economies include so many displaced older workers who have plenty of productive years ahead if they can be matched with the right kinds of positions:

> The place was like a frat house, with refrigerators stocked with cases of beer and telemarketing sales 'bros' drinking at their desks while hammering away on the phones. Thirty-something employees were considered 'old people'... In the tech industry the practice of bros hiring bros is known as 'culture fit', and it's presented as a good thing. The problem with 'culture fit' is that unless you're a twenty-something white person, you don't fit. People of a certain age, people of color,

and women – most of us, in other words – are often unwelcome. This huge, dynamic industry, which is generating so much wealth, has walled itself off from most of the workforce, telling millions of people that they cannot participate. This situation obviously shortchanges a lot of workers, but it also hurts tech companies by depriving them of talent.

Age bias goes hand-in-hand with other forms of bias. HubSpot had many female employees, but few in top management positions. The company was run (and still is) mostly by white men. As far as I could tell, there were no African-American employees. Once, after sitting through a company all-hands meeting and being stunned by the ocean of white faces, I wrote to a woman in HR (the company's human resources office) asking if the company had any statistics on diversity. HubSpot prided itself on possessing numbers for everything, and being a 'data-driven organization'. I received a terse reply: 'No. Why?' (Lyons, 2016b)

Lyons' testimony also underscores how old-line manufacturing is no longer the dominant venue for social democratic campaigns on behalf of workers – and also how social and economic rights must be sought and attained in new kinds of venues – with real teeth, in the form of laws and regulations. Social democrats also need to press the fundamental point that more diverse and inclusive workforces are in everyone's enlightened self-interest – especially the interests of the companies in question.

The voices of beleaguered younger workers are also waiting to be engaged by social democrats; as noted in the first half of this chapter, millions of young adults now bear the brunt of the 'gig' economy often by stringing together a series of temporary jobs, while those fresh out of college often find themselves roving from internship to internship even before they begin landing a paying position of any kind (Perlin, 2011). Even as Hillary Clinton worked to relaunch her presidential campaign's key messages in early 2016 to win over the social democratic supporters of Bernie Sanders, she found herself embroiled in a controversy surrounding the prevalence of unpaid interns on her campaign staff. It turned out her campaign organisation was playing into the same kind of exploitation that Clinton was trying to reposition herself to combat. One of Clinton's former campaign volunteers, Carolyn Osorio, wrote a blistering commentary that attacked Clinton for failing to protect, let alone advance the interests of the younger voters she was trying to attract:

When Hillary announced her second run for the White House, I felt my passion for politics reignite. I quickly applied for and was offered a position as a 'Hillary for America' fellow to work on the campaign. I couldn't have been more excited – until I was told I'd have to move to Nevada and work full time on my own dime. I couldn't believe my ears. I did not apply as a routine volunteer but as a fellow. Its application process with an elaborate screening and interview process was now revealed to be an ugly lie ... Forget arguments about raising the minimum wage. I can't even get a wage. What exactly are Hillary Clinton's priorities and how do I change them? (Osorio, 2016)

Last but certainly not least, schools and educators are obviously venues and voices essential to the task of revitalising social democracy: not only to teach the next generation 'what is real', as Billy Joel put it, but also so they will think carefully for themselves, gain the capacity to formulate normative expectations for politics and society and then critically evaluate the existing political systems according to these expectations – and, of course, get involved for the sake of improvement. One promising educational initiative in the United States has designated numerous schools in economically disadvantaged locations as special community schools, which are then partnered with civil society organisations providing extra services for the students. For example, Morris Academy, located within the poorest congressional district in the United States, in the Bronx, now opens at 6.30 each weekday morning and provides its students with breakfast, along with special tutoring sessions. The programme also offers medical and dental care, psychological counselling and several recreational programmes, from a chess club to competitive dance and robotics teams. Public policy scholar David Kirp (2016) has noted that these programmes bring forward a contemporary version of 'the 19th-century settlement houses founded by the progressive activist and sociologist Jane Addams on the theory that social ills are interconnected and must be approached holistically'.

Some of the early evidence suggests these new community programmes are working; at nearly eighty elementary schools working with the 'City Connects' partnership based at Boston College, standardised test scores in English and mathematics have increased by two-thirds, and in other similar programmes, graduation rates have increased while, likewise, dropout rates have fallen. Not only are these programmes valuable in advancing equity; from an efficiency standpoint, they offer excellent value for money: a study by the Center for Benefit–Cost Studies in Education at Columbia University found that such community partnerships generate a return of at least $3 for every dollar spent. As Kirp noted, 'If City Connects were a company, Warren Buffett would snatch it up.' The programmes in themselves are not expressly ideological in any direction; they simply illustrate what it takes to help today's young people – and especially young people from disadvantaged backgrounds – gain the kind of education they will need to flourish as active and informed citizens and also to improve their career paths. If these kinds of community programmes receive the sustained investment and public support they need to grow and continue for the long term, then our prospects for reinvigorating democratic citizenship and social capital have a better chance at coming to fruition.

Conclusion: toward empowerment, engagement and equity

Empowerment, engagement and equity offer three goals – three lodestars – for a new social democratic citizenship, combining ideals of liberty, self-government, active and responsible participation toward fair and just ends, social inclusion and respect for the inherent dignity of each individual person in today's strikingly diverse societies. While keeping our eyes on these goals, today's social democrats also must reflect on the urgency of the problems we face, both within our respective countries and across our planet. The concentrations of power and wealth in unaccountable and uncaring hands that David Marquand warned about in *The New Reckoning* are no longer new – and the accompanying inequalities, polarisation and alienation have become all the more stark since then. If today's progressives are going to craft a compelling alternative to right-wing populism, the moment has come, with great urgency, to harness the kinds of voices and venues examined in this chapter – and in ever-increasing numbers to build expansive networks of political action.

Social democrats must also bring to the table an expansive moral vision of citizenship that is simultaneously locally minded and globally minded; that is responsive to citizens who naturally situate themselves in multiple, overlapping political and social communities; that lends itself to new and innovative community initiatives to uphold basic social and economic rights and widen opportunities for those hailing from less fortunate backgrounds, and can adapt to new and decentralised forms of governance. It is essential that we shift our societies toward more decentralised and, again, responsive and accountable forms of political and economic power (within states and beyond them) if we are ever going to have a shot at countering today's monopolies and oligopolies in the financial and technological sectors that enable the rich to hold ever more disproportionate access to power. This is also crucial if we are ever going to have a shot at solving the many intractable problems, most notably global warming, that otherwise elude the capabilities of any individual nation-state acting on its own. The current transatlantic drift toward right-wing populism nevertheless leaves our economies and societies configured within neoliberalism, and some of the landmark social welfare programmes that have held on thus far (i.e. Social Security and Medicare in the United States and the NHS in the UK) could be in danger of falling onto chopping blocks in the next few years. Consequently, today's social democrats need careful thinking, constant vigilance (apologies to J. K. Rowling's 'Mad Eye Moody') and, above all, vigorous political organising to create new venues for citizens to raise their voices with high levels of efficacy.

In 2016 the American conservative thinker and *New York Times* columnist David Brooks contrasted, in an essay praising a speech by (then) British Prime Minister David Cameron (2016) articulating a series of social welfare priorities that actually had some affinities with social democracy, what he outlined as 'two natural approaches to help those who are falling behind. The first we'll call the Bernie Sanders approach. Focus on economics. Provide people with money and jobs and their lifestyles will become more stable. Marriage rates will rise. Depression rates will drop. The second should be the conservative approach. Focus on social norms, community bonds and a nurturing civic fabric. People need relationships and basic security before they can respond to economic incentives.' Brooks nicely encapsulates some differences between the competing progressive and conservative approaches, but he was wrong to set up a dividing line between them. It's a false choice. Any serious strategy, by social democrats or any other political actors, to help those who have fallen behind must encompass *both* the approaches. Focusing on social norms and a nurturing civic fabric will simply not work in a climate of economic insecurity and dislocation for all but the most highly advantaged segments of the working population. Especially considering the deep entrenchment of today's social and economic inequalities, more progressive taxation that increases the obligations of the wealthy is certainly in order, and a one-time wealth tax would shift resources in the direction of those on the low end of the socio-economic spectrum. Without the investment funded by such a tax, it will be much harder for many low-income citizens to get a fighting chance.

Finally, today's social democrats need to promote a more pluralist outlook to promote 'a society where all people do well', as Sanders put it plainly. In the immediate aftermath of the November 2016 election of Donald Trump, political writer Derek Thompson pointed out that many white Americans who likely would have supported social democratic candidates and social welfare programmes in the recent past now appear to be rejecting them, partly out of racism: they believe the benefits of such programmes will go mainly to minority groups. In other words, it is quite plausible that Hillary Clinton lost ground in many key states not only because she failed to get her message across to the white working classes but also because the white working classes who *did* hear her message – namely her promises of strengthening publicly supported health care, education and child care – didn't like what they heard. As Thompson (2016) observed:

> The long-term future of the US involves rising diversity, rising inequality, and rising redistribution. The combination of these forces makes for an unstable and unpredictable system. Income stagnation and inequality encourage policies to redistribute wealth from a rich few to the anxious multitudes. But when that multitude includes minorities who are seen as benefiting disproportionately from those redistribution policies, the white majority can turn resentful. (This may be one reason why the most successful social democracies, as in Scandinavia, were initially almost all white.) … So, the country is wobbling between two extremely different futures: pluralist social democracy on the one hand, and white nativist protectionism on the other. The election's bizarre schism, with Clinton winning the popular vote and Trump winning the electoral college, is a sign of how razor-thin the margin between those dramatically opposed futures is.

This is why pluralist social democracy is indispensable for the future yet also a tough nut to crack at present. David Marquand's prescient questions from two decades ago are even more pressing at this very moment:

> Can the left and centre – and, for that matter, the non-fundamentalist right – trump the new tribalism with a tolerant, outward-looking alternative? Can it give the inevitable countermovement against market utopianism a liberal, pluralistic, social – or Christian – democratic form? Can it teach society how to protect itself from fragmentation without turning to a modern version of the man on a white horse or the damnation-spouting prophet? (Marquand, 1997: 32–3)

Regardless of whether today's social democrats can respond affirmatively to these questions, the task of re-making tomorrow's social democrats – and social democratic citizenries – will continue indefinitely, long after the next progressive revival in whatever form it finally emerges. David Marquand has offered us richly and deeply multifaceted ways of thinking about this endeavour that will long endure and, most likely, come to fruition in emergent political forums and circumstances that we have not yet fully anticipated or even conceived.

Note

1 'Allentown'. Lyrics and Music by Billy Joel. Copyright © 1975, Almo Music Corporation on behalf of Joelsongs. Used by Permission. All Rights Reserved.

References

Bartels, L. M. (2007) *Unequal Democracy: The Political Economy of the New Gilded Age* (Princeton: Princeton University Press).

Bartlett, D. L. and Steele, J. B. (1992) *America: What Went Wrong* (New York: Andrews McMeel Publishing).

Brooks, D. (2016) 'What Republicans should Say', *The New York Times* (29 January), A29. at www.nytimes.com/2016/01/29/opinion/what-republicans-should-say.html (accessed 30 January 2016).

Cameron, D. (2016) 'Prime Minister's speech on life chances', *Prime Minister's Office* (11 January). www.gov.uk/government/speeches/prime-ministers-speech-on-life-chances (accessed 30 January 2016).

Citizens Advice Bureau (2015) 'Bogus self-employment costing millions to workers and Government', *Citizens Advice Bureau* (19 August), www.citizensadvice.org.uk/about-us/how-citizens-advice-works/media/press-releases/bogus-self-employment-costing-millions-to-workers-and-government/ (accessed 27 December 2016).

Clinton, W. J. (1992) Campaign brochure. www.4president.org/brochures/billclinton1992brochure.htm (accessed 18 December 2016).

Duane, D. (2016) 'The tent cities of San Francisco', *The New York Times*, 17 December, SR1. www.nytimes.com/2016/12/17/opinion/sunday/the-tent-cities-of-san-francisco.html (accessed 18 December 2016).

Duckworth, A. L. (2016) *Grit: The Power of Passion and Perseverance* (New York: Scribner).

Dweck, C. S. (2007) *Mindset: The New Psychology of Success* (New York: Ballantine Books).

Fifield, A. (2016) 'Young South Koreans call their country "hell" and look for ways out', *The Washington Post*, 31 January. www.washingtonpost.com/world/asia_pacific/young-south-koreans-call-their-country-hell-and-look-for-ways-out/2016/01/30/34737c06–b967–11e5–85cd-5ad59bc19432_story.html (accessed 4 February 2016).

Hardoon, D., Ayele, S. and Fuentes-Niva, R. (2016) 'An economy for the 1 percent', *Oxfam International* (18 January). www.oxfam.org/sites/www.oxfam.org/files/file_attachments/bp210–economy-one-percent-tax-havens-180116–en_0.pdf (accessed 10 January 2017).

Hertz, N. (2016) 'Think millennials have it tough? For "Generation K", life is even harsher', *Guardian*, 13 March. www.theguardian.com/world/2016/mar/19/think-millennials-have-it-tough-for-generation-k-life-is-even-harsher (accessed 19 December 2016).

Hirschmann, A. O. (1970) *Exit, Voice and Loyalty* (Cambridge: Harvard University Press).

Inchley, J. *et al.* (2016) 'Growing up unequal. HBSC 2016 study', *World Health Organization*. www.euro.who.int/en/health-topics/Life-stages/child-and-adolescent-health/health-behaviour-in-school-aged-children-hbsc/growing-up-unequal.-hbsc-2016–study-20132014–survey (accessed 20 December 2016).

Inglehart, R. F. and Norris, P. (2016) 'Trump, Brexit and the rise of populism: economic have-nots and cultural backlash', Harvard Kennedy School Faculty Research Working Paper Series. https://research.hks.harvard.edu/publications/getFile.aspx?Id=1401.

Joel, B. (1982) 'Allentown', Columbia Records. www.billyjoel.com/song/allentown-12/ (accessed 7 September 2016).

Kickstarter (2015) 'Kickstarter is a benefit corporation'. www.kickstarter.com/charter (accessed 4 January 2017).

Kimball, W. and Scott, R. E. (2014) 'China trade, outsourcing and jobs', *Economic Policy Institute*. www.epi.org/publication/china-trade-outsourcing-and-jobs/ (accessed 21 December 2016).

Kirp, D. L. (2016) 'To teach a child to read, first give him glasses', *The New York Times* (6 August), p. SR7. www.nytimes.com/2016/08/07/opinion/sunday/to-teach-a-child-to-read-first-give-him-glasses.html?partner=rss&emc=rss (accessed 8 August 2016).

Kiva (2017) 'Kiva by the numbers'. Accessed on 9 January 2017 at www.kiva.org/about

Klein, N. (2016) 'It was the rise of the Davos class that sealed America's fate', *Guardian*, 9 November. www.theguardian.com/commentisfree/2016/nov/09/rise-of-the-davos-class-sealed-americas-fate (accessed 10 November 2016).

Lee, W. J. (2016) 'Vision and opportunity lead to changes in our neighborhood bakeries', *The Hankyoreh* (4 March). http://english.hani.co.kr/arti/english_edition/e_editorial/733346.html (accessed 7 March 2016).

Lyons, D. (2016a) *Disrupted: My Misadventure in the Start-Up Bubble* (New York: Hachette Book Group).

Lyons, D. (2016b) 'When it comes to age bias, tech companies don't even bother to lie', *LinkedIn Pulse* (5 April). www.linkedin.com/pulse/when-comes-age-bias-tech-companies-dont-even-bother-lie-dan-lyons.

Marquand, D. (1997) *The New Reckoning: Capitalism, States and Citizens* (Cambridge: Polity).

Marquand, D. (2015) 'Can social democracy rise to the challenge of the far right across Europe?' *New Statesman* (8 December). www.newstatesman.com/culture/books/2015/12/can-social-democracy-rise-challenge-far-right-across-europe (accessed 17 November 2016).

Mollick, E. R. (2016) 'Containing multitudes: the many impacts of Kickstarter funding', *Social Science Research Network*. https://papers.ssrn.com/sol3/papers.cfm?abstract_id=2808000. (accessed 4 January 2017).

Moon, K. H. S. (2016) 'South Korea's shamanic panic: Park Geun-hye's scandal in context', *Foreign Affairs* (1 December). www.foreignaffairs.com/articles/

south-korea/2016–12–01/south-koreas-shamanic-panic?cid=soc-tw-rdr (accessed 17 December 2016).

Morozov, E. (2011) *The Net Delusion: The Dark Side of Internet Freedom* (New York: PublicAffairs).

Morozov, E. (2013) *To Save Everything, Click Here: The Folly of Technological Solutionism* (New York: PublicAffairs).

Osorio, C. G. (2016) 'Hillary, pay your interns', *USA Today*, 23 June. www.usatoday.com/story/opinion/2015/06/23/hillary-clinton-unpaid-intern-mill enials-column/28936259/ (accessed 11 January 2017).

Perlin, R. (2011) *Intern Nation: How to Earn Nothing and Learn Little in the Brave New Economy* (New York: Verso).

Piketty, T., Saez, E. and Zucman, G. (2016) 'Distributional national accounts: methods and estimates for the United States', Washington Center for Equitable Growth, Working Paper Series http://cdn.equitablegrowth.org/wp-content/ uploads/2016/12/05095108/120716–WP-distributional-national-accounts.pdf (accessed 8 January 2016).

Putnam, R. D. (2000) *Bowling Alone: The Collapse and Revival of American Community* (New York: Simon & Schuster).

Reich, R. B. (1991) *The Work of Nations* (New York: Knopf).

Reich, R. B. (1998) *Locked in the Cabinet* (New York: Vintage).

Sachs, J. D. (2016) 'The age of impunity', *The Boston Globe*, 13 May. www.bostonglobe.com/opinion/2016/05/12/the-age-impunity/.../story.html (accessed 14 May 2016).

Sandel, M. J. (1996) *Democracy's Discontent: America in Search of a Public Philosophy* (Cambridge: The Belknap Press of Harvard University).

Schlozman, K. L., Verba, S. and Brady, H. (2012) *The Unheavenly Chorus: Unequal Political Voice and the Broken Promise of American Democracy* (Princeton: Princeton University Press).

Schwartz, N. D. (2016) 'In an age of privilege, not everyone is in the same boat', *The New York Times* (23 April). www.nytimes.com/2016/04/24/business/economy/ velvet-rope-economy.html (accessed 19 December 2016).

Smeeding, T. M. (2016) *Gates, Gaps, and Intergenerational Mobility: The Importance of an Even Start* (New York: Springer).

Smith, C. (2016) 'Amazon workers sleeping in tents near Dunfermline site', *The Courier* (10 December). www.thecourier.co.uk/fp/news/local/fife/325800/exclusiv e-amazon-workers-sleeping-in-tents-near-dunfermline-site/ (accessed 14 December 2016).

Sunstein, C. R. (2009) *Republic.com 2.0.* (Princeton: Princeton University Press).

Thompson, D. (2016) 'The dangerous myth that Hillary Clinton ignored the working class', *The Atlantic*, 5 December. www.theatlantic.com/business/archive/2016/12/ hillary-clinton-working-class/509477/ (accessed 6 December 2016).

Wallach, L. (2014) 'NAFTA at 20: One million US jobs lost, higher income inequality', *The World Post* (8 March). www.huffingtonpost.com/lori-wallach/ nafta-at-20–one-million-u_b_4550207.html (accessed 7 September 2016).

Yon, H. B. and Noh, H. W. (2016) 'Already OECD lowest, South Korea's birthrate getting worse', *The Hankyoreh* (28 August). http://english.hani.co.kr/arti/english_ edition/e_national/758664.html (accessed 7 January 2017).

6

A Marquandian moment? The civic republican political theory of David Marquand

Stuart White

Introduction[1]

David Marquand's work emerges from, and engages with, the crisis of social democracy, particularly as this has developed in the UK since the 1970s. As a Labour MP in the 1960s and 1970s, Marquand was well placed to witness the emergence of this crisis and one reason for his leaving Parliament in 1976 was to find the space to reflect upon it. Making use of this space, Marquand has gradually developed a civic republican political theory, a response to the New Right but also to the limitations of traditional Labour politics. My aim here is to explore how this civic republican perspective emerged; to identify its core elements; and to offer an assessment.

The first section traces the way in which Marquand develops a civic republican political theory across four key works: *The Unprincipled Society* (1988), *The New Reckoning* (1997), *Britain Since 1918* (2008) and *Mammon's Kingdom* (2014). The second section tries to identify the core elements of this civic republicanism. The third identifies some criticisms of Marquand's civic republicanism. Finally, I suggest that Marquand's focus on republican political process, centred on discussion and 'mutual education', has considerable relevance in the present UK. J. G. A. Pocock famously wrote of the 'Machiavellian moment' in which the problem of founding a lasting republic is posed (Pocock, 1975). In a related vein, I want to suggest that the UK is reaching a 'Marquandian moment' in which the national deliberation about shared purpose and the common good that Marquand calls for repeatedly in his work potentially has a key role to play in addressing the emerging challenges of national self-definition.

The development of Marquand's civic republicanism

The Unprincipled Society

Let's begin with Marquand's first major attempt to survey the problems of the UK and propose a way forward in his book, *The Unprincipled Society*. The book was written in the mid-1980s, in the context of Marquand's deep involvement with the SDP-Liberal Alliance. It was published in 1988, just as the Alliance project came off the rails. Nevertheless, it was very influential and can be seen as one in a series of key texts in which thinkers on the British left and centre-left started to reappraise the UK state in the light of the governments of Margaret Thatcher (Howe, 2009: 10).

Reflecting the widespread concern with Britain's economic decline, the book takes as its starting point the UK's 'adjustment failure' in the global economy. Marquand argues that the main source of the failure is that the UK has the wrong kind of state. Specifically, unlike countries that industrialised later, it does not have a 'developmental state' able to engage the cooperation of various social groups in joint pursuit of a shared 'public purpose'. The reigning philosophy behind the 'Westminster state' is one of scepticism towards the very idea of shared public purpose. The dominant public philosophy sees only individuals with their preferences and attendant interests, and sees the role of the state as securing fairly these individual interests. Croslandite social democrats and 'neoliberal' free marketeers may differ on what this requires (e.g., regarding the level of tax and spend). But they actually share the same underlying philosophical individualism. To address its economic problems, Marquand argues, the UK must create its own version of a 'developmental state', and this requires a new public philosophy centred on an account of the UK's shared public purpose.

This cannot be thought up by a single author and imposed on British society, however. It must emerge from shared discussion and debate. The logical next step forward, therefore, is to create the institutional conditions in which this kind of discussion and a related 'politics of mutual education' can happen (Marquand, 1988: 12–13, 67–8). For the established structures of the UK state are not set up to foster this kind of dialogue. With the emergence of twentieth-century party politics, they have tended to foster a 'winner takes all' model of government in which an executive drawn from the dominant party in the House of Commons, acting in the name of the sovereign Crown-in-Parliament, asserts its singular will, more or less uncompromisingly, across all the territories of the UK. Institutionally, the need to break with this model points towards an agenda of radical political reform to federalise and otherwise pluralise political power.[2] This was consistent with the ideas of Marquand's comrade in the Parliamentary Labour Party in the 1960s and 1970s, John P. Mackintosh, a political science academic as well as an MP who was an early supporter of creating a devolved assembly in Scotland (Walker, 2013). It was also consistent with a wider emerging critique of the UK state on the left and centre that was shortly to coalesce around Charter 88 (Ascherson, 1988; Barnett, 1988; 1997).

Although Marquand does not describe his viewpoint at this stage as a 'republican' one, it has affinities with civic republicanism in a broad sense in that it emphasises the idea of politics properly aiming, through public deliberation, at some kind of substantive common good. The critique of the British state is also at the same time a critique of what Marquand sees as the dominant mode of citizenship within this state: a mode which emphasises what one is due from the state by way of rights and services, but much less what one properly owes to the community. The pluralised state that he argues for would draw more people into active citizenship. At the level of academic political theory, Marquand's references include Alasdair MacIntyre's *After Virtue* (MacIntyre, 1981; Marquand, 1988: 214–15, 220). This was a major contribution to the so-called 'liberal-communitarian debate' in Anglo-American academic political theory in the 1980s, and one can see Marquand mapping his own argument about Britain on to this debate, aligning his view with the communitarian critique and, by implication, the ruling philosophy of the British state with the liberalism being critiqued.

The New Reckoning

Republicanism is, however, very explicitly centre stage in the essays that Marquand collected in *The New Reckoning* (1997). Many of these essays were written in the late 1980s and early 1990s in the context of a wider public debate around the concept of 'citizenship', which I shall refer to as *the citizenship debate* (Heater, 1991). As Marquand explained in his essay, 'Reinventing Civic Republicanism', from 1991, one important stimulus to this debate was the aforementioned Charter 88, a campaign for a codified, democratic constitution for the UK that emerged in 1988 as an initiative of the *New Statesman* magazine (Barnett, 1988; Evans, 1995; Marquand, 1997a; Howe, 2009). Based on a coming together of the political centre and radical democratic currents from the New Lefts, the Charter called for electoral reform (proportional representation) for the House of Commons, devolution of power to the 'regions', a freedom of information act, a democratic second chamber of Parliament, a Bill of Rights, and a codified constitution to integrate the package of reforms. The focus on the territorial distribution of powers was also stimulated by the emergence of the Scottish Constitutional Convention, a cross-party campaign for a Scottish Parliament supported by many significant institutions of Scottish civil society. This reform agenda was very much in the spirit of Marquand's argument in *The Unprincipled Society*. Marquand was on the first list of Charter signatories published in the *New Statesman* in December 1988, and contributed to Charter 88-related publications (Marquand, 1993; 1994). But there were other voices in the citizenship debate. Douglas Hurd articulated a Tory concern about fraying social cohesion and called for a form of active citizenship expressed in local, voluntary service (Heater, 1991: 140–2; Marquand, 1997a). There was a House of Commons Speaker's Commission on Citizenship and much discussion of the concept in left circles (Mouffe, 1988; Andrews, 1991).

Reviewing this debate in his own 1991 article, Marquand argues that it is helpful to distinguish 'liberal individualist' and 'civic republican' conceptions of citizenship. The former sees citizenship as a 'status', centred on rights, and sees 'no obligation to participate in the public affairs of the community' (Marquand, 1997a: 45). The latter sees citizenship as a 'practice'. It is a practice that is public, political and oriented to the good of the community. Relatedly, 'citizenship is about duties, not about rights' (Marquand, 1997a: 46):

> Citizenship is growing, becoming, *doing*. In an important sense, it is a task: strenuous, stretching, and at first forbidding … While civic republicanism is optimistic in assuming that human beings can grow in this way, it is pessimistic (or perhaps realistic) in recognising that it is hard for them to do so and that they can easily regress. And one of the most insidious threats … is the possessive hedonism which lies at the heart of the free-market model of man and society and perhaps the liberal-individualist conception of citizenship as well. (Marquand, 1997a: 46–7)

From the vantage-point of this civic republican ideal, Marquand finds fault both with Hurd's Tory active citizen and with Charter 88's rights-bearing citizen. The Tory active citizen is active, but depoliticised; he is 'an incomplete, even deformed, creature' because the 'activities in which he is being asked to engage … have nothing to do with citizenship' (Marquand, 1997a: 48). While Marquand hears 'a faint echo of civic republicanism in Charter 88's critique of the culture of subjecthood', he sees it as more expressive of a liberal individualist conception of citizenship for 'the Charter says nothing about duty or activity' (Marquand, 1997a: 49).

Marquand returns to this contrast, and also nuances it, in a 1997 paper, 'Liberalism's Revenge?', which assesses New Labour at its moment of electoral triumph. Marquand is bracingly sceptical. Specifically, he argues that while New Labour is committed to an impressive range of constitutional reforms, including some proposed by Charter 88, it actually seems hostile to the vision of political process, and of active citizenship, which makes sense of them. As a result, it is not clear New Labour understands what a complete and coherent reform programme looks like.

It is worth pausing here to see why, in Marquand's view, historic Labour Party politics is constitutively incompatible with what he understands as civic republicanism. Historically, Marquand argues, Labour has been committed to a politics of 'hegemony': of seeking 'total control of the state' as a means for comprehensive social change. It has held that '[t]he goal of social transformation made hegemony necessary and the pursuit of hegemony legitimate' (Marquand, 1997b: 82). The commitment to hegemony implies a strong aversion to coalition with other parties, rejecting 'a politics of negotiation and coalition-building … as a permanent feature of the landscape' (Marquand, 1997b: 82). But it is precisely in such processes of negotiation – which Marquand associates with deliberation – that republicanism, as a practice, as a mode of politics, lives. Republican politics thus has to be 'pluralist' and thus requires Labour to adopt a 'post-hegemonic' perspective, in which it is prepared to share power 'with other "progressive" forces and to jettison the first-past-the-post electoral system that made Old Labour's hegemonial ambitions appear feasible' (Marquand, 1997b: 83). New Labour's constitutional reforms, notably devolution, do point in this pluralist direction. However, its internal politics, putting a strong emphasis on unity in support of the leadership, is a different matter. This is 'as remote from the liberal ideal of a reflective and deliberative politics of free discussion and debate as was the solidaristic, "collectivist" Labourism of the past' (Marquand, 1997b: 83). Marquand thus identifies an important continuity between Labour and New Labour: an underlying hostility to 'reflective and deliberative politics'. Unable to articulate a republican political philosophy based on this deliberative ideal, New Labour:

> has advocated constitutional reform on liberal-individualist grounds, not on communitarian or republican ones … its constitutional agenda has looked … like a rag-bag of concessions to radical-individualist chic [rather] than a set of

building blocks for a politics of social cohesion and public purpose. (Marquand, 1997b: 89)

A related concern is that New Labour has not fully grasped what is wrong with the British state and therefore just how far restructuring needs to go:

> the British state is not, and cannot be, a proper vehicle for the values of solidarity and common citizenship. It wears the trappings of democracy, but its institutions, its iconography, the symbols and rituals that tell its managers who they are and the operational codes that tell them what to do are all saturated with pre-democratic values. It can deliver... high-quality public goods from the top down, but the very notion of a politics of civic activism runs against its grain. (Marquand, 1997b: 89)

As the title of the essay and the quotes above suggest, Marquand nuances in this essay the very stark contrast between liberalism and republicanism of the earlier essay. Marquand distinguishes now between a 'bastard liberalism' ('thin', 'procedural' and rights-centred) and, referencing the work of Michael Sandel and Michael Walzer, a better liberalism that is informed by 'left communitarianism or republicanism' (Walzer, 1983; Marquand, 1997b: 86; Sandel, 1996). The latter sees how a flourishing political community depends on 'mutual obligations, shared loyalties and civic virtues which the language of individual rights cannot capture' (Marquand, 1997b: 86). A republicanism of this sort is vital, he argues to a 'social-liberal project in the economic domain – a project aimed at "moralizing the market"' (Marquand, 1997b: 87). He reasserts his view, however, that 'the dominant strand in the constitutional reform movement is not republican' in this sense (Marquand, 1997b: 87).

Britain Since 1918

This paper was written at the start of the New Labour era. Marquand's *Britain Since 1918* was written towards its end, appearing in 2008 after Gordon Brown had become Prime Minister (Marquand, 2008). The book is a history of British politics from 1918 structured around the interaction of four competing political traditions: Whig imperialism, Tory nationalism, democratic collectivism and, last and in a sense least, 'democratic republicanism' (Marquand, 2008: 44). Whig imperialism is the dominant philosophy of the British political establishment: 'It came from the heart of the most relaxed and confident political elite in Europe' (Marquand, 2008: 44). Its watchwords are gradual progress, evolution, accommodation and balance. It seeks accommodation between different cultures and between conflicting social interests. It pursues reform judiciously, balanced by conservation. It projects a narrative of empire as the export of liberty. Tory nationalism is a more pessimistic philosophy. It sees politics as the management of permanent and serious threats to order, authority, property and hierarchy. In pursuit of these ends, it tends to be less accommodating than Whig imperialism and less willing to countenance reform. Democratic collectivism is technocratic and managerial, looking to the state as the carrier of scientifically guided social reform. And democratic republicanism? Democratic republicans are 'the awkward squad of British democracy', having 'no truck with Burkean gentlemen or the British tradition of autonomous executive power' (Marquand, 2008: 67). Putting 'their faith in the kinetic energy of ordinary citizens', they stand for 'republican self-respect versus monarchical servility; civic activity versus slothful apathy; and, most of all, government by vigorous discussion and mutual learning versus passive deference to monarch, capitalist or state' (Marquand, 2008: 68).

Marquand's own sympathies are clearly with the democratic republicans, and this is expressed in the first main chapter of the book which reviews the emergence of democracy in Britain from the seventeenth to the twentieth century in a way that also sketches some of the key movements in the democratic republican tradition (e.g., the Levellers, the British Jacobins and the Chartists). At the level of academic political theory, Marquand connects this tradition to Quentin Skinner's work on the republican or 'neo-roman' conception of liberty (Skinner, 1998).

For most of the story that Marquand tells, democratic republicanism is on the margins. Whig imperialism prevails (e.g., in the governments of Baldwin and Macmillan), punctuated by dramatic episodes of democratic collectivism (the 1945–51 Labour governments) or Tory nationalism (the dominant strand in Margaret Thatcher's governments). Marquand sees democratic republicanism beginning to resurface in an unconscious way in the New Lefts and in second-wave feminism in the 1960s/1970s, but emerging more fully into its own in the 1980s/1990s. Unsurprisingly perhaps, Marquand sees it in the SDP-Liberal Alliance of the 1980s, though more so in its Liberal wing (Marquand, 2008: 289–90). But, with an eye clearly on debates that he himself contributed to, Marquand sees it as emerging especially strongly as part of a critical reaction in the later years of the Thatcher governments, in connection with what we referred to above as the citizenship debate:

> Albeit in widely different forms, they [the new wave of critics in the late 1980s] expressed a widely held feeling that Thatcher's counter-revolution, the collapse of Communism and the global capitalist renaissance had, between them, created

a new social world, with which only a new politics could cope. Most of them shared a broadly democratic-republican conception of politics and the good life, as distant from conventional Labour *étatisme* as from Thatcherism. Their chief target was the British state tradition and its impact on the economy and society. They did not agree about what to put in its place, but they were all groping for richer, more inclusive and more pluralistic forms of democratic citizenship and the public realm. (Marquand, 2008: 329)

This review involves some change in perspective and reinterpretation of movements in the late 1980s and early 1990s. As we have seen, while Marquand was supportive of Charter 88 in its heyday, he was also critical of it and hesitant to see it as expressing a republican philosophy. Looking back in *Britain Since 1918*, however, he now sees Charter 88 as clearly in the democratic republican tradition. Under the leadership of Anthony Barnett, he writes:

Charter 88 was part social movement, part pressure group and part secular dissenting chapel. The atmosphere of slightly earnest goodwill would not have surprised the debaters in Putney Church in 1647 or the corresponding societies [British Jacobins] of the 1790s … Its methods were comparatively decorous, but the blood of the British Jacobins and the Levellers ran in its veins. The charter's conception of democracy was law-based, rights-centred, pluralistic and, at least by implication, participatory. (Marquand, 2008: 333–4)

The re-emergence of democratic republicanism finds even more forceful expression in Scotland at this time where, according to Marquand 'the democratic republican tradition of civic engagement and popular sovereignty has always had deeper roots … than in England' (Marquand, 2008: 335). Central here is the 1988 *Claim of Right for Scotland*, drafted by Jim Ross, and the aforementioned Scottish Constitutional Convention that brought together political parties and civil society groups to advance the Claim's assertion of Scotland's right to self-government in the form of a Scottish Parliament. The emphasis on the republican value of popular sovereignty is striking: 'Kenyon Wright, who chaired its executive committee, distilled its purpose in a brilliant soundbite: "What happens when that other voice we know so well [Margaret Thatcher's] responds by saying, 'We say No, We are the State.' Well, We say Yes and We are the People"' (Marquand, 2008: 338).

Marquand also looks back at New Labour. His earlier concerns about the limited and possibly incoherent quality of New Labour's constitutional reforms are seen as vindicated. Blair and his colleagues refused to accept the 'logic of their own intentions'. Although forms of self-government were introduced for Scotland, Wales and Northern Ireland, 'England was not treated at all'. The restructuring of the UK as a federal state, 'with England as one of the constituent states ... required a leap of imagination' that New Labour was not capable of. It also continued to treat local government in England with contempt and adopted a progressively more authoritarian position on civil liberties. The book ends, however, on an optimistic note. The incomplete and incoherent constitutional reforms of the first New Labour government have destabilised the British state. Marquand implies that when we finally come to address the underlying problems, the democratic republican tradition may at last find its moment. Of the four traditions surveyed in the book, it is, Marquand claims, the only one that does not look exhausted and irrelevant.

Mammon's Kingdom

If *Britain Since 1918* conveys this tentative optimism, *Mammon's Kingdom* (2014) is rooted in a perplexed frustration, indeed real anger, at political developments since 2008. The perplexity consists in the way the financial crash of 2008 seems to have strengthened the politics that led to it. Marquand's explanation is cultural as well as governmental. At the cultural level, notions of public service, duty and honour that were part of the ideology of post-war social democracy have fallen before a 'market individualism' and 'moral individualism': 'Slowly, incompletely, but unmistakably, today's hedonistic and relativist culture elbowed aside the old culture of honour and duty' (Marquand, 2014: 57). This is reinforced by 'presentism', a tendency to disparage the past and to celebrate the new as new (Marquand, 2014: 65–6). Reprising some ideas from his *Decline of the Public* (2004), Marquand argues that privatisation and marketisation have weakened the 'public realm' and with it norms of public service and citizenship that are distinct from those of the market (Marquand, 2014: 96–110). This focus on culture reflects a deepening of the concern for the individual-level character and behaviour we see in all the earlier works, and to which the notion of republican citizenship as a virtuous practice is a response. Perhaps given more emphasis in *Mammon's Kingdom*, however, is the power of business over government. Earlier work noted the immense power of the City of London within the UK state, endorsing the argument that this has served British industry poorly. But the City today is stronger than ever. More generally, business corporations exercise enormous influence. The result is a polity in which 'democratic forms conceal an increasingly oligarchic substance' (Marquand, 2014: 170):

> Thanks to party dependence on rich donors, to exceptionally close links between parliamentarians and big firms and, above all, to the revolving door, the corporate

> elite, what remains of the old public-service elite and the handful of politicians who manage to climb the greasy pole have merged into an informal constellation of power with shared values, assumptions and expectations. (Marquand, 2014: 175)

This oligarchical shift is complemented and enhanced by the rise of 'populism' within contemporary politics that denigrates reasoned discussion.

What is to be done? In general terms, the answer is that the economy needs to be remoralised, regrounded in a conception of the common good that people accept places legitimate limits on the pursuit of self-interest. In view of climate change, this is not merely desirable but essential. There are, Marquand argues, 'intimations of a challenge' along these lines in the form of initiatives like Citizens UK, UK Uncut, Occupy, and the green movement. But these sparks need to be fanned into a much bigger flame. How to do this? Here Marquand turns full circle back to the central theme of *The Unprincipled Society*: the need for a wide, inclusive public discussion through which a working account of our common good can be thrashed out: 'The ultimate objective is change, not talk. But there can be no worthwhile change without a new public philosophy; and the last, best hope for discovering such a philosophy lies in talking together and learning from each other' (Marquand, 2014: 187). And, once again, one way to promote this politics of discussion and mutual learning is through new institutions that decentralise and pluralise power. The Scottish Parliament and devolved assemblies created by New Labour have already 'tapped civic energies that were barely in evidence a generation ago' (Marquand, 2014: 219). Going further in this direction, we need to 'rescue local government from its status as the humiliated Cinderella of English governance', make wide use of citizens' assemblies selected by lot, and establish a constitutional convention to discuss the possible structure of a new, federal UK (Marquand, 2014: 219). In this way we can assert a counter-populist conception of democracy, one that is centred on Amartya Sen's notion of public reason, and that involves the practice of the republican virtues of the 'free citizen' (Sen, 2009; Marquand, 2014: 181, 217–19).

The core elements of Marquand's civic republicanism

I have spent some time setting out how Marquand's conception of civic republicanism emerges through the course of his four main works. Before turning to assess it, I want to try to clarify its basic conceptual architecture. I suggest there are three key elements: (1) a normative ideal of deliberative democracy; (2) a related conception of active citizenship and civic virtue; and (3) an institutional commitment to federalising and pluralising power across the polity and economy. Let's take each in turn.

A normative ideal of deliberative democracy

Perhaps the foundational idea in philosophical terms is an ideal of democracy as properly centred on deliberation. By 'deliberation' here I mean reason-giving and, moreover, reason-giving that is aimed at identifying and pursuing a legitimate, shared public purpose or common good. In both *The Unprincipled Society* and *Mammon's Kingdom*, Marquand explicitly eschews putting forward his own detailed reform programme to tackle Britain's economic decline (*The Unprincipled Society*) or roaring inequality (*Mammon's Kingdom*). Instead, he tells us that, in essence, we need to talk about it. More specifically, we need to talk in a way that tries to sort out what purposes or goods we share that can then serve as guides to the development of a concrete policy programme. In so far as Marquand makes prescriptions they focus on political reforms to help get the conversation going.

There is of course a large literature in academic political theory on deliberative democracy (Freeman, 2000). Marquand's conception differs from some influential accounts of deliberative democracy, however, in not making any sharp distinction between considerations of the 'right' and the 'good'. In Rawlsian and related accounts, for instance, the common good is typically elaborated in terms of notions of justice and rights: the 'primary goods' secured through justice, such as specific liberties and a fair share of opportunities and resources, are what citizens hold in common, and these instrumental goods are distinct from citizens' 'conceptions of the good life' – essentially, what they pursue with their liberties, opportunities and resources – which are inevitably very different and sometimes stand in opposition (Rawls, 1993). Marquand seems to think that the common good has to consist of more than this, that it must touch on the nature of the 'good life' itself. In this respect, his conception of deliberative democracy retains a 'communitarian' quality.[3]

Does Marquand value deliberative democracy intrinsically or instrumentally? The argument certainly has an instrumental pitch. In *The Unprincipled Society*, we need a politics of dialogue and mutual education as a precondition for economic renewal. In *Mammon's Kingdom*, we need it to get a fairer and greener economy. Indeed, the instrumental side of the argument is part of what keeps Marquand's civic republicanism connected in a broad way with social democracy, the expectation being that deliberative politics will gravitate somewhat towards social democratic institutions and policies, though not necessarily in a conventional form. However, it seems clear that Marquand also places a great intrinsic value on this ideal. Or, if the appeal is instrumental, it is not simply to extrinsic economic goods, or to social democratic policy, but lies also in the activity that deliberative democracy draws out of the individual as a citizen. This brings us directly to the second core element of Marquand's civic republicanism, perhaps its most fundamental element.

The virtuous, active citizen

When people do the work of deliberative democracy they necessarily enter into a practice, and this practice requires and helps cultivate certain skills and aptitudes – 'virtues' in the language of classical political theory. A repeated theme in Marquand's work is the desirability of this practice and its virtues. This emphasis is distinct from the emphasis that many contemporary republican theorists place either on structural norms (such as freedom as non-domination) and/or on institutional designs, and represents a point of commonality with recent republican theory that focuses more on the *doing* of republicanism in social and political movements and on its attendant practices and qualities of character (Nabulsi, 2008; Gourevitch, 2015). Marquand often describes or implies the relevant virtues by focusing on corresponding vices. Here is an attempt to assemble a list of Marquandian civic virtues and their opposing vices.

Activity: The first virtue, so to speak is that one is active in political, decision-making contexts: 'Citizenship is growing, becoming, *doing*' (Marquand, 1997: 46). Citizenship involves politically centred 'civic activity' (Marquand, 2008: 68); 'the democratic republican tradition' is one of 'civic engagement' (Marquand, 2008: 335). This focus on activity stands opposed to the vices of 'slothful apathy' and '*passive* deference' (Marquand, 2008: 68, emphasis added).

Deliberativeness: More specifically, what does one do when active as a citizen? In Marquand's view, a central part of the answer is that you engage in discussion, with receptivity to others: 'politics [is] … a process of mutual education, in which the members of a community listen to and learn from each other' (Marquand, 1988: 67–8). Democracy should approach an 'ideal of a reflective and deliberative politics of free discussion' (Marquand, 1997: 83); there should be a willingness by citizens to engage in 'vigorous discussion' (Marquand, 2008: 68). This stands opposed to the Labourist emphasis on 'hegemony' with its attendant requirement that 'individual party members … subordinate themselves to the disciplines of the group' (Marquand, 1997: 82); and it stands opposed to 'passive *deference*' (Marquand, 2008: 68, emphasis added).

Equality: The active citizen engages with other citizens, in public deliberation, as an equal. This egalitarianism is related to 'republican self-respect' (Marquand, 2008: 68). It is exemplified in R. H. Tawney's opposition to Labour politicians taking places in the House of Lords (Marquand, 2008: 74). It connects to an appropriate 'disdain for the time-worn traditions and reflexes of British parliamentary monarchy' (Marquand, 2008: 117), and it is also reflected in Margaret Thatcher's 'Paineite contempt for the old, metropolitan establishment' (Marquand, 2008: 278). It stands opposed to vices such as 'monarchical servility' (Marquand, 2008: 68) and to a politics that is 'hierarchical, not participatory' (Marquand, 1997a: 181).

Self-control: Civic activity on the above terms requires self-control. The active citizen must have 'fortitude, self-discipline, a willingness to make hard choices in the public interest and to accept responsibility for them' (Marquand, 2013: 219). The self-controlling active citizen accepts that 'the common good comes before individual appetites' (Marquand, 2013: 222). This stands opposed to just acting for personal pleasure: 'possessive hedonism' (Marquand, 1997a: 47); 'egoistic hedonism' (Marquand, 2013: 2); immersion in a 'hedonistic and relativist culture' (Marquand, 2013: 57).

Reciprocity: Also implicit in the foregoing account of the active citizen, connected to deliberativeness, equality and self-control, are various kinds of reciprocity and solidarity: 'a political community is … a web of reciprocal duties and rights' (Marquand, 1988: 67). 'The ethos [of the public realm]', writes Marquand, 'is Aristotelian: solidarity, its key value' (Marquand, 2013: 97). These stand opposed to 'bastard liberalism' (Marquand, 1997: 85) and to '*egoistic* hedonism' (Marquand, 2013: 2, emphasis added).

Growth: The corollary of being an active citizen who exhibits the above qualities is that one experiences a kind of personal growth: 'growth, activity, learning, and mutuality.… the Self … [is] something shaped through constant interaction with other selves in a common and testing endeavour' (Marquand, 1997: 51). The overall pattern of growth is indicated as follows: '[t]he dialogue that makes persuasion possible requires tolerance, generosity of spirit, intellectual honesty, a willingness to engage with others, a certain magnanimity and above all openness to new ideas' (Marquand, 2013: 159).

I have noted here how Marquand's account of deliberative democracy focuses on deliberation in the search of a common good that implicates the good life itself. Here we see that, for Marquand, the practice of citizenship at the core of this conception of deliberative democracy is itself a great good, almost certainly itself a central part of the good life. The value of deliberative democracy lies, in part, in bringing out of us this good life.

Federalising and pluralising power

The third core element in Marquand's civic republicanism is his persistent commitment to institutional reforms, in the polity but also in the economy, that have the effect of federalising and pluralising decision-making power. This is seen as necessary to create the institutional contexts for deliberative democracy and the associated form of virtuous, active citizenship. In the UK context, this has obviously involved Marquand supporting reform agendas such as Charter 88, particularly moves towards electoral reform and devolution. It is reflected in his commitment to 'rescue' local government in England and, in his most recent work, to sortition. It is also one current in his support for ideas of 'stakeholder capitalism' that aim to create new decision-making structures within firms. As already intimated, this dispersive conception of democracy, as one might call it, puts Marquand's civic republicanism inevitably at odds with both Labourism and Thatcherism as political projects that seek to concentrate power for the sake of facilitating social transformation.

Assessing Marquand's civic republicanism

Having traced the evolution of Marquand's civic republicanism, and identified its core elements, I now venture a preliminary assessment. In this section I note some objections before turning in the conclusion to an argument for its contemporary relevance.

One objection to Marquand's republicanism is that it is too *consensualist*. A related objection is that it is too *perfectionistic* or *communitarian* (to use the language of academic political theory). A further objection is that it too *arduous*.[4] Finally, with an eye on the overarching theme of this volume, we might also ask just how robust is the connection between Marquand's civic republicanism and social democracy.

There seems to be a strong assumption in Marquand's works that the aim of deliberation is a socially agreed understanding of shared public purpose or the common good. This is an explicit assumption of *The Unprincipled Society* and of *Mammon's Kingdom*. It is, however, a recurrent criticism of conceptions of deliberative democracy that they unrealistically and dangerously focus on consensus. Agonistic democrats, such as Chantal Mouffe, also a participant in the citizenship debate of the late 1980s/early 1990s, argue that consensus is something we should be wary of, that it will reflect the suppression of real differences and conflicts of interest and perspective (Mouffe, 1988; 2005). Of course, as we have seen, Marquand also celebrates political and policy-level pluralism. But there also seems to be an expectation of some kind of a shared ethical viewpoint emerging through discussion, and there is not much, if any, consideration of how this fits or stands in tension with ethical pluralism.

Another response to ethical pluralism is the 'political liberal' one of trying to detach notions of the common good, for political purposes, from wider conceptions of the good life as articulated by religious or other 'comprehensive' philosophical doctrines (Rawls, 1993). We have seen how Marquand seems to reject this and that his own republicanism seems, at base, to appeal to a strong conception of the good life. Some will object that makes his republicanism too strong in the claims it makes about the nature of the good life. This connects back to the objection about consensus: is it realistic or reasonable to expect wide agreement on this specific conception of the good life?

In posing such a question, we should note that the status of the good life is itself a matter of controversy within contemporary republican political theory. When Skinner and Philip Pettit started to develop their own 'neo-Roman' account of republicanism they carefully distinguished it from 'neo-Athenian' or 'Aristotelian' accounts (see Pettit, 1998: 83–9, and Skinner, 2002, on how European city-state republicanism developed an intellectual grounding in Roman sources before the recovery of Aristotle's *Politics*). On Aristotelian accounts, the virtues of political practice in the republic are themselves integral to the good life, and the republic is justified by this connection to the good life. By contrast, on the neo-Roman view, the republic is justified as a regime for securing freedom as non-domination. This freedom is not itself the good life, but a fundamental condition for people to define and pursue the good life as they see it. Related to this, the practices and virtues of active citizenship are valued *instrumentally*, as essential means to maintaining freedom as non-domination, not intrinsically as expressive of the good life. Marquand certainly wants to affirm the value of freedom as non-domination, linking his republicanism to that of Skinner. But as we have seen, it also has strong 'Aristotelian' aspects. So far as I can see, Marquand does not see or respond to the possible pitfalls of a specifically 'Aristotelian' republicanism.

A third possible objection is that Marquand's republicanism is too arduous, making unreasonable, or at least unrealistic, demands of us. Marquand's rhetoric frequently alludes to how active citizenship is 'strenuous', 'stretching', 'at first forbidding', requires 'fortitude', involves 'hard choices', responsibility, requires vigour, and so on. An obvious thought is: 'Well, that doesn't sound like much fun.' Why should people take up such a political vision if it is indeed so demanding? Here Marquand's republicanism could perhaps draw strength from its 'Aristotelian' aspect. If the life of the active, virtuous citizen is not only of instrumental value to securing freedom for all, but integral to a life of rich ethical growth, then perhaps this makes it more attractive. The individual is being offered a choice in effect, between an easy life without this personal growth, and a tougher life with it. Marquand's wager must be that, even starting from our current predicament, enough of us can be drawn to the ethically deeper, richer life. That said, does the presentation of republicanism necessarily have to be focused so much on the tougher side of what it demands of us? Does it not have its own – come on, let's use the word – pleasures? What might these be?

Finally, it is worth reflecting further on the connection between Marquand's civic republicanism and social democracy. I began by suggesting that Marquand's intellectual journey is stimulated in large part by the crisis of social democracy as this developed in the UK in the 1970s. As noted, Marquand's argument always has an instrumental aspect in which the republican recasting of UK political structures and practices is seen as building a more promising basis for social democracy. However, I also suggested that Marquand's attachment to civic republicanism is not wholly instrumental. He seems to place a value on deliberative, republican political practice related to the kind of civic character and life that it involves. This emphasis on the value of republican process, with its attendant virtues, is not reducible to a concern with conventional social democratic policy outcomes. Indeed, in some contexts, to some degree, there might be tensions between republican process and social democratic outcomes. (For example, republican process might favour forms of decentralisation in public services that make it harder to secure uniformity in service provision.) Alternatively, one might say that Marquand's aim is perhaps a revisionary one of inviting social democrats to reconceptualise their commitments, through civic republicanism, in a way that gives greater weight to process relative to outcomes.

Conclusion: the UK's Marquandian moment?

In concluding I want to explore a final thought about the relevance of Marquand's republicanism. As we have seen, Marquand argues in *Britain Since 1918* that

New Labour's constitutional reforms destabilised the UK state. If anything, this claim looks even more credible in the wake of the 2014 independence referendum in Scotland and the referendum on the UK's membership of the EU in 2016. In this context, questions about the future of the UK and its constituent nations abound. Individually, and taken together, these nations all face a question of basic, political self-definition. In this situation, Marquand's repeated emphasis on a politics of discussion and mutual education aimed at developing an account of shared purpose arguably has a particular importance.

As a way into this argument, let's consider the so-called 'English question' – though Marquand's own energies are now focused more on Wales (Marquand, 2015). As the legislatures of Scotland, Wales and Northern Ireland acquire greater powers, with Scotland possibly moving towards independence, the question arises as to what form of devolution is appropriate for England. Will England continue to be governed by the UK Parliament? Should England have its own assembly or parliament or strong regional assemblies or parliaments?

In much discussion, the need to address the English question is connected with a call to engage with, and build a sense of, English identity. Although some are keen to emphasise the potential openness and flexibility of 'Englishness', there is a clear danger of definitions, based on highly selective, flattering stories about the English and Anglo-British past, that are nostalgic, dishonest, and ethnically and culturally exclusionary. There is a danger of perpetuating what Paul Gilroy has called 'postcolonial melancholia' in which the loss of empire, the brutal reality of Britain's imperial projects, and the presence of non-white fellow subjects/citizens are suppressed in the collective imagining of what and who 'England' is (Gilroy, 2005). An alternative is to foreground not identity as such, but democracy. We do not ask what 'Englishness' is as some ancestral quality. Instead we ask how we, the people who now live in the geographic unit that is England, in all our diversity, with our multiple, intertwined histories, wish to govern ourselves and build a common life together.[5]

This resonates with the idea that Marquand puts at the centre of his discussion in both *The Unprincipled Society* and in *Mammon's Kingdom*: the idea of a national deliberation focused on defining a shared public purpose or common good. In this form of politics, with its ideal of open discussion, between equal and receptive citizens, achieving mutual education, we can perhaps see the outlines of a constructive approach to the English question. Through the national discussion we can decide how we wish to be governed and, in the process, start the gradual process of building a sense of national identity from how we relate to each other now, and in a way that involves mutual education (not least about our histories).

This process might also have relevance to other nations of the UK, and, indeed, to the UK as a whole, or to whatever political entities succeed the UK.

In concrete terms this connects with an emerging interest in a constitutional convention process for the nations of the UK, an idea to which Marquand briefly alludes in *Mammon's Kingdom* (Marquand, 2013: 219; Hind, 2014; Renwick, 2014; White, 2015; 2017). By constitutional convention I mean an assembly that has responsibility for deliberating proposals for the structure of the political system. The convention might be elected, or else selected on a quasi-random basis from the population so as to create an assembly that is descriptively representative in terms of characteristics such as race, gender, region and social class. These citizens' assemblies can, and should, have some degree of independent power to set agendas in response to popular concerns. They might also be given the power to put their recommendations to binding referendums. One can imagine a convention process, based on such assemblies, that builds up from the UK's regions and nations to the UK as a whole. Its central objective would be to develop recommendations for the government of the regions and nations and for how they might connect at a UK level, while always respecting and affirming the right of nations to independence if they so choose. This process would inevitably have to consider many related questions about political representation, such as whether to have an English Parliament or English regional Parliaments. The process would also offer an opportunity to get to grips with the problem of 'money in politics' that Marquand highlights in *Mammon's Kingdom,* and that is unlikely to find an answer through normal legislative politics. A key to success, in Marquand's terms, would be how far such a process manages to engage not only members of the assemblies, but the wider populations of the UK's nations. Recent constitutional conventions in Iceland and in the Republic of Ireland offer helpful lessons that can inform a convention process in the nations of the UK (Renwick, 2014; Landemore, 2015; White, 2017).

Much depends, of course, on the willingness of existing political elites to step back and create the space for a convention process of this kind. However, if a process can be established that has the necessary independence and integrity, it would have revolutionary significance. Whatever its outcome in institutional terms, a constitutional convention process of this kind would amount to a refounding of the UK, or its successor polities, on the basis of popular sovereignty. In this respect, it would represent a fundamental republican recasting of political life. In so doing, as I began by suggesting, it offers an opportunity for the peoples of the UK to determine their political systems and to define their nations in constructive and inclusive ways. In this sense, we can hope that the nations of the UK will acknowledge that they have reached, and seek to make the most of, this Marquandian moment.

Notes

1 An earlier version of this chapter was presented in the History of Political Thought seminar at Oxford University in October 2016. I am grateful to participants in this seminar, particularly Ben Jackson, Sudhir Hazareesingh and Karma Nabulsi, for their helpful comments. I am also grateful to the editors of this volume for further helpful comments, not all of which I have been able to respond to, and to Anthony Barnett, Dan Hind and Adam Ramsay for many informative discussions of related themes.

2 I take the formulation of 'federalise and pluralise' from Hirst (1994).

3 The integration of political deliberation with conceptions of the good life is a feature of communitarian theories of the polity such as those of Alasdair MacIntyre and Michael Sandel.

4 Another issue, which I set aside here, concerns Marquand's relative lack of engagement with modern republicanisms in other nations (e.g., the French republican tradition). I am grateful to Sudhir Hazareesingh for raising this point.

5 For helpful discussion of the politics of Englishness, see Kenny (2014). Tom Nairn makes a similar distinction in connection with Scotland: 'Just beyond this sound-horizon lies the folklore which counts most, the unimaginable music of the future' (Nairn, 2000: 290).

References

Andrews, G. (ed.) (1991) *Citizenship* (London: Lawrence & Wishart).

Ascherson, N. (1988) 'Ancient Britons and the republican dream', in N. Ascherson, *Games With Shadows* (London: Radius), 146–58.

Barnett, A. (1988) 'A claim of right for Britain', *New Statesman and Society* (2 December), 14–15.

Barnett, A. (1997) *This Time: Our Constitutional Revolution* (London: Vintage).

Evans, M. (1995) *Charter 88: A Successful Challenge to the British Political Tradition?* (Aldershot: Dartmouth).

Freeman, S. (2000) 'Deliberative democracy: a sympathetic comment', *Philosophy and Public Affairs* 29, 371–418.

Gilroy, P. (2005) *Postcolonial Melancholia* (New York: Columbia University Press).

Gourevitch, A. (2015) *From Slavery to the Cooperative Commonwealth: Labor and Republican Liberty in the Nineteenth Century* (Cambridge: Cambridge University Press).

Heater, D. (1991) 'Citizenship: a remarkable case of sudden interest', *Parliamentary Affairs*, 44(2), 140–56.

Hind, D. (2014) *The Magic Kingdom: Property, Monarchy, and the Maximum Republic* (London: Zero).

Hirst, P. (1994) *Associative Democracy: New Forms of Economic and Social Governance* (Cambridge: Polity).

Howe, S. (2009) 'Some intellectual origins of Charter 88', *Parliamentary Affairs*, 62, 1–16.

Kenny, M. (2014) *The Politics of English Nationhood* (Oxford: Oxford University Press).

Landemore, H. (2015) 'Inclusive constitution-making: the Icelandic experiment', *Journal of Political Philosophy*, 23, 166–91.

MacIntyre, A. (1981) *After Virtue* (London: Duckworth).

Marquand, D. (1988) *The Unprincipled Society: New Demands and Old Politics* (London: Jonathan Cape).

Marquand, D. (1993) 'Collaborative capitalism and constitutional reform', in A. Barnett, C. Ellis and P. Hirst (eds), *Debating the Constitution: New Perspectives on Constitutional Reform* (Oxford: Blackwell), 97–103.

Marquand, D. (1994) 'Followers or citizens?', in A. Barnett (ed.), *Power and the Throne: The Monarchy Debate* (London: Vintage).

Marquand, D. (1997a) 'Reinventing civic republicanism,' in D Marquand, *The New Reckoning: Capitalism, States and Citizens* (Cambridge: Polity), 37–52.

Marquand, D. (1997b) 'Liberalism's revenge? Resolving the progressive dilemma', in D. Marquand, *The New Reckoning: Capitalism, States and Citizens* (Cambridge: Polity), 71–90.

Marquand, D. (2004) *Decline of the Public: The Hollowing-Out of Citizenship* (Cambridge: Polity).

Marquand, D. (2008) *Britain Since 1918: The Strange Career of British Democracy* (London: Wiedenfeld & Nicolson).

Marquand, D. (2014) *Mammon's Kingdom: An Essay on Britain, Now* (London: Penguin).

Marquand, D. (2015) 'Returning native', *openDemocracy* (15 December). Accessed online at www.opendemocracy.net/uk/david-marquand/returning-native.

Mouffe, C. (1988) 'The civics lesson', *New Statesman and Society* (7 October), 28–31.

Mouffe, C. (2005 [1993]) *The Return of the Political* (London: Verso).

Nabulsi, K. (2008) 'Mobilisation, representation and republican movements', *Renewal* 16(3/4), 117–25.

Nairn, T. (2000) 'Epilogue: the last day', in T. Nairn, *After Britain: New Labour and the Return of Scotland* (London: Granta), 279–90.

Pettit, P. (1998) 'Reworking Sandel's republicanism', *Journal of Philosophy* 95(2), 73–96.

Pocock, J. G. A. (1975) *The Machiavellian Moment: Florentine Republican Thought and the Atlantic Republican Tradition* (Princeton: Princeton University Press).

Rawls, J. (1993) *Political Liberalism* (New York: Columbia University Press).

Renwick, A. (2014) *After the Referendum: Options for a Constitutional Convention* (London: The Constitution Society). Accessed online at www.consoc.org.uk/ wp-content/uploads/2014/05/J1847_Constitution_Society_Report_Cover_ WEB.pdf.

Sandel, M. (1996) *Democracy's Discontent: America in Search of a Public Philosophy* (Cambridge: MA: Harvard University Press).

Sen, A. (2009) *The Idea of Justice* (London: Penguin).

Skinner, Q. (1998) *Liberty before Liberalism* (Cambridge: Cambridge University Press).

Skinner, Q. (2002) 'The rediscovery of republican values', In Q. Skinner, *Visions of Politics: Volume II: Renaissance Virtues* (Cambridge: Cambridge University Press), 10–38.

Walker, G. (2013) 'John P. Mackintosh, devolution and the union', *Parliamentary Affairs*, 66, 557–78.

Walzer, M. (1983) *Spheres of Justice: A Defense of Pluralism and Equality* (Oxford: Blackwell).

White, S. (2015) 'Building a constitutional convention: Citizens and the UK's constitutional moment', *Juncture*, 22(1), 58–64.

White, S. (2017) 'Parliaments, constitutional conventions, and popular sovereignty', *British Journal of Politics and International Relations*, DOI: 10.1177/1369148117700657.

7

A union of hearts? Republican social democracy and Scottish nationalism[1]

Ben Jackson

The movement of opinion in favour of Scottish nationalism registered by the 2014 Scottish independence referendum catapulted the case for a separate Scottish state to the heart of British political debate. Yet the resulting argument over Scottish independence is often an unsatisfactory one, hobbled by the readiness of both sides to impute bad faith to the other and simply to ignore the stronger points put forward by the opposing camp. For the defenders of the Anglo-Scottish Union in particular, a much more in-depth and forensic engagement with the ideas of Scottish nationalism is badly needed. The advocates of Scottish independence have by necessity already spent a long time scrutinising the case for the Union, whatever else might be said about the quality of their political thought. By contrast, many of their opponents have not reckoned with the fact that Scottish nationalist ideas are in fact now highly sophisticated and, crucially, designed to resonate with important beliefs held by the broader British left. These ideas are also too often misunderstood or even caricatured by the critics of Scottish nationalism, who tend to attack it as a more ethnic and nativist tradition than it actually is, with correspondingly diminishing returns in terms of rebutting its key claims.

This chapter considers how far it is possible to distinguish this progressive strand of Scottish nationalist thinking that coalesced in the 1980s and 1990s from the similar discourse of constitutional reform at the British level associated with movements such as Charter 88 and their leading intellectual advocates such as David Marquand, Paul Hirst and Will Hutton. This latter body of opinion was, in the 1980s and 1990s, generally indifferent or hostile to Scottish nationalism, but it has become harder in recent years to formulate a hard and fast distinction between them. Should those committed to a more democratic and pluralist

British constitutional settlement such as David Marquand in fact 'logically' favour Scottish independence as part of such wide-ranging reform?

Towards a republican social democracy

My answer to this question begins with John Mackintosh, the great Scottish Labour MP and advocate for constitutional reform (and also a close colleague and friend of David Marquand). On the threshold of the Donald Dewar Room of the Scottish Parliament, some words from Mackintosh are cut into the stone. They read: 'People in Scotland want a degree of government for themselves. It is not beyond the wit of man to devise the institutions to meet these demands' (quoted in Walker, 2013: 557). These words were spoken by Mackintosh during the House of Commons debate on the Scotland and Wales Act 1976, and they express the classic case for Scottish devolution espoused by Mackintosh and indeed Donald Dewar himself. Scots, Mackintosh famously argued, have a dual identity, partly Scottish and partly British, and the political institutions that govern Britain should therefore reflect that dual identity by creating a devolved Scottish Parliament to operate within the context of the United Kingdom.

But we should note that Mackintosh's notion of dual identity was more complex than this bald summary suggests. Mackintosh's point was also that at different times one side of the Scots' dual identity assumes greater importance than the other. In the context of the Scottish nationalist surge of the 1970s, Mackintosh observed that the hold of Britishness had been loosened first by the change in Britain's status in the world after 1945 and then by the poor performance of the British economy and government in the late 1960s and 1970s. This left many Scots feeling that the Scottish pole of their dual identity offered a more satisfactory expression of national pride than the British one. Ultimately, Mackintosh argued that a successful British response to the rise of Scottish nationalism would require not just devolution to Scotland but also a period of successful British government, one that would give Scots the feeling that Britain was, as he put it, 'a successful, worthwhile country to belong to for those who do have other places where they can go and other traditions and titles to which they can turn' (Mackintosh, 1998 [1974]: 71; see also Mackintosh, 1982). I think there is still something to be said for this as a reply to Scottish nationalism, although I want to reformulate slightly Mackintosh's prescription.

Before I turn to that, however, I first consider why modern Scottish nationalism presents such a searching challenge to the reforming republican social democracy that authors such as David Marquand delineated during the 1980s and 1990s. Over the last thirty years or so, Marquand, along with colleagues such as the late Paul Hirst and Will Hutton, has eloquently set out the connection between a programme of constitutional reform designed to make the British state more democratic and a programme of economic reform designed to make the British economy more stable and socially just. They have argued that, in order to tackle the pathologies of a short-termist, financialised British capitalism, a more open, pluralist and decentralised British state and political culture will have to be nourished. The creation of a politically durable economic model in which power is shared between labour and capital, and resources pooled more equally between social classes, would in turn require a new British constitution characterised by power-sharing and negotiation rather than classical Westminster majoritarianism (see O'Neill and White, 2014, and Stuart White's chapter in this book, for valuable discussions of these ideas).

Marquand argued in his influential 1988 book, *The Unprincipled Society*, that British economic underperformance in the post-war period could be traced to the failure of the British state to become an effective developmental state, capable of managing the modernisation of the British economy in the way that other leading nations had undertaken successful state-led economic reform programmes. Marquand connected the absence of a suitably dynamic British state to wider pathologies in British public culture and ultimately to the dominance of an inherited ideology and ethos of classical liberal individualism, which, he continued, should be displaced by a politics of 'mutual education' that prioritises a republican commitment to the common good. More precisely, Marquand argued that modern British political and economic culture is organised around an ideal of absolute sovereignty. Politically, he claimed, the absolute legislative sovereignty of Parliament is complemented by its economic counterpart, a belief in the untrammelled rights of a managerial or entrepreneurial class to control the firm. Both are hostile to the notion of power-sharing or division, so that federalism and consensus-building seem alien. Yet in Marquand's view, for Britain to undergo a successful period of economic adjustment and reform – as opposed to the dysfunctional corporatism or Thatcherite shock therapy that had dominated British politics after 1945 – consensus-building and power-sharing was precisely the approach that would have to be taken (Marquand, 1988: 241–2). Indeed, Marquand further remarked that he thought the classical notion of the sovereign European nation state was 'obsolescent' because of the need for economic cooperation and decision-making at a supranational level (Marquand, 1988: 244). But while some powers would have to be transferred upwards to an international level, it was also necessary to devolve powers downwards 'to create neo-corporatist institutions in the regions', effectively creating 'a number of developmental states, region by region', which would be able to respond with greater flexibility than a centralised state to economic change (Marquand, 1988: 243; for Marquand's later reflections and expansions on these arguments, see Marquand, 1997, especially 25–9).

These arguments were an important conceptual breakthrough for the British left, since they postulated a close connection between a revived republican constitutionalism and a fairer and more productive economic settlement. Such ideas were also articulated at around the same time by Paul Hirst, who sought to resuscitate the pluralism of earlier socialist thinkers such as Harold Laski and G. D. H. Cole in a fully-fledged doctrine of 'associationalism'. Hirst followed Marquand in suggesting that the creation of a new culture of social dialogue and bargaining would be critical in shaping a more dynamic and inclusive model of British capitalism. Such a culture could only be created through wide-ranging constitutional reform designed to abolish single-party rule and untrammelled executive power and inculcating instead new norms of power-sharing and coalition-building. As a starting point, Hirst (and Marquand) had in mind such measures as the introduction of proportional representation, a written constitution with entrenched individual rights, a democratised second chamber, and some form of federalism, although Hirst ultimately advocated a more radical programme of economic democratisation and decentralisation designed to make capitalist institutions more accountable and efficient (Hirst, 1989: 39–81, 197–204; Hirst, 1994: 112–57). Hirst saw the cultivation of local political and economic institutions as critical to reviving British industry, since it was at this local level that the most informed economic and social decision-making could take place. Local government and economic actors would collaborate on service provision, industrial innovation and the management of new local investment agencies (Hirst, 1989: 219).

The ideas developed by Marquand and Hirst achieved a significant impact on high political argument when they were synthesised and popularised by Will Hutton in *The State We're In* (1995). Hutton foregrounded the European parallels present in the works of Marquand and Hirst, demonstrating that it was something like the German (or possibly Scandinavian) model of capitalism – with its longer time horizons, integration between industry and finance, and consensual, federalised political culture – that could serve as a practical example of the sort of polity that Britain should aspire to become. Hutton's book was widely read and debated, and even for a brief period thought to offer an intellectual framework for the incoming policies of Tony Blair's New Labour government. But, as Hutton himself would have been the first to acknowledge, the intellectual core of the book drew on the connection between democratic and economic reform first established by Marquand: 'the semi-modern nature of the British state is a fundamental cause of Britain's economic and social problems' (Hutton, 1995: xi–xii; for his debt to Marquand, see Hutton, 2000: 59–60). In Britain, Hutton argued, 'parliament and the firm are sovereign; individuals are subjects and workers. They have no formal stake in the society and economy of which they are alleged to be part' (Hutton, 1995: 287). Hutton therefore proposed a shift towards a republican political and economic settlement of the sort adumbrated by Marquand and Hirst a few years earlier.

It is significant that Marquand, Hirst and Hutton all played leading roles in Charter 88, the pressure group that campaigned for constitutional reform in Britain during the run-up to Labour's return to office in 1997 (Hirst chaired the Charter 88 executive committee, Marquand served as a member of the executive and Hutton on its council). Charter 88 is rightly credited with placing systematic reform of the British constitution back on the political agenda and with winning over a section of the British political elite to the cause of a more democratic polity (see Erdos, 2009). Charter 88's success in promoting debate about the British constitution meant that many of the concrete democratic reforms advocated by figures such as Marquand achieved much greater attention than would otherwise have been the case.

However, Charter 88's energies were, for understandable reasons, chiefly directed at the reform of the central British state. The question of the relationship between the nations and regions of the United Kingdom was given less attention – although the example of the Scottish Constitutional Convention and the wider debate over Scottish devolution was undoubtedly a powerful influence on Charter 88's work. The Charter itself referred to Scotland as being 'governed like a province from Whitehall' and demanded that any new constitutional settlement should 'guarantee an equitable distribution of power between local, regional and national government' (reprinted in Facey, Rigby and Runswick, 2008: 316, 319). The phrasing here was vague, although it seems clear that it was generally understood to entail a commitment to devolution to Scotland, Wales and Northern Ireland and the creation of a much more robust – possibly federal – decentralisation of power throughout the United Kingdom. At any rate, the possibility that Scottish independence might be one desirable outcome of such a process was given short shrift by key figures within the organisation and Scottish nationalists were not generally included within the parameters of the imagined progressive alliance of Labour and the Liberal Democrats that was thought to be the most plausible political vehicle for the realisation of Charter 88's goals (although this was also because the SNP chose to absent itself from the Scottish Constitutional Convention, thus maintaining a hostile stance towards devolutionary proposals). From the perspective of post-2014 political developments, both of these assumptions now look less easily defensible than they did in the 1990s.

The Scottish nationalist challenge

At one level the challenge posed to a British republican social democracy by the rise of Scottish nationalism is simply to question the assumption that the appropriate territorial unit for this sort of political project is Britain. But it runs deeper than that, because the claim of the most articulate exponents of Scottish independence is in essence that, if we take the case made by thinkers such as Marquand, Hutton and Hirst seriously, then we ought to support the dissolution of the Anglo-Scottish Union. How exactly do Scottish nationalists seek to recruit such leading figures of the British left to the ranks of the SNP? They do so by drawing on two strands of argument that are indebted to the constitutional reform discourse of the 1980s and 1990s (for a more detailed analysis of the political ideas of Scottish nationalism, on which the following account draws, see Jackson, 2014).

First, the Scottish nationalist critique of the British state is broadly similar to the one in, say, *The Unprincipled Society*, *The State We're In*, or the discourse of Charter 88. The British state is depicted as pre-democratic and imperial, the product of an idiosyncratic historical path that thwarted a thorough-going bourgeois democratic revolution. Britain is thus an antiquated relic, dominated by the interests of the City of London, and unreformable except by a radical constitutional break, in this case the secession of Scotland. The intellectual provenance of the version of these arguments articulated by Scottish nationalists is more directly indebted to New Left thinkers such as Tom Nairn and Perry Anderson than to Marquand or Hutton, but they ultimately take roughly the same shape (and in any case the latter were to some extent also directly and indirectly influenced by the former's pioneering analysis). Anderson and Nairn famously argued that Britain's unique historical trajectory was determined by the capacity of the aristocracy and the middle class to form a social alliance that staved off a bourgeois revolution, excluding the working class from significant political power. This alliance was cemented by the rise of the British empire and the creation of what became an imperial British state. The British state of the late twentieth century was thus, on this account, the creature of a long and inescapable history of aristocratic power politics, empire, and ultimately post-imperial economic stagnation (Anderson 1964; Nairn 1964a; Nairn 1964b).

These 'Anderson-Nairn theses', as they were later dubbed, formed a set of arguments about the nature of Britain that were subsequently very influential on Scottish nationalist thought and which arrive at a diagnosis of Britain as fundamentally undemocratic that has many affinities with the analysis sponsored by Marquand and his colleagues in Charter 88. Indeed, Anthony Barnett, the first director of Charter 88, was himself a former member of the editorial com-mittee of Perry Anderson's *New Left Review* and a close colleague of Nairn's (see for example Nairn's warm tribute to Barnett in Nairn, 2000: ix). The key difference between the Scottish nationalist analysis of Britain and its counterpart in the writings of Marquand, Hirst and Hutton is the more pessimistic conclusions of the former, namely the Scottish nationalist view is that the regressive character of the contemporary British state is so tied to specifically English hierarchies and inequalities that it won't be possible for Scotland or England to achieve a more democratic and egalitarian settlement while still part of the same political union (see Nairn, 1977, for the most influential statement along these lines). For the advocates of Scottish independence, a developmental state and economy can only be created separately first by Scotland and then subsequently by the rest of the United Kingdom, which will, so the argument goes, have been shocked by the secession of Scotland into a fundamental constitutional and economic reappraisal.

Second, the Scottish nationalist understanding of the concept of sovereignty is, like that of Marquand and Hirst, a pluralist one. Scottish nationalists have learned over the years that a claim for undivided Scottish sovereignty is not credible or convincing as an account of what Scottish independence would look like. Rather than making a claim for Scottish autarchy, Scottish nationalists have elaborated a sophisticated account of how an independent Scotland could simultaneously enjoy self-determination in certain respects but in other respects share institutions, laws and society with foreign nations. Contemporary Scottish nationalism has therefore been deeply influenced by a pluralist view that envisages a diffusion of power across different levels of government and society.

For Scottish nationalists, this approach to sovereignty was developed most fully in the writings of the late Neil MacCormick, the legal theorist and sometime SNP MEP (1999–2004), who advanced the case for what he called the 'post-sovereign state'. MacCormick observed that his own 'diffusionist' theories pointed back towards earlier ideas about associational autonomy associated with figures such as the German jurist and historian Otto von Gierke and the French jurist and sociologist Maurice Hauriou, who had rejected the 'undue pretensions of the state to total mastery of a territory' and were concerned about 'the independence and vitality of the manifold communities, guilds, associations, and corporations to be found in civil society' (MacCormick, 1999: 77). MacCormick argued that European integration had replaced the absolute sovereignty previously exercised by EU member states with a more pluralistic arrangement in which new rules bind together these states at the European level, removing certain of the powers previously exercised nationally. At the same time, the doctrine of subsidiarity – that decisions should be taken at the lowest possible level – mandated that powers should also be decentralised from the state towards regional authorities or even to newly created national institutions that break away from existing large multinational states. On MacCormick's account, the demise of the traditional model of absolute state sovereignty invites Scotland to participate in a new era in which Scottish institutions can take over some important powers previously held at Westminster, while in other domains simultaneously remaining subject to institutions at a European and perhaps even British level (MacCormick, 1999: 137–56).

In some respects MacCormick's analysis left tantalisingly indeterminate how far it would indeed be desirable on these grounds for Scotland to secure independence rather than some form of advanced home rule (Walker, 2012: 163–90). But MacCormick's case was ultimately that a British federalism, because of the disproportionate size of England, could never work, and that asymmetric devolution to Scotland along the lines undertaken in 1999 would ultimately prove to be an unstable settlement, since it would expose the anomalous role of Scottish MPs in determining public policy in England but not in Scotland. Even were England to be divided into regional assemblies, MacCormick noted, this would not tackle the central difficulty of the legislative powers held by the Scottish Parliament. It seemed to MacCormick highly unlikely that English law-making powers of the kind exercised in Edinburgh would, or could, be split between different English regions (for example by splitting up the English NHS into regional units).

A parallel, although more sovereigntist, argument about the instability of devolution was also made by Tom Nairn in 1997. Nairn predicted that once Scottish popular sovereignty was given an institutional form in the Scottish Parliament it would inevitably conflict with the parliamentary sovereignty of the British state. Nairn perceptively noted that the key fact about the new Scottish

Parliament would not be the precise policy domains or fiscal powers it had, but rather its embodiment for the first time of a distinctively Scottish democratic will which would, inevitably, be able to address 'whether to try to alter the conditions of UK affiliation' (Nairn, 1997: 223). While conversant with the increasing salience of debates about federal and 'post-sovereign' power-sharing arrangements between states and regions, Nairn's view ('like MacCormick') was that in the British case there was simply no chance of such a comprehensive recasting of British constitutional practice. Both MacCormick and Nairn therefore argued that the most promising solution to this impasse was an independent Scotland as a member of the EU, complemented by an intergovernmental Council of the Isles to deal with issues specific to the British archipelago. With these arrangements in place, Scotland would secure a relationship of equality with the rest of the UK, and other European states, as an equal member of the European confederation (MacCormick, 1999: 61–2, 193–9; Nairn, 2000: 223–78).

After the 2016 referendum on Britain's membership of the EU, this argument is clearly in need of significant renovation. Indeed, it may even have been rendered irrelevant to current policy debates, since it seems that a more fundamental and irrevocable choice between Scotland's membership of either a European or a British union will now be pressed on Scottish nationalists. But if that is the case, then the republican social democracy associated with David Marquand also faces serious challenges, since this is also ultimately grounded on a vision of shared sovereignty between Brussels, London and Edinburgh (Marquand, 2011). The difference between the two once again hinges on the more pessimistic assessment of the prospects for British federalism on the part of Scottish nationalists.

Responding to the challenge

The extent to which Scottish nationalism has assimilated both the democratic critique of the British state and a pluralist conception of sovereignty is testament to the sophistication of the current campaign for Scottish independence and the skill with which Scottish nationalists have managed to disorientate their unionist opponents. The argument for Scottish nationalism is now, in short, that it is the logical culmination of the British left's arguments about constitutional and economic reform developed over the last three decades.

How might those sympathetic to the creation of a more federal British set-tlement respond to this colonisation of their arguments? One pragmatic view, which tempted a number of English progressives during the 2014 referendum campaign, was simply to concede that, since serious constitutional reform is frozen at the British level and British politics is now dominated by the right, the appropriate response is to wish Scottish nationalists good luck, support Scotland in going its own way, and observe with interest if it can do any better than the rest of the UK in advancing democracy and social justice. This argument has likely gained a number of new adherents in the wake of the 2016 EU referendum. A second response, also espoused by some figures on the left in England, would go even further and argue that in fact Scottish independence is not simply the least worst option available now, but rather a positively desirable outcome of the agenda first set out in the 1980s and 1990s by Charter 88 and other constitutional reformers. This line of argument accepts that the Scottish nationalist use of the ideas I have discussed is in fact correct. This was not the view initially taken by the advocates of constitutional change when Labour took office in 1997. Anthony Barnett, for example, replied to Tom Nairn's scepticism with an optimistic analysis of the new Blair government as initiating a new constitutional settlement for Britain, but Barnett also agreed with Nairn that in the absence of any wider rethinking of British constitutional structures Scottish independence would inevitably command greater credibility (Barnett, 1997a; Barnett, 1997b: 186–93).

A third option, of course, would be to resist the Scottish nationalist conclusion by suggesting that a more federal and decentralised British state remains, in spite of the scepticism of Neil MacCormick and Tom Nairn, an achievable and desirable political goal. And this takes us back to John Mackintosh. I noted earlier that Mackintosh's insight was that it was not enough simply to grant devolution to Scotland; there also had to be something more positive and attractive to say about what Britain stood for, an attempt by unionists to activate and amplify the British element of Scots' dual nationality. If such a strategy to avert Scottish independence is to succeed, then part of such an effort to revivify Britishness will indeed be constitutional; it will rest on creating a more democratic and inclusive British political system, featuring proportional representation, a new second chamber, and so on. It will also face the testing task of resolving the difficult imbalances and anomalies identified by MacCormick and Nairn as severe obstacles to the creation of a successful British federalism. But I would add that this strategy cannot only be constitutional; it also has to encompass political economy. Just as, say, *The Unprincipled Society* spelled out the connections between constitutional reform and the reform of Britain's political economy, the revised case for Britain must also have a socio-economic dimension.

This point has some similarities to the case for the Anglo-Scottish union articulated by Gordon Brown during the 2014 independence referendum campaign (see Jackson, 2016 for a fuller discussion of this point, which the following account draws on). While in office between 1997 and 2010, Brown perceived that Labour's failure to create a new British civic patriotism to accompany Labour's constitutional reforms was a problem, but he failed to articulate an account of Britishness capable of achieving any substantial political or social resonance, instead invoking an impressionistic collection of historical episodes and political values that were collectively said to add up to a progressive British tradition. Until the Scottish independence referendum, few within the Labour Party regarded this failure as a serious problem. Brown's own attention to Britishness tended to be dismissed by allies and opponents alike as chiefly motivated by his need to present a Scottish MP as a legitimate British Prime Minister. But during the hectic spring and summer of 2014, Labour's profound inarticulacy on British identity was clearly revealed. It proved surprisingly difficult for leading Labour figures to give a compelling positive account of British identity to go alongside the ferocious economic critique of Scottish independence. The main exception to this was Gordon Brown, who succeeded in refining his ideas about Britishness to the point where they at last had a significant political cutting edge. Brown's concept of the Union as about risk-sharing and resource-pooling between England, Scotland, Wales and Northern Ireland was a fertile one, which offered a distinctively social democratic characterisation of British institutions and traditions. The best argument for the Union, Brown said, was that it had provided the framework for the creation of 'social and economic rights that the citizens of the four nations have built up and share in common throughout the United Kingdom', including social insurance, the NHS and pensions. In the United Kingdom, 'it is not nationality that decides who benefits, it is need' (Brown, 2014: 231, 227).

The weakness of Brown's analysis, as Scottish nationalists pointed out, is that post-Thatcher the 'pooling and sharing' case for British institutions is harder to make. After rapid deindustrialisation, growing economic inequality, a period of relatively right-wing Labour government, and then Westminster-sponsored austerity, the argument that Britain stands for egalitarian collective action unsurprisingly proved difficult to land with some long-standing Scottish Labour voters. While Brown could point to a number of powerful individual examples of British risk-sharing and resource-pooling that nonetheless persisted even after the Thatcher years, it was undeniable that levels of inequality and poverty remain unacceptably high in Britain in the twenty-first century, even though New Labour in office had made a creditable and effective start on improving them. Campaigners for the Anglo-Scottish Union were therefore left with the uninspiring line of argument that the fiscal and monetary constraints on an independent Scotland would leave a new Scottish state with few options to improve on Britain's dismal record and were indeed likely to make matters worse. This argument was just about politically effective in 2014, but it is hard to see it recreating among Scots the sort of stronger positive affinity for Britain that John Mackintosh recommended as necessary for ultimately diminishing support for Scottish independence.

This places left-wing defenders of the Anglo-Scottish Union in a bind that can probably only be broken by a successful period of left-of-centre government in Westminster. The best way to meet the arguments for Scottish independence is to show through concrete and effective policy action that a new, pluralist British state can also be a state in which poverty, economic insecurity and material inequality will all be lower than under our present constitutional order. So although there has been much discussion about how to renew the case for the Union in the wake of the 2014 independence referendum (and some limited subsequent action), one important way of capturing the initiative from Scottish nationalism would be for a government in Westminster to undertake serious reform to Britain's economic model. Until such a period of (presumably) Labour government can be engineered, the dual identity of many Scots will continue listing to the Scottish side, and the question of Scottish independence will accordingly be a pressing issue of debate for years to come.

Note

1   An earlier and much shorter version of this chapter was first published as my contribution to G. Hassan, B. Jackson, A. Ramsay and D. Torrance (2015) 'Roundtable on the Scottish independence referendum: What happened and what next?', *Renewal*, 23, 68–71. I am grateful to Jeremy Nuttall and Hans Schattle for their comments on a draft of the chapter.

References

Anderson, P. (1964) 'Origins of the present crisis', *New Left Review*, 23, 26–53.
Barnett, A. (1997a) 'Constitutional possibilities', *Political Quarterly*, 68(4), 361–71.
Barnett, A. (1997b) *This Time: Our Constitutional Revolution* (London: Vintage).
Brown, G. (2014) *My Scotland, Our Britain: A Future Worth Sharing* (London: Simon & Schuster).

Erdos, D. (2009) 'Charter 88 and the constitutional reform movement: a retrospective', *Parliamentary Affairs*, 62(4), 537–51.

Facey, P., Rigby, B. and Runswick, A. (eds) (2008) *Unlocking Democracy: 20 Years of Charter 88* (London: Politico's).

Hirst, P. (1989) *After Thatcher* (London: Collins).

Hirst, P. (1994) *Associative Democracy* (Cambridge: Polity).

Hutton, W. (1995) *The State We're In* (London, Jonathan Cape).

Hutton, W. (2000) 'Interview', in R. English and M. Kenny (eds), *Rethinking British Decline* (Basingstoke: Macmillan).

Jackson, B. (2014) 'The political thought of Scottish nationalism', *Political Quarterly*, 85(1), 50–6.

Jackson, B. (2016) 'Labour and the nation', *Fabian Review*, 128(3) (autumn), 8–10.

MacCormick, N. (1999) *Questioning Sovereignty* (Oxford: Oxford University Press).

Mackintosh, J. (1982) *John P. Mackintosh on Scotland*, ed. by H. Drucker (London: Longman).

Mackintosh, J. (1998 [1974]) 'The new appeal of nationalism', *New Statesman*, 27 September 1974; reprinted in L. Paterson (ed.), *A Diverse Assembly: The Debate on a Scottish Parliament* (Edinburgh, Edinburgh University Press).

Marquand, D. (1988) *The Unprincipled Society* (London: Cape).

Marquand, D. (1997) *The New Reckoning* (Cambridge: Polity).

Marquand, D. (2011) *The End of the West: The Once and Future Europe* (Princeton: Princeton University Press).

Nairn, T. (1964a) 'The nature of the Labour Party, part one', *New Left Review*, 27, 37–65.

Nairn, T. (1964b) 'The nature of the Labour Party, part two', *New Left Review*, 28, 33–62.

Nairn, T. (1977) *The Break-Up of Britain: Crisis and Neo-Nationalism* (London: New Left Books).

Nairn, T. (1997) *Faces of Nationalism* (London: Verso).

Nairn, T. (2000) *After Britain* (London: Granta).

O'Neill, M. and White, S. (2014) 'That was the New Labour that wasn't', in G. Lodge and G. Gottfried (eds), *Democracy in Britain: Essays in Honour of James Cornford* (London: IPPR).

Walker, G. (2013) 'John Mackintosh, devolution and the union', *Parliamentary Affairs*, 66(3), 557–78.

Walker, N. (2012) 'Scottish nationalism for and against the union state', in N. Walker (ed.), *MacCormick's Scotland* (Edinburgh: Edinburgh University Press).

Part III

The principled society: mindsets and values

8

The politics of neighbourliness: social democracy on the home front in Britain during the Second World War

Clare Griffiths

We found out in this war as how we're all neighbours. And we haven't gotta forget it when it's all over. (The Dawn Guard, 1941)

In the early days of 1941, projected on the screens of British cinemas, two home guards shared their visions of the future. Roy Boulting's film *The Dawn Guard* lasts just five minutes – one of many short propaganda pieces distributed by the Ministry of Information during the Second World War, dropped into cinema programmes among the feature films and newsreels, with the aim of informing their audience and bolstering morale (Chapman, 2000: 90). Representing different generations, the two characters in *The Dawn Guard* keep their watch beside an old windmill in the southern English countryside, chewing over the lessons they have learned from war. The older man dreams of a return to traditional values and ways of living, and it is left to his younger companion to voice the rallying call for a new Britain – one which would leave mass unemployment, poverty and poor housing behind. Documentary footage juxtaposes images of urban slums and life on the dole with inspiring views of planned housing estates, modern classrooms and playing fields, in a film described as 'arguably the best filmic interpretation of "New Jerusalemism" produced during the early war years' (Paris, 2000: 97). The message is laid on thick, against shots of hands tugging on a rope: Britons had learned the virtues of pulling together for the war effort, and had realised that pooling resources and acting cooperatively could secure a better world in peacetime. But the younger home guard – played by Bernard Miles, in earnest rustic tones – also makes it clear that a key shift during the war had been the development of a new sense of responsibility towards one's fellow citizens, and a willingness to improve the quality of life for everyone (Fox, 2006: 826–7). He expresses this in the language of 'neighbourliness'.

The use of neighbourliness as an image for social relationships and values – as an everyday model for how a good society works – gains much of its power from a seeming universality. Responsibility for, and reliance upon, one's neighbours has been so often referenced as a foundation for functioning communities. Despite abundant evidence that the interactions between neighbours promote hostility as well as mutual support, there is a tendency to idealise these connections, which are commonly imbued with a significance second only to relationships within the family. Invocations of the biblical commandment to 'love thy neighbour as thyself' imply a fundamental concept of neighbourliness that exists outside time and space, while historical studies document significant changes in the lived reality of being neighbours, dependent on patterns of domestic life, sociability and the nature of housing itself (Cockayne, 2013). Between neighbourliness as an ideal, and neighbourliness as a historical experience, was there also scope for neighbourliness to be political? And to be invoked in particular ways in a specific historical context? When Miles's home guard observed that the Second World War had taught Britons that they were 'all neighbours', why choose that particular analogy, and what were its implications?

Inspiration for *The Dawn Guard* is credited to Anna Reiner, a Viennese-born novelist and dramatist who had recently produced the screenplay for a feature film about the Lutheran pastor Martin Niemöller, celebrated for his brave stance against the Nazi dictatorship (Chapman, 2000: 84). Who actually wrote the dialogue for *The Dawn Guard* is less clear, but ultimately the film is the vision of the director Roy Boulting and his twin brother John (who acted as producer), made in late 1940 while they were awaiting their military call-up. In an interview many years later Roy Boulting commented that *The Dawn Guard* 'clearly represented our views at the time' (Burton, 2000: 257). Those views fit well into a familiar picture of the developing public mood during the 'people's war', albeit appearing somewhat earlier than the date traditionally ascribed to a leftward shift in national political opinion, which tended to be linked to the publication of the Beveridge Report at the end of 1942. Almost two years earlier, *The Dawn Guard* was already setting out an agenda for reconstruction, with aspirations for change, for 'something new, and better than what's been destroyed'. The film highlights key areas of policy: housing, employment, public health, international cooperation. The contrast is always with the bad days of the 1930s: with slums, unemployment, poor living conditions and opportunities. The future is characterised by light, clean air, modernity and happy children with space and scope to play and grow. These were features common in left-wing policy programmes and bear strong affinities with the reform agenda presented in

Picture Post's special issue in January 1941, themed as its 'Plan for Britain'. But what is also notable about *The Dawn Guard* is that these ideas and sentiments were being showcased under the auspices of the Ministry of Information, thus acquiring the aura of being officially sanctioned and promoted. And the case for them is made as deriving from common sense and practical experience: the result of rising to the challenge of a war in which both the need for change and the means of achieving it had been revealed through that discovery that 'we're all neighbours'.

Neighbourliness and a 'revolution of feeling'

In any consideration of the history of social democracy in Britain, the immediate aftermath of the Second World War seems to mark a key point in the national political culture. The political atmosphere that enabled Attlee's Labour Party to come to power, and the programme of change pursued by that post-war administration, cement claims for the 1945 general election as a political watershed. And, as Ross McKibbin concludes, the election result 'was undoubtedly a consequence of the radicalisation of opinion: to deny that is to ignore the reality of the war' (McKibbin, 2010: 197). The predominant mood of the 'new Britain' was one in which the values of social welfare were paramount, with a new consensus established about the role of government in shaping a society and economy that offered opportunities for citizens to work and enjoy a decent quality of life. There was much talk about the triumph of democracy and the need to rebuild a country that addressed the needs of everyone, irrespective of background and wealth. Paul Addison has commented on the prevalence of ideas about the 'levelling' of social and economic experience (Addison, 1994: 161–3). In this sense, the 'people's war' had helped to create a 'people's peace' (Morgan, 1991).

In attempting to explain why this should be so, it is difficult to avoid the transformative effect of war itself. Margaret Cole characterised the result of the 1945 general election as a 'real revolution of feeling' (Cole, 1945: 23). What was it about the experience of war that had encouraged such a dramatic change in political sentiment? Did the British (or at least some of the British) *learn* to be social democrats during those years of privation, danger and service? David Marquand identifies the emergence of a new consensus on the principle of making Britain a fair society: 'Wartime sharing – and, not least, the language of sharing – was carried over into peace. "Fair shares" became an uncontested trope of public rhetoric' (Marquand, 2015: 41). Much of the political rhetoric at the time emphasised how the mobilisation of resources and labour had proved an education, shaking the nation out of its earlier complacency, and provoking an explicit break with the past. But running alongside this was a persistent commentary tracing a more fundamental shift, in values as much as policy.

It has always been tempting to locate the roots of this change in the kind of revelation voiced in *The Dawn Guard*. When people rubbed up against their fellow citizens in war work and in facing danger together, they might well have found their opinions and attitudes shaken from old beliefs and prejudices. As middle-class housewife Clara Milburn mused in her diary in October 1940, after a stint of delivering salvage papers in her Warwickshire village, 'I found myself tremendously interested in my neighbours, both well-to-do and otherwise, and the great thing one learns is how very much nicer everybody is than one thought.' The war had apparently opened her eyes, and, at least in the short term, changed her outlook: 'Everybody's house is interesting and I got a smile and kindly words everywhere … And now I shall be able to nod much more understandingly to my neighbours' (Milburn, 1995: 60). Such encounters could stretch beyond the personal. The mixing of classes and cultures might prompt new appreciation of the gulf in living standards, as in Neville Chamberlain's much-cited comments that evacuation had provided a 'shocking revelation' to rural hosts about how their 'town cousins' lived (Welshman, 1998: 36).

There were plenty of statements along such lines. But the basis for such explanations of a changing political climate and social attitudes seems considerably less certain than it once did. Following definitive explosions of 'the myth of the Blitz' (Calder, 1991), attempts to claim that British society became more cooperative, more tolerant, more empathetic as a result of experiences on the home front, make a historian look like the victim of wartime propaganda, buying into the image of a caring, sharing people which was sold back to the British as a form of encouragement and morale-boosting, and to American allies as an inspiring picture of a plucky people who were all in it together. Even the celebrated electoral landslide in 1945 now looks rather less certain as a national commitment to redefining the role of the state in society and the economy (Fielding, 1992).

It would be difficult today to argue a case for characterising the home front as fuelled by altruism and a new sense of communal identity. Investigators for the organisation Mass-Observation were certainly sceptical of attempts to find a renaissance of neighbourliness in the shadow of the blitz:

> [T]he much vaunted 'neighbourliness' alleged to be revived by bombing did not amount to much. You can't shift the centre of gravity of the community life of a nation from office to home simply by making people sleep on mattresses in

someone else's basement or making them carry kettles a hundred yards down the road to fill them from someone else's tap. Such situations give rise not to increased neighbourliness, but to simple irritation and bad temper. (Mass-Observation, 1944: 85)

Another of Mass-Observation's studies, on the subject of housing, registered concern about the levels of bad feeling between neighbours, and a failure to recognise the benefits of cooperating with one's neighbours (Mass-Observation, 1943: 208). Meanwhile, some diagnoses of wartime communitarianism were clearly examples of political wishful thinking, rather than sociological reality. When Richard and Kay Titmuss wrote of how 'In war-time the mass of the people do identify themselves with the community: they live less selfishly … they feel themselves part of something which is larger and more worthwhile than their own selfish lives', this was largely a statement about the world as they would like it to be (Titmuss, 1942).

Yet the language of neighbourliness deserves some further consideration. Even if people were not necessarily behaving in a neighbourly way, or redefining their own interests in solidarity with the community around them, it is interesting that many commentators at the time were keen to identify an upsurge of 'neighbourliness', and to draw implications from this about the potential for popular participation in the post-war reconstruction. One way of looking at the development of the welfare state, planning and economic interventions after the Second World War is to think of this as the outcome of a contest between the prospect of a centralised, bureaucratic system run by experts on behalf of the public, and a more participatory, bottom-up politics. Neighbourliness became a way of talking about the latter approach. David Marquand has written that, 'To change society … ideas have to descend from the lofty empyrean of economists and philosophers to the common or garden world of ordinary citizens talking to and learning from each other' (Marquand, 2015: xvii–xviii). The language of neighbourliness in wartime was often an attempt to do just that: to articulate ideas about common interest and mutual support, and to present these as the basis for a socially progressive politics with its mandate in everyday social relations and the political education which these had afforded.

The importance of being neighbourly

If social historians have sometimes been lured into mistaking the home front for a utopia of cooperation and community spirit, that is partly because such sentiments were being so actively propagated as part of the war effort. Irrespective of whether civilians actually found common purpose and friendship under the exigencies of war, they were continually being pointed in that direction – for purposes both pragmatic and symbolic. On the symbolic side, there were questions of national character at stake. In place of class divisions and a love of privacy, the wartime ideal was far more unifying and engaged. *Ourselves in Wartime*, a morale-boosting publication from 1944, claimed that the greatest lesson of the British home front was 'the lesson that neighbourliness, understanding and unselfishness were the birthright of the British people', celebrating the way that strangers came together to set up canteens and clubs, and to organise parties, entertainments, singing and religious services (Odhams Press, 1944: 84, 86). Neighbourliness here became a weapon on the moral battlefield, not just in promoting constructive communal efforts to keep the home front functioning, but by showcasing positive British virtues. As the physician Lord Horder put it in 1941, whilst observing life in the underground shelters, 'a sense of security and neighbourly kindliness are qualities which characterise life in our particular Commonwealth' (Horder, 1941: 374). In other words, neighbourliness was something that the British demonstrated, and the Nazis did not.

The virtues of being a 'good neighbour', however, were also coopted pragmatically to encourage compliance with government policy and wartime regulations, with home front campaigns on all manner of themes being 'couched in terms of civic duty' (Marquand, 2004a: 70). Potentially unpalatable policies were set out as being dependent on willing expressions of public responsibility and generosity, emphasising an informed voluntarism rather than legal compulsion as the mainspring of national engagement with the war effort. For example, in the effort to make the famously individualistic community of farmers conform to the requirements of wartime agricultural production, government was at pains to foster the idea of a supposed new spirit of cooperation, lauded as 'neighbourliness'. Official accounts described farmers as 'determined not only to pick one another's brains, but to spread the gospel of their experience among their neighbours', including inviting people around for 'Neighbours' Day', giving them the opportunity to walk around the farm and ask questions (Ministry of Information, 1945: 86).

Neighbourliness was explicitly cited in a number of wartime initiatives, including an official 'Help-your-neighbour' scheme, which gave motorists access to additional petrol rations if they offered lifts to members of the public. Some grassroots projects also used the concept of neighbourliness to mobilise cooperative ventures, as seen in the Neighbours' Leagues that were established in Leicester to help victims of bombing, supplementing the work of the official civil defence structures (Hinton, 2002: 83). Herbert Morrison, as Home Secretary, declared a reluctance to force such 'natural' expressions of neighbourly feeling and mutual aid, desirable though it might be to spread such schemes more widely across the country. 'I am anxious to see this praiseworthy movement extended as widely as possible', he commented in response to a question in the House of Commons in November 1940. 'It must be developed for the most part from local initiative and corporate feeling, but I will certainly consider how best I can stimulate its growth' (House of Commons, 1940). Morrison returned to this theme in 1945, in a foreword to Stephen Spender's *Citizens in War – and After*, reflecting on potential outlets for civilians' new-found public spirit. Once again he placed the emphasis on the voluntary nature of neighbourliness, though he held open the possibility of government providing some assistance to help communities give 'organized effect to their spirit as good citizens and good neighbours' (Spender, 1945: 6).

Being a so-called 'good neighbour' in wartime, however, was not necessarily entirely benign. It could be caught up with obligations to do with surveillance and enforcing conformity. The workings of the local War Agricultural Committees, for instance, were frequently glossed as a means for neighbours to 'help' each other, offering good practice to emulate, a source of friendly advice, encouragement and cajoling from someone the farmer knew personally, rather than a distant official (Short, 2014). In such configurations, the responsibilities of 'neighbours' during the national emergency were to support the government's war effort at grassroots level, possibly at the expense of actual local solidarity and fellow feeling. Even neighbourly conversation might be open to suspicion in the light of campaigns to stop 'loose talk' – though the Ministry of Information tried to reassure chatty neighbours that: 'We have no wish to restrict human converse or to damp neighbourly gossip ... We want people to be more friendly and neighbourly than they have been' (Harold Nicholson, July 1940, quoted in Cockayne, 2013: 151).

Neighbours and citizens

When neighbourliness was cited in wartime, it was usually freighted with notions about how it expressed inherent qualities in the British character and contributed to the public good. It was taken as a gauge for solidarity with one's community during the privations and dangers of war, expressed on a personal and essentially voluntary level. Whilst playing on the idea of cosy, supportive relationships with one's immediate neighbours, however, the wartime variation on neighbourliness was often about caring for and acting in concert with strangers, stretching neighbourliness across classes and background. It became a marker for engagement in a broader community and the rejection of narrow self-interest: a practical expression of active citizenship.

If a renaissance of neighbourliness in this sense was welcomed as a pragmatic outcome of the trials of the home front, then what were the prospects of its surviving the war? And could equality of sacrifice, communal expedients and patriotic social duty combine to produce a re-education of Britain's citizens, re-orienting them from a focus on private, domestic, family life to a greater interest and involvement in the public sphere? Some people saw the potential of neighbourliness as a school for citizenship, and as a setting within which social democratic values could be realised and learned. G. D. H. Cole argued that 'Democracy begins at home' and that it should be rooted in the neighbourhood: the place of natural interactions where people lived and worked (Cole, 1942: 167). With the insouciance of someone whose north London house had not yet been hit in an air-raid (though it did suffer damage during the rocket attacks later in the war), Cole's comments about the relationship between neighbourliness and war may seem shockingly cavalier. All across Europe, he observed, small groups of neighbours were coming together and, 'It is worthwhile to be bombed or invaded, if only blitz or invasion can teach us this lesson' (Cole, 1942: 152).

The educative experience of shared suffering and mutual aid on the home front in wartime continued to be evoked as a training ground for citizenship. '[A]midst all the destruction of the "blitz", men and women planned a new and more neighbourly Britain', claimed the National Federation of Community Associations, noting that: 'There was a widespread determination that the neighbourly spirit engendered by the common sacrifice of war should not be allowed to evaporate but should be embodied in some permanent peace-time expression' (National Federation of Community Associations, 1955: 16). Few people waxed so lyrical on this theme as the poet and wartime fireman Stephen Spender, in his writings about the experience of civil defence.

Spender's book *Citizens in War – and After* claimed to be a 'straightforward' account of the development and experience of civil defence, produced in collaboration with the photographer John Hinde, whose rich colour images punctuate the volume (Spender, 1945: 8). It had the official imprimatur of a foreword from Herbert Morrison, the government minister overseeing the civil defence programme. However, Spender's picture of civil defence is in practice far from being a straightforward documentation. The reader certainly encounters a lot of information about what civil defence involved and the experiences of those who took part in it, not least in relation to the work of the fire service, which was the branch Spender knew best and about which he felt most strongly. But the message running throughout the book is about a revolution of attitudes and social experience: an awakening.

The way in which Spender conceptualises this is as 'neighbourliness'. The vocabulary of 'neighbours' and being 'neighbourly' peppers the text, and is hard to avoid. 'The most striking lesson [of the war], particularly demonstrated by whole-time and part-time Civil Defence,' Spender wrote, 'is neighbourliness' (Spender, 1945: 104). The experience of the home front had, in his view, allowed people to combine a greater social empathy with a sense of their own agency. 'In war it is possible to get to know one's neighbour', he observed, in an unlikely echo of the conservative Mrs Milburn, quoted earlier. War overcame conventional barriers and restraints, but it also provided practical reasons and opportunities for social engagement. '[T]he main unifying force in war-time society', wrote Spender, 'is the breakdown of social barriers in order that people may co-operate in a common cause ... They are able to help their neighbours, they are able to give as well as take. They have a deeper insight into the lives of other people' (Spender, 1945: 16).

In Spender's analysis, this neighbourliness connected closely to local patriotism and a particular sense of citizenship. The wartime evocation of national patriotism addressed by most propaganda at the time was countered here by a more communitarian vision of what it meant to be a citizen. Through people's service in civil defence, Spender claimed, 'civilians have become aware that they are citizens, that they have neighbourly responsibilities extending beyond the defence of cities during air raids, that they can educate themselves and help each other in numerous ways' (Spender, 1945: 15).

Spender reiterates throughout the book that this new-found neighbourliness was too good to be set aside once peace returned. 'Civil Defence workers', he observed, 'would probably agree that they have shared many experiences which they do not want to lose after the war. One such experience is the breakdown of social barriers among neighbours: the discovery that at the warden's post, or the depot, or the fire station, men and women leading entirely different lives can become friends and respect each other' (Spender, 1945: 15). Spender's own reminiscences suggest that he actually found 'little spirit of unity' in some of the fire stations where he served (Spender, 1997: 271). But *Citizens in War – and After* presents egalitarianism and common purpose as one of the great revelations of the home front.

Spender terms this 'neighbourliness', but it was really about the social mixing and cooperation of people from different backgrounds, brought together in work for the war effort. 'Unless this relationship can be preserved, the spirit of the war for democracy is lost', he wrote. 'What is necessary is that people of all classes should have some basis for meeting and facing post-war problems on equal terms' (Spender, 1945: 105). One of the major questions posed in the book was how to encourage a continuance of this wider engagement and sense of mutual responsibility into peacetime. In the formal government-sponsored schemes post-war, the notion of civil defence as a 'band of good neighbours' did in fact persist to some extent, with volunteers urged to 'Join your neighbours in Civil Defence' (Grant, 2011: 69, 70). Spender was full of praise for the influence of training, education and practical involvement within the wartime organisations, but the key element that he identified as significant was less institutional, and more to do with a wartime shift in attitudes and social experience. His own proposal was that social clubs and adult education after the war might enable the spirit of civil defence to live on, perpetuating this sort of active citizenship and the satisfaction that people felt in being able to make an active contribution to their community.

Planning neighbourliness

In the post-war period, neighbourliness seemed in some ways to become embedded in ideas of reconstruction and approaches towards aspects of social policy. Although physical planning rested heavily on the verdicts of 'experts' – architects, city planners and engineers – much was made of supposedly democratic consultations with the public and 'ordinary' people's constructive engagement with the process (Cowan, 2013). Planners talked (disingenuously) about the potential for new model housing and towns to emerge from neighbours' conversations about their wants and needs (Royal Institute of British Architects, 1943). One of the tropes of documentary films in the war years and the immediate post-war period was their apparent eavesdropping on citizens in the street – or very often in the pub – talking about reconstruction and their hopes for the new Britain (for example, *A City Reborn* (1945)). This idea of a national conversation, going on at the most local level between work colleagues and neighbours, became part of the bolstering of post-war planning as a democratic process – though it was always in tension with the concomitant emphasis on the role of technical expertise, whether in the Beveridge Report or the schemes put forward by city architects (Tiratsoo, 2000).

Post-war planning also made heavy use of the concept of the 'neighbourhood', cited as a core unit in building communities (Homer, 2000). In the field of town planning, 'neighbourhood' was already established as a key concept by the time of the Second World War (Talen, 2017). But it became a major focus for planning schemes, in both Britain and United States, by the 1950s (Mumford, 1954; Hacon, 1955). The ubiquity of the references can distract attention from the fact that planning 'neighbourhood' units was being interpreted in at least two distinct, and often incompatible ways: as a practical means of organising the provision of services for a community defined by its size and location, and as a more utopian attempt to encourage forms of social behaviour and interaction within a functioning 'community' (Talen, 2017; Hollow, 2012). At a time when the nature of relationships between neighbours was in fact subject to critical scrutiny in community studies (e.g. Black and Simey, 1954), the use of the term 'neighbourhood' was also applied as a positive gloss to the character of life in new, modern developments. When Siegfried Charoux was commissioned in 1957 by the London County Council to produce an outdoor sculpture for the Quadrant housing estate in Islington, the resulting resin sculpture featured two men seated shoulder to shoulder, entitled 'The Neighbours', and praised at the time as an example of public art designed to promote 'social cohesion' (Whiteley, 2011: 140–1).

Some planners at least were committed to the idea that the use of the neighbourhood unit might indeed inculcate the kind of relationships and connections evoked in Charoux's sculpture. For them, the neighbourhood model was more than simply a practical way of structuring housing and facilities, and was in fact capable of fostering greater egalitarianism, building on the social solidarity of the war years and 'erod[ing] class distinctions' (Clapson, 2000: 1–2). The realities of community identities and priorities might even, as in the wartime ideals, feed into the building of these new neighbourhoods. A handbook published to encourage and guide community associations in the early 1950s noted that, since planning was based around the neighbourhood unit, 'It is quite obvious therefore that, if neighbourhood planning is to be sound and democratic, there must be some means whereby the voice of the neighbourhood can be heard and the desires and needs of the people expressed' (National Federation of Community Associations, 1955: 56).

Whilst there was at least some notion that the principles for, and practical expressions of, the new Britain might emerge from such neighbourly exchanges, planners themselves often cherished the hope that planning could foster neighbourliness in return: that 'We may decide for ourselves if we want to get to know our neighbours, but [the planner] provides us with opportunities to do so' (Black and Simey, 1954: 9). Others, however, were doubtful about the potential for a revived neighbourliness to echo the fabled culture of wartime. Professor S. E. Rasmussen, speaking at the International Federation for Housing and Town Planning in June 1948, argued that 'we should make no religion out of the neighbourhood unit. The danger of bombs brought people together, the danger has gone, and so has the neighbourhood spirit. Don't foster too much of local patriotism – it is just as bad as too much nationalism' (Hasegawa, 1999: 156).

One of the ironies of post-war planning was that many new housing developments seemed to destroy rather than nurture the sense of being part of a neighbourhood. A new nostalgia grew up for the 'traditional' working-class communities vulnerable to planners' schemes for clearance and re-housing (Butler, 2015: 206). Influential studies, such as Michael Young and Peter Willmott, *Family and Kinship in East London* (1957), documented the extended family networks that provided a system of mutual support in working-class areas, contrasting these with the sense of dislocation that accompanied moves to new housing estates. From something which had crossed class boundaries in wartime, neighbourliness in the post-war period was often identified, and indeed cherished, as existing within particular communities, most notably a 'traditional' working-class setting. Working-class neighbourliness was broadcast to the nation in soap operas set in the terraced streets and local pubs that were emerging as its most 'authentic' location: *Coronation Street* (Granada Television, 1960), and *EastEnders* (BBC, 1985).

Neighbourliness as social democracy?

Neighbourliness in the post-war period has retained its prominence as a desirable feature of British society, albeit somewhat overwhelmed since the 1990s by evocations of 'community'. References to neighbourliness tend to assume that it operates only at the most local of levels, determining individual relationships but rarely providing the kinds of education and participation associated with its inspirational heyday during the Second World War. It has become more transactional: a form of support waiting in the wings, rather than always on display. Already in the early 1950s, it was being described as taking 'manifest' and 'latent' forms, the first referring to regular experiences of sociability and mutual exchange, and the latter relating to a readiness to help in cases of crisis (Mann, 1954: 164). And in his fieldwork in housing estates in the

Wirral, Peter Mann concluded that this latent neighbourliness was the more reliable indication of a healthy, functioning community (Mann, 1954: 168). A more recent study, by Ray Forrest and Gay Bridge, also defined neighbourliness in these modest terms as 'the exchange of small services or support in an emergency against a background of routine convivial exchanges' (Pilch, 2006: 14).

Even an emphasis on this kind of mutual assistance at the most parochial of levels ran contrary to the direction in which national policy had been developing. As Keith Snell has commented, the general trend in British life seemed to be that 'Sources of security have … shifted from the local arena to national rights and benefits' (Snell, 2016: 244). However, neighbourhood schemes had the potential to supplement or make up for gaps in formal state provision. Some community associations in the 1950s spawned 'Good Neighbours' sections, visiting the sick and organising various forms of 'home help' alongside the development of the National Health Service and other welfare provisions (National Federation of Community Associations, 1955: 55). There was nothing inherent in the mobilisation of neighbourliness that necessarily aligned such initiatives with progressive political sentiments. Indeed, often the reverse. In the 1980s, the Conservative Home Secretary Douglas Hurd encouraged 'Neighbourhood Watch' groups as a form of active citizenship, while the popular uptake of Neighbourhood Watch, though overtly non-political, arguably became a form of grassroots participation in the Thatcherite project of the privatisation of services provided by the state (Moores, 2017).

In the early twentieth-first century, neighbourliness has become something that politicians want to encourage as a component in active 'communities', and often as a potential salve for gaps in the public provision of services: a way of addressing difficult areas of policy, such as well-being in old age, social inclusion, safety and quality of life. The New Labour government set up its Neighbourhood Renewal Unit in 2001, headed by Joe Montgomery, who contended that 'promoting neighbourliness is as vital as improving public services and maintaining the public spaces in our neighbourhoods' (Pilch, 2006: 52). Montgomery, drawing on his background work in urban regeneration, made overt connections between neighbourliness and participation within a civic culture, defining neighbourliness as the 'practical expression of the universal need to feel a sense of belonging with the people around us. It is marked by a shared attitude of mutuality and concern for the well-being and happiness of one's neighbours. It is rooted in individual interactions, but these everyday contacts underpin a broader sense of active civic engagement and a sense of common purpose' (Pilch, 2006: 47).

In other words, neighbourliness could be a building block for wider social responsibility, engagement with the public sphere, and perhaps even a commitment to a social democratic politics.

This connection between neighbourly feelings and a broader scope for participation within public life brings us much closer to the prospects being imagined during the Second World War, and to G. D. H. Cole's idea of a democracy that – like charity – begins at home. All sorts of optimistic projects blossomed in the war years, like the movement for a 'People's Common Law Parliament', evoking the traditions of Magna Carta and calling for an end to poverty and to war, arguing that the 'training' of citizens required the individual to learn how to 'live in harmony with his fellows and to take an active part in self-government with the object of promoting the well-being of his fellows' (Scrutton, 1944: 25). These were the ideals being expressed in the language of neighbourliness. Unlike the blueprint neighbourhoods of post-war reconstruction, this neighbourliness was not restricted to interactions with people living in one's immediate vicinity. It was interpreted in a liberal, expansive way, explicitly encompassing people of varied backgrounds, extending even to the 'neighbourliness' of a new world order of peace and cooperation between nations. Neighbourliness, then, was not a straightforward re-animation of the known, organic community. It was a recognition of common interests and responsibilities between disparate strangers thrown together in the disruption of war.

Historians' debates about the experience of the 'people's war' have tended to throw a sceptical light on enthusiastic contemporary commentaries about social solidarity and a new-found neighbourliness. But, almost irrespective of the reality of any supposed rediscovery of feelings of community in Britain during the Second World War, the *idea* of neighbourliness opened up a different political territory, between the private sphere of the home and the public sector of government. This failed to become mainstream in the immediate post-war years, during a period when welfare and reform tended to be imagined as goods to be provided by the state, rather than in collaboration with an active citizenship. Yet the practice of neighbourliness continued to attract the interest of those considering different ways of thinking about government and society. In 1951, Michael Young, the author of Labour's 1945 manifesto wrote about the need to get back to the 'moral heart' of the party in family and local community, and in the civic virtues of 'solidarity and mutual aid', exploring 'neighbourly socialism' as a potential 'third force' in politics (Briggs, 2006: 22–3). Amidst concerns about citizenship and urban renewal, and the scope for reinvigoration of the 'public domain', it may yet have a contribution to make (Meller, 1995; Marquand, 2004b).

References

Addison, Paul (1994) *The Road to 1945: British Politics and the Second World War* (London: Pimlico).

Black, E. I. and Simey, T. S. (1954) *Neighbourhood and Community. An Enquiry into Social Relationships on Housing Estates in Liverpool and Sheffield* (Liverpool: University Press of Liverpool).

Briggs, Asa (2006) 'The Labour Party as Crucible', *Political Quarterly*, 77(1), 17–26

Burton, Alan, O'Sullivan, Tim and Wells, Paul (2000) *The Family Way. The Boulting Brothers and British Film Culture* (Trowbridge: Flicks Books).

Butler, Lise (2015) 'Michael Young, the Institute of Community Studies, and the politics of kinship', *Twentieth Century British History*, 26(2), 203–24.

Calder, Angus (1991) *The Myth of the Blitz* (London: Pimlico).

Chapman, James (2000) 'Why we fight: *Pastor Hall* and *Thunder Rock*', in Alan Burton, Tim O'Sullivan and Paul Wells, *The Family Way. The Boulting Brothers and British Film Culture* (Trowbridge: Flicks Books), 81–96.

A City Reborn (1945) dir. John Eldridge, Gryphon Films, in association with Verity Films/Ministry of Information.

Clapson, Mark (2000) 'Introduction', *Contemporary British History*, 14(1), 1–2.

Cockayne, Emily (2013) *Cheek by Jowl. A History of Neighbours* (London: Vintage).

Cole, G. D. H. (1942) *Great Britain in the Post-war World* (London: Victor Gollancz).

Cole, Margaret (1945) *The General Election 1945 and After* (London: Fabian Society).

Cowan, Susanne (2013) 'The People's Peace: the myth of wartime unity and public consent for town planning', in Mark Clapson and Peter Larkham (eds), *The Blitz and its Legacy* (London: Routledge), 73–86.

Fielding, Steven (1992) 'What did "the people" want? The meaning of the 1945 general election', *Historical Journal*, 35(3), 623–39.

Fox, Jo (2006) 'Millions like us? Accented language and the "ordinary" in British films of the Second World War', *Journal of British Studies*, 45(4), 819–45.

Grant, Matthew (2011) '"Civil Defence Gives Meaning to Your Leisure": citizenship, participation, and cultural change in Cold War recruitment propaganda, 1949–54', *Twentieth Century British History*, 22(1), 52–78.

Hacon, R. J. (1955) 'Neighbourhoods or Neighbourhood Units?', *Sociological Review*, 3(2), 235–46.

Hasegawa, Junichi (1999) 'The Rise and Fall of Radical Reconstruction in 1940s Britain', *Twentieth Century British History*, 10(2), 137–61.

Hinton, James (2002) *Women, Social Leadership, and the Second World War. Continuities of Class* (Oxford: Oxford University Press).

Hollow, Matthew (2012) 'Utopian urges: visions for reconstruction in Britain, 1940–1950', *Planning Perspectives*, 27(4), 569–85.

Homer, Andrew (2000) 'Creating new communities: the role of the neighbourhood unit in post-war British planning', *Contemporary British History*, 14(1), 63–80.

Horder, Thomas Jeeves (1941) 'The modern troglodyte', *Journal of the Royal Society of Arts*, 89(4586), 365–74.

House of Commons (1940) *Parliamentary Debates*, 365.

Mann, Peter H. (1954) 'The concept of neighborliness', *American Journal of Sociology*, 60, 163–68.

Marquand, David (2004a) *Decline of the Public. The Hollowing Out of Citizenship* (Cambridge: Polity).

Marquand, David (2004b) 'False Friend: the state and the public domain', *Political Quarterly*, 75(1), 51–62.

Marquand, David (2015) *Mammon's Kingdom. An Essay on Britain Now* (London: Penguin).

Mass-Observation (1943) *An Enquiry into People's Homes. A Report Prepared by Mass-Observation for the Advertising Service Guild* (London: John Murray).

Mass-Observation (1944) 'The Crisis', November 1944, file report, Mass-Observation archive.

McKibbin, Ross (2010) *Parties and People. England 1914–1951* (Oxford: Oxford University Press).

Meller, Helen (1995) 'Urban renewal and citizenship: the quality of life in British cities, 1890–1990', *Urban History*, 22(1), 63–84.

Milburn, Clara (1995) *Mrs Milburn's Diaries: an Englishwoman's Day-to-Day Reflections 1939–1945*, ed. Peter Donnelly (London: Abacus).

Ministry of Information (1945) *Land at War. The official story of British farming 1939–1944* (London: HMSO).

Moores, Chris (2017) 'Thatcher's troops? Neighbourhood Watch schemes and the search for "ordinary" Thatcherism in 1980s Britain', *Contemporary British History*, 31(2), 230–55.

Morgan, K. O. (1991) *The People's Peace. British History since 1945* (Oxford: Oxford University Press).

Mumford, Lewis (1954) 'The neighbourhood and the neighbourhood unit', *Town Planning Review*, 24, 256–70.

National Federation of Community Associations (1955 [1950]) *Our Neighbourhood. A Handbook of Information for Community Centres and Associations* (London: National Council of Social Service).

Odhams Press (1944) *Ourselves in Wartime: An Illustrated Survey of the Home Front in the Second World War* (London: Odhams Press).

Paris, Michael (2000) 'Filming the people's war: *The Dawn Guard*, *Desert Victory*, *Tunisian Victory* and *Burma Victory*', in Alan Burton, Tim O'Sullivan and Paul Wells (eds), *The Family Way. The Boulting Brothers and British Film Culture* (Trowbridge: Flicks Books), 97–108.

Pilch, Tony (ed.) (2006) *Neighbourliness* (London: Smith Institute).

Royal Institute of British Architects (1943) *Rebuilding Britain* (London: Lund Humphries).

Scrutton, Robert J. (1944) 'The education of a democracy', in J. Russell Orr and Robert J. Scrutton, *Teach the People to Rule* (London: St George Book Co.), 24–41.

Short, Brian (2014) *The Battle of the Fields: Rural Community and Authority in Britain During the Second World War* (Woodbridge: Boydell Press).

Snell, K. D. M. (2016) *Spirits of Community. English Senses of Belonging and Loss, 1750–2000* (London: Bloomsbury).

Spender, Stephen (1945) *Citizens in War – and After* (London: George G. Harrap and Co.).

Spender, Stephen (1997 [1951]) *World Within World* (London: Faber).

Talen, Emily (2017) 'Social science and the planned neighbourhood', *Town Planning Review*, 88(3), 349–72.

The Dawn Guard (1941) dir. Roy Boulting, Charter Film Productions/Ministry of Information.

Tiratsoo, Nick (2000) 'The reconstruction of blitzed British cities, 1945–55: myths and reality', *Contemporary British History*, 14(1), 27–44.

Titmuss, Richard and Kay (1942) *Parents Revolt* (London: Secker & Warburg).

Welshman, John (1998) 'Evacuation and social policy during the Second World War: myth and reality', *Twentieth Century British History*, 9(1), 28–53.

Whiteley, Gillian (2011) 'Re-presenting reality, recovering the social: the poetics and politics of social realism and visual art', in David Tucker (ed.), *British Social Realism in the Arts since 1940* (Basingstoke: Palgrave Macmillan).

9

As if: contestation, care and the 'temper of the country'

Gideon Calder

The temper of the country

The public interest is not a fixed essence to be derived from first principles through some allegedly value-free calculus of individual costs and benefits, or a kind of Mosaic tablet brought down from Mount Sinai by the great and good. It is inherently contestable, both in the sense that agreement on it can never be final, and in the sense that it is normally defined through conflict and the resolution of conflict. (Marquand, 2004: 33)

We find reminders across David Marquand's writings that a good society is not a destination but an ongoing project, always under reconstruction. To the point he makes above, we might add that the contestation pushing this along plays out across various public settings: in think tanks, on the streets, through public institutions, in research seminars, on social media and in the flux and informality of everyday life. The work is done by theoreticians and practitioners, policy wonks and activists, journalists and novelists, film-makers and dramatists, the 'professional' and the 'lay'. This tells of a complex, pluralistic enterprise. Each setting or role is distinct, in its feel, its purpose and the ways in which people engage with each other. The language used and the kinds of work under way in each will vary and shift, often quite radically. Twitter exchanges or a photographic diary of poverty may be as material to the project as lengthy fine-grained conceptual treatments. And it's not that the definition of such a term emerges fully formed and perfect in the seminar room or through policy documents, while enacting it is a follow-up task to be obediently carried out by the foot-soldiers. What the public interest amounts to is shaped as much through the struggles of citizens and practitioners as at the levels of policy or academic theory. It is defined as much on the streets as at the drawing-board. And, of course, in neither place do those definitions settle, but keep on being contested. What do we share in common? What are our priorities? What does fairness mean? How should we respond to cultural diversity? What is 'well-being', and how might it be socially promoted? The answers here are not self-evident. Rather, they are triggers for a difficult conversation.

Among its very many precious contributions, Marquand's work has thrown searching light on the essential place of such conversation, and – just as urgently – on the waning of its quality under neoliberalism. It punctuates his attention to the lack of a 'philosophy of the public realm' (Marquand, 1988: 11), and his probing of the disconnect between 'the liberal-minded radical intelligentsia' and the core constituencies of progressive parties (Marquand, 1991; Marquand, 1997). For while in early twenty-first-century Britain all of the above things happen, and matter, this does not mean that the conversation coheres or flourishes as it might, or that it is grasped and analysed to the degree that its sheer importance demands. Marquand's claim, quoted above, can be read in a non-partisan way: social democrats, just as democrats, should savour the kinds of contestation at stake. It might also be taken more pointedly as a reminder to social democrats, about both means and ends. The achievement of a progressive agenda is partly about outcome, and partly about process; partly about the architecture of a good society, and partly about what it's like to inhabit one; partly about policy, and partly about street-level dynamics. So as well as coherent doctrine it requires, as R. H. Tawney once put it, a certain 'temper' in the country (Tawney, 1932: 340). It needs more than the tracking of academic or policy debates. It is not enough that economic structures are transformed, or constitutional rules set aright. A good society depends too on the everyday choices and orientations of people inhabiting those structures, the quality of relations between them, and an ethic of public involvement. For Tawney, this means 'the creation of a body of men and women who, whether trade unionists or intellectuals, put Socialism first, and whose creed carries conviction because they live in accordance with it' (Tawney, 1932: 340). Making social democrats, as we might also say.

In some respects, of course, Tawney's point speaks of the time of its making. Labour had lost badly in the general election of 1931. Fertile disputes were afoot on the means by which to achieve a more egalitarian society – a project which seemed both highly fragile and uncertain in shape. It was as part of a then-unfolding argument with 'the Webbs and the communists', as his *New Statesman* obituarist put it, that Tawney insisted on the primacy of human behaviour to the viability of socialism, and rejected as a fallacy any notion that 'a change in the machinery of government was itself enough' (cited in Goldman, 2014: 189; cf. Cruddas, 2009). Yet the stakes of the temper of the country are as high now as they were then, and the hopes of progressives similarly muted. Indeed, during and since the political shifts of 2016, in the climate of the Brexit vote and the election of Donald Trump, whether we are reliving the 1930s has become something of a motif of political commentary. Across Europe and the United States, the mood keeps seeming to confound stock analyses, with shifts to the populist right echoing the darkest periods of the twentieth century. It is uncontroversial that, as Marquand himself puts it, 'all over Europe, social democracy is in retreat, even crisis' (in Calder *et al.*, 2016: 47). The temper of the country is not, in any obvious way, friendly to moves in the direction either of a more fair and equal society, or of a richer, sharper public conversation about what such a society would be like.

Tawney's own work gives us an example of how to work on this terrain, shifting without hiccup between settings, registers and vocabularies. Few modern figures, as his recent biographer Laurence Goldman says, 'have moved so easily between the different arenas and levels of British politics, education and scholarship' (Goldman, 2014: 7). Yet David Marquand is another who has done just this, in a different milieu but with similar dexterity. In recognition of this, this chapter seeks to show why such movement matters, and to press on distinctly Marquandian questions about the state of the public realm and the temper of the country now, four decades into the heavy influence of neoliberalism, and perhaps, indeed, as we move towards its twilight. It comes at this from two different angles.

The first is the relation of academic doctrine to the 'real world'. As a tradition, social democracy has depended on good connections here. But there is a case to be made that academic habits have eroded them. This case is made forcefully by the neo-pragmatist American philosopher Richard Rorty in his 1998 book *Achieving Our Country*. This book has picked up revived notoriety since Trump's political arrival, because of a passage which seems uncannily close to a prediction of his rise:

> members of labor unions, and unorganised unskilled workers, will sooner or later realize that their government is not even trying to prevent wages from sinking or to prevent jobs from being exported. Around the same time, they will realize that suburban white-collar workers – themselves desperately afraid of being downsized – are not going to let themselves be taxed to provide social benefits for anyone else. At that point, something will crack. The non-suburban electorate will decide that the system has failed and start looking around for a

strongman to vote for – someone willing to assure them that, once he is elected, the smug bureaucrats, tricky lawyers, overpaid bond salesmen, and postmodernist professors will no longer be calling the shots. (Rorty, 1998: 89–90)

But this point reflects a wider one, for Rorty, which concerns the severance between different parts of the broad progressive coalition. As for Marquand in *The Progressive Dilemma*, this coalition is vital, but fragile. A large part of its demise, Rorty argues, has been down to the habits of the intelligentsia – and their shift from being agents (politically engaged, proposing programmes of reform) to spectators, using jargon, and inhabiting a milieu, both of which are at a clear remove from the everyday lives of the disadvantaged in society whose interests they claim to have at heart (Rorty, 1998, *passim*; Calder, 2007: 143–7). So it is worth addressing how academic habits might have contributed to this. Specifically, I look at how a certain enthusiasm for models is both a very limited, partial way of approaching social and political questions, and something which, when it becomes the basis for policy, has potentially drastic effects symptomatic of, inter alia, the disconnect between 'professionalised' politics and the publics with whom it purports to engage. The case of neoliberalism is taken as a kind of archetype of this.

The second angle shows that there is nothing necessary about the gap between academic critique and the experience of social change. It reflects a cluster of themes in recent social and political philosophy, concerning the place of care in understandings of the just society. The infrastructures of care are themselves regularly said to be creaking or in crisis, across the regions of the UK. Both the health service and the social care of older people are identified as being under unprecedented strain, and close to collapse. Life expectancy is taking a dip; mortality among older people is rising (Green *et al.*, 2017). We might see this faltering as a kind of culmination of the sustained lack of a coherent philosophy of public intervention, and of a poorly nourished conversation about the public interest. A symptom of these absences is that we are unable to find a language in which to address the public's stake in the intimate, individuated work which care involves – often in a domestic setting, or in residential homes. Like the domestic labour the value of which feminist critics highlighted in their critique of mainstream understandings of the economy and the conditions of it functioning, care work is often unacknowledged, if not hidden. Take it away, and the risks to the common good are drastic.

Broaching these themes does not provide a programme for social democratic renewal. Rather, it points to issues which twenty-first-century social democrats need to fix on and work through, to make good on their own project. And it also highlights the value of a certain vein of critical thinking, from which any such programme will fruitfully draw. It is an orientation epitomised in David Marquand's work. I start by saying a little more about what it amounts to, which also helps explain my title.

Two senses of 'as if'

Mostly, the phrase 'as if' gets used in one of two ways, both illuminating. One is captured in a former strapline of the ever-vital London think tank the New Economics Foundation (NEF) (New Economics Foundation, 2017): 'Economics as if people and the planet mattered'. Here, 'as if' involves a deliberate suspension of the ways about it that we would otherwise be thinking. It is the self-conscious taking of an alternative perspective which offers something different or better. Let's do economics *as if* people mattered, say the NEF – and the planet. (This might sound a rather unarresting proposal, until we are reminded that the dominant models of neo-classical economics have been *defined* by limited thinking about people and the planet.) Regardless of the orthodoxy, they suggest, we should try talking about economics *as if* the discipline had different priorities. The suspension of 'normal service' carries with it a kind of promise: the confirmation of something lost or obscured, but important and real. Here it is also a kind of injunction – a mobilisation to think differently.

The other usage of 'as if' is best achieved with spoken words, with a stress on the second, paired ideally with the pulling of a facial expression (incredulous, affronted by the mere suggestion) deployed often, for example, by Alicia Silverstone in the film *Clueless* (1995). As *if* I would do that. As if *that's* ever likely to happen. As *if* the world were like that. It might suggest 'if only', and carry a sense of regret that the world is not like that. Or it might – as when Silverstone's character Cher brushes off the sudden advances of a fellow student while walking across campus with an 'Ugh – as *if!!*' (Heckerling, 1995) – mean something closer to 'over my dead body'. Either way it equates roughly to 'yeah, *right*'. It conveys savvyness, a lack of naivety, irony, scepticism – and most importantly, a flat rejection of the very plausibility of whatever has just been proposed.

I think it is important to talk about both senses of 'as if', in connection with how we understand and speak about the public interest, and the current horizons of social democracy. Both have their place. Good negotiation of the public interest seems by its nature to involve thinking and acting *as if* the world might be different, and better. So it certainly needs some NEF. Appeals to the common good may also, to many, seem implausibly idealistic, vain, or naive. 'So we'll all converge in a functioning public realm on some shared, coherent notion of the common good? Yeah, *right*.' Yet, while the *Clueless* version of 'as if' may sound like cynicism, or just a diversion, we need it too, in the right measure. Something like it informs some of the most penetrating critiques of modern social norms and structures, or, as in Alasdair MacIntyre's phrase, 'the self-images of the age' (MacIntyre, 1971). This kind of sceptical distancing is not sufficient for good thinking in a social democratic vein, but it's often a necessary element of it. As a way of exploring why, it's worth returning to the question of how scholarly practices and habits hook up (or not) with the world they purport to be about.

Academic doctrine, the public realm and two different kinds of realism

Public intervention implies a public purpose: otherwise, those who do the intervening cannot know what they are trying to achieve. But in a political culture shaped by the assumption that society is made up of separate, atomistic individuals, pursuing only their own private purposes, the notion of a public purpose which is more than the sum of private purposes is apt to seem dangerous, or meaningless, or both. (Marquand, 1988: 10–11)

The most important questions people tend to face in their everyday lives are normative ones of what is good or bad about what is happening, including how others are treating them, and of how to act, and what to do for the best. The presence of this concern may be evident in fleeting encounters, and mundane conversations, in feelings about how things are going, as well as in momentous decisions ... They are matters of practical reason, about how to act. (Sayer, 2011: 1–2)

Social democrats are driven by their normative commitments, but this is mainly because they are human beings. It is banal to say that our view of the world is shaped by our own orientations and preferences. We do not see things from nowhere, through a perfect lens, but always mediated by where and who we are, by background influences and the tools at our disposal. Impartiality is unlikely, and in some senses impossible. This is not because we are necessarily selfish, or incapable of getting outside of our own heads, but because human beings are helpless evaluators: we are *normative* beings. We thrive on doing things we value, or think are right, and in contrasting ourselves with others of whose values we take a dimmer view, perhaps via what Freud (1961) called 'the narcissism of minor differences', or perhaps concerning divergence on a grander scale. This, as Sayer says, is the stuff of practical reason. Reasoning itself may not go smoothly or well. Our normativity is fractured and convoluted by all kinds of factors which make the practice of value judgement a treacherous business.

So it goes, for example, for university researchers. While the idea of a university promises a glorious sharing of expertise, they are also full of territoriality. Academics, just doing their everyday stuff, often seem trammelled within the parameters set by what they themselves are good at. It is not necessarily that they walk around with hierarchies of knowledge in their heads, with their own home discipline installed comfortably at the top. It's just that their habits of thought tend to make some kinds of question, and some kinds of answer, *obviously* more important and valuable than others.

Also, in universities, partiality breeds power. Orthodoxies and models of what counts as wisdom define careers. People have an interest, beyond the pursuit of knowledge itself, in protecting and promoting their 'take' on what counts as appropriate knowledge. It doesn't follow from this that (this would be the inflated, extravagant version) there's no such thing as truth, or that might is right. It does mean, though, that in the university, like anywhere, there is politics and territoriality and that, often, those territories track either disciplinary boundaries, or schools of thought within disciplines, or the (often happenstance) coagulation of subjects into faculties and schools.

This is ironic because the world itself is not disciplinary. It doesn't divide up into tectonic plates, each the province of a separate subject area. Disciplines are not domains, mirrored in separate realities explored by (e.g.) chemists and ceramicists, aeronautics and anthropology. The world is largely indifferent to the disciplinary boundaries which dominate the professionalised domain of knowledge.

This point can be expressed in terms of *realism*. Philosophically, realism comes in two species. On the one hand it refers to ontology, and specifically the stance that the world is as it is, independently of what we know or say about it. So for realists in this vein, planes fly because we figured out some aspects of the way the world was already working, and harnessed these in appropriate ways. Medicines work because of accurate ontological assumptions about bodies, and chemicals. When social policy works, this is because it has captured things about the way human beings and social structures are, and work with the grain of those rather than against them. It has, in Tawney's sense, tuned in to human behaviour, worked with the grain of it to bend it in ways conducive to the fulfilment of good outcomes. This is not to say that very many things aren't socially constructed, and that much of what we see about us is contingent, and could be otherwise. We will not understand gender or race or disability or youth or mental illness without paying hard attention to the ways in which discourses and social perceptions shape and categorise and set boundaries. It is, though, to say that there is more to the world around us than is shaped by discourse, or perceptions, or our ways of describing it. Mere doctrine does not realities make.

The other sense of realism refers to a political starting point. We start from ground level, from where things are, working with the mess of things, rather than from ideal models with at best an approximate relation to that mess. Political realism must be modest, critical and historically honest. The point is not that there is no such thing as the social reality, but that we should be deeply wary of accepting, and installing through policy and practice, any particular picture of it, or expecting it to conform to how we would prefer things to be. Our normative commitments are not the authors of reality, however crucial they are to our engagement with it.

One can be a realist of either species, without being both. But combining the two has much to commend it. One advantage is that it avoids fetishisation of abstract models. Conceptual frameworks are just that. They shed light, but do not give us deep explanations. They help us see problems, but do not deliver answers. And they are always liable to interruption by (to put it simplistically) reality – the stuff which the model-makers left out, or were not precise about, or failed to anticipate.

The limits of 'free' market orthodoxy

As we found out with a bump during the crash of 2008 and the subsequent financial crisis, sometimes the most orthodox of models are profoundly limited in what they will account for or explain. This was particularly true of the neoliberal orthodoxy dominant both in economics syllabuses and the City of London – 'market fundamentalism', as even the Governor of the Bank of England came to call it (see Tencer 2014 – but before that, Marquand, 2014: 74–87). The idea that the 'free market' always knows best, that it is the supreme mechanism for distributing and gauging the value of goods and services, be they biscuits or transport, cars or public parks, depends on a mathematical model, to be taught via graphs and curves. It gives rules of thumb about what to expect, if seeking lower inflation, greater capital mobility, greater labour market flexibility and other items deemed priorities. It is also, of course, a piece of ideology. It is based on partial and highly contestable assumptions about human life, and the choices people make. It depends on simplifying reality, and ironing out all those levels of social structure and individual or group agency which would warp the model or make it less neat. It depends on the eccentric idea that markets are ever actually *free* in the first place.

The idea that they are – as in free from external interference – depends on a definition of 'free' which unravels as soon as it is articulated. As Ha-Joon Chang helpfully puts it:

> The free market doesn't exist. Every market has some rules and boundaries that restrict freedom of choice. A market looks free only because we so unconditionally accept its underlying restrictions that we fail to see them. How 'free' a market is cannot be objectively defined. It is a political definition. The usual claim by free-market economists that they are trying to defend the market from politically motivated interference by the government is false. Government is always involved and the free-marketeers are as politically motivated as anyone. (Chang, 2011: 1)

We will not understand capitalism (everything good or otherwise about it), says Chang, unless we understand this, which is a step as vital for capitalism's biggest fans as for those who would bury it. The idea that markets might be free and that within them it is individual initiative that is the prime or sole generator or wealth is pithily undone in an oft-quoted passage from Massachusetts Senator Elizabeth Warren:

> There is nobody in this country who got rich on their own. Nobody. You built a factory out there – good for you. But I want to be clear. You moved your goods to market on roads the rest of us paid for. You hired workers the rest of us paid to educate. You were safe in your factory because of police forces and fire forces that the rest of us paid for. You didn't have to worry that marauding bands would come and seize everything at your factory … Now look. You built a factory and it turned into something terrific or a great idea – God bless! Keep a hunk of it. But part of the underlying social contract is you take a hunk of that and pay forward for the next kid who comes along. (Warren, 2011)

Here is something you can stick your neck out on: the Warren version of how wealth is generated is simply truer than its individualist opposite, if that is the thesis that somehow, yes, the rich are indeed 'self-made'. Which makes it all the more striking that even since the 2008 crash, so few establishment politicians (whether in the United States or the United Kingdom) will actually say that kind of thing in public, when people are listening, or might write it down. (For more on the journey of neoliberalism into 'commonsense', see Harvey, 2005.)

So the term 'free market' is a kind of conceit – one which serves various interests (particularly, those of the economically most powerful) and neglects others. It is a simplification of reality, but also a distortion. It does not account for the non-market forces – 'the cultural, institutional or political factors' (Marquand, 1988: 4) which must obtain, beyond the radar of the model, in order for things to proceed as they do. Yet it persists. In fact, it does more than persist. As fundamentalisms go, it's the most spectacularly successful of modern times. It has reshaped the way most people look at the world. There are few depictions of all of this as vivid as that in *Mammon's Kingdom* (2014), and few which do as much justice to the realist complaint that models will always be reductive, and that obedience to them requires squeezing complex levels and facets of the social world into a single catch-all rubric, a closed system, which must, by definition, serve to reify and falsify the world for which it is presented as a map.

And this points to another commendation of both realist stances set out here. Sometimes we seek reliable codes, providing firm, strident, all-purpose directions for how to negotiate the messy business of reality. So for example, professions have their codes of ethics, and sometimes it seems as if to be an ethical practitioner is simply to follow the rules, to know what 'the profession' has decided is 'the right thing to do', and do it. But as anyone teaching ethics with professionals will know, any code of ethics is only as good as its practical interpretation by people doing their job. 'Treat service-users with respect' is not some kind of self-explanatory principle which tracks and self-applies itself to every circumstance. If followed, it's a cue for practical reason, a kind of banister when we figure out what to do, rather than something which gives perfect pre-ordained coordinates of our destination. Ethics is about considerably more than knowing the rules, and is never reducible to it. This indeed is why it is worth having classes on ethics at the core of the curricula for professional qualifications, classes in which people get into the messy, sticky, often anxious business of what it is like to make moral decisions involving the well-being and rights – and just the complexity of the situations – of those they will actually work with. It is in this sense that ethics is 'embodied in distinctive practices', in the *practice* of citizenship, in trust, in social learning, in the navigation of complexity, and indeed in the contestation which characterises the public realm (Marquand, 2004: 34, 35).

So being a realist about models and codes and frameworks means recognising their limits. It is to insist on the gap between maps and the terrains they depict. Maps are beautiful, elegant and full of wonder. They are rich and vital aids. Like an eye, they are a part of the world they depict, as well as opening it up for us and helping us make sense of it. But they are not coterminous with that world.

The design of a building is one thing; its use is something else. Blueprints of any kind can be glorious or obscure or flatly dull: how they hook up with the world of practice is another matter. There will always have to be some 'give' in any model we adopt, because there are other models, and because the world itself will never neatly match whichever models we deploy. This is worth bearing in mind by members of any academic discipline or policy think tank, whose favoured maps of the terrain will differ from those in the building (and sometimes the office) next door. But it is just as salient for practitioners, political agents and (if this isn't too grandiose) everyone with a role in understanding the world and making a difference in it. Social democrats have their own good reasons not to mistake models for reality, conflate grand designs and the temper of the country, or make as if negotiating all the nuances of the world can be done by applying the right framework to it, however nuanced the framework. The example of care, and its squeezing out, helps accentuate this.

The neglect of care

Why even use care as an example of something social democrats should think more or better about? Why might care have been neglected in understandings of the good society, and the public interest? How might it have come to represent so glaring an example of an issue central to the flourishing of any society, yet consistently neglected in the conversation about priorities? A powerful means of analysing this comes via work on care by feminist political theorists. On the one hand, the need for care is fundamental. There is no reliable way of conceiving of the human condition without placing care at its basis. Being adequately cared for is a precondition of our development from infancy to adulthood, and of our resilience through illness and as older people. Just in persisting, we move in and out of dependence on the care of others. Yet on the other hand, the significance of care has tended to be elided in models of social justice (see Calder, 2016: 27–31). Long traditions of political thinking, typically by men, have left care relations out of the picture or, at most, addressed them as a footnote. This is partly because of their tendency to neglect the domestic and the intimate, or to park these in a 'private sphere', off the radar of justice. It is also because care has been gendered: taken for granted, understood as women's work and as economically non-productive, when we might alternatively insist, as Nancy Folbre does, that 'success in caring for one another is a precondition for the production of goods and services, but also an end result, a goal' (Folbre, 1994: 1). Caring is not a costless activity. As Tony Fitzpatrick puts it, 'political conceptions of justice are therefore needed as guidance to how and why those costs should be borne' (Fitzpatrick, 2003: 115).

A further reason for care's neglect lies in the way choice has been valorised, sometimes in political theory (where it has been core to voluntarist and contractualist understandings of citizens' responsibilities, for which it is the 'chosenness' of a relationship that generates obligations) but more emphatically still in the rhetoric of marketisation. Here, choice takes on an iconic, a priori status, and stands for much more than the making of meaningful decisions. Marquand depicts it as 'a reified "Choice" with a capital "C", which has little to do with the mundane choices of real-world parents, or patients or students' (Marquand, 2013: 122). It is both an emblem of, and a vehicle for, the extension of the market society, and fundamental to 'a public doctrine that rules out any possibility of fundamental change' (Marquand, 2013: 151). It has become key both to the explanation of how things are, so that we increasingly believe that disadvantage is chosen, rather than due to social injustice, and, as a catch-all metric, to the assessment of how they might be better. Progress will come with choice having been extended further, through the steady commodification of education, health, social care: right across the circumstances of our dependency. For Marquand, this locks us in. In a way that seems likely only to be possible under something like neoliberalism, 'choice has itself become a kind of fate' (Marquand, 2013: 151).

The crisis in social care is perhaps as stark an indicator of this as we might encounter. Its starkest symptom is bed-blocking in the National Health Service. The depletion of local authorities' social care budgets result in older people being more likely to be admitted to hospital due to avoidable injuries or infections sustained at home, and then staying in hospital longer, because there is no suitably supportive set-up for them to return home to, to continue their recovery (Campbell, 2015; Helm, 2016). We must always, of course, take care in inferring causal relationships as we identify correlations. But it is easy to see the steady decline of care for those who are older as a glaring symptom of the reification of Choice with a capital C. Key to the critique of choice-centred models of obligation is that they miss fundamental points about human relationality.

On the one hand, we are all vulnerable across the life-course, and (as we have mentioned) intermittently dependent. It makes starkly little sense, in moral terms, to talk of either of these as deriving from choices. We cannot evade our physiological and other vulnerabilities simply through lifestyle or consumer choices, nor assume that the promotion of choice is the primary way to address them. On the other hand, our responsibilities for others themselves carry unchosen weight. Sometimes these may feel inherent in the very nature of the relationships we hold – we might, for example, see families as just being, by virtue of what they are, a kind of vehicle for unchosen obligations. Yet responsibilities for care are not simply givens; they are also assigned and reinforced by the kinds of society in which we live. There is nothing automatic about fostering, adoption or the care of older people without family. There is nothing automatic either about deciding who among the putatively vulnerable should count as our greatest social priority. In a society which has sanctified Choice, the vocabulary with which we address the care of human beings will have been depleted precisely by the expectation that it is choosing our circumstances which is the key, or only, priority or moral imperative. It is not lack of choice which accounts for the person stuck in hospital because her local authority has run out of cash. It is a failure to assess the public interest in looking after those who are in less of a position to choose, or to respect not just their *choices*, but *themselves*. It is a political deficit.

So the politicisation of care is a vital element of any mapping of the public interest. Partly this is because of the sheer scale of care work. Eva Kittay conveys it like this:

> no culture that endures beyond one generation can be secure against the claims of human dependency. Questions of who takes on the responsibility of care, who does the hands-on care, who sees to it that the caring is done and done well, and who provides the support for the relationship of care and for both parties to the caring relationship – these are social and political questions ... How these questions are answered will determine whether the facts of human dependency can be made compatible with the full equality of all citizens – that is, whether full citizenship can be extended to all. (Kittay, 1999: 1)

For Joan Tronto too, recognising the significances of care as a practice can inform our understanding of democratic citizenship, make us better citizens.

> The qualities of attentiveness, of responsibility, of competence, or responsiveness, need not be restricted to the immediate objects of our care, but can also inform our practices as citizens. They direct us to a politics in which there is, at the center, a public discussion of needs, and an honest appraisal of the intersection of needs and interests. (Tronto, 1994: 167–8)

So it is that attention to care – its ubiquity and primacy – helps us think not just about how poorly we talk about social care, but how much citizenly engagement stands to gain from talking about it better. For the Left, this attention is vital, not least, because of the tendency, among many strains of social democratic thinking, to think that finding the right model, metric or mechanisms for material distribution is enough to secure the good society. Care is, for sure, in terms both of its giving and its receipt, maldistributed in society, as much so as money. But its redistribution is not simply a matter of setting the mechanisms of taxation or cash transfers aright, of 'centrally determined efficiency' (Marquand, 2004: 69). It has just as much to do with civic engagement. Of how we talk, and – just as importantly – listen. It means engaging, critically and committedly, as if we were citizens.

A better conversation about the public interest

What might be called 'governmental' social democracy – the social democracy of the British Labour Party, of PASOK, of the SPD in Germany, of the French Socialists and the Scandinavian social-democratic parties – has been professionalised at least as thoroughly as has the moderate centre right, and is at least as remote from its natural constituency. (Marquand, 2015: 39)

Social learning implies diversity, pluralism, difference. (It would be hard to stay awake, let alone learn anything, in a class consisting of the teacher's clones). (Marquand, 2004: 141)

I have suggested that we need doses of both *Clueless* and the New Economics Foundation, in how we think about social democratic horizons: an ironic raised eyebrow which says '*really?*' alongside a genuine commitment to coming up with constructive visions for the common good. Combined, they amount to a suitably critical realism. I have tried to show that in making a serious fist of achieving a good society there is no avoiding penetrating, critical consideration of questions of value. There are, intriguingly, some who talk as if finding out facts will somehow sort these questions out for themselves. Of course, empirical work in that vein is absolutely vital to progressive causes. But it will never do the whole job, or even most of it. Carys Afoko makes a point reinforced by the recent tendency for national votes to reflect a widespread suspicion about or rejection of, 'experts' and established facts: 'ideas and arguments that convince us, or, better yet, change our minds are not necessarily the ones that are supported by the most facts and figures' (Afoko, 2016: 318). The story and the tone matters just as much to our normative horizons. My case here is in favour of pluralism, particularly as an asset for social democrats but as an orientation more generally for what Marquand calls 'social learning'. Let's open things up and hear *all* the relevant voices, the marginal voice as well as the already enfranchised, the 'lay' voice alongside the professional and expert, and those furthest from being the teacher's clones. As an example, the marginalisation of care in public discourse serves as a pointed reminder of the need for more inclusive contestation.

What might be done, in that direction? Here are some suggestions. They might be for academics, film-makers, social workers, policy wonks, parliamentarians or any other kind of participant in the contestation of the public interest. Imagine the pursuit of the public interest *as if* there were a genuinely deliberative conversation about it, between all the relevant interested parties who are in a position to participate. Here are some rules of thumb and orientations which, I think, would be conducive to that conversation going well. More pompously: they are the kinds of virtue which would help the process of practical reasoning about the public interest and the common good.

1   Listen as if good listening were as highly valued a skill as good speaking.
2   Don't speak as if your own preferred models and frameworks are reality. Speak as if they are partial, provisional, but hopefully still useful ways of apprehending what is going on.
3   Avoid automatically privileging your own language (way of speaking, reference points): don't speak as if yours is the only or necessarily most important one.
4   Don't speak as if the status quo tightly defines all available horizons – or as if we should, as a default, concede to it.
5   Don't speak as if 'the public interest' or 'the common good' are self-explanatory, or as if saying these terms defines them.
6   Don't speak as if theoretical, normative and empirical work are not fruitfully combinable, or presume that one of these automatically takes priority over the others.
7   Don't speak as if knowledge or insight is individual property, as if one person's stance or findings somehow belong to them in anything other than a trivial sense.
8   Deliberate with others as if they are equal partners in the conversation.
9   Deliberate with others as if always acknowledging that we are hugely differentiated in the positions from which we speak, with regards, for example, to levels of social and cultural capital.
10 Treat interruptions to one's own line of thought as if they were a prompt for further thought, rather than a threat.

Contestation needs work. One way to envisage that work is in the form of a good conversation. Conversation skills are by no means all that is required to do the job, of course. Realists know that engaging as if the temper of the country were hospitable to a rounded appreciation of the conditions of good citizenship does not itself bring those conditions about. But in our non-ideal, unjust societies, these might be starting-points for a modelling of civic engagement. Social democrats have every reason to do that – and arguably, more than most.

References

Afoko, C. (2016) 'Communicating a new politics', in L. Nandy, C. Lucas and C. Bowers (eds), *The Alternative: Towards a New Progressive Politics* (London: Biteback), 318–29.

Calder. G. (2007) *Rorty's Politics of Redescription* (Cardiff: University of Wales Press).

Calder, G. (2016) *How Inequality Runs in Families: Unfair Advantage and the Limits of Social Mobility* (Bristol: Policy Press).

Calder, G., Marquand, D., Wood, L. and Lawson, N. (2016) 'Wales, the Corbyn surge, and the Direction of the Democratic Left', *Soundings*, 63, 45–54.

Campbell, D. (2015) 'Number of "fit" patients stuck in hospital hits all-time high', Guardian, 10 December. Available at: www.theguardian.com/society/2015/dec/10/ number-fit-patients-stuck-hospital-hits-all-time-high-nhs#img-1 (accessed 26 November 2016).

Chang, H. J. (2011) *23 Things They Don't Tell You About Capitalism* (London: Penguin).

Cruddas, J. (2009) 'Beware the Liberal drift: equality, always', Guardian, 19 July. Available at: www.theguardian.com/commentisfree/2009/jul/19/labour-open -left-future (accessed 10 December 2016).

Fitzpatrick, T. (2003) *After the New Social Democracy: Social Welfare for the Twenty-First Century* (Manchester: Manchester University Press).

Folbre, N. (1994) *Who Pays for the Kids? Gender and the Structures of Constraint* (London: Routledge).

Goldman, L. (2014) *The Life of R. H. Tawney: Socialism and History* (London: Bloomsbury).

Green, M., Dorling, D. and Minton, J. (2017) 'The geography of a rapid rise in elderly mortality in England and Wales, 2014–15', *Health and Place*, 44, 77–85 http:// dx.doi.org/10.1016/j.healthplace.2017.02.002.

Harvey, D. (2005) *A Brief History of Neoliberalism* (Oxford: Oxford University Press).

Heckerling, A. (dir.) (1995) Clueless. Excerpt at: www.youtube.com/watch?v= VpVoUvLdErw (accessed 12 December 2016).

Helm, T. (2016) 'Care for elderly "close to collapse" across UK as council funding runs out', Observer, 26 November Available at: www.theguardian.com/society/2016/ nov/26/nhs-elderly-care-close-to-collapse (accessed 26 November 2016).

MacIntyre, A. (1971) *Against the Self-Images of the Age* (London: Duckworth).

Marquand, D. (1988) *The Unprincipled Society: New Demands and Old Politics* (London: Jonathan Cape).

Marquand, D. (1991) 'The paradox of British democracy', in his *The Progressive Dilemma: From Lloyd George to Kinnock* (London: William Heinemann), 5–25.

Marquand, D. (1997) *'Liberalism's revenge?'* in *The New Reckoning: Capitalism: States and Citizens* (Cambridge: Polity).

Marquand, D. (2004) *Decline of the Public: The Hollowing-Out of Citizenship* (Cambridge: Polity).

Marquand, D. (2014) *Mammon's Kingdom: An Essay on Britain, Now* (London: Allen Lane).

Marquand, D. (2015) 'A home for the left-behind', New Statesman, 4–10 December, 38–40.

New Economics Foundation (2017) Homepage: www.neweconomics.org (accessed 12 December 2016).

Rorty, R. (1998) *Achieving Our Country: Leftist Thought in Twentieth-Century America* (Cambridge, MA: Harvard University Press).

Sayer, A. (2011) *Why Things Matter to People: Social Science, Values and Ethical Life* (Cambridge: Cambridge University Press).

Tawney, R. H. (1932) 'The choice before the Labour Party', *The Political Quarterly*, 3(3), 323–45.

Warren, E. (2011) cited in Lucy Madison, 'Elizabeth Warren: there is nobody in this country who got rich on his own', CBS News, 22 September 2011. Available at: www.cbsnews.com/news/elizabeth-warren-there-is-nobody-in-this-country-who -got-rich-on-his-own/ (accessed 9 December 2016).

10

Principles and the progressive alliance in a networked society: what we can learn from *Marquandism* in the making and unmaking of social democrats

Neal Lawson

I write in the week that Donald Trump became the forty-fifth President of the United States. His election, which is of little surprise to anyone who listens, rather than just tells, is the culmination of a triple whammy for progressives in the United Kingdom, following Labour's election defeat in 2015, and then the Brexit vote. Predications are now a mug's game but it seems impossible to imagine how the dominant progressive form of the twentieth century – social democracy – can restart itself with any great influence in the twenty-first century. Yes, social democrats can find themselves occasionally in office, but further from real power than ever. If the lurch to the right isn't to continue to even darker places, then the progressive response must surely take a very different form. Enter the ideas and political life journey of David Marquand. What can 'Marquandism' tell us about the political moment, and what we, the people who want a good society that is much more equal, sustainable and democratic, can and should do next?

David has been one of the two most influential thinkers in my political life (the other being the recently deceased Polish sociologist Zygmunt Bauman). I first read the *Unprincipled Society* (1988), the key Marquand text for me, shortly after its publication and its central message of moral, as opposed to mechanical, politics has stuck to me like glue. Because such a moral view of politics of course then cascades into a plural view of change – if politics is essentially moral and not mechanical then the question of how we make change is transformed – it's not the control of the machine that matters as much as how one wins the battle of ideas. And that morality has to be lived and practised. Means always shape ends. In one, for me, celebrated exchange with Anthony Giddens during the high water mark of New Labour in the pages of *Prospect* magazine, David chides Anthony for talking about 'when we get to a social democratic society'. Because of course we can never arrive – we are always on a journey of discovery and the great danger lies in believing there is an end point. As Bauman says, the good society is one that knows it's not good enough.

If notions of moral principles, pluralism and an emphasis on means over ends are the key political learning I take from reading David, then his political life seems to embody those beliefs. From journalist, to academic, to Member of Parliament, Brussels adviser and back to academia, he has sought out the many and sometimes competing places in which ideas and alternatives can be explored. This pluralism of place is reinforced by a pluralism of party. What matters to him is not the machine but the morality.

Any cursory glance at Compass, the organisation I have the honour to chair, can see it is created as much as anything on the basis of Marquandism – the values and practice of pluralism and how pluralism fits with principle. How do we have a sense of moral purpose and direction, but at the same time be open and porous in our approach? It is a key dilemma for any future progressive project, probably best addressed to date by Sue Goss in *Open Tribe* (2014), which is based on a series of interviews with contemporary political figures including David. The book seeks to combine a sense of belief and belonging, the tribe, with a curiosity about what lies beyond the entrance to the cave (Goss, 2014).

So the elements of Marquandism I want to explore here are both the necessity of shifting from a mechanical to a moral politics – why if you like the 'principled society' is needed now more than ever – and why David was so right to make this a cornerstone of his thinking. And then how do we prosecute a politics of principle in a deeply plural way? In particular, I want to end with a rallying cry for a progressive alliance as the means by which we break open our stale and failing party political system to allow the journey to a society that knows it is not yet good enough to go on and on. But to get there we need to start with context and, almost literally, with the nuts and bolts of the world that was.

The age of the machine

David's intellectual endeavour and lived experience is that of the era that spanned the twentieth century, from the Liberal government of 1905 onwards. This is the period that gave birth to the welfare state and the rise of social democracy. It was more than anything the century of the centre, of hierarchy and therefore the big state and the big corporation in which the machine analogy embodied the dominant cultural trend. We explore why and how below. But what is important to recognise here is that there are always dominant and subordinate trends, in this case the more open and less hierarchical forces at work throughout this era, embodied in the likes of the cooperative movement. The central argument I want to make is that the twenty-first century could be the moment when Marquandism, and its belief in plural, democratic and therefore negotiated, as opposed to imposed outcomes, springs to life, flourishes and guides us. And that this bleakest of moments could be looked back on as part of a Gramscian interregnum, the interlude when the old mechanical world is not yet dead and the new moral and networked world is not yet born, and within which all sorts of morbid symptoms appear.

Every political movement and moment is paradoxical, carrying the seeds of competing and contradictory tendencies. Nowhere is this truer than the social democracy of the twentieth century. Labour was a creation of that century, the product of the trade unions, but was born via a deal with the Liberals, built more on Methodism than Marxism, and rooted in the rich cultural fabric of the Left Book Club, the ILP, the Clarion Cycle Clubs, friendly societies, mutuals and cooperatives. In Paul Addison's magisterial *The Road to 1945*, you get a flavour of the richness and diversity that led us to that transformative moment (Addison, 1994). Indeed, David himself called its foundation 'a hundred year conversation' that encompassed a broad and popular front that extended way beyond Labour. The intellectual and policy foundations of the post-war settlement were the product not of Labour thinking, but Liberal, in the form of William Beveridge on welfare, and J. M. Keynes on the economy.

But this rich diversity of organisational culture and intellectual thought was not to be the dominant governing form; because this, more than anything, was the century of Fordism and its political incarnation Fabianism. Named after the organising principles of the Ford car plant in which each worker had and knew their unique and disciplined place on the production line, Fordism became the dominant form of production and governance in the last century. In keeping with the productive insights of Taylorsim, the role of the worker was to preform simple and repeatable tasks, not to think for themselves, or, heaven forbid, imagine. The factory was the cultural metaphor of the age, factories that produced both wage slavery and social solidarity that combined to underpin twentieth-century social democracy.

And if this was the mode of production, then it would create, or at least heavily influence, a social infrastructure in its image. I am not a Marxist, and neither is David, but there is obviously some connection between the mode of production and the social infrastructure. The former largely shapes, but does not determine, the latter. This linear, predictable and controllable theory and practice of Fordism rippled out from the factory shop floor to government, political parties and civil society. From the Fabians to the Soviets, and, in particular, war mobilisation embedded a culture based on the factory – of hierarchy, order, discipline and command and control. Labour and the country slipped with ease from being partners in the wartime coalition to peacetime overlords, winning that peace through centralised national ownership and planning. The creation of the NHS, mass public house building and welfare provision were simply the extension of army and production line discipline. It was an age when pulling the right levers in the right order was the art of politics – to deliver – for the people, to the people. What mattered was control of the machine, and how you got there was at best a moot point.

It is interesting and not unimportant here to note that Henry Ford himself was of course self-enlightened enough to realise that he had to pay his workers at least sufficient to buy the cars they were making. If was therefore Ford and the productive culture his company spawned that probably did as much as anyone to make social democrats in the twentieth century. Perhaps even more interesting is the role of General Motors in the unmaking of those social democrats, because it was the GM CEO Alfred Sloan who in effect was the creator of regular car upgrade models and the need for credit to buy them from the 1920 to the 1950s, thus easing the way for the shift from a society based essentially on production to one essentially based on consumption. If we could buy what we wanted, when we wanted it, then our identities would be predominantly formed by what we consumed, not what we produced. This is the big insight of Bauman, whose *Work, Consumerism and The New Poor* (1998) has been the other guiding text for me (Bauman, 1998).

The DNA of social democracy is a product of this moment and this era. While subordinate traits such as cooperativism lived on in the margins, Labour took the form and culture of the machine. The party existed to elect the managers who would know the right levers to pull. The party members were vote-harvesting cogs to mobilise the mass voting fodder in the wheels of the machine to take control of the state. The art was technocratic, a bloodless and rather cold delivery of what people at the centre thought people not at the centre wanted. And so it went on, from the high point of 1945 to this day, as social democrats try to repeat and rerun the success of a century fast fading in the rear view mirror.

But just at its mid-century high point, everything started to change. The efficacy of the machine started to rust, and as David so starkly warned us in *The Unprincipled Society*, what happens when you can no longer deliver, and there is no morality or principle underpinning your political position? The answer looks like Thatcherism, then Brexit and then Trump. Such a bleak trajectory was interspersed with a long period of New Labour rule, but it did little if anything to avoid the descent into the political chaos that now engulfs us – if anything it cleared the path!

The end of the machine age and the crisis of social democracy

Every political project is both paradoxical and carries the seeds of its own destruction. Thus it was to be with the Fordist social democracy of the last century. In 1978, Eric Hobsbawm penned has famous essay *The Forward March of Labour Halted?*, in which he recounted the demise of the class base of Labour (Hobsbawm, 1978). But the decline did not start then, instead Hobsbawm traced the fall back to a high point of the late 1940s, and from then on it was all downhill. The system of mass production and mass classes had begun to unwind when Labour reached its political height. A new more technical class was emerging, white in collar rather than blue. Production itself was becoming more dispersed because of new technology and the global supply chains and flows of money that came with more instant communication. People didn't want any colour of car as long as it was black. They wanted differentiation and personalisation in a fast-emerging consumerised age.

And a more liberal culture was fighting to emerge from the constraints of post-war austerity and rationing. People wanted to look, feel, behave and think differently. The media was no longer Reithian and was becoming more diverse and satirical. Paternalism and deference were dying. People travelled more, knew more and saw more. Aspirations and experiences grew. The welfare state offered more security, and therefore more freedom. The working class as a class for itself began to unwind. Think of Bob from *The Likely Lads*, not Terry as the social agent of the future, people who no longer knew their place, or were happy with their lot.

Social democracy hung on, believing in the 1950s, via Anthony Crosland, that the class war was over, that social democracy had won, and that the only political issue was how to distribute the proceeds of never ending growth. It received a further fillip in the 1960s, when John Kennedy in the America, and Harold Wilson in the United Kingdom offered to harness the space race and white heat of technology respectively to a common good. But this was just the half-life of a creed losing its life force, of the declining centralised tendencies of that century, and the agency of the working class whose interest could be delivered via the machinery of the state. The oil crisis, and the rise of both inflation and unemployment in the 1970s killed the post-war settlement based on Keynesian demand management and paved the way for neoliberalism, a toxic creed that had been creeping from the margins and marching through the institutions since precisely 1948 when its founders first met and created the Mont Pelerin Society. Social democracy had been failing to keep pace with the new, more individualistic and consumerised culture. It was losing both its instrumental and its intrinsic appeal.

The second-to-last nail in the coffin of social democracy was the fall of the Soviet Union in 1989. Now there was no unique 'third way' space for social democrats to occupy between Washington and Moscow. The threat of communism after the war had helped bring capital to the negotiating table to buy off labour in the form of the welfare state. Now any pretence at such a challenger to global capitalism had gone. Along the way, the technocratic, top-down dream died. Remember, Stalin only had five-year plans. New Labour went for ten-year plans for many of its public service reforms as the new public management kicked in. They endeavoured to mix centralism and targets, with the free market. But neither was appropriate for services based on a public ethos and the common good. Weak in terms of agency and culture, New Labour tried its best to humanise neoliberalism through tax credits and Sure Start centres. But it never confronted the power bases of neoliberalism, and crucially never built its own sources of support in the party, the unions or local government. Its preferred weapon of choice was only spin. It didn't work. Then the final nail in the coffin of social democracy was hammered home in 2008, via the global financial crisis. Freed from the constraints of the Cold War, free market capitalism now ruled supreme: nothing would hold it back, especially from dangerous financial excesses.

Social democrats need capitalism to work in order to distribute the proceeds of growth more equitably. What else is there for them to do? The left thought the crash would benefit them, but so complicit in financialised capitalism had the new 'third way' social democracy of Blair and Clinton become that the social democrats suffered electorally, presumably because they had been caught acting against the interests of those whom they were meant to represent. The right was doing what was expected of them. The Tory claim that it was the big state that had brought the economy down combined with the cultural split between the metropolitan/liberal left and the 'left-behind' white working class has left social democrats weaker than ever. Europe, in the form of the Brexit vote, has broken

Labour, not the Conservatives. The loss of Scotland is maybe a foretaste of the loss of other heartland areas to abstentions or whatever more authoritarian populist movement that comes out of it.

Capitalism isn't over, but it's morally wounded and isn't working for so many. Communism, other than in North Korea and maybe Cuba, is definitely over. Social democracy as a reaction to both is struggling to find a place in the world in which the culture that created it, built it and sustained it is vanishing before our eyes. Today, no social democratic party is on the front foot organisationally, intellectually, culturally or electorally anywhere in the world. PASOK in Greece has for all intents and purposes gone, the rest, such as France, Germany and Spain struggle at around 20–25 per cent of the vote. Even in the Nordics, social democrats look like a spent force. In Britain, New Labour has come and gone. In the words of Alan Finlayson, writing in *Renewal*, New Labour thought it was the start of something new, when it was the end of something old (Finlayson, 2016). In America, the defeat of Hillary Clinton to Donald Trump closed the book on the attempt to humanise neoliberalism. The rise of Corbynism and the Bernie Sanders campaign could be sparks of new life if they adapt to a modernising agenda that combines principles with power. Podemos in Spain, Syriza in Greece, the SNP, the Alternativet in Denmark and the Pirates in Iceland could be signs of new energy or merely the final lease of life of an old sun before it finally burns out.

To date, there are few signs that Corbynism is working. It has rightly rejected Blairism, but rests too heavily on Bennism, a socialism in one country approach that can't get to grips with either globalisation or the more plural nature of politics in an increasingly networked society. What is more, it is failing to find a narrative that joins the interests of the 52 per cent who voted for Brexit and the 48 per cent who wanted to remain in Europe. As the debate is polarised, Labour with a foot in each camp looks like it will fall into the abyss. Corbyn or Corbynism is an enigma. At one level he carries the hopes of a young generation sick of the old politics of spin and deceit. But the very principles he has stuck to hem him in at every turn. To change his mind and develop his approach would be to renege on the past. Thus he lives up to David's desire for a principled society, but can't match the requirement to make it happen, namely an openness to others in the search for alliances that can transform society. The incredible change to the membership of Labour might mean that Jeremy Corbyn remains as Labour leader for some time. But it is hard, if not impossible, to see how he can renew social democracy from such a small cultural, intellectual and organisational base.

Marquandism in new times

In all this gloom, and before we give up completely, I'd like to spend the rest of this chapter thinking through the context of now and the near future, and what the key tenets of Marquandism do to help guide us in this tricky terrain. And in this, it seems to me that the question is: how do we bend modernity to our values, and not operate, as New Labour did, the other way around, or ignore modernity as Corbynism seems to want to do? There are various cultural and environmental factors at play in the middle of the second decade of the twenty-first century. But by far the most important is the rise of what we can call the networked society. This world was explored more fully by Indra Adnan and myself in a pamphlet called *New Times* (2014), to coincide with the twenty-fifth anniversary of the fall of the Berlin Wall, and two other historic events, the publication of Francis Fukuyama's *End of History* and the first protocols for the World Wide Web being written by Tim Berners Lee. Our argument then, as now, is that the fall of the Wall was a metaphor for a society being flatted by technology that increasingly connects everyone to everything: each other, places and ideas.

This flattening world can be counterpoised to the hierarchies of the twentieth century. These are not absolutes. In the last century and in this, there are important counter-narratives, experiences and cultures, but if the predominant governing form was hierarchical in the last century, the dominant governing form of the twenty-first century is increasingly horizontal and networked. And on these flatter planes we have the capacity to be more egalitarian and democratic, because all our voices and views can be heard, organising becomes ridiculously easy and the co-production of goods and service by workers and users becomes possible. Of course, hierarchies and elites like Apple and Facebook can grow in power and influence too. We should expect no less when the networks spring up in a neoliberal legal, economic and cultural paradigm. But networks can be used for democratic and egalitarian ends in ways that old hierarchies – however well meaning – never could. This does not mean they will necessarily be used for such purposes but – given the right conjectural politics – they can be.

People always say technology is neutral. At one level, it of course is. It can be used by left and right. But access to mass communication and information – which were once the preserve of the already rich and powerful – has to be at least potentially of more benefit to the left than the right. The good society was never going to be delivered to the people by elites, only by the people, working together, for the people. The interconnectedness of the twenty-first century makes that possible. There is a potential morality and set of cooperative operating principles about flatness and interconnectedness which progressives can harness. I reiterate for absolute clarity that none of this is ordained or predetermined. We could end up in a techno dystopia of echo chambers and even heightened turbo-consumerism rather than a higher form of democracy, that empowers us not just once every four of five years, but whenever and however we need power in our workplaces, communities and in the state nationally and locally, in forms that are both deliberative and enjoyable. Which future we get is down to politics, our ability to organise and inspire and answer key questions of ownership and access to these critical new commons.

But a new world is definitely and defiantly merging, tentatively at first, but in more and more ways. The Occupy movement was one of the first big manifestations, but it was built on the early works of the social forums and climate camp. The Scottish independence campaign was another example of civil society building its own vision and organisation. But the new times are a lot more than just political expression, the peer-to-peer and sharing economies, social enterprises, community campaign, cooperative platforms and open source movements all contain the seeds of a different future. The art of politics is to sustain this emerging new economy and society through the more vertical institutions of the state. Compass calls this *45 Degree Politics*, the meeting point of the horizontal movements and vertical parties and the state they seek to occupy. The responsibility of the former is to innovate and experiment with new forms of ownership and control, the responsibility of the latter is to resource, enable and regulate this new future into being.

The other aspect of this moment that is crucial to grasp for progressives is the notion of abundance and the finite nature of the planet. Social democrats fail to have an adequate response to planetary boundaries, because theirs is a creed based on 'more'. As such, social democracy goes more with the grain of capitalism, caring more about how the proceeds of growth are shared, than the effect of that growth on the planet and therefore people. In short, there is no limit to how big the worker's flat screen TV should be for a social democrat. There are two problems with this. First climate change always affects the poor most. Their houses tend to be in places that flood, they are more likely to be affected by droughts and crop failures that lead to both rising prices and mass migration, to the detriment of the poor who are moving, and the poor in places they move to, and they tend to live nearer roads and industrial areas where the air is polluted. The poor can't buy their way out of the destruction of our environment. Ultimately the rich can't either, but they have a relative advantage.

The second effect is cultural and political. Our turbo-consumer society rests on the superior buying advantage you have over others. Life is dominated through the consumer race to own the most and the best. It is a war of all against all played out on the high streets, malls and increasingly online. Through our purchasing power, our task is to demonstrate our shopping acumen through our life-long pursuit of more and more things. In that sense, of course, it's not a race, as a race has an end point. The only end point in a consumer society is death, but the funeral will cost as much as possible and be as fancy as possible. Within such a competitive and individualistic culture it is almost impossible to build the bonds of social solidarity. But it is worse than that. Not only are those in poverty left behind, they are stigmatised to such an effect that their lives are turned into a living hell. Because in a consumer society something has to keep the rest of us buying things we didn't know we needed, with money we don't have to impress people we don't know. That something is the fear of being like those living in poverty, the failed consumer. The job of 'the poor' today is not to be the lumpen proletariat that can become useful if and when the labour market needs them. There is no socially useful role for the poor in a consumer society, other than to help police and dragoon the rest of us on to staying on the never-ending treadmill of consumption. What chance for David's principled society in such bleak circumstances?

In the context of David's book *Mammon's Kingdom* (2015), in which money and greed and competition rule, what chance for a social democracy? (Marquand, 2015). Social democracy was the creed that lived between the public and the private, between the market and the state, between capitalism and communism. Its job was to work with the market system, to humanise it and therefore sustain it. But shorn of agency, devoid of a Fabian or statist governing forms and up against a toxic form of capitalism that takes no prisoners and can never be free enough, there is now little if any space for social democracy to take root or even find shelter.

So, what is to be done?

Learning from David, two issues stand out – we have to be moral and we have to be pluralists. What could this means in the context of the twenty-first century as described here?

The precarious and networked society and economy of the future can help create a sense of agency for change. As more and more people struggle to live the consumer dream because of flatlining wages and job dislocation through new technology there will be more people invested in change than the status quo. But such twenty-first-century agents of change, while networked, will not operate solely around work or community locations. They will need something more than place and interest to bind them together, they will need a moral purpose. They must answer the question collectively: what is it to be a fully flourishing human being and to live a good life in a good society? And if the planet and society is to survive, the answer must bring people down on the side of active citizenship over turbo-consumerism. The good, principled and moral life is one that we self-author together, not as lone shoppers but as connected citizens, because it is only as connected citizens that we can change the big things in our lives. Purchasing power doesn't let us transform our public services, communities or workplaces. It is not exit we need, but voice and the art of co-producing our world with others. Ultimately, we must be connected global citizens and we must think and act globally, as well as locally. One simple insight into what this principled society could mean can be taken from the fact that few us, on our death-bed, look back and long for a life in which we could own more things, and instead we look back and wish for more time to do the things we love and be with the people we love. If that insight is given policy life then ideas such as a shorter working week and a universal basic income come straight on to the agenda as do many more.

But while we have to paint a picture of a more desirable world, the pressing issue is not what we want but how we get it – it is feasibility not just desirability we have to explore. Here David has personally shown the way, as he has always put principles before party. British politics has a particularly backward culture. Its lack of any written constitution, its centralisation of power around the executive and the office of prime ministers, the Lords, the role of the monarch, its adversarial nature and first-past-the-post voting system all work to mitigate against progressive and transformative change. Long periods of Tory rule mixed with usually short periods of Labour governance only serve to slow down the destruction of the public realm, social solidarity and the spaces in which we can be democratic citizens over turbo-consumers. The failure of centrist social democracy in 2010 and 2015, the Brexit vote, the rise of UKIP and the existential threat to Labour in its heartland seats impels something different to happen. Jeremy Corbyn is something different. He certainly passes David's morality/principle test, but it is highly questionable whether he is a pluralist or gets the potential of a networked society. He sees the SNP and Plaid Cymru as enemies, not allies and repeatedly says he wants to defeat Caroline Lucas, the only Green MP in the country. To him the Liberal Democrats are beyond the pale, but we forget at our peril that every time Labour has made big advances it has been with the Liberal wing of British politics: in 1906 when Labour made its parliamentary breakthrough because the Liberals stood aside, in 1945 because of the ideas of Keynes and Beveridge, and in 1997 when an implicit pact between the two parties squeezed the Tories almost to death. But today the idea that Labour alone can stem the tide of neoliberalism and right populism given its historic cultural, intellectual and organisational weakness is simply a non-starter.

Instead, the foundation point for a new politics is a progressive alliance of ideas, parties and movements that come together to form a new historic bloc, whose prime job is to change the political system, through the introduction of proportional representation and the maximum devolution of power to the nations, region, cities and communities of the country. Then and only then does the game change. Then the tyranny of a few swing voters in a few swing seats, and the power of the media and political parties to influence those more cautious and conservative people, is gone for good.

But such a move away from a command and control model of politics to negotiated consensus requires what David has called in his 2010 annual Compass lecture, *A Realignment of the Mind* (Marquand, 2010). The emerging progressive alliance in British politics, which found its voice in the post-Brexit gloom, and was given meaning in the Richmond Park by-election in November 2016, when the Greens stood aside to help the Liberal Democrats win, is taking shape in council by-elections and local deals across the country. As ever, the people are ahead of the politicians as they endeavour to find ways around our failing party structures and corrupt electoral system. Given the networked, bottom-up, nature of governance, decision-making and action today, the progressive alliance will happen more to the parties than by them.

Whether today's politicians, as creatures of the twentieth century, can adopt this open, plural and generous mindset remains to be seen. Within and around Labour, the party who must shift, the old tribal ice is melting. From Jonathan Reynolds MP on the Blairite wing of the party, through to Lisa Nandy MP of the soft left, and Clive Lewis MP on the Corbynite wing there has been an embrace of the progressive alliance. Even the unions, the bastions of tribalism, are shifting ground towards proportional representation. Whether they move far enough and fast enough to counter the rise of the regressive alliance on the right remains to be seen. Social democracy could simply be a creature of the century that has gone. But the desire to build a progressive alliance will either transform the party, or it will die and be replaced. Either way the work won't be wasted. David Marquand saw all this coming, and prefigured, intellectually and in terms of his allegiances and actions, the progressive politics of the twenty-first century, an era that will either be defined by morality, principle and pluralism, or by barbarism.

References

Addison, P. (1994) *The Road to 1945* (London: Pimlico).

Adnan, I. and Lawson, N. (2014) *New Times* (London: Compass), at www.compass online.org.uk/wp-content/uploads/2014/11/New-Times-Compass-November -2014.pdf.

Bauman, Z. (1998) *Work, Consumerism and the New Poor* (Buckingham: Open University Press).

Finlayson, A. (2016) 'The present crisis and questions we must ask', *Renewal*, 24(3).

Goss, S. (2014) *Open Tribe* (London: Lawrence & Wishart).

Hobsbawm, E. (1978) 'The forward march of Labour halted', Marxism Today, September.

Marquand, D. (1988) *The Unprincipled Society* (London: Fontana).

Marquand, D. (2010) 'A realignment of the mind', annual Compass lecture.

Marquand, D. (2015) *Mammon's Kingdom* (London: Penguin).

11

Progressivism to democratic socialism: the special case of Dr Christopher Addison

Kenneth O. Morgan

David Marquand's lengthy career and prolific writings have been mainly devoted to championing a mighty cause – uniting and mobilising the forces of centre-left progressivism and thus overthrowing the Conservative dominance of post-1918 British politics. David once termed it 'a marriage of Tom Paine and William Morris', which might have been as stormy as Morris's marriage in real life. It is what Roy Jenkins and the Blairites in the mid-1990s called 'the project'. It is a noble vision in many ways. The problem has been who should carry the torch. Should it be the *arriviste* Labour Party? Marquand has constantly seen it as lacking in vision and purpose ever since the Harold Wilson years when he himself was a dissatisfied Labour MP who left Westminster for Brussels along with Roy Jenkins. Or should it be the heirs of former Liberals who have lingered on since the Lloyd George summer schools of the 1920s? The former, Marquand writes, have turned into an ossified party of 'labourism' and Marxisant bourgeois intellectuals, victims of class transformation and economic globalisation. The latter have become more an amalgam of worthy pressure-groups rather than a coherent party. At their best, perhaps, they were champions of David's favoured 'democratic republicanism', voiced by Milton, Tom Paine and Tawney across the centuries, at worst just a talking shop. David himself has repeatedly shifted his allegiance in this debate. Even his *Ramsay MacDonald* (1977) is an argument for this idea, highlighting the Rainbow Circle and the *Progressive Review* which brought together advanced reformers and early socialists, backed by positivists and ethical reformers, in the 1890s. They attempted a merger of pragmatic collectivism and civil liberty within a tried democratic context. But, like so many other progressive projects over the next hundred years and more, it did not last. The old post-Gladstonian Liberal Party was the casualty.

These miscellaneous reformers, variously Liberals, Wee Frees, Social Democrats and Liberal Democrats, have indeed taken part in inter-party coalitions along the way – but always with the Conservatives. After all, they were free traders committed to capitalism and fearful of the unions. Each time there have been desperate results. In 1918, they split into two. After 1931, they split again into three. In 2015 they almost disappeared, slumping to a mere eight MPs (though also 111 peers). Not surprisingly, perhaps, attempts to form some kind of coalition with Labour have never got very far. It failed again in the 1990s when Roy Jenkins, a historian of Victorian and Edwardian Liberalism (never of the Labour movement, despite his father) attempted to convince the youthful Tony Blair of the value of recreating the glories of pre-1914 progressivism plus proportional representation. In 2010, there was never much prospect of a Lab-Lib coalition. A coalition of David Cameron with Nick Clegg (of the neoliberal Yellow Book school) had a doctrinal solidity which a Brown-Clegg merger never remotely promised. Whether the remarkable Liberal Democrat triumph in the Richmond Park by-election in November 2016, as opponents of Brexit far more committed than Jeremy Corbyn's highly ambiguous Labour Party, would give them a new lease of radical life or whether it was an individual breakthrough in a uniquely 'Remain' suburban constituency, remained to be seen.

Instead of a modern progressive alliance, there has been, over the years, something more piecemeal. At key stages, important individuals have moved from their old Liberal allegiance to inject their passion for social, constitutional and humanitarian reform into the priorities of the Labour Party. Two recent Labour leaders began their political careers within the Liberal Party – Harold Wilson and Michael Foot. In the 1950s, Dingle Foot and Lady Megan Lloyd George brought not only famous names but their own specialist enthusiasms to the Labour cause – civil liberties and colonial freedom in the case of Dingle Foot, Celtic devolution and women's power in the case of Lady Megan. But the most important period came after 1918, when mass disillusion with Lloyd George's Tory-dominated post-war coalition led to an important exodus of Liberal intellectuals into the Labour Party, inspired by Ramsay MacDonald's 'brave new world' aura as a wartime dissenter. But they joined Labour as protesters against the war and the Lloyd George coalition government. They were part of a widely recognised segment of opinion, whose anti-war ethos ran deep, right through the appeasement years.

There is, however, a much more remarkable individual whose influence was profound in dictating British progressive politics for nearly half a century. He was not at all an opponent of the Lloyd George coalition. On the contrary, he had been one of its key members and his leader's intimate ally from 1911 onwards. He showed how a pragmatic brand of British democratic socialism could emerge more naturally from the collectivist Lloyd Georgian version than from the high-minded but inchoate Asquithian variety, distant from organised labour. This was Dr Christopher Addison, the most distinguished medical man ever to enter a British Cabinet, a major figure in both post-war governments, kingmaker (and unmaker) *extraordinaire* (Morgan and Morgan, 1980). He orchestrated Lloyd George's becoming prime minister, he symbolised popular disillusion with the coalition government, he sparked off the rebellion against MacDonald's scheme for a National Government in 1931, he was an outstanding leader of the Lords under the Labour government after 1945. Most of the leading Coalition Liberal ministers of 1918–22 joined the Conservatives – Hilton Young, Grigg, Mond and of course, Winston Churchill. Addison, almost uniquely, went the other way. As a fount of reformist ideas, an executive of power and influence, later, in Harold Wilson's words to the present author, 'a wise old man' in a creative government of socialist reform, he is a key figure in the making of the British progressive left (Interview).

Over the decades, many Liberals felt Liberalism and Labour to be increasingly close for various reasons – religious nonconformity, Welsh or Scottish nationality, rural radicalism, the New Liberalism of social reform. Addison shared these characteristics. He was a Congregationalist, who once published a Social Service lecture on *Religion and Politics* (1931). He was a dedicated Irish home ruler. He was passionate about land reform as a plain countryman from the Lincolnshire Danelaw. He was a radical social reformer, from the campaign on behalf of Lloyd George's National Insurance Act in 1911 to his strong backing for Aneurin Bevan's National Health Service (NHS) in Cabinet in 1945–46. But what makes Addison almost unique was that joining Labour and becoming a champion of democratic socialism was the product not so much of commitment to peaceful reform but of the experience of war. Addison is not a particularly well-known politician to the historians. His name is absent from major works like Peter Clarke's *Liberals and Social Democrats* and David Marquand's *Britain since 1918*. But he fully deserves attention for his distinct brand of social democracy and the values it embraces.

Addison was first drawn into politics by his passion for social reform. An important doctor who had given his name to the surgical discovery of 'Addison's plane', he sought out and won, in the January 1910 election, the Hoxton division of Shoreditch in the East End of London. He was a forceful supporter of the Liberal government's attack on the powers of the House of Lords. More important still, as a rare politician who was also an expert on medical matters, he was a key link in persuading the British Medical Association to take a more positive attitude towards Lloyd George's National Insurance Bill in 1911. It combined all Addison's basic principles – a strong role for the central state alongside a civil chain of connection through individual subscribers via the approved societies and, very importantly, the trade unions. As an instinctive pluralist, he devoted much attention to the work and composition of the local health committees and doctors' panels. The Act for him combined social welfare with citizenship.

The challenges and opportunities of war

Addison was particularly close to Lloyd George in the pre-war years, and attracted to his vision of an alliance between the Liberals and Labour. In return Lloyd George saw him as 'a man to go hunting tigers with' and emerge from the jungle unscathed. Addison gave the Chancellor help in the Land Campaign of 1913–14, supported his radical, redistributive, if procedurally ill-starred, budget of 1914, and encouraged his moves in trying to settle the Irish question in the spring of 1914. He was a pioneer in trying to build on the medical panels set up under the National Insurance Act to create an embryo NHS. He was also keen to push into new areas not yet included in the new Liberal programme, such as housing and education. On the eve of war, a political transition to a new advanced liberalism could be detected within parts of the government. Addison summed it up in his diary: 'We encourage each other to dream dreams, but we base them on existing realities' (Addison, 1924a).

After the war broke out, Addison's political ideology sharpened up a good deal. He had been a member of the dissenting anti-war Foreign Affairs group. But he was no pacifist or Little Englander. The invasion of Belgium made a (predictable) difference and from the start he backed the decision to go to war. He first became a practitioner of wartime collectivism as under-secretary at the Board of Education. He gained an important promotion in May 1915 when he moved to the new Ministry of Munitions under Lloyd George. Here he helped to direct the industrial *dirigisme* of the new department, its controls over production and supply, raw materials and manpower, the managing of its operational costs, its central role in designing and making weapons, and in working with businessmen to ensure efficiency. Years later, in his two-volume book *Practical Socialism* published in 1926, even in the Lords after 1945, he would cite the collectivist approach of the wartime Ministry of Munitions as a model for the running of the economy. As a Liberal, however, he was less at ease in the difficult world of industrial relations and his dealings with the trade unions underwent a series of crises. The complex problems of handling the 'dilution' of labour (frequently with women) within munitions plants, the 'badging' of vital engineering workers engaged upon munitions production and the introduction of something close to industrial conscription would have challenged the skills and determination of any minister. Lloyd George himself had the rare experience of being shouted down at an angry mass meeting of engineering workers in Glasgow on Christmas Day 1915. Addison's role was a subordinate one but his negotiations, conducted with help from Ramsay MacDonald, did bear fruit and the Clyde men returned to work in April (Addison, 1924a).

These wartime difficulties were a pivotal time in the evolution of the idea of democratic socialism. They revealed to Addison and other wartime planners the complex technical problems of adapting war socialism to the sectional needs of the trade unions – a problem even for Ernest Bevin at the Ministry of Labour during the Second World War. But they also suggested new social areas that the emergency of total war had opened up. Of these, those which Addison found the most congenial were the health and physical and moral well-being of workers on the shop floor. The Health of Munitions Workers' Committee, under Sir George Newman, was particularly effective here. For Addison, a naturally consensual progressive, it reinforced his growing view that wartime welfare provided the way ahead for a constructive post-war agenda.

His broad satisfaction with the social and economic approach of his department under Lloyd George now took overt political form. It meant that, when divisions opened up between Lloyd George and Asquith in the spring of 1916, over the issue of military conscription, Addison was a total and whole-hearted supporter of Lloyd George. His role has been badly neglected by historians. In early May 1916, allegedly on his own initiative, he drew up a list of many dozens of Liberal MPs, who would support Lloyd George rather than Asquith as leader if a crisis were to come. As Addison put it, 'they might be relied upon to support an active policy'. It was a decisive moment in the break-up of the Liberal Party. Addison, far more than his backbench allies David Davies and F. G. Kellaway, saw it as a clear choice between collectivist war leadership, and Asquithian piecemeal laissez-faire (Addison, 1924b: 202–3). This pressure was kept up in the autumn when the fortunes of war took an increasingly serious turn. In the ultimate confrontation between the Liberal leaders in December 1916 it was Addison again who assumed for himself the role of kingmaker. He ensured that Lloyd George formed his government on 7 December 1916 with an assurance of backing from the Unionists and (narrowly) the Labour Party – but also certain support from a clear majority of the backbench Liberals. He rejected the muddling through of traditional Liberals like Reginald McKenna and Walter Runciman, all of whom backed Asquith. He was not a dogmatic supporter of the civil liberties argument that generated so much controversy during the conscription crisis.

He felt more sympathetic now to the Unionist leader, Bonar Law, who remarked, in an private talk on 28 November, 'We cannot go on like this Addison, do you think?' (Addison, 1924b: 269). Addison also became far closer to the Unionist leader, Edward Carson, another key figure. 'On our own account', Addison and Kellaway then conducted a private canvass of Liberal backbenchers: 49 were 'out and out' supporters of Lloyd George, and a further 126 would back a Lloyd George government if it came about (Addison, 1924b: 274). The deed was done. Asquith resigned and Lloyd George formed his government twenty-four hours later, on 7 December. The brisk, confident way in which Lloyd George re-shaped the central government machine confirmed his judgement. Addison now moved into the new Coalition government. In the longer term, his progress into the Labour Party was also made the more certain.

Munitions and reconstruction

With Lloyd George now in control in Downing Street. Addison applied himself to entrenching war socialism more firmly. He succeeded Lloyd George as Minister of Munitions and continued much the same policies. Again, he had troubles with the unions. He proved a surprisingly tough minister who backed the dismissal or deportation of unofficial strike leaders. He also set up commissions on industrial unrest to investigate syndicalist or disruptive forces within mining and other unions. After lengthy and wearisome negotiations with the Engineers Union, an agreement was reached over a Schedule of Protected Occupations regarding skilled men and apprentices on 7 May 1917. Shortly afterwards, by agreement with Lloyd George, he left the Ministry of Munitions, probably to his own relief. The American scholar, Bentley Gilbert, has written that Addison was removed 'not for failure but for the reputation of failure' (Addison, 1917; Gilbert, 1970: 72). It is arguable that he was more effective at Munitions, in labour relations for example, than his far more flamboyant successor at the ministry, Winston Churchill.

But he moved on to a very different kind of assignment, important both for his own future and indirectly for the future of British centre-left politics, a very new department, the Ministry of Reconstruction. Whereas his work at Munitions had been immediate and pragmatic, the tasks at Reconstruction were remote, long-term and speculative. Some observers, a number of whom had expected that Addison might be promoted to the War Cabinet when Arthur Henderson left it, saw this as a demotion. Alfred Milner told Addison that the lesson to be drawn was that he needed a 'personal booster' – in the argot of a later age, a spin doctor (Addison, 1924b: 395). On the other hand, his new responsibility gave him an unusual opportunity for blue-skies planning for social reform, working with Beveridge, the Webbs and others on the centre-left. One major project that he and Lloyd George discussed at Criccieth in August 1918 was a powerful Ministry of Health, to replace most of the work done by the time-worn old department, the Local Government Board. It was, of course, an area singularly appropriate for one of Addison's distinguished medical background. Addison recorded in his diary his satisfaction with the state taking on a direct role in promoting the health of the people: 'Why was it not done before?' (Addison, 1924b: 564) It was of immense political symbolic importance, with Lloyd George already considering his programme for the post-war years. The Coalition government, though mainly backed by right-wing Unionists, was, in areas such as public health, social housing, state education and comprehensive insurance, actually paving the way for the first cautious foundations of socialism in our time.

Lloyd George's Coalition government was returned with a landslide majority in the so-called 'coupon election' of December 1918. For Addison, one of the leading Coalition Liberals within it, the vision of 'a land fit for heroes' was no empty rhetoric. The post-war Coalition has had a bad press. Keynes speared it for ever in his sparkling critique, *The Economic Consequences of the Peace* (1919) with his verdict (borrowed from Baldwin) on the Commons looking like hard-faced men who had done very well out of war. The eventual record of the Coalition government, especially in the social and economic sphere when the international economy collapsed and led to mass unemployment in the staple industries, was a grim one. Alongside a cruel period of 'retaliation' in Ireland, many tensions in international policy, notably over Russia and the Near East, and a pervasive sense of casual corruption in high places, especially in 10 Downing Street, the government's later reputation was a bleak one, disreputable, dishonest, perhaps simply corrupt. It helped to prejudice the public mood against the contortions of coalition politics for decades to come. Addison in due time became one of its fiercest critics. But for at least two years he was a staunch executant of the government's priorities, first at local government and then at the first ever Ministry of Health. Almost alone in the government, he led the pursuit of a progressive agenda, using the tried collectivist policies of the war socialism of 1914–18.

The moral that Addison drew from the war was that the old Liberalism, a variation on the themes of pre-war laissez-faire, was played out. The Labour Party, though inexperienced in office, 'do know what they want, which the Asquithians don't'. He added, significantly, 'Heaven knows, we have been socialists enough in war matters' (Addison, 1924b: 602). Compassionate collectivism was the only feasible solution to the immense social problems that the war years had opened up. This was no doubt why Addison leaned towards Lloyd George's politics (and also perhaps why Roy Jenkins, in his biography of his fellow Balliol man, Asquith, leaned the other way).

Post-war social progressivism

Addison became Minister of Health in the spring of 1919, after a brief token spell at the Local Government Board. It was one of the last victories of the pre-war New Liberalism. It embodied many of Addison's good qualities. It showed his talents as a conciliator, working closely in this case with Kingsley Wood of the insurance societies and with the railwaymen's leader, Jimmy Thomas (Addison, 1924a: 221). It revealed also his Fabian zeal for a cohesive planning mechanism to replace health services that were scattered, variously located in the Board of Trade, the Home Office, the Privy Council and the Local Government Board. It entailed bringing in, though ultimately controlling, the local authorities, and building alliances with the British Medical Association. And, always crucial for Addison, it emphasised the need for public education on health, the promotion of medical education and the advancement of knowledge. He avoided creating a departmental juggernaut. Thus, his important creation of a Medical Research Committee was placed under the Privy Council rather than directly under the new ministry (Memorandum, 1919). It was the kind of eclectic approach adopted later – much more effectively – by the Attlee government in creating a welfare state.

The government's claim to be social reformers was certainly not bogus. *Pace* Keynes, this theme played a far more dominant part in the 'coupon election' after the armistice, and in the government's election literature, than hanging the Kaiser or squeezing Germany until the pips squeaked. Its priorities were a form of war socialism, based on the coalition's ideological premises, just like 'unity of command' on the Western Front during the war. To public and press they were summed up in one word – 'Addison', to the centre-left a symbol of a revived

New Liberalism, to the Unionist right, especially its die-hard version, a token of financial waste and the ideological threat of socialism.

If the new Ministry of Health embodied this idea in a relatively consensual way, another area of policy expressed it more controversially. This was housing. Plans had evolved during the war, following the Tudor Walters Committee report, for a dramatic new programme of subsidised state housing, perhaps up to 300,000, to be built by the local authorities (Morgan and Morgan, 1980: 74). The claim by the Lloyd George government to be one of domestic reform largely turned on this one issue. It also suggested new avenues of progressive reform for the future. Housing shortly moved across to the Labour Party's social agenda. Addison himself was soon to move with it.

The urgency of the case for a new housing initiative had become crystal clear during the war. Reports had spoken of severe housing shortages, high rents and huge amounts of slum property, some of it dating from the eighteenth century. The Buildings Material Supply Committee, chaired by Sir James Carmichael, had been working on bricks, timber and other supplies, and enlisting bricklayers and other key workers. What was lacking were a feasible strategy and assured state finance. Addison had favoured a number of housing commissions to obtain sites and prepare plans. But he began work on housing policy in January 1919 with no commissioners, without adequate powers to foster the production of materials and without a foolproof financial policy to penalise extravagance by local authorities (Addison, 1924a: 215). Undaunted, he set forth his ideas in a momentous Housing and Town Planning Bill in March 1919. It empowered – or rather ordered – local authorities to put forward schemes for new housing programmes financed in the first instance by loans raised by local authorities but with losses on housing beyond a penny rate made good by the central government. It was a bold, adventurous programme and met with widespread acclaim in the press and among the politicians.

But this particular New Jerusalem would not easily be constructed. From the start, Addison's building plans faced serious practical difficulties. The minister himself spoke confidently of 100,000 housing starts in the course of 1919, and an escalating total of up to 460,000 houses to be built by the end of 1923 (Cabinet Paper, 1919). But these bold plans were to be frustrated by an immense range of practical problems. The new vision was quite literally obstructed by an absence of bricks and mortar. The building industry was in disarray after the war with a huge inflation in the cost of building materials and loss to the armed services of 200,000 carpenters, joiners, masons and, above all, bricklayers. The local authorities, on whom the progress of house building crucially depended, varied enormously in their capacity and even enthusiasm for undertaking this revolution-ary programme. The private-enterprise building trade itself was a shambles with a lack of cooperation between private and publicly employed building firms. Also, as at Munitions during the war, Addison encountered much difficulty with the trade unions. Here, as in engineering, there was considerable resistance to 'dilution' of the workforce through unskilled labour, and to the provision of more apprenticeships. Critics also noted the immobility of the workforce with many bricklayers and others building warehouses or cinemas, rather than houses for rent.

These criticisms illustrated painfully the technical difficulties of pressing on with bold policies of social reform. At one and the same time, building workers discharged from the armed services were available for work, yet local authorities were unable to meet their housing targets owing to a shortage of labour. There seemed a total lack of coordination on all fronts among private employers, trade unions and local councils. In Cabinet meetings in late 1919, Addison had to admit that a mere 43,299 houses had actually been approved out of the half million needed, though progress did pick up greatly thereafter (Cabinet Minutes, 1919). But Addison encountered an even more implacable obstacle, one often confronting socially minded ministers – the resistance of the Treasury. From the start his schemes met with challenges from the Chancellor, Austen Cham-berlain, committed to a dear-money policy, based on high interest rates, a preliminary to a return to gold some time soon after the war. This inevitably ran up against the potentially inflationary tendencies of a costly public housing programme. Austen Chamberlain was a serial obstacle. He was discouraging over the issue of housing bonds. He was, more understandably, alarmed at the spiralling cost of the new policy of providing subsidies direct to private builders. This was particularly unpopular, with the political right, making Addison the scapegoat of their 'anti-waste' campaign, and working-class tenants vehemently attacking the raising of rents to keep existing homes in decent repair.

The housing programme was becoming increasingly unaffordable, especially so when the minister began to contemplate the even more expensive policy of local authorities undertaking the direct employment of labour themselves. It was the Treasury which delivered the *coup de grâce* with Austen Chamberlain's demand that, to help reduce the floating debt, all departments should cut their expenditure by at least 20 per cent. The future housing programme should be limited to 150,000, half the total urged by Addison (Finance Committee, 1920–21). His policies had finally run into the sand. The politics of 'anti-waste' and the economics of 'sound finance' had brought them tumbling down.

On 31 March 1921, Lloyd George asked Addison to resign from the Ministry of Health and to move to an ill-defined Ministry without Portfolio. He claimed that it was a political necessity; the truth was that Addison and his reforms encapsulated all of the weaknesses of the government on which the political right wing, on whom Lloyd George depended, capitalised. Addison was a helpless victim. A wounding motion for a reduction in his salary was made even harsher when the Prime Minister suggested that the cut in salary should be even more severe than the critics demanded, from £3,000 to £2,500. His successor at the Health Ministry, Sir Alfred Mond, reduced his housing programmes sharply; the Cabinet cut the total even more, to just 176,000 local authority dwellings. Slum clearance was cut back, almost terminally. After a bitter public exchange of letters with Lloyd George, Addison resigned from the government on 14 July, amidst the rejoicing of the Unionist press (Addison, 1921). As *The Nation* observed, he was being dismissed not for waste but to gratify the anti-waste campaign. The last dreams of 'homes for heroes' disappeared.

Yet it is ironic that the stormy ending of Addison's post-war ministerial career marked a stage in the progress of democratic socialism. His years at the Ministry of Health had offered the one serious governmental attempt to promote social reform. Nor were his housing policies anything like a total failure. Between 1 January 1919 and 30 September 1922, his programmes built 210,237 houses. In places such as Manchester and Swansea, the new Addison houses inaugurated a dramatic new phase in urban development. Things became much worse under the Geddes axe. Nor was Addison himself a busted flush. The irony was that his humiliation under Lloyd George in July 1921 had quite differing consequences. It was the all-powerful Lloyd George who would soon be out forever, and the defeated Addison who would enjoy a rebirth with a further thirty years at the highest level.

The move to Labour

Addison's move into the Labour Party was now pre-ordained. He predictably lost his seat in the 1922 general election, and wrote an eloquent pamphlet, *The Betrayal of the Slums*, which condemned the government for breaking their promises to eliminate inadequate and insanitary dwellings existing in their hundreds of thousands in Britain's cities. But as ever he sought a positive role. In 1923 he joined the Labour Party – a natural move. So did many other Liberals. But Addison was unique. He became Labour not as an ex-Liberal opposed to the Coalition but as a democratic socialist who had been one of that Coalition's most prominent ministers. Nearly all his Coalition Liberal colleagues had moved to the right, sometimes the extreme right, from Winston Churchill downwards. Addison rescued his career by advancing boldly to the left. One major legacy he provided for his new party was housing. Even if controversial, his policy of subsidised housing through the local authorities – a theme that had only a vague twelve-word reference in Labour's 1923 election manifesto – now became a leading priority for the party. John Wheatley's 1924 Housing Act under the first MacDonald government, focusing on subsidised working-class houses, was administratively more successful than Addison's though based on much the same principles. Wheatley, unlike Addison, became a reforming hero. Housing required the use of physical controls. The Liberals had failed to grasp this obvious socialist truth.

Addison set out his creed in 1926, in two substantial volumes, entitled *Practical Socialism*. Here he drew on his experience at Munitions and Reconstruction to show how socialist methods had been adopted in allocating raw materials, over costs, prices and employment, the development of mineral resources and the promotion of research. If socialism could save the nation at a time of war, it could promote social recovery at a time of peace. The First World War had been an age of discovery for socialist principles. They should be reasserted to launch a new commonwealth now.

His socialism looked forwards as well as backwards. He now drew on his background as a Lincolnshire countryman to give his party's policies an original new thrust. Labour, a movement born in urban, industrial Britain, found in Addison an innovative politician working to give it new impetus on rural Britain as well. The party had hitherto devoted little attention to the countryside, and made very little impact there other than in Norfolk. Lloyd George's wing of the Liberal Party had been far more active in this area, notably his 'Green Book', *The Land and the Nation* in 1925. In a speech at Tiverton Addison called for nationalisation of the land as the only way to give tenant farmers security of tenure. He also wrote two influential pamphlets, *Why Food is Dear* (1926) and *The Nation and its Food* (1929), which once again turned to wartime collectivism to make British agriculture more productive.

More original was his idea of agricultural marketing boards for basic foodstuffs such as corn, meat and milk. It bridged the cooperative sympathies of an old Liberal and his zeal for a national collectivist approach. He also championed a living wage for agricultural labourers, too often neglected by Liberals in the past, alongside import boards to create a powerful body to regulate the importation of foodstuffs. His broad proposals gained a substantial place in Labour's national programme of 1928, *Labour and the new Social Order*. He hoped and expected that MacDonald would appoint him Minister of Agriculture in the second Labour government but had to content himself with the minor position of Parliamentary Secretary, under Noel Buxton (Addison, 1929). But in June 1930 he succeeded the slow-moving Buxton and now pressed on vigorously for a nationwide system of marketing boards.

The idea of marketing boards was an important addition to the agenda of democratic socialism. It gained support on a cross-party basis – for instance, he worked closely with the Conservative Walter Elliot. It also won backing from sections of society not normally sympathetic to the Labour Party, such as wheat-growers. But it also ran counter to the traditional orthodoxy which underlay Labour's whole approach to domestic policy, especially in the mind of the Chancellor, Philip Snowden. He reflected an unyielding commitment to free trade and a consequent unremitting hostility towards quotas and tariffs. He saw in the Minister of Agriculture's policies the spectre of protectionism and dearer food, the bane of the left for 75 years (Snowden, 1929). Addison's challenging proposals for marketing boards, therefore, produced sharp controversy even though the Prime Minister, Ramsay MacDonald, was himself sympathetic (MacDonald Memorandum, 1930).

His role aroused further concern when he was known to be acting as a liaison figure with his old master and adversary, Lloyd George, about a possible electoral alliance with the Liberal Party. Agricultural policy now became a basis for a possible realignment of the left and a rebuilding of the progressive alliance of pre-1914 days (Lloyd George, 1930). Addison's main achievement was the passage of his Agricultural Marketing Bill which reached the statute book in July 1931, just before the fall of the Labour government. It was a fusion of older Liberal notions of cooperative farming and the socialist wish for national control of production and marketing, with a more sensitive and flexible system for guarantee-ing prices and the production of basic foodstuffs. It was both pragmatic and doctrinal. It became the foundation of Labour's, indeed Britain's, agricultural policy for nearly half a century, until entry into the European Common Market in 1973. It was carried on enthusiastically by Walter Elliot for the National government and was given a major stimulus by Tom Williams, Labour's Minister of Agriculture after 1945.

Addison also played a major part in ensuring that its leadership reflected the movement's basic values. In August 1931, he led the attack in Cabinet on MacDonald and Snowden's support for massive cuts in social spending following a huge international financial crisis. He was the first Cabinet minister to challenge the proposed 10 per cent cuts to unemployment benefit, and was one of the minority of nine who spoke and voted against them. He was also, as A. J. P. Taylor remarks, the only middle-class member of the minority, all the others being trade unionists (Taylor, 1965: 297). It led to a calamitous general election in which Labour's tally of MPs fell to 46; scores of Labour candidates were defeated at the polls, Addison among them. But the rebels had ensured that a mass party of the left would ultimately survive to win power.

He was not an important figure in the 1930s or the wartime years. He was, after all, approaching the veteran stage, entering his eighth decade in 1939. He was re-elected to Parliament in his old seat of Swindon in 1934 but lost it the following year. Two years later he went to the House of Lords and soon became Labour's leader there. He played his part in a variety of left-wing pressure-groups, such as the Socialist Medical Association and the committee to provide assistance for Republican Spain. He wrote with Attlee, Cripps, G. D. H. Cole and others in a volume entitled *Problems of a Socialist Government* (1933). He had, after all, a different approach to social planning. The younger generation of planners, Durbin, Jay and Gaitskell, were all economists, bridging social democracy and the ideas of Keynes. Addison was not a specialist economist but a pragmatic social administrator, drawing not on fiscal theory but personal knowledge of the machinery of government. What gave him continued prominence even in old age, was his closeness to the new Labour leader, Clement Attlee. 'Chris' and 'Clem' shared similar interests including cricket. Addison was very much the kind of free-thinking, pragmatic socialist whom Attlee admired. Furthermore, almost uniquely in Labour ranks, he had an immense knowledge of the practical challenges of being in government. In 1945, therefore, Attlee appointed him both Dominions Secretary and, much more importantly, Leader of the House of Lords.

Attlee's 'wise old man'

As an elder statesman, Addison played a significant, if often overlooked, role in shaping the policies of the Attlee government, both as a minister and a chairman of key Cabinet committees like the Future Legislation Committee. For the Prime Minister he was almost indispensable, a senior adviser of vast experience, playing the kind of role that Lord Granville had played for Gladstone and Lord Crewe for Asquith. It would be difficult to argue that he had a major influence on

Labour's international policy although as Dominions Secretary he played a part in links with Commonwealth countries over food supplies, not least through his strong personal relationship with Mackenzie King, the Prime Minister of Canada. He did play some part, though, in one momentous decision for a Labour government, heir of an anti-militarist past. He served on GEN 163, the secret Cabinet committee dominated by Ernest Bevin which agreed in January 1947 that Britain should develop atomic weapons. Addison, while anti-militarist in spirit, was never a pacifist.

More directly, he was helping to shape the democratic socialism of Attlee and his team. He was an important supporter of Aneurin Bevan's NHS. During debates, often fierce, in Cabinet, he backed Bevan's view that the service should be centralised rather than localised in structure, voicing his characteristic belief that nationalising the hospital service would have a positive effect on medical education and research. He helped to sway the Cabinet against Herbert Morrison's support for a locally based system, and persuaded Attlee to give his backing to Bevan who was duly grateful (Cabinet Conclusions, 1945). On the other hand, he criticised Bevan for undue caution on house-building, and for not giving improvement grants to 'tied cottages' occupied by farm labourers. He had much sympathy with Bevan during his battle with Gaitskell over NHS charges imposed in the 1951 budget and was among those who tried to dissuade him from resigning from the government. He also drew on his ministerial experience in helping Tom Williams, Minister of Agriculture, to making marketing boards and subsidies a central element of Labour's domestic planning.

His main role, though, was in leading the Lords in such a way that the Labour Party now became reconciled to its existence. Addison had been no friend of the upper house in the past, and among its fiercest critics in 1911. Faced with an overwhelming majority of Tory hereditary peers, he managed with remarkable adroitness to get the government's lengthy list of legislative measures safely through a hostile house. With the Conservative leader, Lord Salisbury, with whom he struck up a good relationship, he negotiated the so-called Salisbury-Addison agreement to ensure the safe second reading of measures clearly included in the government's election manifesto (Ballinger, 2012: 55–6). This provided a practical yardstick for many years, though it now seems antiquated.

Addison also played a major part in clipping the influence of the upper house, the Parliament Act of 1949 reducing the Lords' delaying powers from two years to just one. This enabled the government to go ahead with their much-contested nationalisation of iron and steel. In a conference of party leaders in 1948 he turned his hand to the even more contentious issue of the Lords' composition.

His ideas included severely stripping down the number of hereditaries, having life peers appointed, and paying peers a salary. These proved too radical for Attlee and other leading ministers (Ballinger, 2012: 64). They feared that a reformed Lords could now acquire an undue sense of their own importance and challenge the government of the day, and nothing came of it. But what did survive was a more positive view of what the Lords could usefully do under a Labour government. The party for the first time took the Lords seriously. But when Addison died in 1951, just after the Attlee government's electoral defeat, Labour's zeal for constitutional reform was still distinctly qualified.

The legacy

At the time of his death, politics and his party had moved on a long way from those of Addison's political heyday. His influence was now a thing of the distant past. There was, however, one interesting sequel. One very close colleague over many decades, a fellow MP in London's East End, and a surviving Asquithian Liberal until the mid-1920s, was William Wedgwood Benn, later Lord Stansgate. He was greatly stirred by the inability of Addison to press on with his social reform programme after 1918. It impelled Wedgwood Benn into the Labour Party, and he too served as a Cabinet minister under Attlee. He brought with him powerful Liberal convictions which, at least in his earlier period in politics, left its stamp on his more radical offspring Tony Benn in whom it is possible to discern surviving elements of his Liberal past, values which Addison and his father had handed on. There was the nonconformist background, Congregationalism in Tony Benn's case. There was the zeal for civic and institutional reform, shown in Benn's passionate campaign to reform the House of Lords (notably keeping out of it himself), his dedication to civil liberties and freedom of information, and his later enthusiasm for a written constitution and (perversely) for defending the sovereignty of Parliament against the European Union. With Tony Benn, as with Michael Foot, it was important that he was literally a child of the Edwardian Liberal left. It was men like Addison and his father whose early influence loomed large.

The influence of Addison and his generation was thus powerful in giving substance to the progressive ideal in a later age. A second world war would give it greatly added impetus. To adopt Peter Clarke's distinction, strongly endorsed by David Marquand (Clarke, 1978: 5, 14), their 'mechanical reformism' yielded observable results, compared with the older Liberals 'moral reformism', perhaps originating in T. H. Green's Hegelian idealism, which proved to be too often abstract, self-absorbed and ineffectual. It embraced, of course, collectivism and centralised planning, heavily influenced as we have seen by the experience of the First World War. Addison followed a variety of routes to pursue those ideals – the public realm, collaboration with the local authorities as over housing, a social contract with the trade unions, work with the professions as in national insurance, the cooperative ideal underlying the agricultural marketing boards. But since the disastrous general elections of 2010 and 2015, a new centre-left reformism has shown signs of emerging, focusing on democratic and constitutional reform, emphasising regional and civic devolution, local decision-making, democratic accountability, involved citizenship, a break with the party's centralist Fabian past. Jeremy Corbyn's 1970s-style neo-Marxism, and his lack of interest in constitutional issues other than vague pronouncements on human rights, provided serious obstacles to advance, intellectually and electorally. Even so, Addison's pluralist radicalism is perhaps finding renewed momentum, not in the party's leadership, but in a more locally orientated vision of the democratic socialist project, notably in Labour's mayors and leaders in cities and local authorities. The most influential of Addison's successors at the time of writing is Sadiq Khan. A quiet medical man of the Edwardian centre-left could be re-emerging as a prophet of practical socialism in our time, dreaming his dreams but always basing them on existing realities.

References

Addison to Lloyd George, 21 May 1917, [manuscript] Parliamentary Archive, Lloyd George Papers, F/1/3/20.

Addison to Lloyd George, 14 July 1921, [manuscript] Parliamentary Archive, Lloyd George Papers, F/1/6/30.

Addison to Ramsay MacDonald, 9 June 1929, [manuscript], The National Archives, MacDonald Papers, 5/40.

Addison, C. (1924a) *Politics from Within* (London: Herbert Jenkins).

Addison, C. (1924b) *Four and a Half Years* (London: Hutchinson).

Ballinger, C. (2012) *The House of Lords 1911–2011: A Century of Non-Reform* (London: Hart).

Cabinet Conclusions, 18 October, 20 December 1945, [manuscript], The National Archives, CAB 128/1.

Cabinet Finance Committee minutes, 7 December 1920–17 February 1921, [manuscript] CAB 27/7.

Cabinet Minutes, 14 November 1919, [manuscript] CAB 23/18.

Cabinet Paper 3, 27 October 1919, [manuscript] The National Archives, CAB 24/92.

Clarke, P. (1978) *Liberals and Social Democrats* (Cambridge: Cambridge University Press).

Gilbert, B. (1970) *British Social Policy 1914–1939* (London: Batsford).

Interview with Harold Wilson.

Lloyd George to MacDonald, 23 October1930, [manuscript], Bodleian, Oxford, Addison Papers.

MacDonald memorandum, 24 February 1930, [manuscript], The National Archives, MacDonald Papers, 1/244.

Memorandum, 1919, for the Provisions of the Bill as to the work of the Medical Research Committee, [manuscript], *Parliamentary Papers*, 29, 651, Cmd. 69.

Morgan, J. and J. (1980) *Portrait of a Progressive: The Political Career of Christopher, Viscount Addison* (Oxford: Oxford University Press).

Snowden, P. to Noel Buxton, 29 December 1929, [manuscript], The National Archives, MacDonald Papers, 5/40.

Taylor, A. J. P. (1965) *English History 1914 – 1945* (Oxford: Oxford University Press).

Part IV

Prospects, reflections and realities

12

Democracy and social democracy

Tony Wright

One of the enduring themes in David Marquand's work is on the 'democracy' bit of social democracy; and that is the theme explored here. This means saying something about how the social democratic tradition has viewed democracy, in Britain in particular, and where matters stand now. It may then be possible to offer some suggestions for the future, both in terms of thought and action.

Origins and ideas

It was the aim of social democrats to put the 'social' into democracy. If equality and citizenship were good enough for the political sphere, so the argument went, then they were good enough for the social and economic sphere too. Indeed, in some versions of social democracy (whether Marxian or Fabian) there was a historical inevitability about this process of extension, anchored in the organised power of a mass working class. At times there were arguments about whether capitalism would resist such extension, and how such resistance might be overcome, and whether political democracy was adequate for the task. In general, though, the assumption was that the 'socialisation' of democracy would be accomplished by the election of social democratic parties which would implement programmes of social and economic betterment in the interests of those who had elected them.

Where Marxists and social democrats differed was on the nature and possibilities of political democracy. While Marxists stripped off the veneer of political democracy to reveal the capitalist state beneath, social democrats attached themselves to democratic politics both as a value in itself and as the route, through a democratic state, to a socialist future. The original social democratic 'revisionism', when Bernstein dismantled the orthodoxies of Second International Marxism and replaced them with a practical reformism rooted in democratic politics, staked out this territory. In Britain there was no equivalent Marxism to dismantle, but the *Fabian Essays* (1889) set out its own version of social democratic reformism, with Sidney Webb referring to 'the extent of the progress of the economic side of Democracy – that is to say, Socialism itself' (Wright, 1983: 58). Later, in the face of the undemocratic model of socialism represented by the Soviet Union, it deliberately identified itself as 'democratic socialism'. While Marxists denounced the fraudulent infirmities of parliamentary politics, social democrats embraced the parliamentary and gradualist opportunities offered by political democracy.

This was not merely tactical, but a matter of building from the base that political democracy had established. If the principle of equality had been accepted in politics, then it also applied to society and economy. This was also the case in relation to liberalism. If liberalism really believed in the values of liberty it espoused, then it was not enough to protect liberties against the state but to use the state to extend practical freedoms to more people. Just as political democracy implied a process of extension, then a 'social' liberalism was also required. Instead of being the 'bourgeois' concepts that Marxists claimed, for social democrats the traditions of political democracy and liberalism provided the foundations upon which a socialist political project could be constructed. However, an extended liberalism was not enough, for the socialist project was one of community and common purpose. For Ramsay MacDonald (the subject of Marquand's fine biography), it offered the prospect of a transcendent social unity and 'growth towards organic wholeness' (Wright, 1983: 77).

In Britain there is a striking illustration of the success of this line of social democratic argument in a *Times* leader in July 1940: 'If we speak of democracy, we do not mean a democracy which maintains the right to vote but forgets the right to work and the right to live. If we speak of freedom, we do not mean a rugged individualism which excludes social organisation and economic planning. If we speak of equality we do not mean a political equality nullified by social and economic privilege' (quoted in McKibbin, 2010: 118). That catches a particular moment (A. J. P. Taylor once remarked that Britain had become a social democracy in 1940, unlike before and after), but it also encapsulates a whole tradition of social democratic thought.

The post-1945 'settlement' seemed also to have settled all the questions about the relationship between capitalism and democracy that had exercised thinkers on the left in the 1930s. It had provided a definitive answer to the question of whether capitalism could be tamed and domesticated by political democracy. There might be continuing argument about the policies required to secure the taming (and in particular about whether public ownership was still needed), but not about the ability of political democracy to bring capitalism to heel. Crosland's *The Future of Socialism* (1956) stands as the classic expression of the belief that a new kind of capitalism had come into existence and that this required a revision of the policy armoury of social democracy to achieve its traditional egalitarian objectives (Crosland, 1956).

Democracy and the state

What was absent in British social democracy was any interest in the nature of the British state and the character of its democracy. It was simply assumed that the state was the instrument of its purposes and that political democracy would put this instrument into its hands. In fact, the nature of the state in Britain, centralised and without restraining checks and balances, and with prerogative powers transferred from monarchs to elected governments, was seen as particularly suited for social democratic collectivism. There was impatience with those who proposed changes (for example, to the electoral system) that would make the business of governing more difficult. Thus Harold Laski expressed the left's view of proportional representation in describing it as 'a continuous threat to the stability of executive power' (Laski, 1951: 47).

This approach was understandable. The ability to transmit electoral will into legislative action without let or hindrance was a considerable asset for a reforming government. A 'strong' system of government was a natural fit for parties with a strong purpose. So too with its centralised character, which matched the social democratic commitment to a uniform equity and the belief in class as the determinant of attachment. But this approach also had costs. It encouraged a top-down kind of politics, rooted in Westminster and Whitehall, and buttressed by a sovereignty doctrine that discouraged a politics of pluralism, participation and power-sharing.

It also meant that in Britain both left and right, Labour and Tory, had a shared view of the merits of a political system that delivered centralised and concentrated power. As Samuel Beer put it in his classic account of British politics: 'Socialist Democracy and Tory Democracy have a great deal in common', sharing an outlook that 'legitimises a massive concentration of political power'

(Beer, 1969: 91). For the right this reflected a belief in governing authority; for the left, a belief in governing purpose. It also meant that while democracy had become the legitimating basis of the system, it had never become its animating principle. There had never been a moment when the British had been required to decide what kind of democracy they wanted to be. This was a matter of culture, perhaps even more than of structure. Beyond the act of voting, and supporting a party that wanted to govern, a wider and deeper culture of democratic citizenship remained under-developed. As a historian of modern British democracy describes this: 'Britain's more passive form of citizenship has much to do with democracy emerging as a form of government that never greatly enthused the mass of "the people" it purported to represent' (Jefferys, 2007: 9).

It was not always clear that the British version of social democracy would develop in this way. In the first two decades of the twentieth century there was a rich and intense debate on the social democratic left about democracy and the state. The Fabian version of state socialism was challenged by those, notably the guild socialists, who wanted something more decentralised, pluralist and participatory. According to G. D. H. Cole, Fabian collectivism would mean 'the completion of the present tendency towards State Sovereignty by the piling of fresh powers and duties on the great Leviathan' (Cole, 1920: 27). Even if, at times, this debate became bogged down in intricate system-building, it nevertheless had important issues at its core. One of these was how to prevent a socialist state from becoming a bureaucratic leviathan, by dividing power as well as concentrating it. But another was about the need to see democracy as extending beyond the confines of the political system to all the centres of power (especially the workplace).

Although this kind of thinking was destined to become marginalised in mainstream social democratic politics, for a time it found a wide audience. Its influence can be seen in the 1918 Clause Four of Labour's constitution where the party's commitment to public ownership is combined with 'popular control'. It is reflected in the declaration in 1923 by Clement Attlee, newly elected as a Labour MP, that 'no form of society will be satisfactory that leaves the worker a wage-slave' (quoted in Wright, 1979: 107). From time to time this tradition is revisited, if only to be identified as a path not taken, but it lost out to the demands of parliamentary politics and (particularly in the inter-war years) to the imperatives of an economic programme. Besides, it was difficult to persuade social democratic politicians that, when power was won, it should then be given away.

Social democratic collectivism had huge achievements to its credit. The welfare state and National Health Service transformed lives, providing security where none had existed before. Redistributive policies diminished inequality. Planning delivered public goods from clean air to national parks. The power of a centralised state was used for practical betterment. There was little incentive to question the character of British democracy, or to explore ways in which democracy might be extended. Thus the model of a 'national' health service won out against those who wanted to anchor it in local government. At times there were voices arguing for a change of direction – for example, Benn on workers' control, Crossman on a reformed Parliament, Mackintosh on a decentralised regionalism – but these remained noises off. The idea of industrial democracy briefly surfaced, but was soon buried by the forces of old labourism. For as long as the traditional social democratic show was on the road, there seemed no reason to question some of its underlying assumptions.

The show is no longer on the road, and has not been for some time. As the post-war settlement broke down, an aggressive capitalism was again unleashed and with it an ideology of deregulated market individualism. The social democratic toolkit of tax and spend (and redistribution) met a resistance to paying taxes, while a squeeze on public spending displaced a distribution of the proceeds of growth. At the same time, class fragmentation, and the decline of an industrial working class, was undermining the electoral support system on which social democracy had traditionally relied. Then when the reaction against neoliberalism did come, it produced a populist shift to the right rather than to the left and with it a new politics of identity rather than class that left social democracy even more stranded. Social democrats might say that their 'values' were as relevant as ever, but this could sound merely vacuous if they no longer knew how to make them operational.

Some have concluded from this that social democracy is in historic decline; that it is anchored in the conditions and circumstances of the twentieth century and has now lost its moorings as this environment has changed. This is certainly possible. What is clear is that the permanent revisionism that has been a feature of social democracy has never been more needed. It began life as revision of Marxism, then later revised itself in response to changing economic and social circumstances (most notably in the rethinking of the 1950s, and most recently in the 'third way' thinking of the New Labour years) and is now faced with the task of further revision if it wants to remain politically relevant to the world we now inhabit. This is both challenging and liberating. It enables fresh thinking on a whole range of fronts, as the neoliberal promise collapses and leaves an intellectual vacuum to be filled. One of those fronts is the 'democracy' part of social democracy.

Doing democracy differently

Of course this is not just a matter for Britain. As traditional politics runs into trouble, with mainstream parties contracting and electoral participation declining, there is taking place what Peter Mair describes as 'the hollowing of Western democracy' (Mair, 2013). The fact that this trend has been evident more or less everywhere is not surprising, as the factors contributing to it are also widely shared. Yet Britain is nevertheless something of an outlier, where the trends are particularly marked. This suggests that there may be something about the British version of politics that contributes to this democratic malaise. There may also be characteristics of traditional social democratic politics that are part of this problem – and in need of revision.

At the same time, it is important to avoid some of the simplicities that are sometimes in evidence in thinking about these matters. One of these is a generalised call for more 'participation', whereas people (with lives to lead) will only take part with others in collective endeavours if the activity is worthwhile in terms of what it offers. As Colin Crouch puts it: 'We should not puzzle at declining voter turnout and even more strongly declining identification with political parties once we appreciate that a strong interest in politics by the mass of citizens who have no chance of being politically effective needs social supports and that those bequeathed to us by the struggles of the past have declined in salience' (Crouch, 2016: 95). If the old supports for participation have gone, it is futile to expect a revival of participation until new ones are found. For social democrats that means finding a contemporary constituency.

There is sometimes a similar simplicity about the state. Those social democrats who concede that their political tradition has been too associated with 'statism' (which it has) are prone to throw the baby out with the bath water. It is possible to think that social democracy has been too statist in its politics, and to want to revisit and resurrect those minority strands in its tradition that point in more pluralist and decentralised directions, while also recognising that it is only action by the state (and states acting together) that we will have any chance of tackling some of the most daunting and pressing problems of our time. The real issue is therefore not between state and non-state, but what kind of state is most appropriate for what purposes and what its relationship is with other actors. The sort of discussion of these matters that engaged social democrats in the early part of the twentieth century, but was then neglected, should be renewed now.

Similar considerations apply to the question of political leadership. It is possible to embrace the need for democratic renewal through an energised 'movement' kind of politics while also acknowledging that the quality and effectiveness of political leadership matters. These are not opposites, nor should they be. Indeed, the search for a new kind of politics in response to the democratic malaise involves finding new kinds of politicians, while avoiding the excesses of populism. David Marquand's own dissatisfaction with the 'feverish inconsequence' of parliamentary politics (Marquand, 1997: 12) is mirrored in the public's aversion to the way in which political life is routinely conducted. The antipathy to politicians who seem only to be office-seeking members of a political class is matched by the attraction of those politicians who possess the elusive quality of authenticity (which should not be confused with bogus authenticity of those populists who claim to speak for 'the people'). But this only gets them a hearing; they also need to have something to say – and to say it in a way that frames arguments, shapes narratives and wins support. The current tragedy of the Labour Party (in which 'democracy' has delivered an unelectable leadership) is that nobody is listening to what it might have to say.

What is clear is that the sort of top-down and tribal politics that has traditionally been part of the DNA of Labour politics in Britain is no longer fit for purpose. An approach to democracy that simply involved electing Labour politicians who would then pull levers at the centre is not enough. The tribes are no longer there and the levers often do not work. It also produces a democratic atrophy. The party has hollowed out and is now faced with the task of building from the bottom to re-establish the community roots it has lost. A sterile adversarialism which no longer reflects political loyalties does not just turn people off, but prevents the kind of political learning and search for common ground that a more collaborative style of politics would encourage. Different political traditions, with different labels, all have something to contribute to thinking our way through the problems we face and an old bunker mentality only gets in the way.

For a long time the Labour tradition displayed a conservative contentment with the character of British democracy and an antipathy to those who wanted to reform and energise it. This only began to change when Margaret Thatcher demonstrated to what purposes a system of 'elected dictatorship' could be put. The result was the set of sweeping constitutional changes of the New Labour years, which are still working their effects, and the significance of which should not be under-estimated. They created new centres of power and new accountabilities. Yet they remained a series of disparate measures, without a consistent direction and not based upon a coherent idea about how democracy in Britain might be remodelled. They were not presented as the beginning of a democratic revolution, perhaps because they did not spring from conviction or conversion (which is why Tony Blair describes himself as a 'nincompoop' for having introduced freedom of information legislation (Blair, 2010: 516)). British democracy now sits in a kind of limbo, not the system it was, but unsure where it is going.

Social democrats should be those in the vanguard of democratic and constitutional reform, as part of a commitment to putting power in the hands of the people. This is not just a Labour project, but if the party had not disabled itself with its own muddle about democracy it would be well placed to take the lead. There is lots of democratic business to attend to, from the role of money in politics to the future structure of the United Kingdom (and of England). The fact that the second chamber of Parliament is a bloated house of patronage, that peerages can effectively be bought and that politicians can still dish out gongs to themselves and their cronies, provides plenty of democratic ammunition for reformers. The quality of democracy matters. This is not just a matter of structures, and in many ways the culture of democracy is even more important, but the structures should be kept under regular review. There is a case for a democracy commission to lead this work.

One of its tasks should be to start a democratic conversation about the electoral system. This is where the Labour tradition has been at its most constitutionally conservative, opposing any change that would deprive it of the chance of majority government or oblige it to work with others. When parties could command the support of nearly half the electorate then, despite its failure to match votes and seats, there was something to be said for a winner-takes-all system that delivered majority governments. The fragmentation of the electorate has changed that. A majority government can now be formed with not much more than 30 per cent of the vote, leaving most people unrepresented, raising questions about governing legitimacy and confining elections to a relatively small number of seats. This is not a system designed to nourish an active democracy. In 2010 it even failed to do the one thing that was supposed to be its distinctive merit, namely to produce a 'strong' majority government. There is no perfect electoral system, but we can do better than this. If it encouraged parties to learn that it was possible to both compete and cooperate at the same time, then so much the better.

There should also be an exploration of democratic innovations. The digital revolution opens up exciting possibilities for connecting rulers and ruled in new ways, closing the information and communication gap between the represented and their representatives, thereby enriching the quality of representative democracy. These possibilities will not be realised, though, if it simply allows people to inhabit their own digital bubbles, or if democratic conversation and argument is replaced by a culture of abuse and untruth. Referendums are a generally bad way for making complex policy decisions, but there may be occasions (especially at a local level) when they may have a role, as long as they are advisory and have an appropriate framework of rules. For example, there may be a case for testing whether the proposal for new grammar schools has local support. The rejuvenation of local democracy is the most urgent task, as this is where citizenship can most easily be practised. The parties have a role in this by opening up candidate selection through primaries. Elected city mayors should make a difference (the proposed sub-regional ones have a different purpose), especially if new kinds of civic leaders emerge who are not just recycled party politicians.

There is much scope for developing new ways in which people can be involved in the services that affect their lives. School governing bodies have been an example of parental involvement in education (which is why the proposal to remove them was so outrageous), but public involvement in public services should be developed on other fronts. For example, it would be possible to create urban 'parishes' within cities as a focus for community identity and organisation, with their own parish councils to deliberate on local issues and with a budget to spend on local priorities. Members of these city parish councils could be chosen by lot, opening them up beyond the usual suspects to the whole local population. The practice used for jury service, which produces a sense of civic involvement, could in this (and other) ways be applied more widely.

Capitalism and democracy

If democracy is about enabling people to exercise some power and control over the forces that impact on their lives, then social democrats should be those who are constantly looking for ways to make this a reality. A major source of contemporary discontent, providing the fuel for populism, is the pervasive feeling that power has been lost. The financial crash exemplified a world out of control, inflicting hardships on the many while a global elite of the super-rich went on getting richer. The question asked by R. H. Tawney after a previous crash could be asked again:

> The fundamental question, as always, is, Who is to be master? Is the reality behind the decorous drapery of political democracy to continue to be the economic power wielded by a few thousand – or, if that is preferred, a few hundred thousand – bankers, industrialists and landowners? Or shall a serious effort be made ... to create organs through which the nation can control, in co-operation with other nations, its economic destinies; plan its business as it deems most conducive

to the general well-being; override, for the sake of economic efficiency, the obstruction of vested interests; and distribute the products of its labours in accordance with some generally recognised principles of justice? (Tawney, 1932)

The issue of power is at the heart of democracy and the need to assert a public interest in relation to powerful private interests should be at the heart of social democracy. The attack on vested interests, whether state or corporate, should be its natural territory. It should be the enemy of the kind of state power that disempowers citizens and the kind of market power that damages consumers, exploits workers and undermines the public good. Its mission should be to empower people against the powerful, the little people against the big people. If this has an insurgent quality to it, so much the better. In a context in which the services provided by the state have been organised and marketised in ways which make them ever more remote from their users, in which the privatised utility companies often treat their consumers even worse than when they were in the hands of the state, and in which private power is now exercised by global corporations which dwarf many states, the need for a democratic politics of empowerment could not be more evident. There is a crisis of accountability, which in turn produces a crisis of disaffection and alienation.

The relationship between capitalism and democracy, once seemingly settled, again comes into question. The neoliberal surge, with its attendant inequalities, has inevitably produced its reaction. An era of financial deregulation crashed economies and imposed austerity. At the same time the globalisation of economic forces has stripped away old securities. A sense of powerlessness in the face of these developments has produced a political reaction that is still working itself out, often in dangerous and disturbing ways. The promise of democracy involved the control of power in the interests of the many, including economic power. If that promise is not fulfilled, then bad things will happen. Social democrats have seen their task as promoting a kind of capitalism that would fulfil the promise of democracy and the needs of its citizens. That task now has a new urgency.

Brexit and beyond

In Britain the most dramatic example of a reaction is the referendum result on EU membership, seismic in its impact and implications. There is continuing argument about exactly what happened, and why, but not about the fact that it represented a democratic uprising. It was an uprising, as one Leave strategist told a journalist during the campaign, in which: 'Our people are the old, the badly educated and the poor' (Gibbon, 2016: 12). Millions of people voted who had not voted in the preceding general election. They voted in defiance of all the authoritative voices warning of the dire economic consequences of leaving the EU. A social democratic party found itself disconnected from the people it claimed to represent. Whatever view is taken of the result, it is important to try to understand the democratic significance of what happened. It is easy to rail against the deceits and scares of the campaign, but this is not enough if we want to learn some democratic (and social democratic) lessons.

There is general agreement that immigration was the decisive issue, cleverly and ruthlessly exploited by the Leave campaign. Yet this depended for its success on a widespread popular feeling that immigration, its scale and nature, had never been a matter of democratic decision. This extended beyond the recent influx of 'free movement' East Europeans, although this was its immediate focus. Given the chance to vote on it, which the EU referendum provided, people took it; and especially those people who thought their jobs, services and communities were threatened. At the same time they could vote against the political class, in Britain and the EU, who they regarded as having taken decisions on these matters without consulting them. This may have been misguided, but it was not irrational. A referendum provides an opportunity for voters to answer any question they like; and, for many, the question was about immigration.

The whole matter of 'democracy' played a leading role in the referendum campaign and was the banner of those arguing that Britain should leave the EU. It proved remarkably successful and it is important to understand why. The argument was strikingly simple: democracy was about self-government and this meant not being governed by the EU. A democracy should be able to choose and remove its rulers, control its own borders and make its own laws. The sovereignty of the people demanded nothing less, but on each of these fronts the EU had substituted its own authority. However inadequate we might regard this kind of argument, its potency was undeniable. It allowed those wanting Britain to leave the EU to hail the referendum result as the expression of an instinct for self-government on the part of the British people.

It also reflected a failure on the part of social democrats and others to make a case for EU membership that relied on a larger view of democracy. In a country where membership had not been rooted in an adherence to the 'European idea', it needed other supports. One of these was a recognition that sovereignty was not the same as power and that membership of the EU with its pooled sovereignty enabled countries to achieve together what they were less able to achieve separately, including the benefits of a single market. When Britain's relationship with the EU had for so long been presented in terms of a heroic struggle in which ministers 'battled for Britain' against the bureaucrats of Brussels, it was difficult when a referendum arrived to change the narrative to one in which we were participating members of a club designed for mutual advantage. Nor were matters helped by the fact that the EU had developed in a way that made it easy to characterise it as an integrationist project of technocratic elites with a disregard for democracy.

Of course democracy did not stop with the referendum, as the victors liked to claim. It is a continuous process, not an isolated event. Even the event itself had shown a country pretty much split down the middle. The result may have produced a narrow majority for exit, but provided no guidance at all on the nature of any post-exit arrangement. The democratic process has had to take up the slack, with Parliament (and the judges) rightly resisting the government's claim of prerogative power in shaping the country's future. Social democrats should be energetic participants in this process, not least in protecting the interests of those who did not vote to become poorer or less secure. Any final deal should certainly require parliamentary approval; and there is a strong case for putting it to the people in another referendum since that was the trigger for the whole process.

Everyone agreed that the referendum had revealed a country that was deeply divided, although there was less agreement on the nature of the divisions. It turned out to be a more complex picture than some of the instant verdicts (for example, about the 'left behinds') suggested. In many ways it revealed a cultural divide, between those people who had an outlook of easy cosmopolitanism and those who found the modern world a much less comfortable place. This was clearly connected with social class, but it was not just about class. There were suggestions that the real divide was between liberals and authoritarians; and that this was the attitudinal axis along which the EU referendum could most usefully be explained. Yet this raised as many questions as it answered.

For social democrats all this presented particular problems that had always been there, but which the referendum brought to a head. Behind the politics of class that had traditionally sustained social democracy, which could bring with it a centralising indifference to other loyalties, there lurked attitudes that warned of trouble ahead. Even at the height of class-based politics, about a third of working-class voters supported the Conservatives. These were Disraeli's 'angels in marble' (McKenzie and Silver, 1968). This suggested the need for another attitudinal axis in addition to the familiar left/right axis around attitudes to economic inequality. When class fragmentation developed, this further weakened the supports of a class-based politics and strengthened the salience of other attitudes and loyalties. In this sense the referendum did not disconnect Labour from its base, as was asserted, but exposed a disconnection that had been long in the making.

Labour's social democrats too often had a blind eye when it came to the politics of place and of identity. There were good and understandable reasons for this, but it was a weakness of social democratic collectivism nevertheless. The price to be paid was seen in the dramatic collapse of Labour's Scottish fortress when it came under nationalist attack. Antipathy to nationalism in all its forms had excluded the possibility of a 'civic nationalism' that was social democratic. But it was also seen in the limitations of a centralising kind of politics that paid insufficient attention to the local and the particular. In some respects this was surprising for a political tradition that had its roots in the revolt of the periphery. Yet it is no coincidence that worsening regional inequality sits alongside a centralised political system. Everywhere there is a new politics of identity on the part of both individuals and communities, and a resistance to centralised control and unaccountable power. The referendum reflected this, not least in its expression of an English nationalism.

Unless social democracy can find a way to connect with this new environment, it will continue to languish. This emphatically does not mean an embrace of the worst kind of nationalism (or a renunciation of the best kind of internationalism). One of the effects of the referendum has been to open the door to those who trade in bigotry and xenophobia. But even respectable voices have used the referendum to attack those they describe as the 'liberal elite'. This makes it a dangerous moment for the liberal tradition – of tolerance, freedom and openness – that Britain likes to think it has contributed to the world.

No doubt, liberals can sometimes over-reach themselves, insensitive to traditions and familiarities that bind communities together, but the duty of social democrats is to join with others in defence of this liberal tradition, as they have done in times of threat in the past, perhaps in the form of a new popular front. It may not be the answer to the 'progressive dilemma', but it does provide the basis for a progressive alliance among all those (in all parties and none) who recognise the nature of the threat and want to work together to counter it. The British have never needed to express themselves through a noisy nationalism, preferring the understatement of a quiet patriotism. This is a tradition worth hanging on to.

It is also one to which social democrats should attach themselves and make their own. Writing in 1941, George Orwell observed that England was 'the only great country whose intellectuals are ashamed of their own nationality. In left-wing circles it is always felt there is something slightly disgraceful in being an

Englishman.' At the same time he also demonstrated how it was possible to construct a patriotism of the left, with his characterisation of England as 'a family with the wrong members in control' (Orwell, 1941). The flag-waving right has always sought to appropriate patriotism for itself, absurdly but often effectively, understanding its potency. The left has been on the defensive, unsure of its response. The need now is to go on the offensive, drawing on all the resources of a radical patriotism. This is particularly necessary in England, where a sense of Englishness is beginning to make itself felt and demanding some kind of expression. This includes, but goes beyond, the matter of political organisation. A radical patriotism would rally 'the common people of England' against all those groups and interests who are selling the country short. There are rich resources in the radical tradition to draw on.

What is not yet sufficiently recognised is that the democratic revolt that produced Brexit has opened up the whole question of what kind of country we now want to be. This goes far beyond the nature of the relationship with the EU. There will be clear alternatives on offer. One will be of a deregulated market state stripping away protections in a global race to the bottom, with widening inequalities and accelerating insecurities. It is unlikely that the kind of people who could be mobilised in the anti-EU cause will also be mobilised for this kind of future. This creates a real opportunity for those who offer a different alternative, based on the idea of a community of mutual support in which all have a stake. There is a widespread sense, as public services are eroded and life chances curtailed, that it is a moment for some fundamental choices. The potential exists for a constituency to be mobilised that brings together all those people who do not want the kind of future offered by the Brexit ideologues.

Taking control?

On entering Downing Street, Theresa May told people that her intention was to 'do everything possible to give you more control over your lives'. This was the interpretation she had given, rightly, to the referendum result. It was a reaction against a sense of powerlessness that mocked the self-governing promise of democracy and a demand for more control. This is radical in its implications, certainly more than Mrs May seems to understands or intends. Leaving the EU may well result in less control of course, but the wider point remains. It provides an opening for social democrats to explore what 'more control' might actually mean, when applied to all the sites of concentrated power and privilege and to all the engines of inequality and insecurity. In this way the dynamic of democracy could again be mobilised for social democratic purposes. Whether Britain's social democrats are capable of taking this opportunity is another matter.

This would be the 'socialising' of democracy that was central to the intellectual foundations of social democratic politics. Yet the context is now quite different. The real question for the social democratic tradition, which will determine whether it has a future as well as a past, turns on its ability to respond to the kind of world that is now taking shape. This is a world in which the whole nature of work is changing and with it the conditions for a decent life on a sustainable planet. Social democratic values may be enduring, but how they might be applied to this world is a daunting challenge. Social democracy advanced in the last century because it had something to say to the needs of an industrial working class. Its future will be determined by whether it has something to say to the citizens of the very different societies and economies of this century. Never has its capacity for intellectual and political revisionism been more needed.

One of the most refreshing aspects of David Marquand's work is its intellectual honesty, its willingness to question his own previous positions and to embrace uncertainties. Nowhere is this more evident than in his 'Journey to an Unknown Destination', the compelling and autobiographical opening chapter of *The New Reckoning* (1997). Here he still thinks he has been asking the right question ('how can a fragmented society make itself whole?'), but at the same time, 'I cannot suppress a certain pricking in the thumbs – a nagging sense that the path I have followed for the best part of forty years is blocked, and that it is time for a new turning' (Marquand, 1997: 29). It is in that spirit that today's social democrats should approach the task of finding a 'new turning'. It may be, of course, that political traditions will take new forms, and new names, as part of this process. This requires an openness to fresh thinking, and a willingness to cooperate across and beyond party lines. David Marquand's own political promiscuity exemplifies this. Perhaps this is why he likes to quote this passage from William Morris's *A Dream of John Ball*: 'I pondered all these things, and how men fight and lose the battle, and the thing that they fought for comes about in spite of their defeat, and when it comes turns out not to be what they meant, and other men have to fight for what they meant under another name.'

References

Beer, S. (1969) *Modern British Politics*, 2nd edn (London: Faber).

Blair, T. (2010) *A Journey* (London: Hutchinson).

Cole, G. D. H. (1920) *Guild Socialism Re-Stated*, (London: Fabian Society).

Crosland, C. A. R. (1956) *The Future of Socialism* (London: Jonathan Cape).

Crouch, C. (2016) 'Tilted: the familiar axes of politics are changing, with momentous consequences', *Juncture*, IPPR (Oxford: Wiley).

Gibbon, G. (2016) *Breaking Point: The UK Referendum on the EU and its Aftermath* (London: Haus).

Jefferys, K. (2007) *Politics and the People: A History of British Democracy since 1918* (London: Atlantic).

Laski, H. (1951) *Reflections on the Constitution* (Manchester: Manchester University Press).

Mair, P. (2013) *Ruling the Void: The Hollowing of Western Democracy* (London: Verso).

Marquand, D. (1997) *The New Reckoning* (Cambridge: Polity).

McKenzie, R. and Silver, A. (1968) *Angels in Marble: Working Class Conservatives in Urban England* (London: Heinemann).

McKibbin, R. (2010) *Parties and People: England 1914–1951* (Oxford: Oxford University Press).

Orwell, G. (1941) *The Lion and the Unicorn: Socialism and the English Genius* (London: Secker & Warburg).

Tawney, R. H. (1932) 'The choice before the Labour Party', *The Political Quarterly* 3(3): 323–45.

Wright, A. (1979) *G. D. H. Cole and Socialist Democracy* (Oxford: Oxford University Press).

Wright, A. (1983) *British Socialism: Socialist Thought from the 1880s to 1960s* (London: Longman).

13

Social democracy before and after the EU referendum

Lord David Owen

David Marquand and I were part of the new intake of seventy-seven Labour MPs after the sweeping 1966 general election victory. We had never met before and we first talked seriously together at the 1963 Dining Club in the House of Commons. The Club had started after Hugh Gaitskell's tragically early death and around the table were people who all knew Gaitskell well including David, Tony Crosland, Roy Jenkins, Woodrow Wyatt and Gerry Reynolds. I was the only person in the room who had never met Gaitskell, seen him or heard him speak in the flesh. Yet from television and radio I had the highest respect for him and had joined the Labour Party in 1959 after hearing him say on radio, 'the trouble is there are too many armchair socialists'. That described my position exactly, having never gone near a political party during my three years as a medical student in Cambridge, preferring the political background of Great St Mary's Church under Mervyn Stockwood and E. M. Forster's humanists.

Gaitskell's speech on television in 1962 to the Labour Conference had focused on what he saw as the implicit danger in the then European Common Market: federalism. Having engaged in personal debate, a few months before, with its founding father Monnet and then later Spaak, who both wanted a federal Europe, Gaitskell broke with many of his closest political friends when he warned: 'should Britain become only a Texas or a California in the United States of Europe?' His wife, Dora, said to a Labour MP during the standing ovation, 'Charlie, all the wrong people are cheering' (Williams, 1979: 708, 724–5, 734, 736). I was one of the supposedly wrong people cheering, not at the Conference but watching on TV at the Royal Waterloo Hospital as a newly adopted Labour candidate and recently qualified doctor.

This issue of a federal Europe was to become the most personally divisive political issue between David and myself. At times it looked as if our friendship would fracture on this. Particularly when he was with Roy Jenkins in Brussels and I as Foreign Secretary was responsible for a paper ruling out European federalism and endorsed by the Labour Cabinet on 26 July 1977 at an all-day strategy meeting (Owen, 1977).

For all our differences over Europe, and some tough criticisms of me over the years, particularly about populism in the *Progressive Dilemma* (Marquand, 1991), a word which often gives insufficient respect for the democratic need to take account of public opinion, when we meet, sometimes after as long as a few years, it has always been within the context of an underlying affection. He is a gentle, kind man who writes with passion and warmth – a good combination – and uses words like a pianist uses the keys. What binds us together is that we still agree on the overriding importance of reducing inequality and championing the ethical founding principles of the NHS. We used to agree on a federal United Kingdom, but now David has joined Plaid Cymru, I am not so sure.

The first political essay we began writing together was in the late spring of 1967 with John Mackintosh, also a new Labour MP. Entitled 'Change Gear' it was published by *Socialist Commentary* as a fifteen-page pamphlet just before the Labour Party Autumn Conference at Scarborough in September 1967. It received an unprecedented level of publicity because it advocated 'devaluation', the word that few dared to utter in Labour circles. Devaluation was politically too damaging to risk given the Labour government's narrow majority in 1964 but it should have been undertaken within a few weeks of winning a large majority in 1966. In May 1967 David and I had sent a ten-page memorandum to Harold Wilson which owed far more to David's pen than mine. The then Permanent Under-Secretary at the Treasury, later told me he had used it as the peg and excuse for reopening the arguments for devaluation in drafting a reply for Wilson. The pamphlet's detailed advocacy of devolution owed much to John Mackintosh's serious work on devolution as Professor of Politics at Edinburgh. John was, by any standard of eloquence, writing skill, charm, courage and intellect the outstanding politician of our 1966 intake. That he never came into government was a 'scandal' as David termed it in a moving BBC broadcast after his death in July 1978 (Marquand, 1979). All three of us were unashamed re-distributors of income. We wanted to join the Common Market and committed ourselves to VAT, then a controversial issue. The pamphlet ended with this passage:

The moral is clear. No one denies the existence of widespread poverty and injustice in Britain today. What is in dispute is the priority to be given to the assault against them. We believe it should be given the highest priority ... We know only too well that this will be resisted, fiercely and bitterly, by those who have most to lose from such a shift of resources.

One of the many fascinating things we did together was to dine with Enoch Powell, arranged by Dick Crossman: just the five of us. I soon discovered that the weakness of Enoch's apparently impeccable logic was usually his first premise. It was there that his prejudices often defied his later logic. It was the time of the controversy over the Kenyan Asian legislation in February 1968 and on 9 February Powell had called for the 'virtual termination of work vouchers'. While an Asian's entry right was not going to be changed, the issue was whether to delay entry. John had worked in Nigeria and was determined to vote against delay. David on Commonwealth citizens favoured Gaitskell's principled and absolute defence of their right to enter but abstained. I voted for the legislation after much heart searching because of the need to take public opinion into account. Slowing, but not terminating, was I felt the way to contain a growing racial prejudice. There was no need for absolutism. Powell's speech, 'Like the Romans I seem to see the River Tiber foaming with much blood', was made on 20 April and Heath rightly sacked him from the Shadow Cabinet for a speech which was, as he said, 'racialist in tone and liable to exacerbate racial tensions'.

These divisions about immigration and the implications both ways for race relations in the United Kingdom are not new to the Labour Party. Racial tension was mounting then in the East End of London with the dockers supporting Enoch Powell. Despite all the economic constraints on that 1966–70 Labour government, with legislative reform of abortion, homosexuality and divorce, and establishing the Houghton Inquiry into adoption, which laid the foundation for the 1975 Children's Act, that Parliament was a social reforming one, the like of which has not been seen since. It was underlined by Wilson's own commitment to the Open University.

By 2016 London was a multi-racial city although tensions were, in contrast, building up in northern cities and middle England was demanding 'control'. Broadly speaking, in the EU referendum the London Labour Party was against immigration controls, including Corbyn, whereas politicians like Rachel Reeves afterwards warned the Labour Conference in September 2016 that her Leeds West constituency was a 'tinderbox' on this issue. Stephen Kinnock and Emma Reynolds were also trying to open a debate on the freedom of movement of people into the United Kingdom. In 2017 the party was facing, rather successfully, in both ways, but this position will be exposed as immigration, legal and illegal, continues to mount before the next election.

Europe

On 18 June 1970 Labour, somewhat surprisingly to its own supporters, lost the general election. In October 1971 Roy Jenkins, as Deputy Leader decisively led sixty-nine Labour MPs, which included both David and me, to vote against a three-line whip, to support the principle of entry into the European Community. A few months before this David, Judith, his wife who is a distinguished regional economist, and I started to draft material for a series of speeches by Roy which would be chapters in a small paperback *What Matters Now* to be produced by his publisher, Collins. It was intended to be like Joseph Chamberlain's *Unauthorized Programme* in 1885, a distinctive rallying point. Sadly, on Sunday 12 March 1972, Roy backed off in a BBC interview when challenged inevitably about the press headlines saying his speech was a leadership bid. Many of the ideas in the book, however, went into later SDP manifestoes and some still have relevance. David describes in an affectionate essay how we 'became a mini-Think Tank', but also how 'Jenkins himself seemed oddly ambivalent about the operation', and in August 1972 Roy privately wrote, 'the only way through this miasma might be outside the mould of traditional two party politics' (Adonis and Thomas, 2004: 125–31).

Within weeks the Labour Shadow Cabinet, with Wilson, provoked by Roy's speech, did an about turn and decided to vote for a referendum on the European Communities Bill. Both David and I argued for accepting a European referendum and I presented Roy with the argument on paper. When we debated the issue in the context of the European Communities Bill, among those Labour MPs who had voted to join the Common Market, only a few others supported it. The clinching argument against us was that of Roy Jenkins: it would be easier to win a referendum once in the Common Market after the 1974–75 general election with the fear of the unknown having lessened. While still out of the Common Market he felt the issue would be highly divisive inside the Labour Party and the unknown would engender a greater fear factor among the public and a referendum in 1972 would be lost. Roy resigned, and I too, with a few others, followed him, fed up with voting against legislation which we wanted to reach the Statute Book.

David and I both campaigned on a cross-party basis in 1975 to stay in the European Community. Those within the Labour Party supporting 'no' to staying in accepted the result for five years until 1980 when the Labour Conference, spurred on by Peter Shore and John Silkin, who had been Cabinet ministers in Jim Callaghan's government, and by the Tribunite left and most trade unions, voted to come out without even a referendum. Michael Foot had point blank refused before the January 1981 conference to support backing a referendum before leaving when asked to do so by Shirley Williams, Bill Rodgers and myself. Maybe that was because we could at the most assemble thirty Labour MPs to rebel to the point of resigning from the party.

The Social Democratic Party

At the start of the SDP in 1981, in the Open Forum Series, David wrote a polemical pamphlet, 'Russet-Coated Captains: The Challenge of Social Democracy', explaining our 50,000 membership growing at the rate of 500 a week in the early spring. 'Behind this astonishing development lies a long-standing and deep-seated public revolt against a generation of misgovernment', and it had a section entitled 'Moderation is not Enough', accepting that social democracy has to be dynamic and radical.

As leader of the SDP from 1983 I championed the European social market. David did not like my stress on a competitive market, but supported the social policies like merging tax and social security. He allied himself, for too long in my judgement, with Roy Jenkins's incomes policy and the old mixed economy. After the 1987 election David became a Liberal Democrat, then in the 1990s joined New Labour, and after moving to Wales in 2016 became a member of Plaid Cmyru. To the surprise of many, Wales voted to leave the EU in 2016, but UKIP lost support in the 2017 general election to Labour in Wales.

What is social democracy? The best working definition applicable in or out of the EU that I know still remains that of the Polish philosopher, Leszek Kolakowski:

The trouble with the social democratic idea is that it does not stock and does not sell any of the exciting ideological commodities which various totalitarian movements – Communists, fascists or leftists – offer dream-hungry youth [...]

It is an obstinate will to erode by inches the conditions which produce avoidable suffering, oppression, hunger, wars, racial and national hatred, insatiable greed and vindictive envy. (Owen, 1981: 66–7)

It is not Corbynism as it emerged in 2017 and as it is likely to remain until the next General Election.

Corbyn's Labour Party

As Labour leader, Jeremy Corbyn in the 2016 referendum campaigned somewhat half-heartedly to stay inside the EU, despite his own well-known preference to leave. That is not to be condemned; a democratically elected leader cannot ignore the views of the vast majority of its Members of Parliament. By the 2017 general election the stance in Labour's manifesto was to honour the vote to leave which was again a democratic responsibility of its leader. It was vindicated in that Labour began to win back UKIP voters in sizeable numbers. The Conservatives were, therefore, unable to win back as many UKIP voters as they had fully expected, particularly in the North, and this was a significant factor in Labour winning marginal seats and depriving the Conservatives of an outright victory.

In marked contrast to Michael Foot's vocal demand to get rid of nuclear weapons in 1983 both Corbyn and John McDonnell in the 2017 general election manifesto accepted the next generation of Trident submarines would be built while they would continue to champion the Non-Proliferation Treaty commitment to work towards the end of all nuclear weapons. This meant that the 2017 manifesto, when published, was a welcome surprise to many Labour supporters and far more in tune with public opinion than 'the longest suicide note in history', as Gerald Kaufman called the 1983 manifesto. Maybe that was because 150+ Labour MPs had by then been ready to defy Corbyn to the point of threatening to resign from the party and most trade unionists were with them on this issue.

Yet there are clear signs that Corbyn believes he can abandon nuclear deterrence altogether once in government, a view he let slip in a heady moment during his 'rock star' appearance at Glastonbury in 2017. I saw few signs then that he understands the perils and dangers of the world in which the UK has to exist (Owen and Ludlow, 2017). Any incoming prime minister is able to open up nuclear issues with the US President soon after taking office, as I explained in a pamphlet I wrote before the 2015 general election (Owen, 2015). There are different deterrent options to Trident replacement, which I outlined in that paper and which I personally have championed since 1977. A minimum deterrent and stronger conventional defence would be a far more credible defence position for Labour to win the next general election, whenever it takes place (Owen, 2009). Perhaps the Conservatives will last until March 2019 but it will be very surprising if they last as long as Labour did as a minority government from February 1974 to May 1979.

Corbyn as a potential prime minister did come under overwhelming pressure from the press and commentators to commit to define the circumstances in which he would authorise the use of nuclear weapons. He refused to theorise and he sedulously held to his ground, risking the charge of being a pacifist which he refuted. For that reason 2017 did not replicate 1935 when just before the general election Labour ditched its then pacifist leader, Lansbury, when attacked by the T&GWU leader, Ernest Bevin at the party conference. The continuation of Labour support for NATO's nuclear deterrence strategy was essential for Labour MPs. Yet at one stage as many as 170 believed a UK nuclear deterrent of four Trident replacement submarines was necessary. Corbyn, on defence, will never be seen by the public as being like Clement Attlee who was viewed by most people as a patriotic socialist (Owen, 2016), but he has wisely rebutted the charge of being a pacifist. Labour in 2017 fought on as radical a general election manifesto as was produced in 1945. Attlee's election manifesto on social and industrial policy was every bit as radical as Corbyn's and Attlee was never an enthusiast for the Common Market.

Brexit

Brexit is not a purely British phenomenon as some referendum deniers still present it. The Pew Research Centre in June 2016, coinciding with Brexit, showed that in Germany and the Netherlands disapproval of the EU was as high as in Britain and even higher in France, Spain and Greece. Yet while disillusionment was spread across the political parties in the United Kingdom the Labour leader, Ed Miliband, in 2015 did not share this growing disillusionment. As a matter of principle he refused to endorse any In/Out referendum. I tried to convince him to commit to a referendum for many reasons but, above all, because I did not want the UK to become part of a federal state of Europe. While the EU was seen by the British public as becoming ever more dysfunctional at the start of the twenty-first century there was a constant Blairite-led drive to extol the merits of the EU and line Labour up with the EU as a moderate or centrist stance. The fact that Gaitskell as leader in 1962 had warned against a federalist future for the UK within the European Community was brushed out of Labour's history in Blair/Brown's support for what became the Lisbon Treaty, ratified in 2007. Many Labour MPs, after Blair, with Mandelson in the lead, went on pinning their hopes, lifestyle and policies around the EU, deaf to the anxieties of many of their constituents. Labour's unease had always been there in the UK since the Common Market debate in 1962 but with a waxing and waning of enthusiasm for the idea of European unity.

By January 2016, with the EU's social market, which I had long championed, having disgracefully accepted austerity and massive unemployment in Greece, Spain and Portugal, I decided to take the last opportunity in my lifetime to end my long-standing fears of an eventual federal Europe and vote to leave the EU and campaign as a Brexiteer. Because of, first, the referendum and then the Conservative and Labour manifesto commitments to leave that will now happen in March 2019. Corbyn's Labour Party will, meanwhile, play the so-called single market option to keep party differences to the minimum.

There are, however, real difficulties about staying in the single market because of the insistence of the 27 EU Member States that it must involve the four founding principles including freedom of movement of labour for all EU citizens. In fairness, freedom of movement can be helpful economically for an effective Eurozone but it should not be essential for Contracting Parties to the European Economic Area Agreement (EEAA). It is there as a non-EU Contracting Party that the United Kingdom should lodge itself for a few years after leaving the EU in 2019, while negotiating in the implementation period up to, say, 2022 for an EU/UK trade agreement. That measure of continuity would avoid a forced cliff edge decision in March 2019 and allow time to negotiate with the United States and Canada a possible NAFTA Mark II.

The future

After the 2016 referendum many still-committed Labour Europeans were in an understandable state of shock. Their dream had been voted out. A Blairite Labour core wanted to start a new party and a few Conservative MPs were soon tying themselves in verbal knots over their positions. Some Liberal Democrats began calling for a second referendum while hastily adding, though carrying little conviction when doing so, that they respected the views of the British people. Gradually, Labour MPs realised 2016 was not like 1981–83 and they proved this when they fought and won, within the party, a far better manifesto out of Corbyn by 2017 than ever we, who had formed the SDP, were able to get out of Michael Foot before 1981. Also, most of those same Labour MPs began to accept the people's verdict to leave the EU if for no other reason than in the wings lurked UKIP, ready to re-emerge in their own constituencies as they did so strongly when winning the European parliamentary elections in 2014. In effect, there was no serious attempt to buck the 2016 referendum vote to leave.

Owing to Corbyn and McDonnell's EU leave stance in 2017, Labour picked up more of the UKIP vote than would have been expected following the 2016 referendum. Without that position Labour would have lost more seats to the Conservatives in 2017. Also, Labour did very well winning seats and votes with an enthusiasm among the young not seen since the 1964 and 1966 elections, and has a large and expanding membership. Though the young were more favourable to the EU in the referendum in 2016, it did not seem to reduce their commitment to voting Labour in the 2017 election where close to two-thirds of the under 40s voted Labour. In the breakdown of votes cast, in YouGov's post-election analysis of 50,000 voters, women voted equally Labour and Conservatives. While a majority of the electorate voted Conservative their vote was interestingly spread equally across the classes.

The Labour manifesto was cleverly put together. It was designed to be optimistic, promising money for socialist programmes and priorities. It was able to do this by proposing to raise corporation tax from 19 per cent to 26 per cent. Bizarrely, the Conservatives downplayed the real risk of turning off investment in the UK in the light of Brexit. Perhaps they too expected to raise corporation tax? Economic concerns when the next election takes place are likely to dominate the mood of the country. Anger over austerity in the form of pay restraint in 2017 ensured support for an optimistic manifesto akin to that of 1945.

Everything depends on when the next election comes for Corbyn. If Brexit is settled, Labour may find that voters have become more suspicious of such a large increase in corporation tax and they may have to modify this. But it will be hard to resile on abolishing student fees. While in 2017 the Conservatives will not let Labour's economic programme go virtually unchallenged, they will still face what Corbyn got right; namely that a political philosophy is needed which challenges greed and avarice, and appeals to the young's sense of fairness. Corbyn personally identified this issue in 2017 and that feeling was present among affluent voters as well.

That mood change has been long developed in David Marquand's writings, most arrestingly in his book *Mammon's Kingdom* (2014). There is no doubt in my mind that more than any other writer he has contributed to that shift in mood. Fairness is not a neutral word, it does not mean splitting the difference on every issue, nor finding the centre point in opinion polling; or refusing the label left and following a nebulous third way. Fairness means persuading people that poorer people should pay less tax and richer people should pay more tax. It is the act of persuasion that is vital and the left, to their credit, did persist, and there was no voice of conscience coming through from the centre right, no successor to Michael Young or Tony Crosland. Roy Hattersley tried but he was drowned out as Blairism grew. It took conviction and it gave Corbyn victory in two party leadership elections among young Labour supporters. What Corbyn then demonstrated was that a process of persuasion during the election, of taking sides and arguing the case that there needed to be redistribution won voters' support too. In that sense Corbyn changed the zeitgeist. Can he continue to do so?

Social Democrats or people who identify as centre left, myself included, have been too squeamish about undertaking that relentless task of political persuasion. It is the far left of the Labour Party who have kept faith with redistribution. For all its failings – and there are still many – Corbyn's Labour Party in the UK election in 2017 stood for redistribution and on the side of the less well-off and won a sizeable proportion of the votes – some 40 per cent – by doing so. The old Blair slogan 'For the many, not the few' now resonated in a very different way in style, language and with a new authenticity. Corbyn, the allotment holder, carried conviction: the politician, the young saw, who practised what he preached. Had 100 Labour MPs split off, as they nearly did in 2016, that phenomenon would never have manifested itself and that would have been a tragedy. I am glad I argued against such a course.

The years 2015–17 were not like late 1979–81. I believe still we were right to split off then but we left behind a large grouping of Labour MPs who at the time were not fighting, but after we left were forced to make the internal fight for renewal. Over 100 Labour MPs leaving in 2016 would have led to the collapse of Labour as a potential governing party for decades, perhaps forever, and that would have been a very great loss. Labour is now in with a chance of winning the next election. The manifesto will stay, I suspect, without many changes. Labour will be hoping to consolidate support. Instead of the dialogue being all about creating a progressive alliance from now on to the next election, it will be a knock-down fight between Labour and Conservative for outright victory. Only if Corbyn does not stop others foolish enough to force out some prominent Labour MPs through reselection will there be any meaningful split. A split on staying in the EU is less likely because the Conservative MPs are focused on a three-year transition after leaving the EU.

International social democracy

Elsewhere in elections in Europe, the left in 2017 has been hit hard in the Netherlands and in France. No one can be sure how the SPD will do in Germany in the autumn of 2017. But under their proportional voting no party wins outright. Probably the SPD will refuse to work with Die Linke, the German far left party, stronger in what was East Germany but that may change. In the United States the most effective politician who espouses redistribution and can be seen as a European social democrat in many ways is Bernie Sanders who very powerfully challenged Hillary Clinton for the presidential candidacy, and who exposed her credentials as a Democrat. Another social democrat is the Democrat Senator for Massachusetts, Elizabeth Warren. She is unlikely to be a presidential candidate in 2020 but she will be an important figure in the US Democratic Party that has to find values that are not those of Wall Street, New York. Some polls showed Senator Bernie Sanders in 2016 had the potential to beat Donald Trump in the key rust belt states where Hillary Clinton lost to Trump. Sanders, rather than Clinton, would also have found it far easier to harness the general mood of dissatisfaction in the United States but he was running against an established dynasty with a vast budget.

If fairness as a political philosophy is to become an issue in mainstream US politics it will be because people have been convinced by people like Senator Warren. She was elected in November 2012 having overseen, under President Obama, the Troubled Asset Relief Program (TARP). This programme meant handling the big banks' collapse in 2008–10, setting up the Consumer Financial Protection Bureau (CFBP). She therefore understands the US economy and cannot be dismissed as just an idealist. She focused her campaign for the Senate on households making less than $51,371 who in 2012 had suffered a 6.6 per cent decline in living standards. She won her election with a 73 per cent turnout by a margin close to 8 per cent. She now represents 'the Warren wing' of the party and will influence Democratic politics (Tomasky, 2014). But a younger generation of grassroots Democrats will need to emerge in the rust belt states who are not dominated by Wall Street values and have a candidate who will challenge President Trump's appeal. To defeat his appeal they have to first understand it.

The French Socialist Party could not adapt and the right disintegrated in personal scandals, so in a unique collapse of the two old parties President Macron demonstrated that a new party could emerge very rapidly, but he had the French second vote system in his favour. The centrist Prime Minister Renzi's defeat in

Italy on a reform ticket in their referendum on reform may be indicative of deep changes in the Italian mood. But it is too early to be sure.

The trade unions and the left

In *Face the Future* in 1981 in both the hardback and paperback version, which straddled my membership of the Labour Party and then the SDP, I wrote that the SDP is 'an approach built neither on dreams nor on dogmas. In every social democratic country the social democrats have strong links with trade unionists' (Owen, 1981: 59–71). The trade unions proved their worth and held the Labour Party together from 2015 to 2017 and financed the general election. As an independent social democrat now in the House of Lords wanting the return of Aneurin Bevan's NHS I have found Unison, UNITE and the TUC far more committed to repealing the fatally flawed Health and Social Care Act 2012 than the Labour Party. It will be the test case of Corbyn's Labour Party if they can rally the nation to rescue the broken backed marketised NHS in England and they will find it much easier to accomplish outside the EU.

Today's crisis-ridden NHS is the direct result of an external market on top of an internal market in the late 1980s and 1990s in the NHS in England. The external market began in 2002 under Blair's government with independent hospitals which became separated from any geographical area and was massively extended by the Health and Social Care Act of 2012, introduced by the Conservatives and Liberal Democrats. The Liberal Democrat Party, who had a very poor election result in 2017 gaining only four seats from its 2015 low point of eight seats, is no longer seen by many people on the left as being genuinely progressive. It has a choice in the next few years, to stop going along with centrist Labour MPs and the *Guardian* in supporting Simon Stevens, the English NHS Chief Executive, who started to work with Blair in 2002 on the external market and then spent ten years in the United States with a private health care company, and was appointed by the Conservatives to complete a marketised NHS. Or the Liberal Democrats can look for guidance to the clear ethical and vocational NHS brought in by Aneurin Bevan.

Corbyn's Labour Party has a deep aversion to any seat dealing. They have waited for this breakthrough moment with a party they control. They will not be ready to contemplate any substantive initiative over a progressive alliance if their post-2017 election momentum continues. The trade unions who gave them the most support will not want this either. They are confident first-past-the-post will reward them with outright victory at the next election. A key sign of the narrowness of where the Corbyn Labour Party in June 2017 is based was its consistent refusal to negotiate after the election with the smaller parties in a hung Parliament. Repeatedly, they said before and after the election, their policy was to challenge the smaller parties to vote for their Queen's Speech that would be based on their manifesto. They kept reiterating that there would be no deals or negotiations. The 'one more heave' school of politics is still strong in Corbyn circles. They feel they have waited for the alternation of power and now the swing of the pendulum is in their favour and they see that pendulum moving towards them even more after the election of 2017.

In part because of that historic sentiment, the Labour left has been far less frustrated during the long spells out of government. Labour was out of power for nine years from 1931 to 1940, for thirteen years from 1951 to 1964 and eighteen years from 1979 to 1997. Rightly or wrongly, Corbyn's Labour Party senses that a 1945 electoral moment is near. In the reshuffle of Shadow Cabinet posts after the 2017 general election Corbyn did not appoint any former Labour Cabinet ministers to widen the appeal of his Shadow Cabinet, although he did bring back Owen Smith, who had stood against him in a very ineffective leadership campaign. That was a gesture more about being seen as not bearing grudges than realigning the Parliamentary Labour Party. It was not a sign either of a man who expects to win by watering down the appeal of his 2017 manifesto. I would expect Corbyn to stick with the 2017 manifesto and all its radical proposals over the period that lies ahead. It is strangely McDonnell, the Trotskyist, who might be ready to phase the corporation tax rise envisaged into two or more tranches. A big shift in the polls or a clear downturn in the economy might bring that stance but it will not be easy, since it pays for their optimistic programme. For this reason it is necessary to consider the circumstances that would follow a Labour defeat at the next election. Victory is a rational prospect but it is not certain. To become probable it will require a broadening of attitudes and greater flexibility.

Revisiting Labour's past

A good place to start in rethinking social democracy based on Corbyn not succeeding because the base had become too narrow and too doctrinal by the next general election is David's widely acclaimed biography of Ramsay MacDonald published in 1977. He wrote in the Preface this powerful passage:

I believe strongly that the past can have lessons for the present. But I do not believe that its lessons can be learned by forcing it on to a procrustean bed, shaped by present day expectations and present day assumptions. (Marquand, 1977)

The Social Democratic Federation (SDF) emerged in October 1884, and in 1885 the SDF ran three candidates in the November general election. MacDonald, by 1894, was thinking about constituency seat deals but thought it might be necessary 'to bludgeon the Liberals into conceding what they had refused to concede to persuasion; it did not imply isolation, or a squeamish refusal to engage in electoral horse trading' (Marquand, 1977: xiii, 41).

The Labour Representation Committee (LRC), had been formed in 1902 with MacDonald as its Secretary and in that capacity he approached Jesse Herbert, the Secretary to the Liberal Party Chief Whip, Herbert Gladstone, about inter-party cooperation. They asked for a list of constituencies that MacDonald wanted to discuss and wrote to Gladstone, saying that the LRC could directly influence the votes of nearly a million men. MacDonald had seven further meetings with Herbert Gladstone (Marquand, 1977: 79–85). In the 1906 general election the Liberal-Labour seat deal was thought to have won Labour over thirty seats but more importantly it helped to ensure a reforming Liberal government was returned with a majority large enough to challenge the power of the Lords and to start significant welfare reforms. My great-grandfather, Alderman William Llewellyn, was a Liberal leader in Glamorgan County Council. He was also Chairman of the Ogmore Vale Liberal Association and, interestingly, of its Liberal and Labour Association. Liberals made 'seat deals' in Wales believing it would help bring about a great Liberal reforming government. In 1906 it achieved that but also ensured many more Labour MPs were returned than would have been the case without 'seat deals'. Labour ever since has been wary of giving any other party a similar chance.

Coalitions, pacts or electoral deals do not have to involve the merging of parties or the loss of their identity. They are techniques, methods of operating that can be the means to legislative power. They are a way of beating the distorting effect of first-past-the-post voting. The SDP-Liberal Alliance experience of allocating seats between themselves on a broadly 50:50 basis well in advance of both the 1983 general election, when it polled 25 per cent, and in 1987, when it polled 23 per cent, was an ambitious attempt to, in effect, game the system. Yet the SDP won a mere six seats in 1983 and five in 1987. For the SDP, a new party, to come politically so close, so early in 1981, to the Liberal Party was a mistake. It involved a change in identity undertaken within months of emerging from the Limehouse Declaration. All the polling advice was to build our potential stressing the newness of a social democrat party. We should have been more prepared early in the Parliament to fight seats against the Liberal Party. We had a different, and in places stronger, electoral appeal: but we had to prove that to the country and to Liberal activists who were resentful of our emergence.

The SDP did not do what Ramsay MacDonald was ready to do; to strike a bargain with the Liberal Party then in opposition from 1903, namely to 'bludgeon' Campbell-Bannerman's Liberal Party to give them a toe-hold of seats. We in the SDP had at the minimum a considerable spoiling power on the then Liberal Party who were quite weak after the scandal that surrounded its previous leader, Jeremy Thorpe. The SDP should have resolutely refused to change our social democratic identity in 1981 and 1982. Labour, of course, seized on and exploited our early Alliance identification with the Liberals. They fought very hard, as they were bound to do, against the SDP establishing links with Socialist International and the trade unions. In retrospect, we probably should have chosen the title we did consider of 'New Labour', for the word Labour was and remains an identity that is helpful for voters when making up their mind. Labour's response was ruthlessly to reduce over time the appeal of the SDP to potential Labour voters even though they were disillusioned by the party's lurch to the far left, markedly more left than Corbyn's manifesto of 2017.

It was also fallaciously argued from 1981 within the SDP that there was no room for four parties in British politics. Yet ever since 1983 new parties have been emerging, not least the Scottish National Party (SNP). By 2010 the Liberal Democrats had 57 seats gaining eight, the SNP six and Plaid Cymru three. By 2015 the SNP had 56 MPs and were by a large margin the third largest party in Parliament with the Liberal Democrats down to eight MPs and the DUP eight MPs. The Conservative government had a working majority of sixteen with the Ulster Unionists. The House of Commons remains after 2017 a multi-party chamber with the Liberal Democrats having 12 MPs; DUP, 10 MPs; Plaid Cymru, 3 and the Greens one. One wonders if under a Corbyn minority government Sinn Fein might take their seats. It is unlikely but not impossible and in principle they should. Separatism has not stopped the SNP sitting in Westminster which should reflect all opinions in the United Kingdom.

Real proportional representation (PR) is worth continuing to fight for. In the present circumstances, however, there is no chance of Corbyn's Labour Party agreeing to introduce proportional representation after the next general election. The far left believe a first-past-the-post mechanism is the way to produce an outright victory, and they are correct on this.

There has only been one moment in recent history when Labour might have conceded proportional representation and that was in 1992 under Neil Kinnock. By then he had been converted to proportional representation. He should have made a seat deal with the only two SDP MPs, John Cartwright and Rosie Barnes, who were going to fight the general election of 1992, while I had decided to stand down in my own seat of Plymouth. I raised this offer to Kinnock via Alistair Campbell, then a *Mirror* journalist but who was very close to Kinnock. The value of such an arrangement was that it would have signalled to the public that the dispute between Labour and SDP was over and the Sheffield rally could have been presented as the ultimate reconciliation with the SDP, not a triumphalist event. I believe Labour would then have won the election. Alternatively, if a merger between the SDP and the Liberal Party had been called off as too divisive after the 1987 election, and the Alliance had held together with its separate elements but with a Liberal as leader, such an Alliance could have held the balance in 1992 and negotiated the introduction of proportional representation.

Labour was in government from 1997 until 2010. It was elected on a very SDP programme but Blair never forced through the recommendations from the Jenkins Commission, established by the Labour government, for a changed electoral system involving an AV+ method (Independent Commission, 1998). I had been asked to rejoin Labour in the summer of 1996 by Tony Blair, and nearly did, but was put off by his support for the euro. In retrospect, it was the best political decision I ever made but it did not feel like it until the debacle over Iraq in 2003. Then the start of the destruction of the NHS with its fragmentation and marketisation laid the foundation for Cameron and Clegg's US style health market. What slowly went wrong for Labour after their second general election victory was that it lost its moorings in social democratic theory and practice. An ideological free zone was established; what works was the test without asking what was power for and establishing principled criteria and weighed evidence for social democratic reforms. That left the way open for Corbyn's Labour Party that is an ideologically dominated party but has attracted people, especially the young, to join.

A federal UK

What hope for a federal UK and no separation? The SNP's loss of seats in 2017 suggest that separatism may be losing its appeal but that cannot be assumed. Those who believe the UK is a federation of Scots, English, Welsh and Northern

Irish need to be more positive now about a federal future and show the hesitating separatists that there is a better way forward. I have suggested that the German federal Bundesrat model should be adapted to create a federal UK. Both countries have to deal with considerable asymmetries in their federal geography. The Bundesrat has to approve constitutional changes and all legislation that affects their sixteen federal states or Landers. It also sends delegates rather than elected members to represent them on specific issues in the Bundesrat. There are, of course, huge differences between Germany and the UK. But there are also some significant similarities. Bavaria, in German Bayern, is the largest Lander with seemingly the most similarities to Scotland, not in the nature of their political complexion but in their mountainous landscape and their long histories as independent countries. There is no Lander with a similar equivalent of Wales with its Welsh language, though Saxony does protect the Danish language close by.

The devolved governance in the UK within a federal context involves not just the 10 million people in the three devolved nations of Scotland, Wales and Northern Ireland within its boundaries but the 8 million people living in London and the 15 million people in the eight core cities currently being established under the Core Cities initiative. Provision is already made for a collective voice for those who live contentedly within county councils and do not wish to become regions in non-metropolitan councils, which together account for 21 million, as well as for those who live in unitary authorities, in which currently over 8 million live. They may or may not wish to develop a regional identity that could lead to separate representation. However, there should, and would, under a Federal UK Council, be no pressure to move to an all-regional pattern away from the current English local government structures. The skill, as the Germans have done with their Bundesrat, is to retain existing representational structures where they already carry support in representing large numbers of people's interests to central government but add federal powers. I would hope that, eventually, Conservatives, Liberal Democrats and Labour in Scotland will see merit in these ideas but I doubt there will be much movement before the next general election which, because its timing is now so unpredictable, will mean parties focusing on short-term rather than medium- to long-term initiatives.

The existential separatists in Scotland and Wales will not settle for a federal UK council or any other UK-wide constitutional reform aimed at recognising a federal future but they cannot ever be satisfied. The challenge is to engage with utilitarian separatists in Scotland and in Wales over asymmetrical federal reforms. To unite fully the UK post-Brexit will need some kind of structural interrelationship between all its parts and not just an ad hoc series of relationships with Whitehall.

I believe the SNP, if they lose more seats to the Conservatives, Labour and Liberal Democrats at the next general election, will negotiate a federal UK and the reason lies in a speech Nicola Sturgeon made in 2012 when not yet leader of the SNP. Her speech in Strathclyde said how Neil MacCormick, the son of one of the SNP's founders and a distinguished academic at Edinburgh University, had distinguished between 'existentialist' and 'utilitarian' varieties of Scottish nationalism, the first demanding independence simply because that is what nations should have, and the second seeing it as a route to a better society. This was described in a perceptive article in the *Guardian* on 23 April 2015 by Ian Jack. He returned to the same theme in late September 2016 still seeing its potential despite the adverse Scottish reaction to Brexit. Nicola Sturgeon has recognised that while some (by implication older) SNP members were existentialists she was a utilitarian; for her, she said:

> The fact of nationhood or Scottish identity is not the motive force for independence … nor do I believe that independence, however desirable, is essential for the preservation of our distinctive Scottish identity. And I don't agree at all that feeling British – with all of the shared social, family and cultural heritage that makes up such an identity – is in any way inconsistent with a pragmatic, utilitarian support for political independence.

Nicola Sturgeon has also said that Scotland has to focus on 'the most effective political and economic unit to achieve the economic growth and the social justice that the Scottish people want. It is, in many ways, our version of the same question being asked across all mature western democracies: how to build a thriving but sustainable economy that benefits the many, not the few. The Westminster system of government has had its chance – and failed. Today, independence is the pragmatic way forward.'

On this basis Sturgeon can, at least, conceive of a progressive alliance forged through a Convention establishing a better pragmatic way forward than Scottish separation from the UK. Already many of the gas and oil revenue assumptions on which the SNP campaigned in the 2014 referendum have been shown to be invalid. Many want a constitutional convention to determine critical constitutional questions and techniques for cooperation before any agreement could be reached. But there is little chance of reaching an agreement before the next general election.

Corbyn might offer a constructive way forward to a federal UK if in government but with a small majority and wanting SNP support. It may be easier for Corbyn to do this as UK leader, now that Labour's Scottish Party may be asking for greater freedom and focus on Scottish issues.

It will probably be impossible for Corbyn, this side of the next general election, to convince even himself, let alone potential Labour voters, of the priority for constitutional reform. Who knows which will be the third largest party in the Westminster Parliament after the next election, but they may become an inescapable factor in Labour's calculation of their chances of creating a majority government. Corbyn has shown he has an appeal to the young, he seems to many authentic and interested in extending democracy outside Westminster. He appeared initially a committed republican but he accepted the role of official leader of the Opposition and gives respect to the Queen. After 2017, and after more than just surviving the personal press criticism, it is no longer credible to claim he can never be elected prime minister. I have already mentioned his one very distinctive hobby as an allotment holder. My experience of allotment holders in Plymouth was that they are very independent figures, all of a piece, content in their own skin and not a typical Trotskyist. Corbyn is not someone that the right-wing press have been able, despite hurling every form of abuse at him, to depict as a hater of his country.

A progressive alliance

Building a progressive alliance would have been very much on the political agenda had Labour not done so well in 2017 and with such a left-wing programme. The tragic Grenfell Tower fire in a Conservative-controlled council helped to reinforce Labour's immediate post-election claim that there had been a seismic shift in political attitudes to the left which underpinned their electoral support in that general election. But it soon emerged that Labour-controlled councils, like Camden, were also guilty of using the same cheap combustible cladding materials. It is hard to escape the likelihood that after 2017 cynicism will return to engulf UK politics. Labour gained the youth vote helped by campaigning on the immediate abolition of student fees. This is a policy remembered by students with some bitterness, given the Liberal Democrats pledge never to introduce/increase student fees, but who in coalition with the Conservatives during 2010–15 reneged and supported the Conservatives' increasing of student fees. The experience of the student loan system has been a very depressing one; many students have built up large debts and many seem resigned to being unable to repay them and central government have limited capacity to chase and the cumulative level of debt is high. It is not a success, the graduate tax – which I favoured – was dismissed.

If there was to be a progressive alliance would it repeal the Health and Social Care Act 2012? It is hard to see a 'progressive alliance' worth the name credibly being formed under a Labour government and the SNP if the Liberal Democrat party is still supporting an external market for the English NHS.

David Marquand has Welsh roots. His party, Plaid Cymru, is a radical progressive force. His father was Welsh and a Labour MP for Cardiff. He also has Scottish roots. Both his grandmothers were Scottish. One of them died when he was a child. But the other – Roberta Leckie before her marriage, and then Roberta Rees – played a huge part in his young life together with his grandfather, David James Rees, who was the son of his great-grandfather Ebenezer Rees, founder editor of the first socialist newspaper in Wales (and possibly in the UK) *Llais Llafur* ('Labour Voice'). His proudest possession is a copy of the very first issue. It is half in Welsh and half in English. And as for his Scottish leanings, his dearest friend in Parliament was John Mackintosh, closely followed by Donald Dewar. David has found a radical progressiveness in Plaid Cymru which makes him very happy. But are they long-term separatists? I doubt if they will ever be more than devolutionist and cultural and Welsh language champions.

If Labour cannot be persuaded now to commit to a cross-party constitutional convention would they establish one if a Labour government needed the support of smaller parties after the next election? The biggest problem for a minority Labour government in Westminster is that it would face demands for an extension of proportional voting to the Westminster House of Commons and House of Lords if that was to become a federal Parliament.

A UK Federal Council modelled on the Bundesrat has the advantage that it does not involve direct elections. That mechanism will have merit to those Labour MPs against proportional representation. If the correct balance were to be achieved within a federal council it could become a powerful unifier for the UK. The alternative, so often touted and so often blocked, of an elected second chamber would, of course, be discussed in any constitutional convention. But the dismal record of the House of Commons in preventing any such elected chamber emerging is there for all to see, most recently in 2011. Labour MPs are not united on supporting an elected second chamber but probably ready to have it studied, yet again, safe in the belief it will never happen.

A warning of both the unpredictability and the capacity for the manipulation of a referendum, if it were needed after the next election, is the national Alternative Vote (AV) referendum conceded by the Conservative Party in the negotiations with the Liberal Democrats as the price for a coalition government in May 2010. Every poll in the second half of that year showed AV being won in a referendum. By February 2011 Ipsos/MORI had 'Yes' on 49 per cent and AV looked certain to be endorsed ten weeks later, much to the chagrin of many Conservatives, and to predictions of adverse electoral consequences despite initial claims by Cameron that AV would have few consequences.

Suddenly, Cameron was forced to focus on the dangers to the Conservative Party of the Liberal Democrats triumphing over AV. Osborne is reported to have said, 'we have to win this ... thing; who cares what Clegg thinks?' (Seldon and Snowden, 2015: 118). Cameron, true to his reactive 'Flashman' character moved fast. Money was found to overpower the 'Yes to Fairer Votes' campaign. Also, more and more people became aware that AV was neither truly proportional nor fair and could have bizarre results. Some saw it as another manipulation agreed post-election inside the coalition by Conservatives with no electoral mandate. The 'No' campaign spent the last few weeks exposing the three 'Cs': cost, complexity and Clegg. Clegg, despite being Deputy Prime Minister, was lampooned and Cameron talked of AV being 'bad for democracy'. On 5 May the referendum resulted in the 'No' campaign achieving 67.9 per cent support with 30.1 per cent voting 'Yes' to AV. The turnout was a miserable 42.2 per cent.

Cameron then fought the Scottish referendum, and 'Project Fear' emerged, some believed, as a powerful weapon in the rejection of separatism. Over-confident, Cameron felt he could do the same on the EU referendum but here 'Project Fear' backfired during the Remain campaign and Leave managed to demonstrate it was too doom-laden. To many people's surprise, the decision was taken by voters to leave. Referenda are but a device, part of the struggle for power in democratic politics, likely to be used when political parties are deeply divided in the House of Commons. It tends to be forgotten that first-past-the-post is kept by MPs because it best suits the two main parties. The Conservative Party strongly favour it, but also many Labour politicians believe it helps their party too and they will be fortified in this belief if they have just won power under it after the next election. The smaller parties all want proportional representation; besides its merits, it is a means for them to gain seats. There is nothing disreputable in this but when politicians advocate what is to their advantage, non-political voters are more sceptical.

The appointed House of Lords, which now numbers 850 members, presents an indefensible combination of patronage and privilege where peerages clearly have their price. Yet here too abolition or even reform is fraught with difficulty. A new Act of Union Bill has been developed that may have appeal to some constitutional reformers. But it represents a huge legislative commitment and I see no prospect of it being put on the statute book until after at least two more general elections. A more feasible and also proven reform, I believe, is to build up support for a Federal UK Council in the next Parliament.

In summary, the *realpolitik* after the 2017 election is that the hard left are in a position of greater influence inside the Labour Party since Labour's very early history. Labour is presently not interested in anything other than outright victory in a general election which may be held at any time through to 2020. It is very hard to see this Parliament lasting beyond then, let alone its full term of June 2022. There will be no movement of significance in the Labour Party towards any progressive alliance until the next election, whether a federal UK, proportional representation or seat deals in particular constituencies. Labour is poised to go for broke on the basis of their 2017 manifesto and with broadly the Shadow Cabinet that is in place now. This strategy is very risky; they are not assured of victory but it has the precious enthusiasm of youth behind it.

Even though they gained over 30 additional parliamentary seats in 2017 they still remain 64 seats short of an overall majority. Even so, they managed to convince one in ten previous Conservative voters and one in five previous UKIP voters to vote for their manifesto. Their greatest cause for optimism is that Labour is not polling its full potential strength among former Labour voters. According to an Ipsos/Mori analysis of voting in the 2017 general election, Labour had a 15-point lead among graduate voters and it was the Conservatives who had a 17-point lead among people with no qualifications and 6 per cent lead among those educated to below degree level. The swing to Labour was strongest in the 25–34 age range, at 13 per cent, and in the 18–24 years, the swing was 10.5 per cent. If, as I fully expect, Corbyn remains totally committed to taking the UK out of the EU they should be able to take more votes from UKIP.

Before the next general election there will be much juggling of policies to attract those under the age of 40. The immediate momentum with the young is with Labour. Yet the Conservatives may decide to pre-empt Jeremy Corbyn's promise to get rid of student fees and simply abolish them before the election. Cynical? Certainly. Electorally attractive, but only if they pre-empt the attack from Labour that the Conservatives were giving a huge financial boost to their own supporters if simultaneously they match the abolition with a tax increase for the higher paid.

Theresa May did try during the election to face up to the need to address intergenerational injustice, whether pulling back from the triple lock on pensions, or trying to avoid fixing the maximum cost exposure on the individual and thereby the family contribution to a dementia tax. The truly bold and fair policy is to refuse to introduce such a misguided concept as a dementia tax and place dementia care in the community with the NHS and fund health in and out of hospital by a new hypothecated general health tax. This is what Labour should support by the next election. It would win the support of many Conservative voters and be the basis for holding the high percentage vote Labour won among AB voters.

By focusing on shifting the emphasis away from austerity, championing a return of a true NHS in England and making health care in the community, as in hospitals, an NHS priority paid for out of general taxation they could escape all the tortured compromises of how to finance and handle dementia care. A drive for low-cost housing and a higher priority for social reforms could ensure an even greater increase in Labour's appeal.

Are we poised as a country to invoke again the spirit of 1945? Time alone will tell. But this is not the Labour Party politically built up by Arthur Greenwood, an unsung hero, and Clement Attlee, a man of unshakeable integrity, from 1935, tempered by five years in coalition, which I wrote about in my book *Cabinet's Finest Hour* (Owen, 2016: 4–30). It may be that Corbyn's vision of the Labour Party wins an outright victory. But it will not be a party that social democrats will feel comfortable in. I may cheer such an outcome if it restores our NHS but it will come to power accompanied by fear as well as hope. We have not been well governed so far in the twenty-first century and the prospect of that changing is not high. Let us hope that the commitment of the young will broaden the Labour Party's vision, not deepen the dogma, that their idealism settles for the 'obstinate will to erode by inches the conditions which produce avoidable suffering, oppression, hunger, wars, racial and national hatred, insatiable greed and vindictive envy'.

References

Adonis, A. and Thomas, K. (2004) *Roy Jenkins. A Retrospective* (Oxford: Oxford University Press).

Marquand, D. (1977) *Ramsay MacDonald* (London: Jonathan Cape).

Marquand, D. (1979) 'In memory of John P. Mackintosh 1929–1978', The Political Quarterly.

Marquand, D. (1991) 'The Progressive as Meteor', in *The Progressive Dilemma. From Lloyd George to Kinnock* (London: Heinemann).

Marquand, D. (2014) *Mammon's Kingdom: An Essay on Britain, Now* (London: Allen Lane).

Owen, D. (26 July 1977) 'The European Community', Memorandum by the Secretary of State for Foreign and Commonwealth Affairs.

Owen, D. (1981) *Face the Future* (London: Jonathan Cape).

Owen, D. (2009) *Nuclear Papers* (Liverpool: Liverpool University Press).

Owen, D. (2015) 'Reshaping the British nuclear deterrent', COMEC Occasional Paper,5, www.comec.org.uk/publications/occasional.

Owen, D. (2016) *Cabinet's Finest Hour. The Hidden Agenda of May 1940* (London: Haus Publishing).

Owen, D. and Ludlow, D. (2017) *British Foreign Policy After Brexit* (London: Biteback).

Report of The Independent Commission on the Voting System (October 1998), Cm 4090–I & Cm 4090–II.

Seldon, A. and Snowden, P. (2015) *Cameron at 10. The Inside Story 2010–2015* (London:William Collins).

Tomasky, M. (2014) 'A woman of the people', *Foreign Affairs*, 93(5), 63–8.

Williams, P. (1979) *Hugh Gaitskell* (London: Jonathan Cape).

14

From Bodmin Moor to Cardiff Bay: a European education?

David Marquand

First, I should thank Jeremy Nuttall and Hans Schattle for the honour they have done me by editing this volume. I am more grateful to them than I can say. Thanks, too, to the many contributors, and for their thoughtful (and thought-provoking) essays. I'll try to describe the way in which my thinking and writing have developed over the sixty-five years since I started my national service, against the background of the attitudes and values I absorbed – mostly without realising it – from my parents and grandparents.

I was born in 1934, in Cardiff. My father was the first Professor of Industrial Relations in what was then the University College of Cardiff. When he was appointed, he was the youngest professor in the United Kingdom. His family were unthinkingly Conservative, but he joined the Labour Party at the age of 18, and used to sell the then rumbustious and far left *Daily Herald* outside Cardiff's dock gates on his way to school. He became a Labour MP and a minister in the Attlee Government. He was one of the most tolerant people I have ever met. He never told me what to think; he showed me, by his example, that no one person or school of thought had a monopoly of the truth and that dogmatic self-righteousness – whether of the right or the left (or, for that matter, of the centre) – was incompatible with the open society.

My mother's family history was more flamboyant. In 1898 her grandfather Ebenezer Rees – my great grandfather – founded *Llais Llafur* ('Labour Voice') the first socialist newspaper in Wales, and perhaps even in the United Kingdom. One of my proudest possessions is a somewhat dilapidated copy of the very first issue. Half of it is in English, half in Welsh. To my shame, I haven't yet managed to learn Welsh: it is a beautiful language to listen to, and the Welsh national anthem, 'Mae hen wlad fy nhadhau yn annwyl i mi', when sung in Welsh, beats even the *Marseillaise* when sung in French. In *Llais Llafur*, Ebenezer preached a magnificent, blood-red socialism, which would make Jeremy Corbyn look pale pink. 'Never, in the history of the world has mankind shown, in a greater degree, the lustre of its genius and the magnificent sweep of its powers, than in our present day and time', he wrote in his first editorial, 'and never more than in these closing years of the nineteenth century has it been enslaved'.

David James Rees, Ebenezer's son and my grandfather once told my mother that he disapproved of women curtseying to the Queen because he hated the thought of one woman bowing her knee to another. Perhaps because of this heritage, I've always hated flummery and flunkeyism. One of my heroes is R. H. Tawney, whom I interviewed as a young editorial writer on what was still *The Manchester Guardian*, on the occasion of his eightieth birthday. Tawney's biting contempt for 'the servile respect for wealth and social position which remains even today the characteristic and contemptible vice of large numbers of our fellow countrymen' thrilled me when I retrieved the letter to the *New Statesman* in which the passage appeared. It thrills me still. When I asked him whether the Britain of the 1960s was closer to his vision of democratic socialism than it had been in his youth, he said regretfully that it wasn't. But then he added mischievously: 'At least shop assistants are less polite.'

Shop assistants may be less polite than they were when Tawney was young, but in other ways flummery and flunkeyism are still alive and well. Examples include the preposterous honours lists that appear from time to time, with their companionships of honour, knighthoods, damehoods, KCMGs, CMGs, CBEs, OBEs and the rest; the monarch's multiple palaces and the archaic rituals of the court; the trooping of the colour on the monarch's official birthday; and, not least, the grotesquely swollen and unelected House of Lords. Some years ago I was half-offered a peerage, but I turned it down. (Of course, the half-offer might never have become a full offer.) Many of my friends *are* peers: the distinguished Welsh historian, Kenneth Morgan; my sometime parliamentary colleague and old friend, Robert Maclennan; and until his untimely death, Ralf Dahrendorf, a public intellectual as well as a distinguished academic both in Germany and in Britain. I'm an easy-going and on the whole a tolerant person, so I don't hold their peerages against them. But I'm still mystified by their failure to see that they are propping up a quintessentially anti-democratic culture.

Another early influence was my national service itself. It was very un-military. Out of my twenty-four months as a conscript in the RAF a total of twenty months was spent in the intense, highly competitive hothouse of the Joint Services Russian course. (Russian is a difficult language too, though not as difficult as

Welsh.) By the time I finished the course I could speak it moderately well, but I've now forgotten most of what I learned, though on infrequent visits to Russia I find I can remember snatches of it. What has stuck in my mind for more than 60 years is the extraordinary, almost shaming contrast between the life histories of our teachers and our own lives. Some of them were Poles, some were Ukrainians, some were White Russians who had escaped from Russia after the Bolshevik putsch, some were refugees from Stalinist Russia and one was an Estonian. All of them had been uprooted from homes, families, careers and legitimate expectations and swept hither and thither like driftwood in a river in spate. I couldn't help realising that, but for the lucky chance of a few miles of salt water, their fates might have been mine. As a result, I came to feel that the smug, condescending and self-righteous notion that Britain was different from and better than the rest of the European continent was both false and disgraceful. The seeds of my lifelong commitment to the vision of a united Europe were sown in the unlikely setting of a camp of leaky wooden huts perched on the edge of Bodmin Moor.

University followed national service; and at Magdalen College, Oxford between 1954 and 1957 the seeds sown at the edge of Bodmin Moor flourished mightily. I was astonishingly lucky. I was taught by two great historians – K. B. (Bruce) Macfarlane and A. J. P. Taylor, universally known as 'A. J. P.'. With the possible exception of Richard Crossman, Taylor was the best lecturer I've ever heard. He was the only person I can think of whose eyes really twinkled. He was also an inspirational tutor. His technique was to say something outrageous, and force you to knock it down. Once, I remember, I teased him by saying nothing after an outrageous statement. So he said something even more outrageous. After three outrageous statements, my nerve cracked, and I knocked it down. But that's by the by. Under Taylor, I spent an academic year reading books and writing essays on European history from 1815 to 1914. Taylor himself was no friend of the European project. But even my rather skimpy acquaintance with the revolutions of 1848, the Franco-Prussian War, the Italian Risorgimento and the internal conflicts of the Habsburg Empire that led to the First World War, by way of the murder of the heir to the throne in Sarajevo, reinforced the lessons of the Services Russian course: that Britain's fate was inextricably bound up with the fate of mainland Europe and that it was both stupid and wicked to pretend otherwise.

Other university influences pointed in the same direction. In my first term at Oxford, Aneurin Bevan – then in Opposition and a thorn in the side of the Labour Party leadership – spoke to a packed meeting, attacking German rearmament. I can still hear his characteristic mixture of wit and passion, as he mocked the idea that 'German f-f-foot soldiers' would help to deter the Soviet Union. The Suez war broke out early in my third year, and I was present at the monster Trafalgar Square demonstration against it, in which Bevan was the main speaker. Again, I can hear his voice in the deadliest quip of the afternoon. 'If Sir Anthony is sincere – and he may be and he may be – then he's too stoopid to be Prime Minister.' At the end of the demo my brother and I were part of a crowd surging down Whitehall towards Downing Street, only to be checked by a detachment of mounted police. On the way back to Oxford, I remember, I took part in an excited discussion about the best way to use marbles to force the police to dismount. More sedately I was part of what became known as the 'First New Left', and contributed an article to *Universities and Left Review*, the ancestor of today's *New Left Review*. For the New Left, Europeanism and socialism were different sides of the same coin.

Back to Bevan – the greatest leader Labour never had. He was a tough-minded social patriot as well as a constructive statesman. He was in favour of sending tanks to break the Berlin blockade of 1948–49; in one of the greatest speeches of his life he denounced the supporters of unilateral nuclear disarmament for wanting to send a future British foreign secretary 'naked into the conference chamber' and described their policy as 'an emotional spasm'. He was also an internationalist – and, above all, a *socialist* internationalist. He died before the question of British membership of the European Economic Community (the ancestor of today's European Union) had reached the political agenda in the United Kingdom. Many of his surviving followers opposed membership, but I don't think Bevan would have done so if he had lived. He was not a bigoted Atlanticist like Hugh Gaitskell or a hysterical, 'reds-under-the-bed' anti-Communist like the unlovely trade union barons who constituted Gaitskell's Praetorian Guard. Still less was he an instinctive little Englander like Douglas Jay, Gaitskell's closest friend in politics. He was after all a Welshman, born in Tredegar, in the eastern edge of the South Wales coalfield. The communitarian values that underpinned the National Health Service whose master builder he was were those of the mining valleys of South Wales.

These values, he believed, were alien to the vulgar materialism and hyper-individualism of the United States. But he was a man of power as well as of protest. I think he would have realised that his values were closer to those of mainland Europe than to those of the United States, and that only a united Europe could countervail the overweening power of the American hegemon. Be that as it may, my own experience of the United States led me to the same conclusion, albeit by a different route. I spent the academic year 1958–59 as a graduate student and teaching assistant at the Berkeley campus of the University of California. I didn't object to American culture in the way that Bevan did, but my sojourn in the heavenly Bay area made me realise that I was a European. I remember lolling by the pool and listening to some French students talking to each other in French. I realised that I had more in common with them than I had with my American fellow-students. When I got back to England (by this time I was working as a leader-writer on *The Manchester Guardian*) I listened with horrified disgust to Gaitskell's conference speech opposing British membership of the European Community on the preposterous grounds that it would mean the end of 'a thousand years of history'. (I didn't then know that, as Gaitskell's wife Dora told me years later, Gaitskell had come to the conclusion, well before his speech, that Britain wouldn't be allowed to join the Community in any case and had therefore decided, with cool calculation to stir the anti-European pot.)

In any event, Gaitskell's speech was a textbook example of the dangers of trusting economists who know no history: in 962 CE, a thousand years before his speech, Britain did not exist, and England's existence was problematic. Non-economists who know no history are, of course, equally dangerous. One obvious example is Tony Blair whose ignorance of the tormented history of the Middle East led him to embark on the disastrous invasion of Iraq alongside the equally ignorant Bush administration in the United States. More damagingly, the same is true of the motley crew of 'Leave' campaigners in the 2016 referendum on EU membership. They pray in aid a myth of British exceptionalism, but seem blissfully unaware of the self-evident truth that Britain has been part of what Edward Gibbon called the 'great republic of Europe' since 'Britannia' was a Roman province more than 1,600 years ago.

My time at Berkeley had another legacy. The constitution of the state of California was drawn up when American populism was riding high. (There was even an American People's Party during the late nineteenth and early twentieth centuries.) The referendum and the recall were both enshrined in it. It was possible for a group of citizens to put a 'proposition' calling for this or that on the ballot paper; and citizens could also put a demand for the recall of an allegedly unsatisfactory office holder to the vote of the people. During a course in American politics, my class was visited by a senior representative of the notorious public relations firm Whitaker and Baxter. She explained that one of the firm's ground rules was that you should always attack (shades of the Brexiteers in Britain's EU referendum) and never allow yourself to be forced on to the defensive. Almost all the referenda in the history of California had been won by their clients. They had also masterminded successful campaigns against health care reform, both during Roosevelt's presidency and during Truman's. Once the firm had been retained by a dodgy mayor of San Francisco whom a group of citizens sought to recall. How, the firm asked, could it square its essentially aggressive philosophy with the need to defend its client? The answer was a stroke of genius. San Francisco was plastered with hoardings proclaiming the message 'Defeat the faceless man' and depicting a sinister figure with a trilby hat hiding the top half of his face and a coat collar hiding the bottom half. The mayor was not recalled.

These experiences vaccinated me against the populist virus which has done so much damage to pluralist democracy from Mussolini to Hitler, from William Jennings Bryan to Joe McCarthy, from Louis Napoleon to Pétain, from Enoch Powell to Margaret Thatcher and from Tony Benn to Boris Johnson. As a Member of Parliament in the 1970s I followed Roy Jenkins in agreeing reluctantly to take part in a nationwide referendum on continued membership of what was then the European Community. I was even drafted in to act as political adviser to Charles Guggenheim, a brilliant American practitioner of *cinéma verité*, who made the television films for Britain in Europe, the umbrella organisation which ran the campaign for a 'yes' vote in the referendum. But though I enjoyed the campaign – partly no doubt because I could see that opinion was moving steadily towards us – I did not forgot the lessons of California: that referenda are invariably subject to manipulation and, much more importantly, that the basic premise of all the many varieties of populism – that the unmediated voice of a homogeneous 'people' should carry all before it – is both false and dangerous.

In truth, the 'people' do not exist. What exist are individual *persons*, with fluctuating moods and a variety of identities. Populists claim to listen to the people. The claim is a lie. The truth is that they *speak* to them. They seek to mobilise a group of individual persons by pretending that the group is in fact the whole, and that they have a direct line to the whole, by-passing the intermediate institutions that protect the individual citizen from an over-mighty central state (and over-mighty private firms) as the ozone layer protects the earth from harmful rays of the sun. For populists, wisdom and virtue – an intuitive, unschooled wisdom all the more profound for being unschooled – reside in the people, and not in any elite or institution. 'Romania?' said an anonymous Romanian philosopher at an international conference. 'The Romanian contribution to philosophy is the immemorial wisdom of the Romanian peasant.'

That is the populist mentality in a nutshell. Peasants are wiser than philosophers: the people are right and the 'experts' traduced by the 'Leave' campaigners in the referendum are wrong. Pluralists inhabit a world of dilemmas, of tensions between conflicting and incommensurable goods, and of negotiation between the bearers of different values. For populists dilemmas are impermissible. The people know best. Values are not in tension with each other, and there is no need for negotiation. The people decide which values are to prevail. In extreme versions of the populist approach, they even decide what is scientifically valid, as when that archetypal American populist, William Jennings Bryan, insisted that evolution should not be taught in the public school system because 'not one in ten of those who accept the Bible as the Word of God' believed it to be true.

By the same token, populists assume that legitimate power springs from the uncorrupted people, and only from the people. Oppression by power-hungry rulers is indeed a danger, but the solution is simple: empower the people. Moreover, the people are a homogeneous and monolithic whole. There is no need to protect minorities from the tyranny of the majority. Minorities are either part of the whole, in which case they don't need protection, or self-excluded from it, in which case they don't deserve to be protected. Apparent differences of interest or value that cut across the body of the people, that divide the collective sovereign against itself, are products of elite manipulation or, in Margaret Thatcher's immortal phrase, of the 'enemy within'. For there is a strong paranoid streak in the populist mentality. Against the pure, virtuous people stand corrupt, privileged elites and sinister, conspiratorial subversives. The latter are forever plotting to do down the former. A case in point is the Leavers' claim that the only way to keep the United Kingdom out of a federal Europe is to stand aloof from the rest of the continent to which we belong and whose civilisation we have shared since Julius Caesar's troops landed on the shores of Kent.

Is there an alternative? I think there is, but it is not easy to put into practice, or even into words. As a Labour Member of Parliament, my dearest friend was the ebullient, brilliant, courageous, and gloriously indiscreet John Mackintosh. He was a distinguished academic – a professor of politics first at Strathclyde and later at his alma mater, Edinburgh, and author of a classic study of the British Cabinet. He was five years older than me; and I loved him like a brother. His untimely death at the age of 49 was a terrible blow. I still think of him a lot. In one of our many conversations he told me that for him Gladstone was the greatest political leader in British history. I couldn't understand how that could be. How could Gladstone, with his intense religiosity and fascination with Homer, be a hero to the bawdy, irreverent John Mackintosh? His answer was that Gladstone never talked down to the vast popular audiences that he attracted, that he paid them the compliment of appealing to the better angels of their nature, and that he proceeded on the basis that ordinary people could understand and respond to complicated arguments. To put it simply, Gladstone (and Mackintosh) appealed to the best in people. Populists appeal to the worst.

Can a Gladstonian (and Mackintoshian) vision of politics – of politics as open debate, as mutual learning, as dialogue through which people learn from each other and from which they emerge as different people – fly in the age of the sound-bite, the tweet and Facebook? The only answer is that I don't know. What I do know is that, like James Madison, John Stuart Mill, Amartya Sen, R. H. Tawney, and, above all, de Tocqueville, the greatest analyst of democracy in the history of western political thought, I have believed, ever since I can remember, that populism and pluralism are deadly enemies. It follows that, as Jan-Werner Müller has argued, populism is not just illiberal; it is also anti-democratic (Müller, 2016).

The narrow 'Leave' victory in the EU referendum in the summer of 2016 horrified me – not just because I thought it an act of national self-harm unparalleled since France surrendered to Nazi Germany in 1940, but because the Leave campaigners plumbed depths of ignominy not seen in the United Kingdom since the anti-Jacobin panic of the late eighteenth century. Their campaign was the most dishonest I can remember. The results have been disastrous. The old betrayed the young; the English betrayed the Scots and the people of Northern Ireland; and the Welsh betrayed themselves. The rule of law, the foundation stone of democratic governance, has been called into question. The Anglocentric policies of the government which took office after the referendum are pulling the four nations of the United Kingdom apart. The Scottish government may well hold another independence referendum when the Brexit negotiations between Britain and the EU are over. The delicate balance of forces that brought peace to Northern Ireland in 1998 has been disrupted. Plaid Cymru (the party of Wales, to which I am proud to belong) has insisted that, if Scotland votes for independence Wales should do the same.

British democracy is now in crisis – not just because of Brexit itself (though that bears a large part of the blame) but because of the shameful conduct of its advocates. This is not a case of 'Forgive them, Lord, for they know not what they do.' The leading Leavers knew only too well what they were doing. They were appealing to a xenophobic, little England nationalism, ignorant of, and indifferent to, the attitudes, cultures and self-understandings of two of the four nations of the United Kingdom. The problems raised by the contradiction between the project of the hard-line Brexiteers and the manifest needs of the peoples of Northern Ireland and the Irish Republic were perfectly foreseeable, and were in fact foreseen. They were treated with blithe indifference, verging on contempt.

The same applies to the economic costs, which are already beginning to bite in the form of a plummeting pound and falling real wages.

Not only is British democracy in crisis; so too is social democracy. Social democracy in one country is a contradiction in terms. It is quintessentially outward-looking and at the same time quintessentially European. The oldest social democratic party in the world is the German SPD; the great German revisionist, Eduard Bernstein, learned his revisionism from the British Fabians. Keir Hardie, the first independent Labour MP, was a pall bearer at the funeral of August Bebel, one of the greatest leaders in the long history of German social democracy.

The great questions for the future are whether social democracy can recover and, if so, how. Great man though he was, uplifting quotations from Kolakowski will not get us very far. In a globalising world, in which inequality between nations is gradually diminishing, while inequality within nations is steadily increasing; in which the choice is between the free market and the free society; and in which the sovereign nation-state of old days can no longer shield its citizens from the wild gyrations of the global market, the core values of social democracy will have no purchase on the real world unless social democrats embody them in a governing philosophy fit for a world which has changed out of all recognition since Kolakowski wrote.

I can't pretend I know how to do this: no single person could. But one thing is clear. Classical social democracy – the social democracy of Leon Blum. Willy Brandt, Anthony Crosland, Aneurin Bevan and Kurt Schumacher – was both child and parent of the classical nation-state. Its underlying assumption was that social democratic values could be realised only by winning power over the central state in democratic elections, and then implementing social democratic values from the top down. That assumption was always full of holes, but in its heyday it seemed fairly plausible. Today, it is patent nonsense. The classical nation state is under threat. Pre-modern ethnicities – Welsh, Scottish, Lombard, Provençal, Breton, Corsican, Basque, Catalan and the like – have come in from the cold. The choice facing twenty-first-century social democrats is starkly clear: either we recognise that the top-down social democracy of the past is a busted flush and behave accordingly, or we dwindle into a marginal sect like the Jacobites in eighteenth-century England or the Bourbons in nineteenth-century France.

The implications go wide. Behaving accordingly must mean that the social democracy of the future will have to be bottom-up instead of top-down: that social democratic values will have to be implemented (if they are to be implemented at all) by much smaller polities than the ones social democrats relied on in old days. This implies a huge leap of imagination of which there is little sign at present. More important, it also implies that the smaller polities in question will have to collaborate in new ways if they are to withstand the tempestuous gales sweeping through the increasingly integrated global marketplace. Yet, in fact, Europeans already have at their disposal an instrument with which this can be done. It is known as the European Union. The choice is, in fact, what it has been ever since Britain joined what was then the European Economic Community: either a sovereign global market or power-sharing between the nation-states of Europe and supra-national European institutions.

Against that background the current debate on the outcome of the EU referendum is hopelessly inadequate. Among former Remainers as well as former Leavers, the prevailing assumption is that, because around 37 per cent of the eligible electorate voted Leave, there is nothing more to be said. Article 50 of the Lisbon treaty has been invoked; and that is the end of the story. But as Lord Kerr, who wrote Article 50, has pointed out, the British government's Article 50 application is revocable. In fact, the future is open. We are not doomed to suffer the economic, psychological and moral damage that leaving the European Union would inflict on us. For social democrats the choice is between craven acceptance of an alleged fait accompli which need not, in fact, be accepted, and resistance. It remains to be seen whether British social democrats will step up to the plate. If we don't, history will not forgive us. Antonio Gramsci once called for a combination of pessimism of the intellect and optimism of the will. We have had all too much pessimism of the intellect. It is time for some optimism of the will.

Not least in Wales, the land where I was born and which I love. Wales voted 'Leave' in the EU referendum. But it stands to lose more from leaving the EU than any of the other four nations of the United Kingdom; and it's pretty clear that opinion in Wales is already shifting towards 'Remain'. Though I've spent most of my life in England, I feel Welsh first and European second. I have never felt English. It's not an accident that the politicians I've most admired – Aneurin Bevan, Roy Jenkins, Leo Abse, Donald Dewar, John Mackintosh, John Smith and Robin Cook – were all either Scottish or Welsh. Nor, for that matter, is it an accident that the two anglophone poets of the twentieth century whose work has moved me most are the Irishman Yeats and the Welshman Dylan Thomas. Brexit has shone such a fierce light on the archaic, corrupting and contemptible absurdities of the British state that I no longer feel as British as I did in the days of my innocence.

Ideally, I would like to see a federal United Kingdom, with an elected senate replacing the House of Lords, straining every nerve to undo the economic, cultural, intellectual and – above all – psychological damage that leaving the European Union would bring with it. But if that turns out to be impossible (and the omens are not propitious) I would throw what little weight I have into a campaign for Wales to become an independent nation within a confederal European Union instead of being chained for ever to a hard-right, chauvinistic and xenophobic England. 'Take back control', proclaimed the Brexiteers. If it's right for the United Kingdom to leave the European Union in order to take back control, why should it be wrong for Wales to leave the United Kingdom in order to win the control it has lacked since the murder of the last Welsh Prince of Wales in 1282?

Reference

Müller, J. W. (2016) *What is Populism?* (Philadelphia: University of Pennsylvania Press).

15

David Marquand and liberal social democracy

Will Hutton

David Marquand is right. He has been right for the last forty years. Successful capitalism rests on a subtle and complex interplay between the public and private. Both are vital, not merely for capitalism but for a healthy civilisation. Effective public institutions are needed to socialise risk, create the ecosystem for enterprise and workers to flourish and perhaps more importantly, stimulate a culture of common purpose. Equally, you need companies, who put a purpose to promote human betterment before profit, to work within this publicly created architecture and culture to drive the economy forward. Neither happens spontaneously; they need to be self-consciously created – and Britain's tragedy, rooted in its particular history along with systematic intellectual mistakes by liberal left strategists and thinkers, is that it has done neither.

From that follows Britain's ongoing crisis, first of the resulting continuing economic and social decline, but second of the left's failure to build a coalition and shared programme to turn it around. It is even more obvious that any successful social democratic drive to shape capitalism so that it both captures the new while benefiting the mass of people requires an effective capacity to act publicly through a smart state – and a tradition to support it. This involves a much more complex and sophisticated conception of the state than Britain boasts: it has to be responsive and accountable as well as smart and agile – again underpinned by a recognition that it embodies common public goals. Equally the free market as a stand-alone idea is a nonsensical construct; markets sit in a wider social architecture which can be better or worse designed. A dysfunctional state and a dysfunctional economy are symbiotically interlinked. But in a British context you might as well as bay for the moon in arguing in this way – and David has been baying and raging all his working life.

The British state is a gothic, feudal horror, and the British corporate and financial system deeply biased against long-term wealth generation. Both feed off each other. But progressive liberal opinion in Britain has never managed to find a philosophic basis to make common ground for the state's root and branch reform, the precondition for any action – whether over the electoral system, reforming the House of Lords or ambitiously creating a written federal constitution in which power is properly handed back to the country's cities, regions and constituent countries. The left want to use the grand old British state, which curiously legitimises them, to do top-down statist things in the name of 'socialism', which inevitably only works poorly, while liberal opinion does not know whether it wants to hobble the idea of government in multiple checks and balances or simply curtail it in the name of liberty.

Name any issue you like – creating publicly owned companies, a national identity card system (allowing us to know who is in Britain and which would have done much to lower the hysteria over immigration), offering Scotland a federal settlement, deciding on a voting system to replace first-past-the-post, accepting a role for the European Court of Human Rights over press regulation, or just the daily business of politics – the same fissures appear. With the left unable to coalesce, power is handed by default to the Conservatives – both practically because in a first-past-the-post system they are the consistent beneficiaries of a divided vote between Labour and the Liberal Democrats, and culturally, because in the absence of a strong civic, community culture what becomes the ascendant culture is the tone, breeding and assumptions of the upper class. As ever, Tories morph into a ruling class as part of the natural order of things, and Britain's feudal state structures – from the state opening of parliament to the network of Lords Lieutenants representing the Crown in the counties (all of which are Conservative) – are their hidden supporters.

Marquand has been saying this with mounting force and conviction since the 1980s. His great book – *The Unprincipled Society* – laid the intellectual foundations, along with Axel Leijunhufvud's *Keynesian Economics and the Economics of Keynes*, of my own, *The State We're In*. Marquand's account of Britain's tragic failure in the 1960s and 1970s to use the state creatively to reform industrial relations, or make partnerships between state, business and the union movement work in any respect struck me forcibly. There was simply too weak a belief in the idea of the public interest or common good to which successive governments could appeal. Britain's public culture, deriving from its winner-take-all voting system, unwritten constitution and an executive branch of government wielding de facto monarchical power, is built on adverserialism and party interest. The public interest had come to be understood as what a particular governing party defines as policy in the name of the Crown and can then ram through the House of Commons. It is, in the immortal words of Quintin Hogg, an 'elective dictatorship' – a far cry from any conception of good governance and its associated public culture. Of course, this state could not make post-war Keynesianism work or refashion the British economy. The embrace of Thatcherism, allegedly not needing a proactive state except to build the foundations of a privatised, less regulated economy, was thus inevitable.

Labourism's complete disinterest in the constitutional question horrified Marquand: its only interest was to capture state structures to advance its agenda of public ownership, welfare and defending trade union privileges. But this would always be under the threat of dissolution because the process of garnering wide consent has not been undertaken. Unlike Scandinavian capitalism or the German social market economy whose roots went deep into civil society, the Labour Party engaged in no such effort – it had neither the responsive state structures nor, more importantly, the accompanying culture of common purpose with which to work. With shallower roots, it was always possible for another government – using the same top-down power – to dissolve and repeal what Labour had done. So it has proved.

Marquand's pessimism that a Labour government might never get elected was dispelled by Blair, but as of this time of writing in 2018, thirteen years since the party's last victory, for all Jeremy Corbyn's higher than expected showing in 2017, his warnings still seem prescient. New Labour's achievements, such as they were, have been eliminated by its successors' desire to shrink the state, which they are in the process of achieving with precious little opposition. The social contract is being unpicked and ordinary working-class people being exposed to new workplace risks and uncertainties: funding for health and education is as low as can be got away with politically. The principles of liberal social democracy seem a distant dream.

Even more of a dream seems a government ever able to implement them. The Conservative hegemony has been re-established, sealed by the referendum on Brexit. The left's bankruptcy was dramatised by the election of Jeremy Corbyn as leader of the Labour Party, to whom Marquand's ideas – even if he knew of them – would be an anathema. Yet Corbyn has nothing to say about the state, the constitution or how to build values that support the ideas of the public interest and common purpose. Equally, he has nothing to say about how to craft a more purposed, investment and innovation friendly capitalism. He has no conception about how to manage the alchemy between private and public. He wants to reinvent Labour as a social movement that one day will control the state on a first-past-the-post voting system and legislate for socialist transformation. He, and those who back him, have learned nothing. Yet the sheer magnitude of the political failure may yet provoke a rethink. When the thinking begins, there will be no better place to start than the body of work of David Marquand.

16

Not just any social democracy: 'Marquandism' and the primacy of pluralism and republicanism

Hans Schattle and Jeremy Nuttall

The myriad essays in this collection have set forth the habits, mindsets and qualities of social democratic citizens as well as the political circumstances and economic conditions necessary for a robust version of social democracy to take hold. Several authors have also explored how the writings of David Marquand throughout the past five decades have offered a distinct interpretation with regard to social democratic as well as civic republican endeavours: whether the United Kingdom might be on the cusp of a 'Marquandian moment' of democratic renewal, as Stuart White proposed, or whether 'Marquandism', as Neal Lawson argued, offers a pathway for progressive politics to spring forth once again in the networked post-industrial era.

Our conclusion to this volume seeks to discern the extent that 'Marquandism' has emerged as a coherent body of thought, offering an alternative course to neoliberalism and its influences across the world's constitutional democracies, with particular force in Britain. One could question, for sure, whether 'Marquandism' is an inflated claim, falsely evoking conceptual clarity where there is disarray, as David Marquand throughout his 50 years as a public intellectual has changed his party allegiances several times and has modified his thinking on key issues as well as his historical analysis of many illustrious political figures. Indeed, since Marquand, over the years has taken an ecumenical approach by singling out, as sources of inspiration, numerous thinkers of seemingly incompatible philosophical and ideological stripes, conservative, liberal and socialist – among them, the Levellers, the Chartists, Thomas Paine, William Morris, Edmund Burke, John Stuart Mill, and R. H. Tawney – one might argue that Marquand has drawn upon such a breadth of perspectives that any notion of 'Marquandism' might elude us. Nevertheless, we argue that Marquandism withstands critical scrutiny given its overriding emphasis on pluralism and republicanism as two crucial, consolidating elements that must be incorporated into any kind of democratic political system worth having. Moreover, although David Marquand does not specifically privilege social democracy (in any form) as the most ethically desirable political system, the balance of his ideas throughout the past half century seem to place the greatest emphasis on how pluralism and republicanism are essential in fostering a very specific model of social democracy that hinges on the character and mindsets of the citizenry and its political leaders as well as the configurations of governing institutions. The premium Marquand places, then, on a pluralist, republican social democracy serves as the unifying thread in his political thinking.

In light of this, we first stitch together the main elements of pluralism and republicanism as Marquand sees them, and then we examine how pluralism and republicanism both inform Marquand's perspective on the 'social' in social democracy and, finally, on the essence of democracy itself. Examining what 'Marquandism' really means – its principles and prescriptions – helps us better understand how Marquand has envisioned the good polity and the good society, and what kinds of citizens and governing institutions are vital to advancing not just any kind of social democracy but an ethically inspired and politically effica-cious social democratic project to nurture and sustain. The intersecting themes of citizens, mindsets and realities in the making of social democrats have occupied the minds of our authors, whether normative political theorists, comparative political scientists or intellectual historians; whether scholars or practitioners; and across ideological convictions and policy preferences. A foray into the enduring aspects of 'Marquandism' thereby helps us reckon with the question, as noted in the introduction to this volume: what unacceptable realities must today's social democrats confront most forcefully, and, correspondingly, what kinds of new realities should progressives strive to bring into existence?

Pluralism

Pluralism is not a doctrine. It is a disposition, a mentality, an approach. Like most approaches to politics, it is a matter of feeling as well as of belief … Pluralists like the clash and clang of argument; the monochrome sameness of the big battalions horrifies them; so does the sugary conformism of the politically correct. Instinctively, they are for the 'little platoons' that Edmund Burke saw as the nurseries of 'public affections,' and they want to protect them from the homogenising pressures of state, market and opinion. For them, a good society is a mosaic of vibrant smaller collectivities – trade unions, universities, business associations, local authorities, miners' welfares, churches, mosques, Women's Institutes, NGOs – each with its own identity, tradition, values and rituals. (Marquand, 1999)

David Marquand's thinking on pluralism cuts across three interconnected realms: politics and government, social and cultural contexts, and the economic arena. With regard to politics and government, for starters, Marquand has regularly issued clarion calls for federalism in both the United Kingdom and the European Union. For Marquand, federalism is not an end in itself but a means, through the distribution and decentralisation of jurisdictions, in order to facilitate a multitude of open access points across multiple levels of governing institutions. It thereby fragments political power through constitutional checks and balances, keeping it out of the hands of any particular faction or narrow clique – the opposite of the 'elected dictatorship' that drives the Westminster parliamentary system – while maximising the opportunities for citizens and their respective interest groups to shape laws and public policy decisions. When pluralism works well, elected officials across the range of governing institutions are conditioned to make decisions in ways that account for the cacaphonic yet widely encompassing voices of everyday people that cover close to the full spectrum of views radiating from the body politic.

Federalism is simultaneously horizontal and vertical: distributing political power more widely across multiple branches of the national government (consider Marquand's calls, for example, for an elected second chamber and proportional representation) and redistributing authority both upwards and downwards. In the case of the United Kingdom, with its resolutely centralised national institutions, this means transferring some competencies to regional and local governments while delegating other powers to the European Union. Devolution, in which Westminster (under the Blair government) granted varying degrees of authority to regional Parliaments and Assemblies in Scotland, Wales and Northern Ireland (but not England) and the London metropolitan government yet retains the ultimate jurisdiction to grab these powers back again, if it so chooses, is not enough to satisfy David Marquand. The federalism he advocates, if carried to its fullest extension, would also lead to the drafting of a new written constitution for the United Kingdom. Once again, this new constitution would not be an end in itself but a means to the vision of pluralism for Britain that Marquand articulates in his writings. The aftermath of the Brexit referendum, with Britain now poised to leave the European Union and the spectre of Scotland and possibly Northern Ireland breaking away from the United Kingdom as a result, has thrown Marquand's federalist vision into jeopardy; it suggests that much of England has turned its back not only on Europe but also on federalism, decentralisation, and, by extension, pluralism. This is why Marquand would just as soon see Wales also secede from the United Kingdom, if Scotland ends up leaving, and deploy its political culture oriented toward citizen voice and institutional collaboration as an outpost of the European Union rather than as an appendage of a diminished and inward-looking England.

Concern as to whether considerable segments of England are capable of harnessing the many aspects of pluralism already flourishing in its increasingly diverse society rather than drifting into nativism leads to the value Marquand affords to pluralism in social and cultural contexts: he seeks a political culture of consensus building, negotiation across different kinds of value systems, and a readiness to adapt to, and even foster, nonconformity rather than stamp out differences; then, in the economic arena, Marquand's pluralism entails genuine power sharing between labour and capital. Marquand's endorsements of pluralism in these varied contexts also takes us full-circle back into political interaction, as well, given his long-time advocacy for progressive alliances to build bridges across political parties on the left and centre-left – namely Labour, the Liberal Democrats, and now the Greens as well as the Scottish National Party and Plaid Cymru. The hesitancy shown toward pluralism that Marquand laments in the wider political culture of Britain, and particularly in England, applies especially to the Labour Party.

Just as Marquand's writings, taken together, offer a coherent picture of how pluralism ideally would gain ground in a vibrant, diverse and open polity, he has also articulated forcefully through the years what kinds of institutional arrangements and cultural attributes he is against, for being too closed, narrow and stilted to allow for pluralism; as a laundry list, culled from the various chapters in this book: absolute Crown-in-Parliament sovereignty; an adversarial political culture; decision making by majority rule (thereby downgrading minority rights and interests); first-past-the-post, winner-takes-all elections; centralisation within 'feudal' state structures; and a brand of populism that sees the public as a homogeneous, monolithic, uniform whole. All these negative realities of the British state and British politics, enduring after devolution and its accompanying destabilising effects, have left Marquand and several of the authors in this book sceptical of the ability of the Labour Party and its present leader, Jeremy Corbyn, to bring about the sort of political transformation that would prompt a genuine social democratic re-awakening. Like many of his Labour predecessors, Corbyn is seen as too willing to use Britain's democratically impoverished mechanisms for the party's short-term goals of gaining and then leveraging power rather than taking on the task of fixing the underlying problems and bringing about long overdue, thoroughgoing change.

Republicanism

In contrast with Marquand's priority placed upon pluralism, which points to complex changes (at least in the immediate term) in the governance of the United Kingdom, Marquand's emphasis on democratic republicanism is mainly about the people. As several chapters in this volume have made clear, Marquand favours a polity with actively engaged citizens willing to pay attention to what is happening in politics and government, speak out about their interests and concerns regarding what is happening, relate these concerns with their understandings of what would constitute the good society, and take responsibility for the larger public good. Indeed, holding out for a public good or common good that amounts to more than the sum of a polity's constituent parts is yet another essential aspect of republicanism.

In *Britain Since 1918*, the book in which Marquand presented democratic republicanism as a political tradition warranting a higher profile in British politics, he encapsulated its key themes, dating back to John Milton and the Levellers, as 'republican self-respect versus monarchical servility; civic activity versus slothful apathy; and most of all, government by vigorous discussion and mutual learning versus passive deference to monarch, capitalist or state' (Marquand, 2008: 68). While Marquand has never decisively called for an end to the monarchy so to make an outright transition to a republic, he is no friend of the monarchy, given the ways in which it centralises political power and also sets the tone for elements of subservience in the political culture. Keep in mind also that the title of Marquand's most recent book, *Mammon's Kingdom*, takes critical aim not only at Mammon but also at the kingdom: he seeks a republic of self-governing citizens rather than a kingdom of voracious yet politically languid consumers. All this boils down to what Marquand has tried to get across to his readers in the terms and phrases he has employed in his writings to capture what he means by democratic republicanism: democratic civic culture, public purpose, public realm and so forth.

Marquand's republicanism also connects itself with pluralism. Although Marquand places the most weight on citizenship as deployed in the context of national politics, he also sees the need for active public engagement in multiple political communities – beneath the state, in cities and towns, hamlets and villages – and also beyond the state, in the continental arenas of EU politics as well as the wider global spheres of civic activism, ranging from holding international institutions accountable to democratic norms to all the contestation and debate that now unfolds online. Hence Marquand's view of the political world lends itself to multiple, plural and dynamic citizenships rather than a fixed model of citizenship attached exclusively to the state.

Throughout his writings, Marquand has often expounded upon the kinds of personal qualities necessary for good citizenship, in the republican sense of the concept. Marquand's affinities with pluralism once again become manifest here, sometimes to the point of seeping into elitism. In *Mammon's Kingdom* he devotes considerable space to lamenting the decline of the 'clerisy' and the professional service elite as exemplars of a fading culture of honour and duty. Just as for Marquand pluralism involves meaningful interaction among fellow citizens with radically different interests, outlooks and values, public deliberation is also important for Marquand in clarifying what the public's interests might be – or, in civic republican parlance, what the common good might be and what genuine commitments to the common good would entail across an entire array of policy domains – and then having extended public conversations about how to advance such common goals. Furthermore, following the ancient tradition of republican thinking, going back to city states when citizenship among limited, selected members of the population was an office as well as a status – citizen-legislator, citizen-warrior, and so forth – Marquand sees modern citizenship as universally inclusive yet, similar to the ancients, dependent on mutual education and mutual learning; the resulting enlightenment indeed bears the fruit of public deliberation that Marquand cherishes.

What republican citizenship is not, for Marquand, comes down to individualism and subjection. That Marquand would prefer active citizenship over passive subjecthood is obvious and needs no further explanation here. What warrants a closer look is his apprehension of individualism. Marquand has long railed against several variants of individualism; among them, hyper-individualism, market individualism, moral individualism and radical individualism. He clearly has affinities with so-called communitarian thinkers, such as Alasdair MacIntyre and Michael Sandel, in that he regards everyday people as inescapably embedded in their social environments and argues for individual citizens to bring their whole being actively into political life, not abstracting their identities out of politics. And yet, similar to many contemporary critics of individualism, Marquand is a liberal republican as much as a republican social democrat; he is thoroughly and unabashedly in favour of human rights, thereby underscoring how social democracy in the twenty-first century might end up situated closer to liberalism than socialism. All in all, Marquand is more of a friendly critic of liberalism's excesses – its leanings toward a warped individualism that atomises human beings and removes them (or motivates human beings to remove themselves) from their social environments and descends into greed, egoism and selfishness.

The 'social' in social democracy

What, then, does 'Marquandism', and its emphasis on pluralism and republicanism have to say about the 'social' in social democracy? Here David Marquand has gone much further than the writings of communitarian thinkers in the United States, who tend to remain agnostic as to what kinds of economic arrangements are best suited to fulfil principles of social and economic justice. Recall that it was the liberal thinker John Rawls, in his magisterial text *A Theory of Justice*, who placed far more emphasis than communitarians ever have on searching for ways to alleviate social and economic inequalities.

On matters of social welfare and economic inequality, Marquand bridges liberal and republican schools of thought, having devoted tremendous attention to how capitalism should be tamed and how European approaches to taming capitalism (both social democratic and Christian democratic) offer lessons to the Anglo-American world in countering the pervasiveness of neoliberalism. Marquand is also for inclusion and internationalism; he eschews the solutions of (and, in fact, was early to sound the alarm bells about) resurgent right-wing populism with its scapegoating and exclusion of immigrants; nor is Marquand seeking anything close to a relapse of the 1930s with nations closing their borders to trade. Rather, he is seeking more innovative and dynamic solutions suited to today's globally interconnected network societies; as Marquand has suggested, at least implicitly, technological change does not render obsolete the need to socialise risk; as Hutton has argued, following Marquand's footsteps, this is the job of effective public institutions.

What Marquand is against in the economic arena, accordingly, are economic arrangements that are inherently anti-social, and Marquand's objections to neoliberalism and its effects often echo and redeploy into the economic realm his reservations about individualism. In a nutshell, 'Marquandism' stands against laissez-faire capitalism or 'bastard liberalism' (Marquand, 1997: 85), the consumer society and its resulting greed, the 'ethic of profit' (in contrast with the republican ethic of public service), market fundamentalism, marketisation, the market state, the market society, 'vulgar materialism' and, as Ben Jackson's put it, in Chapter 7, 'short-termist, financialised capitalism'. This last element is very important as it ties into the need for stewardship and concern not only for the next quarterly financial statement but for the long-term common good.

Democracy with pluralist and republican sensibilities

All of the above adds up to 'Marquandism' and its pluralist and republican sensibilities. Marquandian thinking has never been entirely in sync with the Labour Party as it was – not even 'New' Labour – but instead has evoked something newer and also more radical to the status quo, at least in Britain – something more innovative and cutting edge. It is nothing less than a blueprint for a possible future of Britain. Whether or not Britain remains in Europe – and for that matter, whether or not Britain remains Britain – this essential question remains: Will the public and its leaders take the cumulative thinking of David Marquand and seize the moment – in our parlance, make social democracy, as well as forthcoming generations of social democrats – so to shape new and more inspiring realities?

The obvious antidote to the economic inequities Marquand has long and relentlessly decried is carefully crafted pluralist and republican social democracy tuned into a political culture that inspires the people to give their best to the political arena, opting for voice and efficacy rather than silence and apathy. Here a series of contrasts serve to clarify what 'Marquandism' is all about: Marquand champions political institutions, leaders and citizens responsive to bottom-up (or at least middle-range) initiatives rather than top-down 'political paternalism' or some sort of 'neosocialist alternative'; a moral politics rather than either a mechanical politics or an unmediated politics; democratic activism that nevertheless is sufficiently informed by and mindful of history, at times even to the point of erudition, as opposed to 'unschooled wisdom' betraying an ignorance of history. Marquand's democratic thinking also lends itself to a willingness to adjust and adapt with the times; he has sought, never flinching, to foster a dynamic (as opposed to static) political system in which the citizens and leaders both exhibit and exercise the constant capacity for growth, change, reconsideration and innovation.

One of the most interesting aspects of Marquandian thinking is how it has crossed the boundaries between ideas and practical action. At times, Marquand has engaged with relatively idealised and abstract political theory, in other instances he has provided a more middle range intellectual agenda to inform actually existing governments, and at yet other times he has acted directly as a political practitioner and operator. In some respects, these competing genres and arenas in which Marquand operated have created tension, and Marquandism can at times lose sight of the politics of the possible and the practicalities of constraint. But at its finest, it attained that synthesised optimum, by which the best of high ideals and constructive practical politics became mutually supportive. This synergy was clearly evident in those reforming social democratic moments of 1945, 1964 and 1997, all of which illustrated, in their different ways, elements of Marquandism, as well as the critiques he made of key social democratic political figures.

This raises the question of whether Marquandism is fundamentally optimistic or pessimistic about the march of modern British political history. As is fitting of a progressivism defined by mindset as much as specific ideological or policy prescriptions, Marquandism has often been as interested in the posing of questions as in the providing of answers. He concluded his 1997 introduction to *The New Reckoning* by asking: 'Can the left and centre – and, for that matter, the non-fundamentalist right – trump the new tribalism with a tolerant, outward-looking alternative? Can it give the inevitable counter-movement against market utopianism a liberal, pluralistic, social- or Christian-democratic form?' Twenty years on, in the time of Brexit and Trump, this is a further reminder of Marquand's ability to foresee some of the larger political trends and dilemmas: these questions could be posed almost verbatim today. But what of the answers? Marquand's own response at that time, characteristically, was that 'there are no certain answers' (Marquand, 1997: 32–3).

In this position somewhere in the middle of that spectrum between optimism and pessimism, Marquand represents something of a duality, one that defines both social democracy, and the intelligentsia as a class. If the nonconformist critic's need to pinpoint societal shortcomings allied to a determination at all costs not to be thought of as naive or unworldly (that frequent charge against the intellectual) foster a certain gloominess, this is countered by a burning underlying enlightenment optimism in the power of reason, joined with a sense that there is something deep down in the human condition that makes it want to grow, improve and strive.

If the current bitter fruits of democracy make it difficult for many scholars to feel inclined to laud the demos for their political wisdom, there is also a modish danger in missing countervailing, sometimes more subtle, grounds for optimism. One is that both Brexit and Trump remain, as yet, short-term phe-nomena; their rootedness in something more profound and lasting remains as yet unproven. A second consideration is that at the time of writing, in October 2017, the rightward shift in British politics evident in 2015 and 2016 has already been somewhat mitigated. The Conservatives lost their majority at the 2017 general election, in part as a reaction to the threefold vices of 'hard Brexit', austerity and a measure of prime ministerial hubris. At the same time, UKIP almost completely collapsed as a serious electoral force, echoing the fate of the neo-fascist British National Party when it had momentarily seemed ready to flower almost a decade earlier.

The progressive, social democratic, liberal and indeed one-nation Conservative response to this rapidly changing political environment remains uncertain and divided. But it seems likely that at some point a moderate yet also visionary progressivism will put its house in order. Since the dawning of democracy in 1918, Britain has rarely, if ever, been a country of the unyielding hard right. Even Thatcherism, in its earlier years, represented, in some aspects, a pulling back to the centre or centre-right, after some of the statist and trade union excesses of the 1970s, and when, in its latter half, it turned more zealously ideological, it lost momentum, and ultimately Thatcher found herself deposed by her still 'one nation' Cabinet.

It is ultimately in the good spirit and constructive decency of 'the people', not the machinations of their rulers, on which rests a sense that the present despair may prove unfounded. This, ultimately, has served as Marquand's most profound and sustained insight. Political and social progress was, at its heart, about neither state structures nor bustling markets, but rather the very ethics, aspirations and political culture of the people. The people would benefit from that progress, but most fundamentally they would determine and shape its very occurrence. Hence, the profoundly democratic, egalitarian conclusion of this most cerebral of members of the British public intellectual 'elite': in the end, we would have to do it ourselves.

References

Marquand, D. (1997) *The New Reckoning* (Cambridge: Polity).

Marquand, D. (1999) 'Pluralism v populism', *Prospect*, 20 June. www.prospectmagazine.co.uk/magazine/pluralismvpopulism.

Marquand, D. (2008) *Britain Since 1918. The Strange Career of British Democracy* (London: Weidenfeld & Nicolson).

Index

EU authorised representative for GPSR:
Easy Access System Europe, Mustamäe tee 50,
10621 Tallinn, Estonia
gpsr.requests@easproject.com

www.ingramcontent.com/pod-product-compliance
Lightning Source LLC
Chambersburg PA
CBHW051952270326
41929CB00015B/2621